Learning Disabilities
Bridging the Gap Between
Research and Classroom Practice

ew Jersey
o

Vice President and Executive Publisher: Jeffery W. Johnston
Executive Editor: Ann Castel Davis
Editorial Assistant: Penny Burleson
Production Editor: Sheryl Glicker Langner
Production Coordination: Penny Walker, Techbooks
Design Coordinator: Diane C. Lorenzo
Cover Design: Candace Rowley
Cover Image: Fotosearch
Photo Coordinator: Maria B. Vonada
Production Manager: Laura Messerly
Director of Marketing: David Gesell
Marketing Manager: Autumn Purdy
Marketing Coordinator: Brian Mounts

This book was set in Garamond Book by Techbooks. It was printed and bound by R. R. Donnelley & Sons Company. The cover was printed by R. R. Donnelley & Sons Company.

Chapter Opening Photo Credits: Anne Vega/Merrill, p. 1; Krista Greco/Merrill, pp. 17, 141; Anthony Magnacca/Merrill, pp. 37, 127, 157, 227; Scott Cunningham/Merrill, pp. 47, 85; Laima Druskis/PH College, pp. 67, 107, 207; Patrick White/Merrill, pp. 173, 269; George Dodson/PH College, p. 189; Todd Yarrington/Merrill, p. 247.

Pearson Education LTD.
Pearson Education Singapore Pte. Ltd.
Pearson Education Canada, Ltd.
Pearson Education–Japan

Pearson Education Australia Pty. Limited
Pearson Education North Asia Ltd.
Pearson Educación de Mexico, S.A. de C.V.
Pearson Education Malaysia Pte. Ltd.

10 9 8 7 6 5 4 3 2 1
ISBN: 0-13-111656-8

In Memory of Patrick J. McNamara

Dedicated to Fran, Melissa, Tracy

TEACHER PREP

MERRILL
PRENTICE HALL

TEACHER PREPARATION CLASSROOM

Your Class. Their Careers. Our Future. Will your students be prepared?

We invite you to explore our new, innovative, and engaging website and all that it has to offer you, your course, and tomorrow's educators! Organized around the major courses pre-service teachers take, the Teacher Preparation site provides media, student/teacher artifacts, strategies, research articles, and other resources to equip your students with the quality tools needed to excel in their courses and prepare them for their first classroom.

This ultimate on-line education resource is available at no cost, when packaged with a Merrill text, and will provide you and your students access to:

Online Video Library. More than 150 video clips—each tied to a course topic and framed by learning goals and Praxis-type questions—capture real teachers and students working in real classrooms, as well as in-depth interviews with both students and educators.

Student and Teacher Artifacts. More than 200 student and teacher classroom artifacts—each tied to a course topic and framed by learning goals and application questions—provide a wealth of materials and experiences to help make your study to become a professional teacher more concrete and hands-on.

Research Articles. Over 500 articles from ASCD's renowned journal *Educational Leadership*. The site also includes Research Navigator, a searchable database of additional educational journals.

Teaching Strategies. Over 500 strategies and lesson plans for you to use when you become a practicing professional.

Licensure and Career Tools. Resources devoted to helping you pass your licensure exam; learn standards, law, and public policies; plan a teaching portfolio; and succeed in your first year of teaching.

How to ORDER *Teacher Prep* for you and your students:

For students to receive a *Teacher Prep* Access Code with this text, instructors must provide a special value pack ISBN number on their textbook order form. To receive this special ISBN, please email: **Merrill.marketing@pearsoned.com** and provide the following information:
- Name and Affiliation
- Author/Title/Edition of Merrill text

Upon ordering *Teacher Prep* for their students, instructors will be given a lifetime *Teacher Prep* Access Code.

PREFACE

This is an exciting time to be a teacher of students with learning disabilities. Consider the following:

- The number of students with learning disabilities continues to grow rapidly.
- Students with learning disabilities spend the majority of their school day in regular education classes.
- There are numerous opportunities for professional collaboration between regular and special educators.
- The 2004 recent reauthorization of the Individuals with Disabilities Education Act (IDEA) allows changes in the way students with learning disabilities are identified.
- The research base for teaching students with learning disabilities continues to grow rapidly.

The field of learning disabilities has changed dramatically since its inception in 1962. It has been marked by controversy, disagreements, and confusion regarding policies and practices. This multidisciplinary field generates so much information that a classroom teacher can be overwhelmed. What works? What is the current thinking on a particular approach? What does the research say? This book attempts to make sense of this wealth of information so that teachers can base their classroom practice on the best information available.

This comprehensive textbook addresses the nature and needs of students with learning disabilities throughout their lives, from early childhood to adulthood. It is intended for undergraduate and graduate students who are interested in becoming teachers of students with learning disabilities. It is also appropriate for general and special educators who are currently teaching these students in a variety of educational placements, such as resource rooms, self-contained classrooms, and inclusive classrooms.

Chapters 1 to 4 deal with the definitions, characteristics, and early stages of the field, as well as the causes of learning disabilities and underlying process disorders. Chapters 5 to 8 address prereferral practices, identifying students with learning disabilities, collaboration, and educational placements. Specific populations from early childhood through adulthood are discussed in Chapters 9 to 11. And finally, specific disabilities, such as those involving spoken language, reading, written language, and mathematics, as well as social-emotional and behavioral aspects, are covered in Chapters 12 to 16.

FEATURES

Each chapter includes a list of objectives at the beginning and a Summary and Springboards for Reflection and Discussion at the end. These features enable students to check for their understanding of the chapter, reflect on their practice, and expand their learning beyond the classroom. Throughout the book, there are highlighted materials that bring the information to life (Best Practices, Practical Considerations, and Implications for Teachers). The focus is on practical ways in which teachers can determine the impact that public policy, advocacy, and science have on their lives in the classroom and the lives of their students.

This book addresses the practical needs of teachers of students with learning disabilities. Attention deficit hyperactivity disorder, functional behavioral assessment, behavior intervention plans, and the social-emotional aspects of learning disabilities are thoroughly covered. Prereferral practices are discussed using examples of student referral and interventions. All the chapters on specific disabilities employ the same format, describing characteristics, assessment, and interventions. The reauthorization of IDEA is discussed, with an emphasis on its impact on teachers of students with learning disabilities. Finally, the concepts and application of inclusion, collaboration, and diversity are emphasized throughout the textbook.

The field of learning disabilities came about through the confluence of public policy, advocacy, and science, with a good dose of politics thrown in along the way. It is my hope that you will be as enthusiastic about this dynamic field as I am and base your classroom practice on the best information available.

ACKNOWLEDGMENTS

The willingness of students with learning disabilities, their teachers, and their families to share their experiences has had a profound impact on me, both personally and professionally, and I want to acknowledge their contribution. The professionals who reviewed the manuscript at various stages of development provided thorough, thought-provoking comments and enhanced the usefulness of this book. I thank them. They include David Anderson, Bethel College; Karen Applequist, Northern Arizona University; Lynne S. Arnault, Mississippi State University; Tamarah Ashton, California State University, Northridge; Dave Bass, Valley City State University; Judy L. Bell, Furman University; Joyce Williams Bergin, Armstrong Atlantic State University; Joan Bonsness, Minot State University; Elizabeth Borreca, University of St. Thomas; Kathleen Briseno, Northern Illinois University; Maryann Dudzinski, Valparaiso University; Jean Faieta, Edinboro University of Pennsylvania; Kathryn A. Lund, Arizona State University; Nancy Mamlin, Appalachian State University; Maurice Miller, Indiana State University; Robert F. Moore, University of Miami; Rita Mulholland, California State University, Chico; Miriam H. Porter, George Mason University; Diana N. Pyle, Eastern New Mexico University; Sheila Saravanabhavan, Virginia State University; Ted Schoneberger, California State University, Stanislaus; Malcolm L. Van Blerkom, University of Pittsburgh at Johnstown; and Donna Wandry, West Chester University.

Allyson P. Sharp was my Editor throughout most of this process. Her genuine concern was apparent at every stage. Her advice, support, and encouragement are truly appreciated. Kathleen S. Burk, Editorial Assistant, was always available to respond to my questions and concerns. In the final stages of the process, Ann Davis, Editor, and Penny Burleson, Editorial Assistant, made the transition seamless, and I appreciate their professionalism and competence.

This book was written in memory of my father, Patrick J. McNamara, a hard-working, kind, and gentle man. And it is dedicated to my wife, Fran, and our daughters, Tracy and Melissa. Fran was never too busy to help me resolve any issue related to this book. When she could have easily (and justifiably) said "Enough with the book!" she sat down, listened patiently, and helped me clarify my concerns. Knowing that I could depend on her immeasurably helped the writing of this book. Her love and belief in me have always sustained me, and this time was no different. Melissa and Tracy are remarkable young women who bring enormous pleasure to me. They have always brought joy and purpose to all I do. Our innumerable conversations and e-mails invariably ended with their genuine offers of help. They both have very busy lives and yet were always available to help, which meant a great deal to me. Simply knowing that was remarkably reassuring. For these reasons, and so many more, this book is dedicated to Fran, Tracy, and Melissa, with love, devotion, and appreciation. I also want to acknowledge my son-in-law, Todd J. Hirsch, not only for being a wonderful addition to our family, but also for his enthusiasm and interest in my work. And finally, I acknowledge my loving mother, Ursula McNamara, for being my loving mother.

DISCOVER THE MERRILL RESOURCES FOR SPECIAL EDUCATION WEBSITE

Technology is a constantly growing and changing aspect of our field that is creating a need for new content and resources. To address this emerging need, Merrill Education has developed an online learning environment for students, teachers, and professors alike to complement our products—the *Merrill Resources for Special Education* Website. This content-rich website provides additional resources specific to this book's topic and will help you—professors, classroom teachers, and students—augment your teaching, learning, and professional development.

Our goal with this initiative is to build on and enhance what our products already offer. For this reason, the content for our user-friendly website is organized by topic and provides teachers, professors, and student with a variety of meaningful resources in one location. With this website, we bring together the best of what Merrill has to offer: text resources, video clips, web links, tutorials, and a wide variety of information on topics of interest to general and special educators alike. Rich content, applications, and competencies further enhance the learning process.

The *Merrill Resources for Special Education* Website includes:

- Video clips specific to each topic, with questions to help you evaluate the content and make crucial theory-to-practice connections.

- Thought-provoking critical analysis questions that students can answer and turn in for evaluation or that can serve as a basis for class discussions and lectures.
- Access to a wide variety of resources related to classroom strategies and methods, including lesson planning and classroom management.
- Information on all of the most current relevant topics related to special and general education, including CEC and Praxis™ standards, IEPs, portfolios, and professional development.
- Extensive web resources and overviews on each topic addressed on the website.
- A search feature to help access specific information quickly.

To take advantage of these and other resources, please visit the *Merrill Resources for Special Education* Website at

http://www.prenhall.com/mcnamara

BRIEF CONTENTS

CONTENTS

Chapter 3
CAUSES OF LEARNING DISABILITIES   37

Chapter 4
ATTENTION DEFICIT HYPERACTIVITY DISORDER AND UNDERLYING PROCESS DISORDERS   47

Chapter 5
PREREFERRAL INTERVENTION STRATEGIES   67

Chapter 6
IDENTIFICATION OF STUDENTS WITH LEARNING DISABILITIES 85

Chapter 7
COLLABORATION WITH COLLEAGUES, FAMILIES, AND THE COMMUNITY 107

Chapter 8
EDUCATIONAL PLACEMENTS 127

Chapter 9
PRESCHOOL STUDENTS WITH LEARNING DISABILITIES 141

Chapter 10
MIDDLE SCHOOL AND HIGH SCHOOL STUDENTS WITH LEARNING DISABILITIES 157

Chapter 11
TRANSITION PLANNING AND ADULTS
WITH LEARNING DISABILITES   173

Chapter 12
SPOKEN LANGUAGE DISORDERS   189

Chapter 13
READING DISORDERS   207

Chapter 14
WRITTEN LANGUAGE DISORDERS   227

Chapter 15
MATHEMATICAL DISORDERS   247

Chapter 16
SOCIAL-EMOTIONAL AND BEHAVIORAL ASPECTS OF LEARNING DISABILITIES   269

Note: Every effort has been made to provide accurate and current Internet information in this book. However, the Internet and information posted on it are constantly changing, so it is inevitable that some of the Internet addresses listed in this textbook will change.

DEFINITIONS, CHARACTERISTICS,

CHAPTER 1 # AND CURRENT ISSUES

CHAPTER OBJECTIVES

At the end of this chapter you will:

- be able to define learning disabilities.
- understand the major issues related to the definition.
- know the major characteristics of students with learning disabilities.
- explore the current issues in the field.

If a friend, colleague, or family member asked you, "What is a learning disability?" how would you respond? Learning disabilities is the most well-known special education classification, so it is not surprising that many people have heard or read about it or know a student who is classified with a learning disability. Therefore, when asked to define a learning disability, how will you respond? You can recite the federal government's definition found in the Individuals with Disabilities Education Improvement Act (IDEA) of 2004 or describe characteristics of students with learning disabilities, and it still might not be clear exactly what a learning disability is. For most fields of study the definition is fairly straightforward. Sociology is the study of . . . History is the study of . . . Learning disabilities, by contrast, is an interdisciplinary field combining science, advocacy, and public policy, with a dose of politics thrown in along the way. Therefore, it is virtually impossible to find agreement on some of the basic issues confronting the field, such as identification, assessment, placement, and instructional practices (see Practical Considerations in Defining a Learning Disability). However, perhaps the most problematic issue has been that of definition. If learning disabilities cannot be defined adequately, how can we know what they are? How can we identify students? How can we conduct research? How can we describe the best practices in the field? How can parents, educators, and policy makers communicate with one another?

These and other concerns will be addressed in this chapter. In addition to discussing definitional issues related to learning disabilities, this chapter will describe the characteristics of students with learning disabilities, as well as current issues in the field. Wiederholt (1974) was prophetic when, over 30 years ago, he wrote, "it is unlikely that the problem of definition will be solved in the near future" (p. 146). Recent discussions in the professional literature on the definition of learning disabilities indicate that this statement is as true today as it was in 1974.

Practical Considerations in Defining a Learning Disability

The interview was going well. Then, all of a sudden, the Director of Special Education asked a rather simple question: "Do you think a student who is classified as mentally retarded can have a learning disability?" "No" came the rapid response from the interviewee "because students who have learning disabilities have average intellectual ability, and students with mental retardation are excluded from the classification." After that, the rest was a blur, except that the author was involved in a seemingly endless discussion of what a learning disability was and was not. And why couldn't a student be classified as both mentally retarded and having a learning disability? And is it more of a concept than a specific disability? That same discussion could occur today, over 35 years after the author was offered the job!

WHAT IS A LEARNING DISABILITY?

The term **learning disability** is so general that many employ it as synonymous with learning problems, school failure, and the like. In fact, it refers to a specific diagnostic category.

Learning disabilities has been referred to as the most heterogeneous special education classification. An examination of its definitions suggests that this heterogeneity refers more to the wide range of academic deficits found in the population than it does to cultural and linguistic diversity.

In 1990, Hammill examined 28 textbooks on learning disabilities published between 1982 and 1989. In all, 11 different definitions were discussed.

THE DEFINITIONS OF LEARNING DISABILITIES

Kirk and Bateman

Samuel Kirk is often referred to as "the father of learning disabilities" because he defined the term in a widely used textbook, *Educating Exceptional Children* (1962, p. 263):

> A learning disability refers to a retardation, disorder, or delayed development in one or more of the processes of speech, language reading, writing, arithmetic, or other school subjects resulting from a psychological handicap caused by a possible cerebral dysfunction and/or emotional or behavioral disturbances. It is not the result of mental retardation, sensory deprivation, or cultural and instructional factors.

The term became popularized when Kirk (1963) used it in a meeting of parents of children with **perceptual handicaps** a year later. As a result of his speech, the parents became so energized by the concept of learning disabilities that they formed the Association for Children with Learning Disabilities (ACLD), which is now the Learning Disabilities Association of America (LDA). Three years later, a former student of Kirk, Barbara Bateman, formulated another definition. Whereas Kirk discussed

processes that affect learning and causes of learning disabilities, Batemen ignored causes and focused primarily on children (Hammill, 1990). The most notable part of her definition is the inclusion of a discrepancy between performance and potential (Hallahan & Mercer, 2002). Although hotly debated, this continues to be a major issue in the definition of learning disabilities.

Minimal Brain Dysfunction: National Project on Learning Disabilities in Children

The federal government, along with the Easter Seal Research Foundation, established two task forces to study the definition of learning disabilities. Task Force I (mainly medical professionals) and Task Force II (mainly educators) each developed definitions. Task Force I (Clements, 1966) listed 99 signs and symptoms of students with minimal brain dysfunction (MBD). The 10 most frequent ones closely resemble the characteristics of students currently classified as having a learning disability. They are:

1. Hyperactivity
2. Perception impairments
3. Emotional lability
4. General coordination deficits
5. Disorders of attention
   Short attention span
   Distractibility preservation
6. Impulsivity
7. Disorders of memory and thinking
8. Specific learning disabilities
   Reading
   Arithmetic
   Writing
   Spelling
9. Disorders of speech and learning
10. Equivocal neurological signs and EEG irregularities

Task Force I defined MBD as a disorder affecting

children of near average, average, or above average general intelligence with certain learning or behavior disabilities ranging from mild to severe, which are associated with deviations of function of the central nervous system. These deviations may manifest themselves by various combinations of impairments in perception, conceptualization, language, memory, and control of attention, impulse, or motor function. . . .

These aberrations may arise from genetic variations, biochemical irregularities, perinatal brain insults or other illnesses or injuries sustained during the years which are critical for the development and maturation of the central nervous system, and from unknown causes. (Clements, 1966, pp. 9–10)

Task Force II could not agree on a single definition, so they proposed two (Hallahan & Mercer, 2002). These definitions were slightly different in that one cites specific underlying processes. They both include the notion of a discrepancy between potential and performance, and the possibility of central nervous system dysfunction, and exclude other causes.

The National Advisory Committee on Handicapped Children

This committee, chaired by Samuel Kirk, defined learning disabilities as follows:

Children with special (specific) learning disabilities exhibit a disorder in one or more of the basic psychological processes involved in understanding or in using spoken and written language. These may be manifested in disorders of listening, thinking, talking, reading, writing, spelling or arithmetic. They include conditions which have been referred to as perceptual handicaps, brain injury, minimal brain dysfunction, dyslexia, developmental aphasia, etc. They do not include learning problems that are due primarily to visual, hearing, or motor handicaps, to mental retardation, emotional disturbance, or to environmental disadvantage. (NACH, 1968, p. 34)

Hammill (1990) notes that "without a doubt this was the seminal definition of learning disabilities, for it was the basis for the 1967 United States Office of Education definition that was incorporated into Public Law 94–142" (p. 75). It is essentially the same definition that is employed in IDEA, and despite debate regarding its viability, it remained

the same in IDEA 2004. It differed from Kirk's original definition in that emotional disturbance was no longer stated as a cause of learning disabilities, and thinking disorders were included. It should be noted that in this definition, learning disabilities apply only to children. Later on, both parents and professionals responded to this exclusion of learning disabilities in adolescence and adulthood and formulated a definition that extended beyond childhood.

Northwestern University

The U.S. Office of Education funded an institute at Northwestern University to help resolve definitional issues regarding learning disabilities. Kass and Myklebust (1969) reported on the work of the institute. Northwestern University's definition is as follows:

- Learning disability refers to one or more significant deficits in essential learning processes requiring special education techniques.
- Children with learning disability generally demonstrate a discrepancy between expected and actual achievement in one or more areas such as spoken, read, or written language, mathematics, and spatial orientation.
- The learning disability referred to is not primarily the result of sensory, motor, intellectual, or emotional handicap, or lack of opportunity to learn.
- Significant deficits are defined in terms of accepted diagnostic procedures in education and psychology.
- Essential learning processes are those currently referred to in behavioral science as involving perception, integration, and expression, either verbal or nonverbal.
- Special education techniques for remediation refers to educational planning based on the diagnostic procedures and results. (Kass & Myklebust, 1969, pp. 378–379)

The discrepancy between expectation and performance was reintroduced, and there was no mention of causation. Hammill (1990) states that this definition formed the basis for the federal government definition developed in 1976.

The U.S. Office of Education (1976)

The federal government's definition was as follows:

> A specific learning disability may be found if a child has a severe discrepancy between achievement and intellectual ability in one or more of several areas: oral expression, written expression, listening comprehension or reading comprehension, basic reading skills, mathematics calculation, mathematics reasoning, or spelling. A "severe discrepancy" is defined to exist when achievement in one or more of the areas listed above falls below the expected achievement level, when age and previous educational experiences are taken into consideration. (USOE, 1976, p. 52405)

When the term **severe discrepancy** was introduced, the federal government defined it as a 50% discrepancy and provided a formula. This notion was not widely accepted, and there was heated opposition (Hammill, 1990). The notion of discrepancy continues to be very controversial (see Bradley, Danieson, & Hallahan, 2002). The reauthorized IDEA 2004 no longer requires schools to establish a severe discrepancy in order to classify students as having a learning disability. In making such a classification, schools "shall not be required to take into consideration whether a child has severe discrepancy between achievement and intellectual ability" (614 [b][6](A). A report from the U.S. Senate provides the rationale for this change:

> The committee believes that the IQ-achievement discrepancy formula, which considers whether a child has a severe discrepancy between achievement and intellectual ability, should not be a requirement for determining eligibility under IDEA. There is no evidence that the IQ-achievement discrepancy formula can be applied in a consistent and educationally meaningful (i.e., reliable and valid) manner. In addition, this approach had been found to be particularly problematic for students living in poverty or culturally and linguistically different backgrounds who may be erroneously viewed as having intrinsic intellectual limitation when the difficulties on such tests really re-

flect lack of experience. (S. Rept. 185, 108th Cong., 2nd Sess. 26, 2003)

The U.S. Office of Education (1977)

The 1977 U.S. Office of Education definition for learning disabilities was developed to identify more precisely children with learning disabilities. The definition is as follows:

> The term "specific learning disability" means a disorder in one or more of the basic psychological processes involved in understanding or in using language, spoken or written, which many manifest itself in an imperfect ability to listen, speak, read, write, spell, or to do mathematical calculations. The term includes such conditions as perceptual handicaps, brain injury, minimal brain dysfunction, dyslexia, and developmental aphasia. The term does not include children who have learning disabilities which are primarily the result of visual, hearing, or motor handicaps, or mental retardation, or emotional disturbance, or of environmental cultural, or economic disadvantage. (USOE, 1977, p. 65083)

The major purpose of the definition was to guide funding for schools and federally funded programs. Hence, it is the most widely used and most popular definition of learning disabilities (Mercer & Pullen, 2005).

The National Joint Committee on Learning Disabilities (NJCLD)

The NJCLD includes representatives from national organizations in the field of learning disabilities. These include the American Speech-Language-Hearing Association (ASHA), the Council for Learning Disabilities (CLD), the Division for Children with Learning Disabilities (DCLD), the International Reading Association (IRA), the Learning Disabilities Association of America (LDA), the National Association of School Psychologists (NASP), and the International Dyslexia Association (IDA, formerly the Orton Dyslexia Society). The NJCLD's original definition was proposed in 1981 and modified in 1988.

The major differences in its definition are the inclusion of learning disabilities "across the life-span" and the notion that learning disabilities "may occur coincidentally" with other disabilities. This is the official definition of NJCLD, although DCLD abstained and LDA voted against it, formulating its own definition.

The LDA definition included examples of the types of learning disabilities and excluded coexisting conditions.

The Interagency Committee on Learning Disabilities (ICLD)

The ICLD definition, formulated in 1987 by a committee of 12 agencies within the Department of Health and Human Services and the Department of Education, added social skills deficits as a specific learning disability. This continues to be a topic of

TABLE 1-1 Definition of Learning Disability

Proposed By	Key Components
Kirk (1962)	• Retardation, delay, or disorder in a psychological process • Possible cerebral dysfunction • Excludes other causes
Batemen (1965)	• Ignored causation • Focused on children • Introduced the concept of discrepancy
Task Forces I and II (Clements, 1966)	• Task Force I (mainly medical) Task Force II (mainly educational) • May/may not have central nervous system dysfunctions • Excludes other causes
National Advisory Committee on Handicapped Children (1969) Northwestern University (Kass & Myklebust, 1969)	• Continues the notion of discrepancy • More educationally oriented • Mentions special education techniques • Does not mention causation • Focuses only on children
U.S. Office of Education (1976)	• Introduces the term *severe discrepancy* • Lists area in which the discrepancy can be manifested
U.S. Office of Education (1977)	• More precise • Includes terms previously employed • Most widely used
National Joint Committee on Learning Disabilities (1981; Revised 1988)	• Introduces the notion that learning disabilities exist across the life span • May occur coincidentally with other disabilities
Learning Disabilities Assocation of America (1986) (Previously ACLD)	• Provides no examples of the types of learning disabilities • Does not include coexisting conditions
Interagency Committee on Learning Disabilities (1987)	• Adds social skills • Recognizes the wide variety of coexisting conditions
U.S. Office of Education (1977)	• Assumes average intellectual ability • Significant discrepancy • Exclusionary clause • Central nervous system dysfunction
U.S. Office of Education (2004)	• The same as 1977 • Students do not have to demonstrate a discrepancy between intellectual and academic functioning

debate within the learning disabilities community. Should social skills be included? Can a student be identified as having a social skills learning disability alone, with no learning disability in any other area? Chapter 16 provides additional information on this topic.

THE CURRENT DEFINITION OF LEARNING DISABILITIES

"Specific learning disability" means a disorder in one or more of the basic psychological processes involved in understanding or in using language, spoken or written, which may manifest itself in an imperfect ability to listen, think, speak, read, write, spell or to do mathematical calculations. The term includes such conditions as perceptual handicaps, brain injury, minimal brain dysfunction, dyslexia, and development aphasia. The term does not include children who have learning problems that are primarily the result of visual, hearing, or motor handicaps, or mental retardation, or emotional disturbance, or environmental, cultural, or economic disadvantage. (34 C. F. R. §300.7)

This is essentially the same definition that was included in Public Law 94-142, the Education of All Handicapped Children Act of 1975, and is included in the 2004 reauthorization of IDEA. And while there has been considerable dissatisfaction with this definition, Mercer, Jordan, Allsopp, and Mercer (1995) found that 71% of the state departments of education surveyed used major components of it. However, there are those who argue that it is necessary to radically alter the federal government's definition of learning disabilities (Fletcher et al., 2002) and others who want to make the definition more general (Shaw, Cullen, McGuire, & Brinckerhoff, 1995). Table 1–1 summarizes the definitions discussed above.

MAJOR COMPONENTS OF THE DEFINITION

The definition of learning disability assumes (a) at least average intellectual capacity; (b) a significant discrepancy between achievement and potential; (c) exclusion of mental retardation, emotional disturbance, sensory impairment, cultural difference, or lack of opportunity to learn as primary factors in the student's learning difficulty; and (d) central nervous system dysfunction as the basis of the difficulty. Given the problems in determining the intellectual capacity of students, especially those with diverse linguistic and cultural backgrounds, and of matching a specific achievement score to intellectual capacity and to classroom instruction, the diagnosis of specific learning disabilities is very often one of exclusion.

Intellectual functioning is a critical element in the definition and diagnosis of specific learning disabilities. Individuals with learning disabilities must demonstrate, by definition, at least average intellectual ability. Therefore, intellectual ability becomes the yardstick by which the student's acceptable level of academic achievement is calculated. However, the concept of easily definable and quantifiable areas of general intelligence is not without its critics.

ACHIEVEMENT–INTELLECTUAL FUNCTIONING DISCREPANCY

The definition of specific learning disabilities no longer requires that a significant discrepancy exists between some area of academic achievement and intellectual potential. However, it remains to be seen how many states will continue to employ the notion of discrepancy. The degree of discrepancy may vary from state to state, making it possible for a student who takes the same test and achieves the same score in two different states to be classified as having a specific learning disability in one state and not in the other. This also happens in school districts within the same state; more affluent districts provide services for students who have smaller discrepancies. A discrepancy between achievement and intellectual performance is established by tests administered to students who have basic experiential differences from the population on which the instrument was normed. Thus, the result of such testing cannot be considered an accurate index of achievement of potential (Salvia & Ysseldyke, 1995). This is a critical issue in urban areas where students who are suspected of having a learning disability may include a variety of linguistic and experiential backgrounds. Furthermore, inherent in the assessment of academic areas is the assumption that the test items reflect what was actually taught in the classroom.

CENTRAL NERVOUS SYSTEM FACTORS

The assumption of central nervous system dysfunction is perhaps the least observed component in the diagnosis of specific learning disabilities. Because central nervous system dysfunction is so difficult to demonstrate, specific learning disabilities are often defined by the exclusion of sensory deprivation, mental retardation, emotional disturbance, cultural differences, or economic disadvantage as primary factors in the student's underachievement.

For students from poor urban areas, for students whose acculturation is different from that of the standardized population of the assessment instruments used, for students whose native language is not English, and for students with no opportunity to learn, the diagnosis of specific learning disabilities *should* be an extremely complex process. Ironically, it often appears that these very students are the ones most frequently classified as having learning disabilities. In fact, it is relatively easy to classify culturally different students in urban areas as having learning disabilities when evaluators do not consider the appropriate match between students and the normative population, and do not consider the social-cultural and instructional factors that, by definition, should preclude such a classification.

In general, a major problem lies in the attempt to identify an atypical learner who, although assumed to have at least average intellectual ability and no primary deficits in sensory reception, intellectual capacity, emotional adjustment, or cultural and economic factors, does not appear to learn specific types of information in the typical manner. The problem is exacerbated in large, diverse urban

areas. In many instances, evaluators in such areas are faced with the question "With what type of error do we feel most comfortable: a false positive, in which large numbers of students may be classified as having learning disabilities when they do not, or a false negative, in which large numbers of students who do have learning disabilities must go without services?"

HOW SCHOOLS DEFINE LEARNING DISABILITIES

MacMillan and Saperstein (2002) state that "it is evident that the *concept* of LD used by the schools deviates markedly from the original concept of LD articulated in authoritative definitions" (p. 319). Therefore, as a teacher of students with learning disabilities, you may find that the situation of your students does not necessarily align with the federal definition. You may find that their intelligence level is lower than you anticipated; that there are environmental, cultural, and/or linguistic factors that contribute to their underachievement; and that there is no evidence of central nervous system disorder. This may be especially true if you work in a culturally and linguistically diverse urban environment. Gottlieb, Gottlieb, and Trogone (1991) found that students with learning disabilities in New York City were very different from students with learning disabilities in affluent suburban school districts. In New York City, 90% of students with learning disabilities received some form of public assistance, most students had low achievement, and English was not the primary language of 44% of their parents.

As noted earlier, learning disabilities is the most heterogeneous of all special education classifications. There will never be a definition that will satisfy all of the stakeholders. Professionals in the field of learning disabilities frequently apply the medical model, in which science informs public policy and public policy influences practice. To be sure, there have been many missteps that could have been avoided if that model had been in place. Learning disabilities is a field that came about through the synergy of science, public policy, politics, and advocacy. No doubt it is moving in the right direction by attempting to validate empirically the processes of identification, classification, and instruction. And yet, so much more has to be done.

When school personnel view the definition of learning disabilities differently from researchers, the result is an "unhealthy schism." MacMillian and Saperstein (2002, p. 326) note:

> There exists an unhealthy schism between research and practice fueled, in part, by the discrepancy between SI [School Identified] and RI [Research Identified] students with learning disabilities. Public school personnel perceive the research community as out-of-touch, while the research community often views those in the public schools as uninformed. In truth the research does not inform practice, as the database derives from a population of "LD" students only vaguely resembling SI "LD" students. An analogy to medicine may clarify our point. Research on the treatment of diabetes informs physicians treating diabetics because the researchers and the practitioners agree on who is diabetic. Researchers studying subjects with LD and the practitioners serving students with LD do not agree on who is LD and, as a result, research does not inform practice.

Until there is some resolution to this conflict, there will continue to be a disconnect between research and classroom practice. As IDEA 2004 is implemented in schools, you will play a critical role in bridging the gap between research and classroom practice.

PREVALENCE

As the previous section stated, many definitions of learning disabilities have been proposed. And while there continues to be disagreement, there is consensus on the major components. It may seem that the debate over definitions would make the classification of students with learning disabilities relatively difficult. However, the opposite is true.

The number of students classified as having learning disabilities continues to increase. In 2001, over 208 million schoolchildren were identified as having a learning disability (U.S. Department of Education, 2002). This represents 50% of all special education students. The closest category is speech language impairment at 19%.

Male versus Female

Most teachers of students with learning disabilities will tell you immediately that there are more boys in their classes than girls. Do learning disabilities occur more often in males than in females? A 1998 Office of Civil Rights survey indicated that 70% of students with learning disabilities are boys. Smith (2004) states that regardless of research suggesting that the male:female ratio may be equal, boys are 6 to 105 times more likely to be identified as having learning disabilities. It may well be that girls who exhibit unexpected underachievement are not identified as rapidly or as often as boys. Mercer and Pullen (2005, p. 27) provide a sample of medical, maturational, and sociological hypothesis concerning gender differences.

Medical Factors
1. The male appears to be more biologically susceptible to brain damage during prenatal and postnatal periods than female.
2. Because males typically have greater birth weights and larger heads than females, they are more at risk for brain injury during the birth process.
3. Males experience one and one-half to three times as many head injuries as females.
4. The left hemisphere, which is associated with language and reading achievement, is particularly vulnerable in males because abnormalities in the immune system's development are associated with too much testosterone, a male hormone.

Maturational Factors
1. From birth through adolescence, males mature more slowly than females.
2. The male brain's protective sheath tends to mature more slowly than that of the female.

3. The neural maturation of the male's cortical regions associated with attention and language occurs more slowly than that of the female.

Sociological Factors

1. The slow maturity rates of males often translate into a lack of school readiness and poor early-grade-level performance.
2. Because teachers expect males to exhibit more learning problems than females, bias in referring males for assessment and identification results.

Learning Disabilities and Minority Status

In their report "Minority Students in Special and Gifted Education" (2002), the National Research Council (NRC) states, "from the enactment of the 1975 federal law requiring states to provide a free and appropriate education to all students with disabilities, children in some racial/ethnic groups have been identified for services in disproportionately large numbers" (p. 1). This typically occurs in high-incidence categories such as mild mental retardation, emotional disturbance, and, to a lesser degree, learning disabilities. The NRC reports that data from the Office of Civil Rights (OCR, 1998) suggest that all racial/ethnic groups are more at risk than whites for classification as having learning disabilities, much more so than those classified as mildly mentally retarded. In discussing trends over time, the NRC notes that the OCR national projections for the learning disabilities category include a dramatic increase in the risk to children of all racial/ethnic groups except Asian/Pacific Islanders. It is interesting to note that there is not significant overrepresentation of Blacks or Hispanics in the population with learning disabilities nationwide. However, the rate of increase for all racial/ethnic groups has been dramatic.

This may be why the issue of disproportionality is not often raised in discussions of learning disabilities. For example, Harry (2002) states that "for several decades, LD was a disability category reserved for middle class children, mostly white, whose poor academic achievement stood out as

unexpected in the context of their family and community setting and of their own verbal and general skills" (p. 77).

For teachers, especially those in urban areas, there are some issues to consider. There is a considerable difference among states and in urban versus suburban areas. For example, when examining the referral pattern for parents and teachers in New York City, Gottlieb et al. (1991) found that of the 328 students referred by teachers, 15.5% were White, 42.4% were African American, and 42.1% were Hispanic. There was a 95% chance that teachers referred African American or Hispanic students more often than White students. Consider the following article from the *New York Times* on May 31, 1997, titled "Special Education Practices in New York Faulted by U.S.":

> The Federal Government last night warned New York City school officials that they must reduce the disproportionately high number of Black and Hispanic students in special education or face a lawsuit and ultimately the revocation of tens of millions of dollars in Federal aid. (p. 1)

The article went on to say that the perceived overrepresentation of minority students was true. It also noted that approximately 75% of the 120,000 students receiving special education were classified as "learning disabled" or "emotionally handicapped."

An agreement between the New York City board of education and the OCR will address these concerns through a series of corrective measures including staff development and parent training. The article concluded with a statement from a lawyer familiar with the agreement: "The reason this case is important is that it sends a message out to school districts throughout the United States that the issue of minority students in Special Education is not one the Federal government is ignoring" (p. 22).

The overrepresentation of minority students classified as having learning disabilities, and the problems in defining and diagnosing specific learning disabilities, require significant changes in traditional special education assessment and instruction. These changes must occur so that professionals can give appropriate attention to the factors of cultural and linguistic diversity and their impact on how students represent and demonstrate knowledge. There is a critical need to incorporate sensitivity to issues of diversity in educational assessment, curriculum planning, teacher training, and interactions with parents, especially in large urban areas characterized by cultural and linguistic diversity.

CHARACTERISTICS OF STUDENTS WITH LEARNING DISABILITIES

Now that we have reviewed the definitions of learning disabilities promulgated by federal agencies, professional groups, and parent groups, you are probably wondering what students with learning disabilities look like in the classroom and in their homes. What characteristics enable us to differentiate them from other groups of underachieving students? Due to the heterogeneity of this population, it is difficult to describe one type of person with learning disabilities. Rather, the literature has described a number of characteristics that, taken together, present a fairly well accepted picture (Lerner, 2006; Mercer & Pullen, 2005; Smith, 2004; Wong, 2004).

Motor Problems

Students with learning disabilities may have trouble with tasks involving fine or gross motor skills. Fine motor tasks involve using hands and fingers, whereas gross or large motor skills involve arm and leg movements or the larger muscles of the body. Students with learning disabilities may have trouble playing with blocks, puzzles, or beads; using a spoon, fork, or knife; and coloring or copying shapes and objects. Their handwriting may be poor, and they may have difficulty with activities that require coordination, such as gym and playground activities and sports. Parents often report that their child with a learning disability frequently bangs into objects, knocks things over, and is awkward.

Perceptual Deficits

Some students with learning disabilities have difficulty with perceptual tasks. Perceptual deficits can be divided into two major categories: auditory and visual.

Perception is the interpretation of information from the environment. If this information comes to us through hearing, it is referred to as **auditory perception;** if it is derived from vision, it is known as **visual perception.**

Most information is not strictly visual or auditory, but rather a combination of the two. Students with learning disabilities have difficulty with different components of perception. For example, they may have trouble differentiating between letters that look alike (*b* for *d, w* for *m*) or words that are similar (*was* for *saw),* or understanding what someone is saying in a noisy environment.

Early in the study of learning disabilities, many problems students encountered were attributed to their perceptual deficits. Subsequent research has not supported such contentions, yet it is clear that these deficits do exist for some students with learning disabilities.

Attention Deficits

It is estimated that approximately one third of all students with learning disabilities have an attention deficit hyperactivity disorder (ADHD; see Chapter 4). The majority of students with learning disabilities are not diagnosed with ADHD. Their attention difficulties are related to the processes of learning. For example, they may have difficulty staying on task, deciding what is important and what is not in listening to a lecture or reading a passage, and sustaining attention on particular tasks. This may not happen all the time, as it does for students with ADHD, but may instead be related to specific tasks. Many experts believe that many, if not most, students with learning disabilities have attention problems, but for most (two thirds) such problems are not severe enough and do not occur often enough to be diagnosed as ADHD.

Memory Disorders

Some students with learning disabilities have memory problems. Some of these problems involve short-term memory (STM), which lasts for 30 to 60 seconds. If one does not attend to the information from the environment, it will never become part of STM. Clearly, that is what happens to many students with learning disabilities. If we attend and the information reaches the STM, it must then be transferred to long-term memory (LTM). For example, you are introduced to someone at a party, and you do nothing to remember the person's name; consequently, when you see this person the following week, you have forgotten it. However, if you did something to remember the name when you were introduced (STM), a process psychologists call **rehearsal,** you would have had a higher probability of committing it to your LTM and being able to retrieve it when you saw the person.

Memory is a complicated process that is not completely understood. However, it is clear that students with learning disabilities need assistance in this area.

Language Disorders

Students with learning disabilities frequently have difficulty with the reception, processing, and expression of language. These problems appear to be persistent and continue throughout life for about half of these students. Examples of difficulty with receptive language include failure to understand specific sounds, words, or sentences or difficulty understanding the structure of language. Receptive language problems always result in expressive language problems. If students do not understand what they hear, they will have difficulty expressing themselves (input precedes output). Some students with learning disabilities have trouble coming up with the correct words, frequently talking around something or describing it. Others have trouble with the grammar of the language (syntax); they may not use the correct sequence of words or proper noun–verb agreement. Still others have very little to say about the world in which they live. They tend to say very little spontaneously and even less upon demand.

Social Perceptual Disorders

Social perception can be defined as understanding the constraints of a social situation. For many students with learning disabilities, this is a major problem. Many parents and teachers notice that students with learning disabilities have a hard time making friends; they say the wrong thing at the wrong time and make impulsive comments. These are just some of the characteristics of a child who has difficulty with social perceptual skills.

Emotional Overlay

It is not surprising that emotional issues are closely related to learning disabilities. Children with learning disabilities come to school wanting to succeed like everyone else. Often they soon realize that their best efforts are not good enough. Couple that problem with teachers and parents who may not recognize the disability, and it is obvious that undetected learning disabilities can lead to social-emotional difficulties. These students do not have behavior disorders or significant emotional problems. However, many professionals know that it soon becomes impossible to detect which condition came first.

All these characteristics will be discussed more thoroughly through the book.

Academic and Instructional Characteristics

In the preschool years, it is difficult to identify students with learning disabilities. There are a number of variables that put a child at risk for school failure (see Chapters 3, 4, and 9), but it is hard to differentiate between learning disabilities and other disabilities/disorders (Bender, 2004). Additionally, there is no federal or state requirement to employ the IDEA 2004 classifications before students enter kindergarten. Chapter 9 will discuss the specific academic characteristics of this population.

In elementary school, students with learning disabilities, by definition, display difficulties with spoken language, written language, reading, and mathematics. Specific academic and instructional characteristics and interventions will be provided for each of these areas (see Chapters 12 and 15). And because there are unique issues related to middle and high school students with learning disabilities, the academic and instructional characteristics of these students are covered in Chapter 10.

CURRENT ISSUES

Some researchers suggest that the field of learning disabilities is in constant flux. Definitions change; identification procedures vary; instructional approaches frequently go in and out of vogue. However, as a teacher of students with learning disabilities, you may be above (or below) the fray. You are charged with meeting the needs of your students. This introspective, self-critical approach has marked the field since its inception, and it is unlikely that the situation will change soon. However, it may impact your practice, and therefore it is critical that you are cognizant of the major issues of the day. What are the issues you will face based on current public policy and research on learning disabilities? This section will briefly discuss some of these issues, which will be elaborated on throughout the book.

Identification of Learning Disabilities

There has been dissatisfaction with the identification process for some time (Bradley et al., 2002; Siegel, 1989; Torgesen, 1979; Ysseldyke, 1983, 2005).

This is not surprising given what you have just read about the issues related to defining learning disabilities. As the field grappled with a variety of definitions, many methods were proposed to operationalize them and establish specific criteria for classification (Hammill, 1990; Learning Disability Roundtable, 2002).

The new regulations in IDEA 2004 no longer require the determination of a discrepancy between intellectual ability and academic achievement. Several approaches have been proposed to replace the discrepancy model (Donovan & Cross, 2003; Fletcher et al., 2002; Vaughn & Fuchs, 2003). One of the most widely discussed approaches is responsiveness to intervention (see the Special Series in *Learning Disabilities Research and Practice, 18*[3], 2003 and the Special Series in *The Journal of Learning Disabilities, 38*[6], 2005).

At this point, continued research is needed on the utility of these approaches. IDEA 2004 requests 15 states to submit proposals on how they will operationalize the definition of learning disabilities without establishing a discrepancy. Will this mean that more students will be classified as having learning disabilities? How will it impact your students in the future? Will they be similar to the students who are currently classified as having learning disabilities? Ongoing research into new ways to identify students with learning disabilities will provide new answers and new questions. Chapter 6 provides more information on this topic.

Disproportionality

A major concern in special education is the disproportionately large number of minority students who are classified as having learning disabilities (Artiles & Ortiz, 2002; Donovan & Cross, 2002; Losen & Orfield, 2002). This issue focuses on minority groups, and it is a major concern when viewed in the context of urban special education (McNamara, 1999). Culturally and linguistically diverse students living in urban areas may need carefully constructed educational interventions.

Whether they need to be classified as having learning disabilities is the question. If you are a teacher in an urban area, this will impact your classroom practice. As the identification process is refined, it will be critical to monitor it and evaluate whether the new procedures increase the probability that students from culturally and linguistically diverse urban areas are more likely to be classified as having learning disabilities (see Chapters 3, 5, and 6 for a more thorough discussion of this issue).

Bridging the Gap Between Research and Classroom Practice

The emphasis on validated practices for students with learning disabilities is not new (see Lyon, 2005). However, it has gained impetus from the No Child Left Behind Act, where the term **scientifically based** is used over 100 times. There is an increasingly large database on effective instruction for students with learning disabilities (Gersten, Schiller, & Vaughn, 2000; Swanson, 2000; Vaugh, Gersten & Chard, 2000).

Using these data to inform classroom practice is the challenge (Crockett, 2004). The history of learning disabilities provides ample evidence of the schism between research and practice (see Chapter 2 for a thorough discussion). The roles of science, advocacy, and practice need to be more fully integrated. Will the current momentum of scientifically based practices continue? Most likely this will be a "current" issue for years to come, impacting what you teach and how you teach it. It will provide evidence to inform your instruction, and it will enable you to evaluate its effectiveness.

As Lloyd and Hallahan (2005), in a special issue of *Learning Disability Quarterly* (*28*[2]) on "the Future of Learning Disabilities" note, "Although learning disabilities probably will continue to be awash in controversy, it will stand for a model of promoting the empirical basis for effective teaching" (p. 135). Clearly, this is an exciting time to be a teacher of students with learning disabilities.

SUMMARY

This chapter has focused on a central question in our field: "What is a learning disability?" It should be clear that there is no simple answer. A number of definitions were presented, ranging from Kirk's early definition to the current one in IDEA 2004, to demonstrate the complexities involved in formulating a definition that is acceptable to all stakeholders. There is now wide acceptance of both the NJCLD and federal government definitions. As the body of research continues to grow, this will be an ongoing debate. This chapter has also presented information on the prevalence of learning disabilities and the characteristics of students so classified. As a teacher of students with learning disabilities, you will see that while the characteristics vary, there is a common core. Finally, current issues in the field were presented. Given the history and nature of the field of learning disabilities, this list will continue to evolve.

SPRINGBOARDS FOR REFLECTION AND DISCUSSION

1. Define learning disabilities.
2. Interview a group of regular educators and ask them "What is a learning disability?" How accurate are their answers? Is there great variability in their definitions?
3. Interview a group of special educators and ask them, "What is a learning disability?" How do their definitions differ from those of regular educators?
4. Interview parents of students with and without learning disabilities and ask them, "What is a learning disability?" What are their answers? Are the answers similar or dissimilar? Are they different from those of the educators? How accurate are the definitions?
5. Do you think there will ever be one definition of learning disabilities accepted by the majority of parents and professionals? Why or why not?

6. Describe the major characteristics of students with learning disabilities as manifested in the classroom.

7. Observe classes of students with learning disabilities (both self-contained and inclusive). Are there more boys than girls? If so, what do you think is the reason? Ask the teachers about their views regarding gender differences.

8. Interview classroom teachers about current issues. Are the issues the same as the ones listed in this book? How similar or different are they?

2
CHAPTER

THE HISTORY OF LEARNING DISABILITIES

CHAPTER OBJECTIVES

At the end of this chapter you will:

- understand the early foundations of learning disabilities.
- understand the transitions in the field up to the present.
- know the federal initiatives on behalf of students with learning disabilities.
- understand the role of advocacy in the development of the field of learning disabilities.
- understand the relationship between advocacy and science.

Y ou are probably wondering, "Why do I have to know about the history of learning disabilities? I just want to know how to teach these kids." Wiederholt (1974) provides a succinct rationale for examining the history of learning disabilities: "Unless we use the past as a point of reference and guidance, investigators of LD may either recommit past follies or 'rediscover' the contributions of their professional progenitors when they should instead extend and correct the works of those who pioneered before them" (p. 103). Clearly, there have been many changes in the field since Wiederholt's classic historical statement, but his words of caution are as appropriate now as they were over three decades ago. Learning disabilities did not appear in the early 1960s. Much of the foundational work occurred during the 1800s when physicians, psychologists, and educators in Europe and the United States provided a framework that has influenced the current leaders in the field. Perhaps now more than ever, when some question the very existence of learning disabilities, the need for a historical perspective on the field is crucial. You will recognize that many of the instructional practices you use every day have their roots in the early developmental stages of the field.

HISTORY OF LEARNING DISABILITIES

Learning disabilities is a relatively new category in the field of special education. However, as Hallahan and Mercer (2002) point out, "the origins of its conceptual foundation are as long standing, or nearly as long standing, as [those of] many of the other disability categories" (p. 1). The history of learning disabilities is typically divided into generally agreed-upon phases or periods (Hallahan & Mercer, 2002; Lerner, 2003; Mercer & Pullan, 2005; Myers & Hammill, 1990; Wiederholt, 1974). Hallahan and Mercer's chapter ("Learning Disabilities: Historical Perspectives") in their 2002 work provides the most thorough historical perspective to date. They divide the history of the field into five periods (see Figure 2-1).

European Foundation Period (1800–1920)

Early research that laid the groundwork for learning disabilities occurred in the medical field. Investigators attempted to find a relationship between brain physiology and brain function (brainbehavior research). Typically, this involved performing autopsies on individuals with observed difficulties, most often in language functions. Franz Joseph Gall, the first to investigate this relationship, noted the effect of brain damage to a particular part of the brain (the left temporal lobe), a condition now called **Broca's aphasia.** Wiederholt (1974) notes that his views were not widely accepted, in part due to his association with the field of phrenology (which believed that behavior was the result of the shape of the skull), which many considered quackery.

Later (the 1820's), John Baptistc Bouillaud continued the work of Gall by performing autopsies

European Foundation Period 1800–1920	U.S. Foundation Period 1920–1960	Emergent Period 1960–1975	Solidification Period 1975–1985	Turbulent Period 1985–2000

FIGURE 2–1   Historical Timeline of Learning Disabilities

on brain-injured individuals. He hypothesized that certain areas of the brain controlled specific motor and speech functions. Perhaps the first researcher many teachers have heard about is Paul Broca (1879), who identified the part of the brain (left frontal lobe) that is responsible for speech. You may know someone who has had a stroke, resulting in speech that is slow, laborious, and disfluent—Broca's aphasia. Another type of aphasia was identified by Carl Wernicke (1874). **Wernicke's aphasia** (due to damage to the left temporal lobe) is characterized by incomprehension of language and fluent but meaningless speech. Individuals with this disorder often use 'nonsense' words for everyday items, making communication frustrating and difficult. Someone who has suffered a stroke and cannot communicate effectively may want a comb and call it a *gleam* or some other nonsense word, failing to realize that it is not a word or that the person being communicated with has no idea of what he or she is saying. Chapter 12 provides examples of students with learning disabilities who display similar disorders.

During this period, a number of researchers started to examine reading disorders (Hallahan & Mercer, 2002). Broadbent (1872), Kussmaul (1877), Morgan (1896), and Hinshelwood (1917) reported observing individuals with apparently normal intellectual ability, with no other disabilities other than in the area of reading. Hinshelwood's book, *Congenital Word Blindness* (1917), considered to be a classic in the field, provided information on his findings. There were two major findings: more males than females were affected, and reading disorders may be inherited. Hinshelwood emphasized training in visual memory for words and intensive individualized instruction.

U.S. Foundation Period (1920–1960)

Hallahan and Mercer (2002) divide this period into two areas of research:

Language and reading disabilities
Perceptual, perceptual-motor, and attention disabilities

The major figures in the area of language and reading were Samuel Orton, Grace Fernald, Marion Monroe, and Samuel Kirk.

Samuel Orton.   Orton was probably the premier researcher in the United States in the area of reading. The organization named after him (the Orton Society, later the Orton Dyslexia Association and now the International Dyslexia Association) continues to be a powerful and influential organization of professionals and parents. Orton was a neuropathologist who focused on students with reading disorders. His classic book *Reading, Writing, and Speech Problems in Children* (1937) reports his findings. One of his major theories concerned cerebral dominance. He believed that the student with a reading disorder did not establish dominance in the dominant hemisphere of the brain; therefore, when reading, information from the nondominant hemisphere would emerge. For example, rather than reading *was,* the student would read *saw.* By contrast, the efficient reader, with established dominance, would read the correct word. Orton observed this phenomenon not only on the word level, but also with individual letters (e.g., *b* for *d*) and syllables of words.

Orton coined the term **strephosymbiolia,** which referred to the use of twisted or mixed syllables to describe the reversals he observed in his subjects. Subsequent research did not support

Orton's contentions, but his influence remained due to his emphasis on phonics and multisensory training (see Chapter 13). The **Orton Approach,** also referred to as the **Orton-Gillingham Approach** (see Gillingham & Stillman, 1970, for a description of this multisensory phonics-based method), continues to be as popular as other approaches, such as the **Wilson Reading Program,** which fall under the umbrella of the **Orton family** approaches.

Grace Fernald. Fernald worked at the University of California at Los Angeles Clinic School (Fernald & Keller, 1921) and developed a multisensory approach to reading. Unlike Orton's approach, the **Fernald Approach** (see Chapter 13) focused on the whole word, not phonics. Fernald's classic textbook, *Remedial Techniques in Basic School Subjects* (1943), describes her experience in the clinic and the experimental classroom at UCLA.

Marion Monroe. Marion Monroe worked as a research associate of Dr. Orton. Her book, *Children Who Cannot Read* (1932), describes the results of her experiments with her methods and diagnostic techniques. She is credited with introducing the notion of **discrepancy,** measuring the difference between actual achievement and expected achievement as a way of identifying students with reading disabilities (Hallahan & Mercer, 2002). This approach was a precursor of diagnostic-perspective teaching. Monroe's work had a direct impact on classroom teaching.

Samuel Kirk. Kirk is recognized as the father of learning disabilities. An interesting story is reported by Hallahan and Mercer (2002, pp. 13–14) about Kirk's experience as a graduate student and instructor at the Institute of Juvenile Research, describing how it changed his life and the field of special education.

> At this school I taught in the afternoon and served as a recreational worker after school. In the evenings I helped the nurses put the boys to bed and see that they stayed there. In reading the clinical folders of one of these children from the famous Institute of Juvenile Research, I noticed that the boy was labeled as "word blind," a term I had never heard before in my psychology courses. He was ten years old, a nonreader and had a recorded IQ of 82. This clinical folder referred to Marion Monroe's monograph (Monroe, 1928) on reading disabilities, Hinshelwood's book (1917) on congenital word blindness, and Fernald's kinesthetic method. After reading these references, which I found the next day in the university library, I arranged to tutor the boy at nine o'clock in the evening, after the boys were supposed to be asleep. This boy was eager to learn, sneaked quietly out of bed at the appointed time each night and met me in a small space between the two dormitory rooms, actually, in the doorway of the boys' toilet. By making this arrangement we both knew we were violating a regulation, since the head nurse had directed me not to allow the boys out of bed after nine. In the same vein as the Boston Tea Party, and knowing the consequences of civil disobedience, I decided to take a chance and violate the directions since the cause was good. I often state that my first experience in tutoring a case of reading disability was not in a school, but was in a clinic, in the boys' lavatory. (Kirk, 1976, pp. 242–243)

In addition to studying reading disorders, Kirk developed procedures to assess particular disabilities more specifically. Later, during the emergent period of the field, it was Kirk who was credited with coining the term **learning disabilities.**

The European influence was still prominent during this period because pioneers in the field such as Kurt Goldstein, Henry Werner, and Alfred Strauss had immigrated to the United States. Other influential contemporary researchers were Laura Lehtnin, William Cruickshank, and Newell Kephart.

Goldstein was a medical doctor in a hospital that treated soldiers who had received head injuries during World War I. He noted that these men were perceptually impaired, distractible, and preservative—many of the same characteristics that were later used to describe students with learning disabilities. Unlike some of his predecessors, Goldstein was not interested in localized brain function; rather, he looked at the whole picture (an approach referred to as **gestalt psychology**).

Werner and Strauss continued the work of Goldstein and applied it to children. Their classic work on endogenous (hereditary) versus exogenous (brain injury) mental retardation led to differentiated instruction for these two populations. They discussed specific environmental accommodations and teaching methods. Their classic books (Strauss & Kephart, Vol. 2, 1955;56 Strauss & Lehtinen, 1947) are essential reading for any teacher of students with learning disabilities. The distraction-free environment, sometimes referred to as the **Strauss classroom,** still exists in many special education settings.

Just as Goldstein influenced the work of Werner and Strauss, these researchers influenced the work of William Cruickshank. Hallahan and Mercer (2002) note that Cruickshank was the bridge between children with mental retardation and those with normal intelligence, "many of whom today would be identified as learning disabled" (p. 19). Cruickshank's early work was done at Syracuse University with students who had cerebral palsy. Based on his findings, one of his recommendations for teaching these students was a distraction-free environment. The results of his groundbreaking demonstration pilot study in Montgomery County, Maryland, were published in *A Teaching Method for Brain-Injured and Hyperactive Children* (Cruickshank, Bentzen, Ratzeburg, & Tannhauser, 1961). Cruickshank and his colleagues provided extensive case studies and specific recommendations for the teacher, including how the classroom should be organized, going so far as to suggest that the teacher refrain from wearing distracting clothes, jewelry, and so on.

Emergent Period (1960–1975)

You might think that the early 1960s marked the beginning of the field of learning disabilities. However, it is apparent from the previous discussion that the foundations of the field were laid much earlier. Clearly, the key event of this period was the introduction of the term **learning disabilities,** defined by Samuel Kirk in 1962 and 1963. Kirk first defined the term in an introductory textbook, *Educating Exceptional Children* (1962), but it was his presentation to a parent organization that is credited with its wide acceptance. Parents requested help from Dr. Kirk regarding the name for their new national organization; Hallahan and Mercer (2002, pp. 22–23) cite his remarks:

> I have felt for some time that labels we give children are satisfying to us, but of little help to the child himself. We seem to be satisfied if we can give a technical name to a condition. This gives us the satisfaction of closure. We think we know the answers if we can give the child a name or a label—brain injured, schizophrenic, autistic, mentally retarded, aphasic, etc. As indicated before, the term "brain injury" has little meaning to us from a management for training point of view. It does not tell me if the child is smart or dull, hyperactive or underactive. The terms cerebral palsy, brain injured, mentally retarded, aphasic, etc. are not actually classification terms. In a sense they are not diagnostic, if by diagnosis we mean an assessment of the child in such a way that leads us to some form of treatment, management, or remediation. It is not a basic cause since the designation of the child as brain injured does not really tell us why the child is brain injured or how he got that way.
>
> Recently, I have used the term "learning disabilities" to describe a group of children who have disorders in development in language, speech, reading, and associated communication skills needed for social interaction. In this group, I do not include children who have sensory handicaps such as blindness or deafness, because we have methods of managing and training the deaf and blind. I also exclude from this group children who have generalized mental retardation. (Kirk, 1963)

Motivated by Kirk's speech, the parent immediately accepted the term **learning disabilities** and formed the Association for Children with Learning Disabilities (ACLD). Now known as the Learning Disabilities Association of America (LDA), it is generally acknowledged as the largest and most influential learning disabilities parent organization in the United States.

The emergent period was also marked by an explosion of educational programs for students with learning disabilities on all levels, starting with elementary school. Most of these students were educated in self-contained classrooms (all special education students were grouped together), but the resource room model (in which students were educated in regular education classes and were provided supplementary instruction in resource rooms) was beginning to surface (McNamara, 1989). The specific interventions recommended during this period focused predominantly on underlying psychological processing disorders (see Chapter 4).

Kirk's attempts to assess these processes through the development of the Illinois Test of Psycholinguistic Ability (1968) were not successful. Although widely used, this test lost its popularity due to its poor psychometric properties and questionable training procedures (see Hammill & Larsen, 1974). However, it was important to the field of learning disabilities because "it reinforced the notion that children with learning disabilities have intra-individual differences . . . and it underlined the concept of using assessment to guide instruction, sometimes called diagnostic-perspective teaching" (Hallahan & Mercer, 2002, p. 28).

Doris Johnson and Helmer Myklebust, at their clinic at Northwestern University, applied Myklebust's work with deaf children to children with learning disabilities. Their textbook, *Learning Disabilities: Educational Principles and Practices* (1967), still provides the classroom teacher with vivid descriptions of the characteristics of various types of learning disabilities and educational interventions that are still valuable. The visual and visual-motor theorists had a major impact on the field of learning disabilities. Individuals such as Kephart, Frostig, Gilman, Barsh, Doman, and Delacate influenced much of what went on in classrooms for students with learning disabilities.

Newell Kephart's *The Slow Learner in the Classroom* (1960, 1971) did much to popularize this approach. Kephart believed that motor development precedes visual development and that kinesthetic sensation provides feedback. This perceptual–motor match was at the core of his theory. Unfortunately, this theory was taken as fact and used throughout the country until researchers began to question Kephart's findings (see Hammill & Larsen, 1974).

Other researchers such as Marianne Frostig, Gerald Getman, and Raymond Barsh developed training programs to be used in the classroom. Like Kephart's theory, their theories were just that: theories. Yet, unfortunately, many teachers used them in their classroom without any proof that they were effective.

Glen Doman and Carl Delacato (Delacato, 1959, 1963, 1966) are often placed in the category of perceptual motor theorists, yet they should not be viewed in this light. Their program of neurological organization was widely criticized for a number of reasons, including lack of research and the use of unacceptable promotional techniques (see Robbins & Glass, 1968, for more information). Even in the face of negative findings, Doman and Delacato used questionable techniques to encourage parents to enroll their children in their program.

Solidification Period (1975–1985)

The U.S. Department of Education funded five research institutes from 1977 to 1982 to empirically validate educational interventions for students with learning disabilities. The institutes were located at Columbia University, Teachers College, the University of Illinois at Chicago, the University of Kansas, the University of Minnesota, and the University of Virginia. What is remarkable is that it was not until the middle to late 1970s that the notion of empirically based programs become a concern. From the time the term **learning disabilities** was first introduced to the general public in 1963 until the mid-1970s, many students with learning disabilities were educated by teachers utilizing educational practices whose value was largely unproven. Some would argue that this may be just as true today, even with the proliferation of evidence of best practices. Hallahan and Mercer (2002, pp. 34-37) describe the focus and key personnel.

Columbia University Teachers College. Dr. N. Dale Bryant was the director of the institute that focused on information processing. Dr. Margaret J. Shepherd led the team that conducted research on memory and study skills. Dr. Jeanette Fleishner and her colleagues focused on arithmetic. Three areas of reading were studied: (a) basic reading and spelling, led by Dr. Bryant; (b) interaction of the text and the reader (Dr. Joanna Williams); and (c) reading comprehension (studied by Dr. MacGinite and his team).

University of Illinois at Chicago. Dr. Tanis Bryan and her colleagues focused on the social-emotional aspects of learning disabilities (see Chapter 16). Prior to this time, there had been very little examination of this area of learning disabilities. Bryan and her colleagues conducted seminal work in this area and continue to keep it in the forefront of discussions on learning disabilities.

University of Kansas. Dr. Donald Deshler directed the institute at the University of Kansas and focused on adolescents with learning disabilities. As was the case with the Illinois team, there was little research evidence on this population (see Chapter 10). Deshler and his colleagues developed the Learning Strategies Curriculum, which has had a major impact on the education of adolescents with learning disabilities. They also demonstrated effective ways to engage in applied research and make it teacher friendly.

University of Minnesota. Dr. James Ysseldyke and his colleagues at the University of Minnesota focused on two areas: identification of students with learning disabilities and curriculum-based assessment. Their findings are somewhat controversial because they suggested that they cannot differentiate students with learning disabilities from other low-achieving students and that special education services are ineffective, in addition to their belief about when intervention should be provided. Some of their findings regarding the identification of students with

learning disabilities have generated discussion in the field (see Kavale, Fuchs, & Scruggs, 1994; McKinney, 1983; Ysseldyke, 2002). The work on curriculum-based assessment indicates that it is effective and more useful than typical standardized tests.

University of Virginia. The attention problems of students with learning disabilities were the focus of this institute, directed by Dr. Daniel Hallahan. These researchers examined metacognitive problems and developed cognitive behavioral interventions. Additionally, Dr. John Lloyd and his colleagues at the University of Virginia researched the use of academic strategies.

The five institutes have been remarkably productive in disseminating information to the field and have had a tremendous impact in the classroom. During this period, Hallahan and Mercer (2002) note that direct instruction (Engelman, Becker, Hanner, & Johnson, 1978, 1988) was found to be highly effective. This approach continues to have an impact on instructional strategies. During this period, the field experienced a major shift away from approaches that were driven more by theory than proof, developing a body of empirical findings that could be built upon.

Turbulent Period (1985–2000)

Dissatisfaction with definitions of learning disabilities continued to plague the field (see Chapter 1). Research proceeded at the five institutes and continues to have a strong impact on current practices. While Hallahan and Mercer (2002) characterize this period as turbulent, there are areas that provide further solidification, such as the institutes' research on phonological processing (see Chapter 13) and neurobiological causes (see Chapter 3). The problems that continue to plague the field are identification, disproportionality, and the need for evidence-based practices. Table 2–1 provides a quick reference to influential reasons and events throughout the various periods of development in the field of learning disabilities.

TABLE 2–1   Influential Persons and Events in the Field of Learning Disabilities

European Foundation Period (1800–1920)
- Gall
- Bouillaud
- Broca
- Wernicke
- Broadbent
- Kussmaul
- Moran
- Hinshelwood

Emergent Period (1960–1975)
- Kirk
- Myklebust and Johnson
- Perpetual–motor theorists

Solidification Period (1975–1985)
- Columbia University, Teachers College
- University of Illinois at Chicago
- The University of Kansas
- The University of Minnesota
- The University of Virginia

Turbulent Period (1985–2000)
- Dissatisfication with definitions of learning disabilities
- Dissatisfication with identification

FEDERAL GOVERNMENT RECOGNITION AND FUNDING

Concurrent with research and program development during the emergent and solidification periods was the involvement of the federal government, whose recognition of learning disabilities was critical to the growth of the field. Through the infusion of funds as well as legislation, learning disabilities was able to establish itself as a recognized, credible special education classification. Figure 2-2 provides

a timeline for federal government legislation that impacted the field of learning disabilities, from the Children with Specific Learning Disabilities Act of 1969 through the reauthorization of IDEA in 2004.

Prior to P.L. 94–142

Many cite P.L. 94-142 (the Education of All Handicapped Children Act [EAHC] of 1975) as the major legislation responsible for recognizing learning disabilities as a special education category. However, several acts of Congress prior to 1975

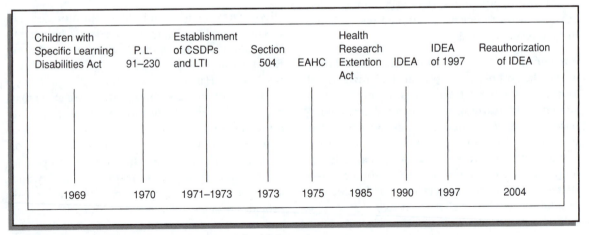

FIGURE 2–2   Timeline for Federal Government Legislation

helped place the field of learning disabilities on the national stage (Hallahan & Mercer, 2002; Martin, 2002). The first was the Children with Specific Learning Disabilities Act of 1969. This was the first time that model programs for students with learning disabilities were funded. The Education of the Handicapped Act of 1966 (EHA) did not include the category of learning disabilities, but it provided funds for colleges and universities to train teachers of students with learning disabilities under the existing category of "other health impaired." (For an account of the politics involved in these decisions, see Martin, 2002.) Dr. Edwin Martin was Deputy Director of the Bureau for the Educationally Handicapped (BEH) at the time. The name was later changed to Office of Special Education Programs.

In 1970, P.L. 91-230 consolidated federal grant programs for students with disabilities and in Part G provided funding for learning disabilities (for teacher training, research, and model programs).

Two other initiatives on the federal level provided funds for the relatively new field. From 1971 to 1973, 43 states set up Services Demonstration Projects (SDPs) for students with learning disabilities. During this period, the Leadership Training Institution (LTI) in Learning Disabilities was established at the University of Arizona. It provided documentation on a number of topics related to learning disabilities. Wiederholt (1974) also noted that the staff of the LTI provided consultation services to professionals in the field.

Education of All Handicapped Children Act of 1975

Federal legislation mandating special education services is relatively new. As of 1975, with the passage of the Education of All Handicapped Children Act (also referred to as P.L. 94-142), all children with special educational needs must be provided with a free, appropriate public education. Before 1975, the quantity and quality of services provided were dictated by where one lived; some states had programs, others didn't. Some families with children with special needs moved to a different state

or a different community so that their child would receive the needed educational services. During the congressional hearings that led to the passage of P.L. 94-142, it was found that half of all children with special educational needs were not being provided with any service whatsoever.

National consciousness was raised with the passage of federal legislation ensuring that students with disabilities would receive special education services from age 3 until age 21. However, school districts were not required to provide services to the 3 to 5 age group unless they had a school program for 3- to 5-year-olds without disabilities. In 1986, P.L. 99-457 extended these services to all children with disabilities in the 3 to 5 age group. Four major components of P.L. 94-142 are:

- a right to an education
- a right to a free, appropriate public education
- a right to a nondiscriminatory evaluation
- a right to due process

A Right to an Education. Most parents take it for granted that they can bring their 5-year-old child to kindergarten and have the child enrolled. Before P.L. 94-142, however, parents of children with special needs did not have this basic right. They paid the same school taxes as their neighbors and their portion of federal and state taxes used for education was the same, but they could not count on their children receiving an education.

Many schools felt that they were unable to provide an education for special education students; they did not have the personnel, the facilities, or the equipment. Moreover, this issue concerned the value of an education and what constitutes an education. Should a severely retarded child, a child with learning disabilities, a deaf-blind child, or an autistic child receive an education?

Also questioned was the definition of an education. Should it be defined as the acquisition of academic skills? If so, what about those who would never acquire those skills? The hearings surrounding the passage of the Education of All Handicapped Children Act provided a focus for experts, parents, and legislators on all sides of the issue. The conclusion was that if *any* child in a school district is entitled to an education, then *all* children are so entitled. The needs of each child must be considered. Children must receive an education, and it is the responsibility of the local school district to develop an appropriate educational plan. The recognition that all children must be provided with an education set the stage for provisions regarding the quality of such an education.

A Right to a Free, Appropriate Public Education. The education of special education students must be appropriate for their needs and provided at no cost to their parents. If the most appropriate placement is a special school with a wide variety of support services, such as speech therapy, physical therapy, and psychological services, then the student must be placed there. The spirit of the law was clear: all children are entitled to an education, and this right should not be dictated by the parents' ability to pay.

To ensure that all special education students are provided with an appropriate education, the authors of P.L. 94–142 required the inclusion of an Individualized Education Program (IEP). The format of the IEP differs from one school district to another but must always include the following:

- The student's current level of performance in the areas of concern.
- Annual and short-term objectives.
- The specific education services to be provided and the extent to which the student will participate in regular education.
- The projected date for initiation of the program and the anticipated duration of such services.
- A description of the schedules and evaluation procedures for determining what objectives are being met.

An important component of the IEP is the Least Restrictive Environment statement. The school must state to what extent a child is being educated in the **mainstream,** that is, receiving regular classroom instruction. The law is very clear; it states that "the handicapped child should be educated with his non-handicapped peers to the maximum extent possible." The point of the Least Restrictive Environment statement is that all children have a continuum of services and have the right to learn in an environment consistent with their academic, social, and physical needs. By providing for individual needs, the letter and the spirit of the law are observed.

A Right to a Nondiscriminatory Evaluation. In the past, students who could not speak English were evaluated in English and placed in special education classes based on that evaluation. This can no longer happen; students must be evaluated in their native language. In addition, if the student or the student's family does not speak English, these all written information must be translated into that language at all school meetings that his or her parents attend. If a student's mode of communication is sign language, then the same holds true. An interpreter must be present to sign the entire evaluation, and if the parents need an interpreter, the school must provide one at no cost to them. All of these provisions have been established to ensure that students are referred, identified, and placed in special education settings using a nondiscriminatory process.

A child cannot be evaluated without parental permission, and if the parents feel that an evaluation solely in English would be unfair to the child, they can request an evaluation in the child's primary language. A simple translation of the test is not sufficient. Rather, the evaluators must be aware of the linguistic and cultural needs of the student, and it is up to the school district to ensure that these services are provided.

A Right to Due Process. Parents have the right to:
- Review all school records.
- Review assessment procedures (underlying tests).
- Refuse or permit evaluation.
- Be informed of the results of the evaluation.
- Be provided with an independent second opinion at public expense.

- Participate in multidisciplinary team meetings. Parents who disagree with the findings of the school district are entitled to a *due process hearing,* also referred to as an *impartial hearing.* In general, the law stipulates the following:
  - Parents must be informed of free or low-cost legal or other relevant services.
  - An unbiased, impartial hearing officer (who is not employed by the school district) will review the case.
  - Parents are entitled to a written or topic-recorded, word-for-word record of the proceedings.
  - Parents are entitled to interpreters of the deaf and/or of the language spoken in the home at no expense.
  - Parents are entitled to be represented by an attorney and/or other professionals, and any other persons can accompany them to the hearing.
  - Parents and their attorney can cross-examine officials from the school district.
  - All information presented must be shared with parents at least 5 school days before the hearing.
  - Parents will be informed of the hearing within 45 calendar days of the request. They may appeal the decision to the Commissioner of Education. The child remains in his or her current placement until all proceedings are completed.

Individuals with Disabilities Education Act (IDEA)

Prior to IDEA, Congress passed P.L. 99-158, the Health Research Extension Act of 1985, which also had an impact on the field of learning disabilities. Cannon (1997), who provides a concise description of the law. This law mandated that the Director of the National Institutes of Health establish an Interagency Committee on Learning Disabilities (ICLD) to review and assess federal research priorities, activities, and findings regarding learning disabilities (including central nervous system dysfunction in children). This mandate further required the ICLD to report to Congress on its activities and include in the report the number of persons affected by learning disabilities and the demographics data describing such persons; a description of the current research findings on the cause, diagnosis, treatment, and prevention of learning disabilities; and recommendations for legislation and administrative actions to increase the effectiveness of research on learning disabilities and to improve the dissemination of information on their diagnosis, treatment, and prevention.

In 1990 Congress passed the Individuals with Disabilities Education Act (IDEA), P.L. 101–479, which reauthorized P.L. 94–142 (the Education of All Handicapped Children Act of 1975). It contained a number of important additions, not the least of which related to language. The term **disability** replaces **handicapped** and advocates "students-first" terminology. So, rather than using the term **learning-disabled student,** the law states that we are to use **student with learning disabilities. Individuals** also replaces **children.** The law also adds two categories of students who are entitled to receive services under IDEA: those with **autism** and those with **traumatic brain injury.** Additionally, it requires schools to provide transition plans for adolescents with disabilities. This last provision will be discussed further later in this book (see Chapter 11). IDEA also emphasized programs for infants and toddlers.

IDEA of 1997

IDEA was reauthorized in 1997 (P.L. 105-17). As with the previous reauthorization, the spirit of the law remains intact; however, changes were made. The Council for Exceptional Children, in their publication *CEC Today* (April–May 1999), summarized the highlights of IDEA 1997. Those related to learning disabilities and ADHD will now be described.

Other Health Impairment. Attention deficit disorder (ADD) and (ADHD) may result in eligibility for special education services under the "other health impaired" category. This is the first time ADHD has been specifically noted in IDEA.

Supplementary Aids and Supports. Supplementary aids and services include aids, services, and other supports that are provided in general education settings to enable children without disabilities to be educated with children without disabilities to the maximum extent appropriate. These can include a computer, a one-to-one aide, and/or an auditory training, to name only a few.

Service Plans. A school may use funds for special education, related services, and supplementary aids and services provided in a general education setting for a child with a disability, even if children without disabilities receive incidental benefit from the services.

Mediation. School and state education agencies must ensure that procedures are established and implemented to allow parents and schools to resolve their differences through mediation.

Individualized Education Program. IDEA 1997 added new IEP requirements and expanded existing ones. The IEP must include:

- A statement of the child's present levels of educational performance, including how the child's disability affects his or her involvement and progress in the general education curriculum. For preschool children, it must describe how the disability affects the child's participation in appropriate activities.
- A statement of measurable annual goals, including benchmarks or short-term objectives related to:
  a. Meeting the child's needs that result from his or her disability and enable the child to be involved in and progress in the general education curriculum.
  b. Meeting each of the child's other educational needs that result from the child's disability.
- A statement of the special education, related services, and supplementary aids to be provided to the child or on behalf of the child. Such statement should also include any program modifications or supports for school personnel that are

needed for the child to be involved in and progress in the general education curriculum; to participate in extracurricular and other nonacademic activities; and to be educated and participate with children with and without disabilities.
- The extent to which the child will not participate with children without disabilities in the general education class.
- Any modifications in the administration of statewide or districtwide assessments that are needed for the child to participate in the assessment.
- If the child will not participate in the assessment or part of the assessment, a statement explaining why that assessment is not appropriate and how the child will be assessed.
- The projected date for the beginning of the service and modification and their frequency, location, and duration.
- The child's transition service needs (beginning at age 14 and updated annually) that focus on his or her courses of study. This should include, when appropriate, the interagency responsibilities of needed linkages (beginning at age 16 or younger) and a statement that the child has been informed of the rights that will be transferred to him or her on reaching the age of majority under state law.
- How the child's progress toward the annual goals will be measured and the extent to which the child's progress will enable him or her to achieve the goals by the end of the school year.
- How the child's parents will be regularly informed of their child's progress at least as often as the parents of children without disabilities are informed.

Including Parents in the IEP Team. Each local education agency (LEA) or state education agency (SEA) must ensure that the parents of each child with a disability are members of any group that makes decisions on the educational placement of their child.

Including General Education Teachers in the IEP Team.

- If the child participates or may participate in the general education environment, the IEP team must include at least one of the student's general education teachers. The teacher must participate in the development, review, and revision of the child's IEP The general education teacher must also help determine appropriate behavioral interventions and strategies for the child, as well as any supplementary aids, program modifications, and supports for school personnel that will be provided on the child's behalf.

Access to the IEP. The IEP of a child with a disability must be accessible to all general education teachers, as well as to all special education teachers, related service providers, and other service providers who are responsible for implementing the IEP.

- Each teacher must be informed of his or her specific responsibilities related to implementing the IEP and the accommodations and supports the child will receive.

Reauthorization of IDEA. On December 3, 2004, President George W. Bush signed P.L. 108–446 (see Table 2–2 for a brief legislative history of IDEA 2004). The basic structure and civil rights guarantees of IDEA 1997 remain; however, significant changes were made. The Congressional Research Service (CRS) Report for Congress (Apling & Jones, 2005) summarizes the changes:

- An extensive definition of "highly qualified" special education teachers and a requirement that all special education teachers be highly qualified.
- Provisions aimed at reducing paperwork and other non–educational activities (for example, a paperwork reduction pilot program).
- Extensive provisions aimed at ensuring special education and related services for children with disabilities who are homeless or otherwise members of highly mobile populations.

- Increased funds and increased requirements for statewide activities.
- Authorization for states to use IDEA funds to establish and maintain "risk pools" to aid local educational agencies (LEAs) that provide high-cost IDEA services.
- Modifications to requirements for parents who unilaterally placed their children with disabilities in private schools to help ensure equal treatment and participation for such children.
- Revised state performance goals and requirements for children's participation in state and local assessments to align these requirements with those in the Elementary and Secondary Education Act of 1965 (ESEA) (No Child Left Behind Act).
- Authority for LEAs that qualify to offset some expenditures for special education with annual increases in their federal IDEA grant.
- Authority for LEAs to use some of their local IDEA grant for "early intervening services" aimed at reducing or eliminating the future need for special education for children with educational needs who do not currently qualify for IDEA.
- Significant changes to procedural safeguards, including:

The addition of a resolution session prior to a due process hearing to encourage the parties to resolve their dispute. Revised test regarding the manifestation determination. Addition of a new category—where a child has inflicted serious bodily injury on another person—to the school's ability to place a child with a disability in an interim alternative educational setting.

- Major changes in compliance monitoring to focus on student performance, not compliance with procedures.
- Authority to extend Part C services for infant and toddler services beyond the age of 2.

TABLE 2–2 A Brief Legislative History of IDEA 2004

- On April 30, 2003, the House of Representatives passed H.R. 1350 by a vote of 251 to 171.
- On May 13, 2004, the Senate incorporated its bill (S. 1248) in H.R. 1350 and passed H.R. 1350 in lieu of S. 1248 by a vote of 95 to 3.
- The conference committee filed its report on the bill (H. Rept. 108–779) on November 17, 2004.
- The House agreed to the conference report on November 19, 2004, by a vote of 397 to 3.
- The Senate approved the conference report on November 19, 2004, by unanimous consent.
- President Bush signed the bill on December 3, 2004 (P.L. 108–446, IDEA 2004).

Impact on Learning Disabilities

In addition to the changes cited above, there are specific changes that will impact students with learning disabilities, their parents, and their teachers. Most provisions of IDEA 2004 went into effect on July 1, 2005.

One of the major changes for teachers of students with learning disabilities is the way in which such students are identified. The establishment of an intellectual functioning academic achievement discrepancy is no longer mandated. IDEA 2004 (Section 1414 [b] [6]) states that schools "shall not be required to take into consideration whether a child has a severe discrepancy between achievement and intellectual ability in oral expression, basic reading skill, reading comprehension, mathematical calculation, or mathematical reasoning." Senate Report 185 (108th Cong., 2d Sess. 26, 2004) states the rationale for this change (*CRS Report*, 2005, p. 21):

> The committee believes that the IQ achievement discrepancy formula, which considers whether a child has a severe discrepancy between achievement and intellectual ability, should not be a requirement for determining eligibility under the IDEA. There is no evidence that the IQ achievement discrepancy formula can be applied in a consistent and educationally meaningful (i.e., reliable and valid) manner. In addition, this approach has been found to be particularly problematic for students living in poverty or culturally and linguistically different backgrounds, who may be erroneously reviewed as having intrinsic intellectual limitations when their difficulties on such tests really reflect lack of experience or educational opportunity.

In response to frequently asked questions regarding the changes in IDEA 2004, the National Center for Learning Disabilities (2005) noted that Congress recognized the lack of validity of the IQ-achievement discrepancy approach and supported the use of other factors that point to the existence of a learning disability.

Schools are required, as in the past, to use a variety of assessment procedures to determine whether or not a learning disability exists. Included is a determination of whether the student responds to scientific research–based intervention (see Chapter 6). This is an option—however, one that is encouraged. The NCLD notes that this approach could help reduce the disproportionately large number of minority students in special education.

Another change that will directly impact teachers of students with disabilities is the development and implementation of the IEP. There is no longer a requirement for benchmarks and short-term objectives. However, the teacher's goals still must be measurable, and schools may still utilize short-term objectives and benchmarks to measure progress toward the annual goals.

To reduce paperwork and streamline the IEP process, a few changes were made. If parents and schools agree, any changes that need to be made after the annual review can be made in writing rather than by reconvening the IEP team. Also, there is the possibility of a 3-year IEP. This will be written so that it follows typical transition points in school (natural transition points). Up to 15 states can submit proposals to use 3-year IEPs, and those states that are chosen for the demonstration project (pilot project) must make it optional, not mandatory, for parents. Also, if it is deemed that the student's progress is insufficient, reviews must be more frequent than every 3 years.

A change that will impact teachers of students with learning disabilities is the new definition of *highly qualified teacher* (§602[10]), which is aligned with that of NCLB. All special education teachers must have a BA and be fully certified by their state or possess an equivalent license. The new definition gives specific requirements for various categories of special education teachers, such as those who teach one or more core academic subjects to students with disabilities (see Apling & Jones, 2005, for more specific information on the topic).

Other changes noted at the beginning of this section will probably not impact teachers directly. Smith (2004) notes that "in many instances practices will remain relatively similar" (p. 318). However, all of the changes are important in providing students with a free, appropriate public education. Even though teachers are not responsible for specific compliance issues or funding allocation, they need to keep abreast of the ways in which all the new provisions of IDEA 2004 are implemented. As SEAs and LEAs (schools) begin to develop policies and procedures, there will be questions and issues of interpretation. As in the past, there will also be lawsuits regarding specific provisions. Over time, a clearer interpretation will emerge (see the following section).

Practical Considerations: What You Need to Know About IDEA 2004. The Council for Exceptional Children (CEC) Council on Administrators in Special Education (CASE) division provides a short summary of IDEA 2004 **(http:// www.casecec.org/idea/short_summary.htm):**

Protects the civil right of students with disabilities to a free appropriate public education

- Vigorously enforces provisions by giving the U.S. Secretary of Education and state education agencies greater power and new tools to measure compliance and impose sanctions when schools fail to meet standards.
- Requires states to develop a plan, establish targets and meet them in the delivery of a free appropriate public education, general supervision, transition services, and disproportionate representation of minorities.
- Makes agreements in dispute resolution and due process binding.
- Establishes competency standards for the training of hearing officers.

Makes IDEA work for students, parents, teachers, school administrators, and school districts

- Provides new opportunities for parents and schools to address concerns before the need for a due process hearing and encourages parents and schools to resolve differences by clarifying that mediation is available at any time.
- Provides greater flexibility for parents and schools by allowing them to agree to make minor changes to a child's IEP during the school year without reconvening the IEP team, and encouraging the consolidation of IEP and reevaluation meetings.

- Increases parental involvement in IEP meetings by allowing the use of teleconferencing, video conferencing, and other alternative means of participation.
- Provides increased resources to assist parents with complaint resolution and due process through Parent Training Institutes.
- Requires that initial evaluations occur within 60 days of referral unless the state has a policy that establishes a timeline for evaluation.
- Encourages Parent Training Institutes to focus on improving parent–school collaboration and early, effective dispute resolution.
- Enhances the preparation, professional development, and support for special educators and other school personnel working with students with disabilities to ensure that these educators possess the necessary skills and knowledge to provide instruction to students, including by creating a new grant program for institutions of higher education focused exclusively on training beginning special educators.

Provides quality services and instruction at all stages, from early childhood through graduation from high school

- Maintains early intervention and preschool special education programs for infants, toddlers, and preschoolers with disabilities, including allowing states to create a system that gives parents the choice to have their child continue early intervention services until the age of five.
- Requires that infants and toddlers who are abused, neglected, drug-exposed, or have experienced family violence be referred for early intervention.
- Allows for the development of new approaches to determine whether students have specific learning disabilities by clarifying that schools are not limited to using the IQ–achievement discrepancy model.
- Authorizes local educational agencies to use up to 15% of IDEA funds to develop a comprehensive educational support system for students without disabilities in grades K-12 who require additional academic and behavioral supports to succeed in a general education environment.
- Establishes a state-level risk pool fund to assist local educational agencies in providing FAPE to high-need children.

- Requires schools to provide short-term objectives for students with significant disabilities, and for all students, quarterly reports to parents on their child's progress toward meeting annual IEP goals and how that progress is being measured.
- Emphasizes academic achievement and functional performance within a child's individualized education program (IEP).
- Simplifies the rules for transition services (activities that help a student begin planning for life after high school) by requiring that substantive transition services and planning begin at age 16.
- Provides an option for 15 states to develop a 3-year IEP for children with disabilities to focus parents and schools on long-term goals for helping the student transition to postsecondary activities.
- Provides for the establishment of a National Instructional Materials Access Center, to provide schools with a one-stop provider of textbooks or other materials for students who are blind or with other disabilities.
- Strengthens the involvement of the State vocational rehabilitation system with disabled students who are still in secondary school.
- Provides new flexibility for special education teachers to meet the highly qualified teacher requirements in the No Child Left Behind Act.
- Improves outreach and services to homeless, foster care and other youth by clarifying state child find responsibilities, simplifying parent or guardian involvement and improving coordination between schools.

Improves discipline and ensures safety

- Improves current discipline provisions by simplifying the framework for schools to administer the law while ensuring the rights and the safety of all children.
- Requires schools to determine if a child's behavior was the result of their [sic] disability or poor implementation of their [sic] IEP when considering a disciplinary action.
- Requires that schools conduct functional behavioral assessments and give behavioral services to students who are disciplined beyond 10 days in order to prevent future behavior problems.

- Requires that schools continue providing services that enable students who are disciplined to participate in the general curriculum and meet their IEP goals.
- Establishes a new program to develop and enhance behavioral supports in schools while improving the quality of interim alternative education settings.

Integrates the Individuals with Disabilities Education Act with the Elementary and Secondary Education Act

- Provides for a national study of valid and reliable alternate assessment systems and how alternate assessments align with state content standards.
- Ensures that local educational agencies measure the performance of students with disabilities on State or district-wide assessments, including alternate assessments aligned to the State's academic content standards or extended standards.
- Clarifies the IEP team's role in determining whether a child with a disability should take regular assessments with or without accommodations, or alternate assessments, consistent with State standards governing such determinations.
- Aligns the personnel preparation and personnel certification with No Child Left Behind.

The specific areas that will affect students with learning disabilities and their teachers are:

- Eligibility of the learning disabilities classification.
- The use of an instructional, intervention-based approach for learning disabilities identification and eligibility.
- Flexibility concerning attendance at IEP meetings.
- Multiyear (3-year) IEP's.
- No requirement for short-term objectives on the IEP.
- Becoming a highly qualified teacher.

Other Legislation that Impacts Teaching Students with Learning Disabilities

Section 504 of the Rehabilitation Act of 1973 (P.L. 93–112). Section 504 requires any institution that receives federal funds to make accommodations for individuals with disabilities. This is not a special education law but rather a civil rights law for all students. Disability is defined in broader terms than in IDEA 2004 as "any physical or mental impairment that substantially limits one or more major life activities" (included are walking, talking, seeing, hearing, speaking, breathing, learning, working, performance, manual tasks, setting, reaching, and staying). If the student has a disability under Section 504, the school is required to develop an Accommodation Plan. This can include extended time, a scribe, and/or a separate setting for tests. As a teacher of students with learning disabilities, you may teach students diagnosed with ADHD (see Chapter 4), who are struggling academically but are not classified as having a learning disability. The Office of Civil Rights (OCR) Department of Education (1989, p. 8) provides a list of requirements for schools under Section 504 that protect the civil rights of individuals with disabilities. The school must:

- Annually identify and locate all children with disabilities who are underserved.
- Provide a "free, appropriate public education" to each student with a disability, regardless of the nature or severity of the disability. This means providing general or special education and related aids and services designed to meet the individual educational needs of persons with disabilities as adequately as the needs of nondisabled persons are met.
- Ensure that each student with disabilities is educated with nondisabled students to the maximum extent appropriate.
- Establish nondiscriminatory evaluation and placement procedures to avoid the inappropriate education that may result from the misclassification or misplacement of students.
- Establish procedural safeguards to enable parents and guardians to participate meaningfully in decisions regarding the evaluation and placement of their children.
- Afford children with disabilities an equal opportunity to participate in nonacademic and extracurricular services and activities.

The Americans with Disabilities Act (ADA) of 1990. ADA protects the civil rights of individuals with disabilities in a wide variety of settings outside of education. There have been accounts in *U.S. News and World Report*, the *New York Times*, and *Newsweek* regarding adults with ADHD who are utilizing ADA to file discrimination lawsuits (see Chapter 11 for more information).

No Child Left Behind Act (NCLB) of 2001. NCLB is the current version of the Elementary and Secondary Education Act of 1965. It was signed into law in January 2002 by President George W. Bush. The four major components are:

1. Accountability for results.
2. Improved teacher quality.
3. Research-proven effectiveness of instructional methods and materials.
4. Influence, information and choice for parents. (Cortiella & Horowitz, 2004)

Many of the components of NCLB are included in the reauthorization of IDEA 2004. States are required to specify annual measurable objectives to measure student progress. Students must be disaggregated by economic status, race, ethnicity, disability, limited English proficiency, and proficiency in reading and math. They must demonstrate proficiency in math, reading, and science by 2014 (with annual testing of students in Grades 3–8). These requirements, combined with the mandate of highly qualified teachers, proved (scientifically based) instructional methods, parental rights, public school choice, and local state report cards, all ensure that no child will be left behind.

A number of professional organizations related to learning disabilities (the CEC's Division for Learning Disabilities, International Dyslexia Association, the LDA, and the National Center for Learning Disabilities) formulated a position paper in 2002 entitled "No Child Left Behind and Students with Specific Learning Disabilities." They recognize the need for accountability while acknowledging the need for students with specific learning disabilities (SLD). They state:

We believe students with SLD must be provided full participation and equal accountability in NCLB. These students both need and deserve the full benefits that can be realized by NCLB's focus on:

- Raising student achievement in the areas of reading/language arts and math, particularly in the early grades.
- Improving the quality of general education teachers in core academic subjects, including reading.
- Improving the quality of special education teachers and paraprofessionals.
- Requiring all students to participate in state assessments, with the appropriate accommodations, so that schools are accountable for achievement of all students.
- Enhancing the public's awareness of the achievement of at-risk groups of students through disaggregated subgroup data.
- Expanding parent involvement and public awareness through local report cards and information on teacher qualifications.
- Increasing options for parents of students in poor performing schools such as making supplemental services available and allowing parents to transfer their child to higher performing schools in the area.

We recognize [that] schools are facing challenges in implementing NCLB for students with disabilities, but these challenges should be met. For example, NCLB regulations issued on December 9, 2003, allow school districts to assess up to one percent of all students using alternate assessments based on alternate standards; this will provide sufficient flexibility for schools to include those students unable to participate in a state's general education assessment system even with accommodations. This limited exception provides adequate flexibility to states.

The U.S. Department of Education should provide a comprehensive plan to provide technical assistance, guidance, capacity building, information, resources and other supports that states will require to ensure that students with SLD have the maximum opportunity to meet AYP (adequate yearly progress).

We applaud the continued dedication of both the Administration and the Congress to maintaining their commitment to all students. Given the early stage of NCLB implementation, we resist any actions, be they regulatory or statutory, that will compromise the benefits that NCLB holds for students with SLD. Instead, we hope that states, school districts and schools will rise to the challenge to ensure that NO child is left behind.

It should be noted that there are critics of NCLB. Time will tell if all the provisions will remain intact and if it fulfills its expectations of leaving no child behind.

Case Law

How does statutory and case law affect the field of learning disabilities? Herr and Batemen (2003) focus on three areas:

1. The evaluation/eligibility process
2. IEPs and free, appropriate public education
3. The least restrictive environment (LRE)

Most lawsuits between school districts and parents related to evaluation/eligibility have to do with whether the student has a learning disability. Due to controversy over discrepancy and the lack of a clear definition of this condition, the authors believe that neither "the law nor LD practice has positively influenced the other" (p. 60).

The field of learning disabilities has been influenced by issues related to IEP and a free, appropriate public education in that practitioners have a heightened awareness of what is required. However, this does not necessarily mean that students are provided with appropriate services. Cases regarding placement and, more recently, methodology have been litigated.

In the last area, LRE, most cases have involved parents requesting reimbursement for private school tuition because they felt that the public school was not meeting their child's needs. The findings have been mixed and reflect the complexity of these decisions.

Herr and Batemen (2003) conclude that the impact of specific cases on learning disabilities is "vast and sometimes conflicting" (p. 70). As IDEA 2004 is implemented in schools, additional cases will impact on practice, most likely in the areas of identification and methodology (see Herr & Bateman, 2003, Appendix 401 for a complete list of IDEA cases and issues).

ADVOCACY

The field of learning disabilities has been greatly influenced by advocacy. From Kirk's presentation to a group of parents using the term **learning disabilities** to the present, advocacy has played a critical role in the development of the field. The formation of the ACLD, now the LDA, in 1963 signaled the beginning of a strong relationship between advocacy and public policy and a weaker relationship between advocacy and science. Scruggs and Mastropieri (2004) note that the field is more a product of advocacy than of science. Brigham, Gustashaw, and St. Peter Brigham (2004, p. 206) provide a useful perspective on the difference between the two:

> Special education is a very young profession, and it is still closely aligned with its roots in advocacy. Science, however, differs from advocacy in many ways. The scientist must remain doubtful, whereas the advocate must be certain. The scientist may only speak of what the evidence supports, whereas the advocate must act in the absence of complete knowledge. Scientific evidence is dispassionate and intentionally removed from the personality of the scientist, but advocacy operates in an "up close and personal" manner. Scientific understanding is harder to acquire, and practices based on the advocacy of a trusted individual may be very resistant to change. We are certainly not casting aspersions on advocates. We understand that our profession is based on advocacy under the circumstances just described. However, as the field of special education matures, its future will depend on the transition from advocacy to justification by scientific evidence. The role of the advocate in special education has not evaporated and is unlikely to do so; however, we hope that the distinction we have drawn between advocates and scientists remains, for if our scientists become certain and our advocates are filled with doubts, we will truly be lost.

LEARNING DISABILITIES IN THE 21ST CENTURY

Hallahan and Mercer's (2002) thorough historical review of the field of learning disabilities covers the review from the early 1800s to the present. The emphasis on empirically validated practices has been evident in the field for many years (Vaughn & Linan-Thompson, 2003). However, the increased emphasis on results of the federal government (in NCLB and IDEA 2004) will characterize the field for the foreseeable future. As Chard (2004) notes, "current political rhetoric promotes practices that are based on scientific reading research" (p. 215). NCLB mandates, and the political climate dictates, that all of our practices in the identification, placement, and intervention must be based on empirically validated findings.

The field has come a long way since its early stages, but it must continue to validate its existence. To answer the question "What is special about special education for students with learning disabilities?" Vaughn and Linan-Thompson (2003, p. 145) state:

> For most students with LD, it is not the curriculum. Students with LD should have access to the same curriculum, including higher order processing and problem solving skills, as their non-disabled peers. What should be special is the delivery of instruction, given that their needs are rarely met through general education instruction alone. Students with LD benefit from explicit and systematic instruction that is closely related to their area of instructional need. How much additional instruction do students need, how thorough and in what format? As researchers continue gathering evidence of how variables such as group size, duration, and intensity interact, the key issue will be the extent to which schools can implement and sustain special education for students with LD.

This recognition that evidence-based practices are here to stay was noted in a special series in the *Journal of Learning Disabilities* entitled "Supporting Science in the Schoolhouse: Fostering the Delivery of Effective Institution in Contemporary Schools—Part 1" (2004, *37* [3]). In this issue, Crockett (2004, p. 190) discusses four ideas for linking practice with research:

1. Turn to science as the best trick we know for solving educational problems.
2. Specify clearly what we hope to achieve in our instructional decision for students with LD.
3. Rely on instruction the best tool we have for improving student performance.
4. Cultivate—and keep—competent and caring personnel.

And while there are many barriers to the implementation of these ideas, there is really no alternative. As Scruggs and Mastropieri (2004) point out, "a scientific practice is the same as best practice, we must continue to overcome these barriers and to promote scientific practices as the best policy for students with LD" (p. 276).

SUMMARY

This chapter has focused on the history of the field of learning disabilities from its foundation in the early 1800s to the present. It has examined the major research efforts of pioneers in the field, as well as the contributions of contemporary leaders. In addition to the field's research and primary development activities, the involvement of the federal government was explored. The role of the federal government in recognizing and funding the field of learning disabilities cannot be overemphasized. The 2004 reauthorization of IDEA was discussed, as well as NCLB of 2001. Both of these laws will govern teaching practice for many years to come. Finally, this chapter has discussed the advocacy component of the field. Clearly, understanding the importance of research and program development, federal legislation, and funding and advocacy

is critical to understanding the field of learning disabilities in the 21st century.

SPRINGBOARDS FOR REFLECTION AND DISCUSSION

1. Read Wiederholt's (1974) historical overview of the field of learning disabilities. How has the field changed since this book was written?
2. Think back to when you were in elementary school. Were there students with learning disabilities in your classes? Were they mainstreamed? Were they classified as having learning disabilities? Were they taught in separate classes?
3. Speak to an adult with learning disabilities. How was his or her education different from the one he or she would receive today? When did this person first realize that he or she had a learning disability? What was the parents' reaction?
4. Speak to the parents of a student with a learning disability. How has federal government legislation impacted the education of their child? Are they members of a parent organization?
5. Ask a few teachers of students with learning disabilities if they think it is important to know about the history of learning disabilities. Why or why not?
6. How will you deal with the pressure to provide scientifically based interventions in your classroom? How will you know which ones are effective and which are not?
7. Attend a meeting of a professional organization on learning disabilities. What are the current themes? What can you apply in the classroom? How will you bridge the gap between research and practice?

3 CHAPTER CAUSES OF LEARNING DISABILITIES

CHAPTER OBJECTIVES

At the end of the chapter you will:

- understand the complexity involved in identifying causes of learning disabilities.
- understand the prenatal, perinatal, and postnatal factors related to causation.
- know the medical causes of a learning disability.
- know how to diagnose neurological functions.
- know the genetic causes of learning disabilities.
- understand the vulnerability of parents to controversial approaches.

Historically, it was assumed that students with learning disabilities were neurologically impaired. And while there has recently been much more emphasis on diagnosis and treatment, Torgesen (2004) believes that the "ultimate integrity [of learning disabilities] as a separate field of education depends upon finding answers to questions about the extent of brain pathology in the population it serves" (p. 25).

Adam's parents were concerned about his inability to read. He was the youngest of three children, and the other two did well in school. Both parents were college graduates and had successful careers. School failure was never an issue for their children. Adam's language development was slower than that of his siblings, but his parents attributed this to his being the youngest child. His motor skills seemed fine, but he had a little difficulty using scissors and coloring. When he entered kindergarten, it was apparent that reading would be difficult for him. He simply could not keep up with his classmates. And while there was a wide range of abilities in his class, he appeared to be one of the students who were having the most difficulty. When Adam's parents discussed their concerns with the teacher, they were reas-sured that he was "coming along." However, this didn't allay their anxiety regarding his performance. They brought him to a university-based medical center, where a full psychoeducational evaluation was performed and their suspicions were confirmed. Adam was diagnosed with a learning disability.

When this happens, one of the first questions parents ask is, "What causes a learning disability?" Teachers are also often curious about the causes of learning disabilities even though they realize that the answers probably will not help them teach their students. How would you respond when Adam's parents' ask that question?

The exact cause of a learning disability is unknown. This frustrates many who ask, "Why?" The problem is that so many things can occur before (prenatal), during (perinatal), or after (postnatal) birth that it is virtually impossible to pinpoint when the difficulty begins. Moreover, certain children experience considerable difficulty during these stages and yet have no school-related problems.

This chapter will examine various causes of learning disabilities and present recent findings on learning and the brain. After reading it, you will be better able to answer Adam's parents' question.

WHAT CAUSES A LEARNING DISABILITY?

A number of hypotheses exist regarding the etiology of learning disabilities, most of them medical in nature. The field has a long history of relying on the medical model of learning disabilities (see Chapter 2), hence the overreliance on trying to find a medical 'cause'. The field of learning disabilities has moved away from this perspective, especially with the passage of NCLB and IDEA. These two acts focus on 'results', not causation, and place the responsibility for education directly on the school. It is interesting to note that in the recent discussion regarding the definitions of specific learning disabilities (SLD) in Congress, some House of Representatives members wanted to include "medically detected" in the definition. That is, if there was no medical proof, there was no SLD. That provision was defeated and was not included in the reauthorization of IDEA 2004.

As a competent professional, you need to be aware of the information on etiology even if it does not directly impact on your teaching. You may receive reports from medical doctors regarding your students, and you should have a basic understanding of their perspective. Also, there is considerable ongoing research on the brain and on ways to diagnose learning disabilities, specifically reading disorders, and all teachers should keep abreast of these findings. Other factors related to the diagnosis of learning disabilities, such as underlying process disorders and early indicators of learning disabilities, such as poverty, are discussed in Chapters 4 and 9, respectively.

FACTORS RELATED TO PRENATAL, PERINATAL, AND POSTNATAL DEVELOPMENT

One problem related to the discussion of these factors is that difficulties encountered during any stage of development may cause a variety of disabilities, not learning disabilities alone. Also, many children experience some of these problems and yet have no problems in school. You need to be aware of these factors, but you should also be cautious in your interpretation.

Prenatal Factors

The NRC and the Institute of Medicine (IM) (2000) issued a report on early childhood development indicating that the most common causes of fetal complications and future difficulty in learning are alcohol consumption, drug use, and smoking. Fetal alcohol syndrome (FAS) occurs in 1 out of 1,000 live births. These babies have growth retardation, craniofacial changes, and central nervous system dysfunction. This is an extreme manifestation of the use of alcohol during pregnancy. Donovan and Cross (2002) note that research in this area is limited. However, there appear to be differences in racial/ethnic groups that have implications for schools. The rate of alcohol consumption during pregnancy is reportedly higher among American Indian/Alaskan Native and Black women than among White, Hispanic and Asian/Pacific Islander women (Abel, 1995), as cited in the NRC report (Donovan & Cross, 2002), which states that the incidence of FAS births is 10 times higher among Blacks than Whites.

Smoking also puts the fetus at risk for learning disabilities. The NRC/IM (2000) and the NRC (2002) have provided data on the relationship between maternal tobacco use and learning problems, citing mild attention problems, cognitive effects, lower receptive language scores, and poor performance on memory tasks. The NRC reports higher cigarette smoking among American Indians/Alaskan Natives than among any other social/ethnic group. Asian, Black, and Hispanic women have lower rates of smoking during pregnancy than White women.

There have been discussions in popular media, such as magazines, newspapers, and television programs, on the effect of cocaine use. Problems include low birth weight, abnormal electroencephalograms (EEGs), irritability, low rates of social interaction, and increased impulsivity, according to the NRC/IM (2000) report. Yet, a report from the NRC Committee on Minority Representation in Special Education (Donovan & Cross, 2002) suggests that due to the illegal status of the drug, it is difficult to conduct research. Another problem is confounding, since cocaine is often used with alcohol and tobacco.

Autopsies performed on individual who had learning disabilities (Duane, 1989; Galaburda, 1988; Hynd, Marshall, & Gonzalez, 1991) revealed abnormalities in the structure of language-related areas of the brain. These studies suggest that the anomaly occurs during the fifth to seventh months of pregnancy. As Smith (2004) points out, if it occurred after birth, the brain might have been able to compensate. These are interesting studies, but to date they have had little impact on clarifying the causes of learning disorders.

Perinatal Factors

Problems that occur during the birth process may affect the newborn and subsequent development. These include prematurity, anoxia (lack of oxygen), prolonged labor, and injury from medical instruments (Mercer & Pullen, 2005). Yet, these difficulties may not necessarily cause learning disabilities. As previously stated, the majority of babies who had difficulty during the birth process do not have a learning disability. At this time, "no direct causal links have yet been established" (Bender, 2004, p. 56).

Low birth weight has been studied as a cause of learning disabilities. On the one hand, the evidence suggests that the majority of these babies have normal outcomes. On the other hand, as a group, they encounter more neurodevelopmental and behavioral problems than normal-birth-weight babies. Stanton-Chapman, Chapman, and Scott (2001) studied the records of very-low-birth-weight (VLBW—below 2 lb) children in Florida, examining the records of almost 250,000 children who were born between 1989 and 1990 and attended Florida public schools during the 1996–1997 school year. VLBW was a reliable predictor of future learning disabilities. Low birth weight needs to be viewed within a sociocultural context. It is more common among Blacks than in any other social/ethnic group (occurring about twice as often). There is also a link between income and low birth weight. The NRC/IM (2000) report notes that the rate of low birth weight was decreasing but has increased lately due to the advances in neonatal technology and the increase in multiple births among White women.

Postnatal Factors

The most common postnatal factor associated with learning problems is head injury (Mercer & Pullen, 2005), although due to the plasticity of the brain, the outcome of injury is not always poor. Poor nutrition in the early stages of life can lead to serious problems. This factor is difficult to study because it typically occurs together with poverty, poor schooling, and neglect (Sigman & Whaley, 1990). One line of research points to iron deficiency in children. Donovan and Cross (2003, pp. 108, 111) drew the following conclusions from the work of Eysenck and Schoenthaler (1997) and Sigman and Whaley (1998):

1. Inadequate levels of vitamins and minerals in the bloodstream reduce a child's IQ, and supplementation of the child's standard diet can raise nonverbal IQ significantly.
2. A consistent effect of supplementation on young infants is on motor skills (Politt et al., 1994). Infant motor skills are predictive of later cognitive abilities among children in developing countries (Sigman & Whaley, 1998).
3. The younger the child, the greater the effects of supplementation. There is little effect beyond the teenage years.
4. Approximately 20 percent of children in the United States respond to supplementation with IQ increases of 9+ points over test-retest increases in a placebo group. However, no effects are found for children with adequate levels of vitamins and minerals in their diets. The concentration of effect is likely to be greatest among disadvantaged children.
5. Effects of micronutrient supplementation have been demonstrated to continue for one year and may last longer.

Lead poisoning has been implicated as a cause of learning problems. And while there has been a decrease in the use of lead in paint and gasoline, children in urban environments tend to have higher levels of lead (see The NRC's report "Minority Students in Special and Gifted Education," 2003, for a detailed review of the research).

It is clear that environmental factors such as poverty contribute to poor prenatal care, low birth weight, and poor nutrition. Children living in poverty are more likely to exhibit school-related problems, which may or may not be learning disabilities. (see Chapter 6 for more information on the problems associated with the diagnosis of learning disabilities when environmental factors are introduced).

MEDICAL CAUSES

Simple Neuroanatomy

According to Smith (2004), experts agree that "learning disabilities are caused by neurological differences in the way that human brains are constructed and function" (p. 54). Therefore, it is helpful to understand simple neuroanatomy and brain functions (Bender, 2004; Mercer & Pullen, 2005; Sousa, 2001). The brain has three major regions: the brain stem, the cerebellum, and the cerebrum (Figure 3-1).

Brain Stem. The brain stem is located in the lower part of the brain and is responsible for respiration, heart rate, and what have been called **life-sustaining functions.** It is the oldest, most primitive part of the brain. This region controls sensory input and motor output. It is also responsible for wakefulness and perhaps attention.

Cerebellum. The cerebellum receives and integrates sensory input and controls most of the motor nervous system. It is responsible for balance, posture, and walking.

Cerebrum. The cerebrum is the part of the brain that makes us human. That is, while all mammals have this region, it is most fully developed in human beings and is responsible for the higher-level functions. The cerebellum is divided into two hemispheres, left and right, which are connected by the corpus callosum, a diverse network of nerve fibers that allows communication between the hemispheres. In general, the right hemisphere controls most functions on the left side of the body, and the left hemisphere controls most functions on the right side. This has been referred to as a **cross-wired** or **cross-lateral** arrangement. In Chapter 2, much was made of the notion of **laterality;** Orton believed that lack of hemispheric dominance caused reading and writing problems. And while this theory has been refuted, some teachers still believe that the lack of hand dominance (mixed dominance) is a reason for learning disabilities. The

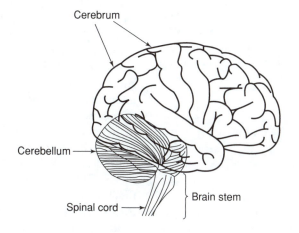

FIGURE 3-1 The brain

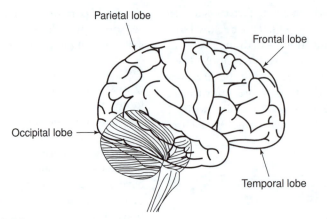

Parietal lobe

Frontal lobe

Occipital lobe

Temporal lobe

FIGURE 3–2 Hemispheric lobes.

hemispheres are not totally independent of each other. As Mercer and Pullen (2005) note, the overall function of the central nervous system is the major concern, more so than laterality and dominance.

Hemispheric Lobes. The brain is also divided by hemispheric lobes. Each hemisphere has four lobes: temporal, frontal, parietal, and optical. The temporal lobe is responsible for auditory memory. The frontal lobe controls abstract thinking, bodily movement, and speech. The parietal lobe controls the tactile sensations that come from different bodily parts. And finally, the optical lobe is responsible for vision and visual perception. As was noted earlier, the corpus callosum allows communication between similar lobes in each hemisphere (Figure 3-2).

DIAGNOSIS OF NEUROLOGICAL FUNCTIONS

Neurological Exam

The neurological exam is utilized more often in some parts of the United States than others. Neurologists are medical specialists trained in the

function of the central nervous system. The typical neurological examination attempts to rule in or rule out "soft neurological signs" that may explain the child's difficulty in learning. Mercer and Pullen (2005) cite Kandt (1984), Schor (1983), and Shaywitz and Shaywitz (1988) when describing the major components of the exam.

Mercer and Pullen (2005) note that the validity of the neurological exam is uncertain. Smith (2004) states that "examining hard and soft neurological signs has been fruitless in predicting or explaining learning problems" (p. 75). And yet, parents may ask you if their child should have a neurological exam. How should you respond? Typically, it is advised that parents speak to their pediatrician. Parents need to weigh the advantages and disadvantages of the exam. It may not provide information that will be helpful for instructional purposes, but it may allay some anxiety. It can eliminate concerns regarding seizure activity or tumors. "The fact that a child's brain has been injured raises red flags, it does not automatically means [that] learning disabilities will follow. The brain is plastic and often can compensate for losses" (Smith, 2004, p. 75). Many students with no school problems whatsoever display soft neurological signs.

Neurodiagnostic Testing

Early in the history of learning disabilities, parents and school personnel attempting to find a medical basis for a learning disability supplemented the neurological exam with an EEG. In addition to the EEG, there are four other tests that medical doctors can utilize to examine brain functioning: brain electrical activity mapping (BEAM), the computerized axial tomography (CAT) scan, the position emission tomography (PET) scan, magnetic resonance imaging (MRI), and functional MRI (fMRI) and functional MRI (Bender, 2004; Mercer & Pullen, 2005; Sousa, 2001).

- *EEG:* Records electrical activity in the brain. Electrodes are taped to different parts of the scalp, and a running record of activity is recorded.
- *BEAM:* Provides computer-constructed images of the information provided by the EEG.
- *CAT Scan:* Measures the structure of the brain through the use of many x-ray beams at different angles. It allows the radiologist to form a picture of the brain and identify various activity levels.
- *PET Scan:* Radioactive sugar isotopes are introduced into the brain through the bloodstream. When the patient performs various tasks, blood flow is recorded and specific sections of the brain are identified.
- *MRI:* A neuroimaging (nonradiological) procedure that creates a magnetic field to record specific measurable changes in brain tissue. These changes are measured by radio frequencies and computerized enhancements, allowing the radiologist to view the shape and location of parts of the **brain.**
- *fMRI:* Measures blood flow throughout the brain. As the student (child or adult) engages in a task, such as reading, fMRI identifies the brain areas involved. By comparing these finding to those of efficient learners, researchers can identify specific areas of efficiency and/or inefficiency in brain functioning.

fMRI has been cited frequently as the neurodiagnostic test of choice (see Shaywitz & Shaywitz, 2003, for a thorough review). When examining students with dyslexia, Shaywitz and Shaywitz (2003) identified the left occipitotemporal region as the site responsible for skilled automatic reading observing a failure of the "left-hemisphere posterior brain systems to function properly during reading" (p. 524). Students with dyslexia had overreliance on the frontal lobe and right hemisphere. These authors cite a convergence of evidence to support their findings and note that "fMRI has supplanted all other kinds of functional brain imaging for the examination of cognitive systems in the brain" (p. 22).

In summary, neurodiagnostic techniques hold great promise for the diagnosis of learning disabilities. However, some believe that they have "not contributed greatly to the understanding of the etiology of learning disabilities" (Bender, 2004, p. 57). Others (Miller, Sanchez, & Hynd, 2003; Shaywitz & Shaywitz, 2003) believe that there is a large body of evidence to support a neurological basis for learning disabilities, specifically in reading. This is a fascinating area of inquiry, and continued research may help to elucidate the etiology of these disabilities.

GENETIC CAUSES

Researchers have examined the genetic causes of learning disabilities (Raskind, 2001; Wood & Grigorenko, 2001), and there appears to be evidence to support the notion that some learning disabilities may be caused by a genetic problem. If a parent has a reading disability, there is a 30% to 50% chance that the child will also have one. This percentage is even higher for boys (Smith, 2004). Scarborough (1990) cited family history as one of the most important risk factors. Siblings have a 40% risk of dyslexia (Pennington & Gilger, 1996). Thompson and Raskind (2003) conclude their review of genetic influences on reading and writing disabilities by citing substantial progress in research in this area. They note that the Human Genome Project has provided useful information and powerful statistical methods for studying genetics. Currently, chromosomes 1, 2, 6, 15, and 18 have been implicated as possible sites of reading and writing disorders.

Twin studies have examined the relationship between genetics and learning disabilities. Identical twins have the same genetic constitution, whereas fraternal twins do not. The research indicates that identical twins are more likely than fraternal twins to have a learning disability (Smith, 2004; Thompson & Raskind, 2003).

It is important to recognize that the environment also influences learning. As Smith (2004) notes, "despite the evidence for genetic links in learning disorders, it's important to remember that what's been served up by the genes can be modified by the environment" (p. 80). This is a particularly important message for teachers working in an urban environment with culturally and linguistically diverse students with learning disabilities. The NRC report "Minority Students in Special and Gifted Education" (2002) notes that the dichotomy between biological and environmental factors is artificial. This is most evident when the role of poverty is introduced. The report states that issues related to poverty clearly impact the field of learning disabilities. As environmental factors such as poverty, race, language, and culture are introduced into the equation, issues related to etiology become murky. However, they cannot be ignored. If you teach in an urban setting, neuroenvironmental factors will impact your daily life in the classroom.

CONTROVERSIAL APPROACHES

The search for the causes of learning disabilities has led professionals and parents to use approaches that are unsupported by research. Some suggest that visual defects cause a learning disability, and others point to allergies or vitamin deficiencies. You need to be aware of such theories in order to help parents sort out fact from fiction.

Parents are vulnerable to a variety of practitioners who claim success without any reliable and valid documentation. McNamara and McNamara (1993) cited three approaches that continue to be popular:

1. Scotopic sensitivity training
2. Visual training
3. The Feingold diet

Scotopic Sensitivity Training

This approach was developed by Dr. Helen Irlen (1983), a psychologist, who uses colored lenses to correct for light sensitivity, which she suggests interferes with learning. The Irlen Institute for Perceptual and Learning Disabilities has branches in many cities throughout the United States and screens students for scotopic sensitivity syndrome (SSS). The characteristics of SSS are very broad. They include headaches, burning or itchy eyes, dry eyes, fatigue, and words perceived as doubling, moving, looking fuzzy, and disappearing.

Dr. Irlen suggests that individuals with SSS may rub their eyes, blink excessively, squint, open their eyes wide, shade the page, hold the reading material close to their eyes, cover one eye, read word by word, or use a finger to hold their place. Once it is determined that the individual responds well to particular colored lenses, he or she is advised to get such glasses.

To date, there are no empirical studies supporting this approach. The results provided so far are from individual case studies or testimonials from clients. Until this treatment can be supported by impartial scientific evidence, it cannot be recommended to the parents of children with learning disabilities (Fletcher & Martinez, 1994).

Visual Training

Students whose visual difficulties affect learning may move ahead when reading, use a finger to keep their place, skip lines, skip words, ignore punctuation, have difficulty coloring a ball, have a short attention span, develop fatigue when reading, read only short books, or have trouble with reading comprehension. Once the diagnosis has been made, students receive training (from an optometrist) in eye movement and eye-hand coordination.

Most experts in the field of learning disabilities believe that reading is not merely a visual task and that learning disabilities are not caused by visual defects. Therefore, visual training cannot cure a learning disability, as proponents of this approach suggest. And, as with scotopic sensitivity training, there is no credible evidence to suggest that visual training works.

There is a long history of controversy surrounding visual training. A policy statement on learning disabilities, dyslexia, and vision approved in 1992 by the American Academy of Pediatrics, the American Association of Pediatric Ophthalmology and Strabismus, and the American Academy of Ophthalmology notes that there is no known eye or visual cause for dyslexia and learning disabilities and no effective visual treatment.

Feingold Diet

In 1975, Dr. Benjamin Feingold published his best-selling book *Why Your Child Is Hyperactive*. His theory, based on his clinical observations as an allergist, was that food additives cause hyperactivity and learning disorders. His solution was simple— eliminate food additives. Dr. Feingold was a charismatic and powerful speaker, and parents responded to him. At the time he proposed his diet, many people were concerned about the food they ate and how it affected them. Before long, Feingold Associations were cropping up throughout the United States. Following is a list of the foods Feingold recommends eliminating.

Group 1

Green pepper	Peaches
Nectarines	Tangerines
Oranges	All teas
Plums and prunes	Tomatoes

Group 2

Foods containing artificial flavors

Baked goods (except bread)	Ice cream
Beverages	Condiments
Candy	Gelatin
Chewing gum	Preserves

Group 3

Foods containing artificial colors
Blues #1 and #2, Green #3, Reds #3 and #40, and Yellows #5 and #6. Two food colors should be limited in use to one produce each: Orange B for hot dogs and Citrus Red #2 for orange skin.

Group 4

Foods containing preservatives
Butylated hydroxy toluence (BHT)
Butylated hydroxy anisole (BHA)

Group 5

Foods containing natural salicylates

Almonds	Coffee
Apples	Cucumber and pickles
Apricots	Currants
Cherries	Grapes and raisins
Cloves	

Although parents reported remarkable success with the diet, the scientific community expressed considerable doubt about its effectiveness. Patients say it works; researchers say there is little, if any, support. Studies have been criticized for their poor execution, and parents have been criticized for seeking quick cures. Well-controlled studies have not found that food additives cause hyperactivity in 98% to 99% of children (Bender, 2004).

Mercer and Pullen (2005) point to megavitamin therapy and anti-motion sickness medication as additional controversial therapies, citing Worrall (1990) on ways of detecting health fraud in "cures" of learning disabilities. The following questions are a good start (p. 59):

1. Does the theory have a logical connection to the problem or condition being treated? Simply, does it meet commonsense standards?

2. Is the theory or therapy consistent with the related body of knowledge? Does it make sense in light of known facts in areas such as anatomy, psychology, and medicine?
3. How reasonable is the objective evidence? Does the study include control or placebo treatment groups? Is the therapy isolated in the study? Are the groups large enough to make statistical comparisons? How many studies are there?

Other researchers have commented on controversial therapies as well (Silver, 1995). What is apparent is that during your teaching career, you will encounter other possible causative factors that are equally controversial. Too many parents spend considerable time and money trying to help their children with learning disabilities, only to be disappointed by the results. They also lose valuable time that could have been spent on scientifically documented interventions.

SUMMARY

This chapter has addressed the many factors cited as causes of learning disabilities—environmental, medical, and genetic. What is apparent is that while there are optimistic reports from many in the fields of medicine and neuropsychology, we are far from identifying specific causes of learning disabilities. However, as Cutting and Denckla (2004) note, "with advances in behavioral, neuroimaging and genetic methodologies, the next few decades should yield a deeper understanding of the complexities of cognition and different types of LD, with the end goals of producing effective, proven, school-based treatments for students with an array of cognitive weaknesses" (p. 174). Presently, our response to Adam's parents regarding the cause of his learning disability may not be what they want to hear. That is, it is unknown. And while researchers continue to explore possible causes, at this time we must continue to be aware of the current findings regarding etiology.

SPRINGBOARDS FOR DISCUSSION AND REFLECTION

1. How would your respond to a parent who asked, "What causes a learning disability?"
2. Interview a parent who took his or her child for a neurological exam. Did it meet the parent's expectations? How did it impact the child's education?
3. Read the special series in *Learning Disabilities Research and Practice* on genetic disorders with a high incidence of learning disabilities (*19*[3], August 2004). Discuss it with colleagues. What is your reaction? Their reaction?
4. Visit a medical facility for the evaluation of learning disabilities. How does its evaluation differ from a school evaluation? What are the implications for instruction?
5. How would you address parents who are using controversial treatments for their children with learning disabilities?

ATTENTION DEFICIT HYPERACTIVITY DISORDER AND UNDERLYING PROCESS DISORDERS

CHAPTER 4

CHAPTER OBJECTIVES

At the end of this chapter you will:

- understand the rationale for examining underlying process disorders.
- understand the processes of attention, memory, and cognition.
- know the characteristics, diagnosis, and treatment of ADHD.

Alicia is having difficulty with geometry due to her visual perceptual problems. Ron appears to be off task, but he simply can't process auditory information. It's not clear whether Aaron's attention problems are affecting his memory or the reverse. These are just a few examples of the reasons you may give to explain a student's learning disability. It is not unusual to look for underlying process disorders—of perception, attention, and memory—to explain learning disabilities in academic areas. In the early stages of the field's development, the **process approach** was very much in vogue.

Training students in isolated processes (particularly perceptional training) to improve their academic skills was one of the defining characteristics of the field. A compelling body of research put a halt to the process approach, but the notion of underlying processes is still a major component of the definition of learning disabilities. This chapter examines these processes, reviews the relevant research, and discusses implications for instruction. Additionally, ADHD is discussed because you as a teacher will probably have considerable contact with students who have both learning disabilities and ADHD.

Torgesen (1998) notes that learning disabilities' "unique professional identity" (p. 16) came from the identification and remediation of specific psychological processes. It is apparent from the history of the field (see Chapter 2) that early pioneers such as Kirk, Frostig, and Kephant focused on isolating specific psycholinguistic and/or perceptual processes. Early criticism (Mann, 1979; Mann & Phillips, 1967) was followed by a host of studies indicating that process training did not transfer to basic academic skills (see Myers & Hammill, 1990, for a detailed discussion of this criticism). Torgesen (2002) suggests that the field may have been premature in discussing psychological processes and that we have progressed greatly since the late 1960s and early 1970s):

> These advances have occurred not only in understanding the basic processes that underlie development, but also in identifying those processing limitations that produce individual differences in learning outcomes for children exposed to the same learning opportunities.

The reason for these advances is that the information processing paradigm, as a way of studying and explaining human behavior, has matured during this time, and it has contributed important methodologies and theoretical constructs to the understanding of human learning and behavior. (p. 569)

This new knowledge led to renewed interest in examining the underlying psychological processes (attention, memory, and cognition) that impact on learning, and this research is continuing. However, we must be careful not to jump on the bandwagon and make the same mistakes made in the early years where perceptual training was widely used with no empirical evidence to support it. McGrady (2002) urges caution because we still do not have a validated taxonomy of intrinsic psychological processes, and Torgensen (2002) notes that "the foundation for reliable and valid measures of intrinsic psychological processing weaknesses of children with LD is not strong enough to recommend it for widespread application in schools" (p. 591).

Basic research in these areas is necessary if we are to have a better understanding of how to identify and remediate these processes.

PERCEPTION

Early researchers in the field of learning disabilities believed that motor learning (walking, hopping, jumping, throwing, etc.) was a prerequisite to higher-level learning methods such as talking, reading, and writing. To communicate, read, and write, a child must be proficient in motor learning. Therefore, in the 1960s and 1970s, many educational programs resembled what we now call **adaptive physical education,** focusing on motor activities such as hopping, skipping, jumping, throwing, catching, obstacle courses, and the like.

The rationale was that these skills had to be learned so that students could progress to other, more academically oriented skills. Research conducted in the early 1970s did not support this contention, and while some people continue to espouse this approach, current theories in the field do not support the use of isolated training in perceptual-motor activities.

This does not mean that students with learning disabilities do not have motor problems. Many parents report that these children are awkward or clumsy, or that they were delayed in walking or bike riding. Others state that their children are always bumping into things, have a hard time with sports, and do not enjoy physical activities. Teachers often note that these students have difficulty with handwriting, using scissors, buttoning a coat, or tying a shoelace. They may not be able to catch a ball, may drop their books, and never play with anyone on the playground.

Clearly, there are students with learning disorders who have motor problems. What has changed over the years is our approach to remediation. For a child with a motor problem, multifaceted intervention may now include adaptive physical education to modify the existing physical education program and meet the student's needs; occupational therapy to improve the student's fine motor skills; and physical therapy to promote the student's gross motor skills.

Students with motor problems may become easily frustrated because they cannot express what they have learned. They often write little because writing is so difficult. Their handwriting can be sloppy and illegible. This can also cause difficulty with mathematics. Due to misalignment and illegibility of the numbers they write, they make mistakes.

Children with spatial relation problems have trouble sequencing letters in words and words in sentences. They may also have trouble walking through a crowded classroom or store without knocking things over.

Visual perceptual problems can involve visual discrimination, figure–ground discrimination, closure, and visual closure. **Visual discrimination** is the ability to distinguish one object from another. A typical example of difficulty in this area is the reversal of letters (*b* for *d*, *p* for *q*) or words (*was* for *saw*).

Figure–ground discrimination is the ability to distinguish an object from the background. Students struggling to master this skill may also have trouble concentrating on one word or tracing objects when they overlap. Focusing on important information on a blackboard with a lot of writing can be difficult, too.

Visual closure is the ability to identify the whole when only a part is shown. Activities in children's workbooks that require them to find all the socks or all the fish. The child has to identify the correct number of items even though only parts of them can be seen. A child with a visual closure problem has difficulty with this activity. Identifying a partially covered word is also difficult. Finally, children with visual memory problems may have trouble identifying letters, numbers, and words, as well as shapes and objects.

Auditory perceptual problems can be divided into auditory discrimination, auditory figure–ground discrimination auditory memory, and auditory blending problems. **Auditory discrimination** is the ability to distinguish similarities and differences between sounds. Students with auditory discrimination problems have a hard time following directions and have problems with all aspects of phonics. Students with difficulty in **auditory figure–ground discrimination** cannot identify the major source of the information they are hearing from the background. Teachers may comment, "He knows exactly what is going on all around him but does not hear a word I say." Parents often report that she "listens to everything but what she is supposed to listen to." These students cannot distinguish the relevant from the irrelevant in a lecture or conversation. An **auditory memory** problem is manifested as inability to recall information the child has heard. These children may have trouble recalling the days of the week, a phone number, and a sequence of words, as well as commands (especially if there is more than one). Many children with learning disabilities have difficulty blending the isolated sounds of words together. This skill, called **auditory blending,** is critical for success if a child is being taught using a phonics-based approach. It is less important if other approaches are employed.

As with motor problems, leaders in the field of learning disabilities felt that these skills were critical for future success. Once again, this belief was not supported by research.

Despite the lack of empirical evidence for perceptual disorders in students with learning disabilities, teachers know that they exist for some students (Mercer & Pullen, 2005). Teachers must be cognizant of these problems and use content and basic skills instruction, not isolated process training.

ATTENTION

Attention is an inferred construct. As a classroom teacher, you may think that the child who is looking right at you, nodding his head in approval, and apparently focused is attending. The truth is, you really don't know until he or she demonstrates that attention by performing a task. Bender (2004) divides attention into three areas:

1. Time on task
2. Focus of attention
3. Selective attention

The area that has received the most research is **selective attention,** the ability to focus on what is important and ignore irrelevant stimuli. Even if you have only limited experience with students with learning disabilities, you will notice that many have difficulty with this skill. They may focus on unimportant aspects of a lecture or what they read. Frequently, parents or students report that they studied all night for a test, only to have targeted all the wrong information. An early investigator, Alan Ross (1976), examined research on students with learning disabilities and concluded that the inability to attend selectively to a task is one of the major hallmarks of a learning disability. Hallahan, Gajar, Cohen, and Tarver (1978) adapted Hagen's (1967) task of central and incidental learning to study attention in students with learning disabilities. Students were presented with seven posters of household items on the top divided by a line. On the bottom half were drawings of animals. Bender (2004) describes the experiment and the results:

> Each stimulus card was presented for 12 seconds to children who were learning disabled and to others who were not. There were 18 different posters. Students were asked to attend only to the animals and to remember the order in which they were shown the animal pictures. The first 4 posters were used as practice trials and the last 14 as actual test items. The percentage of correct responses was used as the measure of central recall because the children were told, in effect, to center their attention on the animals. At the end of this task, the children were presented with seven paired boxes with the animals drawn in at the bottom and blank spaces at the top. Also, the students were given seven pictures of the household items to be matched to the animals and placed in the blanks. This was considered the measure *of incidental recall* because the children remembered these stimuli only incidentally. By subtracting the incidental recall score from the central recall score, the researchers obtained

a measure of selective attention. Results showed that the students with learning disabilities were similar to the other group on incidental recall, but both central recall and selective attention scores for the group with learning disabilities were lower than for the other group. Hallahan and his co-workers stated that this selective attention deficit among children with learning disabilities supported Torgesen's conceptualization of these children as inactive learners. (p. 78)

There are many unresolved issues regarding attention and learning disabilities (Conte, 1998). Part of the problem is in the selection of study subjects. Most studies include a variety of subjects who have learning disorders—some with ADHD, some without. Other studies examine students with ADHD—some with learning disorders, some without. It is still unclear if the ability to attend selectively or to sustain attention is responsible for the learning problems of students with learning disabilities.

The bulk of the evidence has demonstrated that students with learning disabilities are deficient in every aspect of attention behavior. They are on task less often than other children. In the majority of studies, children with learning disabilities are perceived as being more distractible than others. Finally, selective attention is lower among these children, and they demonstrate a lag in developing this important attention capability. Clearly, attention deficits among children with learning disabilities warrant further research attention—the only way of clarifying these important issues. As a teacher, you should follow the continuing research in each of these areas.

ATTENTION DEFICIT HYPERACTIVITY DISORDER

There is an overlap between learning disabilities and ADHD. Learning disabilities may precede ADHD, ADHD may precede learning disabilities, or they may co-exist. Teachers need to be familiar with ADHD because attention problems, impulsivity, and hyperactivity occur often in students with learning disabilities (Hallahan, Lloyd, Kauffman, Weiss, & Martinez, 2005). Clearly, learning disabilities and ADHD are not synonymous, but their overlap and comorbidity make ADHD a topic to be aware of.

The terminology has changed over the years and has varied across disciplines. In the 1960s, a child with an attention problem evaluated by a physician would most likely be labeled as having **minimal brain dysfunction** (MBD), whereas the school might use the term **learning disabled** or **hyperactive.** Currently, the term most frequently employed is **attention deficit hyperactivity disorder** (ADHD). Some experts suggest using the more general term **attention deficit disorder** (ADD) because it includes all kinds of attention problems, not just those involving hyperactivity.

The most frequently cited characteristics of children with ADHD are **hyperactivity, distractibility,** and **impulsivity.** They have difficulty staying on task and focusing on important aspects of conversations and/or school-related tasks. Frequently, they do not complete tasks because they are moving rapidly from one activity to another or are distracted by extraneous stimuli. Parents talk of children who require little sleep, are very restless, and are constantly in motion.

Hyperactivity is a central nervous system disorder that makes it difficult for children to control their motor activity. These children are not necessarily constantly on the go, but they appear to be restless and fidgety. Parents describe children who can't sit through a meal, or who move from one activity to another very rapidly, or who "never shut up." Other teachers report that these students are always doing something—getting up to sharpen their pencil, tapping their pencil or fingers on the desk, tapping their foot on the floor, finishing assignments very rapidly and often incorrectly, running around on the playground, and squirming in their chairs. These behaviors are often without purpose or focus. Frequently, someone will say, "I don't know where he gets his energy" or "I wish I had his energy." This is not the type of energy that allows someone to accomplish a great deal. Quite the opposite: it interferes with productivity.

Children who are distractible have difficulty staying on task and filtering information from the senses. They are not good at discriminating between relevant and irrelevant information; thus, everything competes for their attention. They are unable to focus on specific tasks for long periods of time; hence, the term **short attention span** is often used to describe them.

You've seen children and adolescents who are easily distracted. A slight noise in another part of the room will draw their attention. They hear someone talking outside the house and are distracted by it. A car goes by the window, and they rush to look out. They may walk into the bedroom to get something, but their attention shifts to a picture on the wall and they forget why they are there. Many of these children experience difficulty in places where a great deal is going on, such as birthday parties, shopping malls, carnivals, circuses, and the like. They often become irritable and restless because of the increased stimulation in their surroundings. Some classrooms can cause the same problem. So much may be going on that the child can't attend effectively.

Some children with ADHD are impulsive, acting first and thinking later. They may say things that are offensive but may not realize it until it is pointed out to them. They may hit classmates and then apologize profusely. They lack the ability to anticipate the meaning of their behavior and merely act out. Impulsive children ask questions that have nothing to do with the current subject of conversation. In class, they call out answers before the questions have been asked—usually the wrong answers. These children and adolescents appear to be accident prone because they do not attend to the consequences of their actions. The child with ADHD manifests these behaviors both at school and at home. One hallmark of the disorder is the pervasiveness of the behaviors displayed. If a child displays these characteristics in only one setting—school or home—then it can probably be attributed to causes other than ADHD.

Prevalence and Causation

Most experts estimate that 3% to 7% of school-age children can be diagnosed with ADHD (Barkley, 1998; Du Paul & Stover, 2003; Pastor & Reuben, 2002). As a teacher of students with learning disabilities, you can be expected to teach students who have both learning disabilities and ADHD. The prevalence of comorbidity (two or more disorders occur simultaneously) for learning disabilities and ADHD ranges from 20% to 40% (Du Paul & Stover, 2003; McNamara & McNamara, 2000).

What causes ADHD? The same causal factors implicated in learning disabilities are implicated here. "The most prudent conclusion regarding the etiology of ADHD is that multiple neurological factors may predispose children to exhibit higher rates of impulsivity and motor activity along with shorter than average attention spans compared to other children" (Du Paul & Stover, 2003, p. 15). These authors note that we need to be cautious about these conclusions due to methodological difficulties with research, the importance of the environment, and the lack of a connection between cause and treatment.

Terminology

Some suggest that the term *ADHD* is misleading because there is no deficit in attention (Cutting & Denckla, 2004). They cite Barkely's (1997) work as evidence that there is a "deficit in [students'] development or allocation of attentional resources" (p. 126). Denckla and her colleagues at the Learning Disability Research Center at the Kennedy Krieger Institute at Johns Hopkins School of Medicine have done considerable work on ADHD employing a behavioral neurogenetics (gene to brain to behavior) approach. See the special series in *Learning Disabilities Research and Practice* (*19*[3], 2004) for a description of their work. Du Paul and Stover (2003) also note the work of Barkley (1997, 1998) in the conceptualization of the deficits in ADHD. Barkley's model suggests that ADHD is a disorder of behavioral inhibition rather than of attention. Barkley notes that research in this area is ongoing. Despite the dissatisfaction with the terminology, it must be recognized that what is going on here is a convergence of science, policy, and advocacy. There is a powerful advocacy component influencing public policy, and its identity (and power) would be threatened by the elimination of the term *ADHD*. Research needs to continue, independent of parent and professional organizations, to refine our understanding of ADHD. However, it must be acknowledged that awareness of ADHD has been greatly enhanced by this constituency.

Identifying ADHD

The criteria for identifying ADHD, as stated in the *Diagnostic and Statistical Manual on Mental Disorders* (DSM-IV) of 1994, are as follows:

A. Either (1) or (2):
1. six (or more) of the following symptoms of inattention have persisted for at least 6 months to a degree that is maladaptive and inconsistent with developmental level:

(1) Inattention
a. often fails to give close attention to details or makes careless mistakes in school work, work or other activities
b. often has difficulty sustaining attention in tasks or play activities
c. often does not seem to listen when spoken to directly
d. often does not follow through on instructions and fails to finish school work, chores, or duties in the workplace (not due to oppositional behavior or failure to understand instructions)
e. often has difficulty organizing tasks and activities
f. often avoids, dislikes, or is reluctant to engage in tasks that require sustained mental effort (such as school work or homework)
g. often loses things necessary for tasks or activities (toys, school assignments, pencils, books or tools)
h. is often easily distracted by extraneous stimuli
i. is often forgetful in daily activities

(2) Hyperactivity-Impulsivity
a. often fidgets with hands or feet or squirms in seat
b. often leaves seat in classroom or in other situations in which remaining seated is expected
c. often runs about or climbs excessively in situations in which it is inappropriate (in adolescents or adults, may be limited to subjective feelings of restlessness)

d. often has difficulty playing or engaging in leisure activities quietly
e. is often "on the go" or often acts as if "driven by a motor"
f. often talks excessively
g. often blurts out answers before questions have been completed
h. often has difficulty awaiting turn
i. often interrupts or intrudes on others (e.g., butts into conversations or games)

Code based on type:

314.01 Attention-Deficit/Hyperactivity Disorder Combined Type: if both Criteria A1 and A2 are met for the past 6 months.
314.00 Attention-Deficit/Hyperactivity Disorder, Predominantly Inattentive Type: if Criterion A1 is met but Criterion A2 is not met for the past 6 months.
314.012 Attention-Deficit/Hyperactivity Disorder, Predominantly Hyperactive-Impulsive Type: if Criterion A2 is met but Criterion A1 is not met for the past 6 months.

The criteria list three types:

AD/HD's combined type
AD/HD Predominantly Inattentive Type ADHD

Predominantly Hyperactive-Impulsive Type
Most children are diagnosed with the combined and the predominantly hyperactive type. Note the qualifiers that these symptom must be present before the age of seven, and they must be present in at least two settings. They must impact on social, academic, and occupational functioning and must not be the result of other disorders.

AD/HD, Predominantly Inattentive Type
Many experts believe this is an overlooked population, and children who are described as "out of it," "spacey," and the like may have ADHD. Moreover, some have suggested that more girls than boys are this type and not properly diagnosed.

When you examine the criteria, you can readily see why many professionals and parents have a difficult time deciding on a particular point—for example, "fidgets with hands or feet or squirms in seat." How much? How many times? During what tasks? What do you mean by *squirms?* Barkley

(1998) cites a number of concerns regarding the DSM-IV criteria. However, he notes that it is a vast improvement on previous criteria and is closer to the literature on ADHD. He advises professionals not to be dogmatic when adapting the criteria and to use good clinical judgment.

Identifying a child with ADHD is often a process of exclusion. That is, when other difficulties have been ruled out and the child exhibits characteristics such as distractibility, hyperactivity, and difficulty staying on task, the diagnosis is commonly ADHD. However, this diagnosis should never be made in isolation or by one person. A proper assessment uses the team approach, whereby professionals from medicine, psychology, education, and social work evaluate the child/adolescent together.

Diagnosis of ADHD

A thorough multidisciplinary evaluation is crucial for the accurate diagnosis of ADHD. Medical, psychological, educational, and social history evaluations must be undertaken. Each component of the evaluation, as well as ways to evaluate all the findings, will be discussed. Disorders occurring simultaneously, known as **comorbidity,** will also be considered.

ADHD is a complex disorder. To ensure a proper diagnosis, information must be gathered from a variety of sources. The evaluation should be undertaken by a group of professionals referred to as a **multidisciplinary team,** consisting of a physician (neurologist), a psychologist, a special educator, and a social worker. Team members work together make a diagnosis that will provide a total picture. Without a multidisciplinary approach, an important factor may be missing, and without that factor, the diagnosis may be wrong.

The **neurologist,** preferably a developmental or pediatric neurologist, will evaluate the functioning of the central nervous system. This is not an invasive examination (see Chapter 3). Depending upon the nature of the problem, certain laboratory tests may be desirable. For example, if there is a suggestion of a seizure disorder, the neurologist may request an EEG, which measures brain wave activity.

The **psychologist** will evaluate the child's intellectual and social-emotional functioning, looking for disorders such as learning disabilities, emotional disturbances, or other psychological or psychiatric disorders that may coexist with ADHD or may be the main problem.

The **special educator,** trained in psychoeducational assessment procedures, will administer a battery of tests to explore the existence of a possible learning disability or other school-related disorders. The student's basic psychological processes (attention, memory, perception) and basic skills will be assessed to determine specific strengths and weaknesses. In some parts of the country, a school psychologist will administer the test.

The **social worker** will meet with the family to obtain information about the child's social history, including birth information, developmental milestones, family dynamics, medical information, and school placement. The social worker will also explore the child's behavior at home and at school to acquire information that will help determine the cause of ADHD.

The need for a multidisciplinary evaluation cannot be minimized. When information is accumulated by a variety of professionals, the true nature and needs of the child can be determined. For example, a child may be referred for an evaluation because of excessive motion in the classroom. Upon evaluation, the neurologist may not find a satisfactory explanation for the behavior, but the special educator notes the school problem, as does the psychologist. The social worker may request a home visit, and the parents may confide that there are marital difficulties and great stress. In this case, there does not appear to be a neurological basis to ADHD. Rather, the child's anxiety about her parents is causing her to act disruptively in the classroom. The treatment would be markedly different for this child than for a child who appears to be hyperactive because of a central nervous system dysfunction.

When all professionals have accumulated their findings, they generally meet to discuss their results, to determine the existence or absence of ADHD, and to develop a treatment plan and ways to monitor progress. See Du Paul and Stover (2003) for a thorough description of a school-based assessment of ADHD.

Learning Disabilities and ADHD

As noted previously, most teachers of students with learning disabilities have considerable contact with students who also have ADHD. Approximately 40% of students with learning disabilities are also diagnosed with ADHD, and about 30% to 40% of students with ADHD also have a learning disability (Barkely, 1998; Pastor & Reuben, 2002).

If a student is classified as having both a learning disability and ADHD, he or she can receive services under IDEA 2004. If the diagnosis is ADHD without a learning disability, the classification may be other health impaired (OHI). IDEA 1997 allowed for the classification of a student with ADHD as OHI. If the student is not eligible for classification as OHI, he or she may receive services under a Section 504 plan (see Chapter 2).

Medical Intervention

In the foreword to *ADHD in the Schools* (Du Paul & Stover, 2003), Dr. Russell Barkley, a leading expert on ADHD, employs rather strong language on the topic of medical treatments for ADHD. He states:

It does not matter whether one "believes" in medicine or not, as the question is so often phrased by the naïve. Medication management is not a religious belief requiring a leap of faith to endorse it. Contrary to the political propaganda and scientifically illiterate blather one may discover in the popular media, some Congressional hearings, and zealotry-tainted websites against medication and even ADHD as a diagnosis, medication management of ADHD is a more well-established intervention in denial science that in any other treatment strategy. . . .

Medication has been determined to be effective for most students with ADHD (Bender, 2004; Du Paul & Stover, 2003). Du Paul and Stover (2003) point out that given its widespread use, school personnel need to be familiar with the side effects of medication, factors in recommending medication, how to assess treatment, communication with medical professionals, and the limitations of medication. Based on an extensive review of the literature, they summarize the findings on psychotropic medication:

Various psychotropic medications have been used to enhance the attentional, behavioral, and academic function of children with ADHD. CNS stimulant medications are the most effective medications for the symptomatic management of children with ADHD. Among positive treatment responders, stimulant medications significantly enhance the attention span, impulse control, academic performance, and peer relationships of children with ADHD, although effects on the latter two functioning areas must be replicated further. Side effects (e.g., insomnia, appetite reduction) are relatively benign and are more likely to occur at higher dose levels. Given that the behavioral effects of stimulants are moderated by dose and individual responsivity, each child's treatment response must be assessed in an objective manner across a range of therapeutic doses. School professionals can play a major role in evaluating stimulant-induced changes in the classroom performance of children with ADHD and providing objective outcome data to the prescribing physician. Because the overall efficacy of stimulant medication treatment is limited by a number of factors, other interventions (e.g., behavior modification) are likely to be necessary to optimize the probability of long-term improvements in the behavioral and academic status of children with ADHD. (p. 222)

Teachers need to employ empirical evidence to inform their opinions. Decisions related to medicine should be based on the same kinds of decisions you would make for a reading or math intervention. Whether you believe in it or not is unimportant. Whether there is support in the professional literature is the real issue. Other interventions such as diets, food restriction, megavitamins, herbal medicines, and other new "crazes" have not been demonstrated to be effective. Teachers need to keep abreast of the research and these controversial interventions. For a thorough understanding of ADHD, consult Du Paul and Stover (2003).

MEMORY

Many teachers and parents of children with learning disabilities say that they have memory problems. They often remark, "She forgets everything" or "If I don't remind her, she never remembers" or "When I mention something we discussed for an entire week, she looks at me like she doesn't have a clue about what I'm talking about."

Memory is a complex process that involves much more than the number of items to be remembered. It encompasses knowing what should be remembered, strategies for remembering, and methods for access information stored in one's memory bank. Knowing how memory works can help us use it more efficiently.

The ability to understand the demands of the task, to know what strategies to use, to use them effectively, and to learn how to retrieve information may be at the core of the problem for students with learning disabilities. A simple visual model (Figure 4–1) will help explain this process.

Information comes to us through the environment. If a child has a perceptual processing disorder, this information deficit may be compounded and affect memory functioning. If there is no problem with interpreting the information (perception), then the child must attend to the information

in order to move it into **short-term memory** (STM). Some children and adolescents with learning disabilities do not transfer information to their STM. They don't forget it; they never had the opportunity (or strategy or process) to remember it.

Once information enters STM, students must do something to transfer it to **long-term memory** (LTM). STM is very short, possibly lasting for only about 15 seconds. Therefore, if the student doesn't employ a strategy to recall the information, it will be lost. In order for information to proceed to LTM (sometimes referred to as **LTM storage**), students must act on the information or "rehearse" it, also referred to as **working memory** (WM). For example, you are introduced to someone you think you will never see again, so you don't do anything to remember his name. Then you run into him next week and cannot recall his name. If you had thought of a way to remember it, such as associating a characteristic with the first letter of the name or associating the person's face with someone with a similar name, then your would probably remember it.

In school, students with learning disabilities are required to recall information far more complex than someone's name, but the process is the same. They must act on the information in order to transfer it to LTM and retrieve it at a later date.

Memory is a complex task involving much more than the rapid recall of facts and figures. It is a developmental process involving the ability to attend to, perceive, organize, store, and retrieve information. The problems that students with learning disabilities have with memory may involve any or all of the parts of memory, as well as the complexity of the information they have to remember.

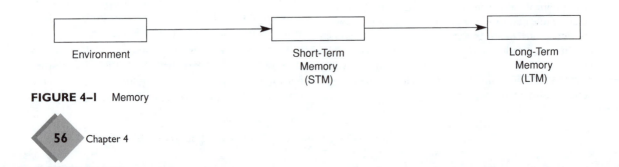

| Environment | Short-Term Memory (STM) | Long-Term Memory (LTM) |

FIGURE 4–1 Memory

Swanson (1999) defines memory as "the ability to encode, process and retrieve information" (p. 107). He believes it is a critical focus in learning disabilities and cites three reasons:

1. It reflects *applied* cognition: that is, memory functioning reflects all aspects of learning.
2. Several studies suggest that the memory skills used by students with LD do not appear to exhaust, or even to tap, their ability, and therefore we need to discover instructional procedures that capitalize on their potential.
3. Finally, several cognitive intervention programs that attempt to enhance the overall cognition of children and adults with LD rely on principles derived from memory research. (p. 107)

Current memory research focuses on the analysis of nonstrategic processing, that is, processing that is not consciously performed. Earlier, the focus was on the acquisition of mnemonic strategies. Swanson and Saez (2003) reviewed the research on memory and summarized their findings. Students with learning disabilities have WM deficits. They also have difficulty with attention allocation and with shifting and updating information in WM. Finally, they have phonological system deficits.

STM has been the most widely researched area of memory. Swanson and his colleagues have conducted several studies in this area (see Swanson & Saez, 2003, for additional information and references). Students with learning disabilities are inferior to their counterparts without such disabilities on STM tasks, and when they are required to memorize information in sequential order, they perform even more poorly. There is a relative dearth of information on the LTM functioning of students with leaning disabilities. The area of LTM that has received the most attention is WM. Swanson (1999) cites Baddeley's (1986) description of work "as a limited capacity central executive that interacts with a set of two passive store systems used for temporary storage of different classes of information, the speed-based articulatory loop, and the visual sketch pad" (p. 134).

The current state of research can be summed up as follows (Swanson & Saez, 2003, p. 195):

Prior to 1989, memory research in LD was strongly influenced by the hypothesis that variations in memory performance are rooted in the children's acquisition of mnemonic strategies (Cooney & Swanson, 1987; Swanson, Cooney, & O'Shaughnessy, 1998). Strategies are deliberate, consciously applied procedures that aid in the storage and subsequent retrieval of information. Research in the last 10 years has moved in a different direction, toward an analysis of non-strategic processes that are not necessarily consciously applied. The major motivation behind this movement has been that important aspects of memory performance are often disassociated with [sic] changes in mnemonic strategies. The most striking evidence has come from strategy-oriented research, which shows that differences between children with and without learning disabilities remain after the use of an optimal strategy (i.e., a strategy shown to be advantageous in the majority of studies).

It is clear from our synthesis of the literature (Swanson et al., 1998), however, that children with LD can benefit from mnemonic instruction when training is sufficiently rigorous. However, strategy training does not eliminate ability group differences between students with LD and their peers with disabilities in a multitude of situations. Some of the causes of strategies' ineffectiveness or utilization deficiencies may be related to individual differences in information processing capacity (i.e., children without LD benefit more from the strategy than do children with LD) and/or a particular level of strategy effectiveness may have different causes in different children. A child with LD, for example, may be unable to benefit from a strategy because of his or her limited capacity, whereas another child may be constrained by his or her lack of knowledge relevant to the task. Thus, different children may follow different developmental routes to overcome their utilization deficiencies.

COGNITIVE PROCESSES

Are particular cognitive processes involved in learning disabilities, specifically in the area most frequently studied—reading? Siegel (2003) postulated five basic cognitive processes that are significant in reading development: phonology, syntax, WM, semantics, and orthography. (These are covered in Chapters 12 to 14.) Phonological processing is believed to be the most significant process, as it relates to the development of reading skills. Siegel concludes that this process, as well as syntax and WM, are strongly deficient in students with reading disabilities, whereas, semantic and orthographic processes are less significantly disrupted. She recommends that the assessment of learning disabilities include these three processes.

INFORMATION PROCESSING

In the previous discussion, cognitive processes were examined in isolation to some degree. However, it is very difficult to isolate specific abilities in students with learning disabilities. The information processing approach focuses on the overall system rather than specific abilities. It has been viewed as the most influential model in cognitive psychology (Mercer & Pullen, 2005; Swanson et al., 1998). As Mercer and Pullen (p. 80) note, it is somewhat similar to a computer system.

Information processing theories and models may vary, but they have the following characteristics in common:

1. Information processing is characterized as being part of a system.
2. Information processing occurs when information is coded and recoded as it enters and moves through the information processing system.
3. The information processing system is believed to have structural or capacity features that are not under the individual's direct control and cannot be changed.
4. The information processing system is believed to have structural or capacity features that can be changed through experience and training. Some of these features are under the individual's conscious control, and others are not.

Swanson et al. (1998) summarize the information processing approach as one that "focuses on how input is transformed, reduced, elaborated, stored, retrieved and used" (p. 118).

A number of models have been proposed (see Mellard, 1998; Swanson, 1987; Swanson et al., 1998) regarding the way in which students with learning disabilities process information, transfer it, and employ learning strategies. How much of their difficulties with high-level functioning can be attributed to the inability to employ cognitive strategies or to deficits in basic processes? Ongoing research is needed to answer this question.

IMPLICATIONS FOR INSTRUCTION

Instructional Strategies for Attention

The following teaching tips may increase the use of attention skills (Bender, 2004, p. 80):

1. Offer numerous cues to attend to task during lecture and discussion. Cues such as "The next point . . .", "Point number three . . ." or "There are four specific examples of this I want you to have. First . . ." will cue students to attend to the points you make.
2. Visually monitor a child's eye contact with the assigned task at all times. You should always wander around the room when students are doing seatwork independently in order to scan visually and make certain that students stay on task.
3. Keep external distractions to a minimum. Draw shades if another class is on the playground outside your window. Consider using background music in your class to cover the routine classroom noise.
4. Question students on how they knew what aspect of a stimulus to attend to. Discuss the selective attention strategies in class.
5. Use special attention strategies. For example, use a colored marker to code the instructions on each worksheet for students who demonstrate attention problems.
6. Discuss the meaning of *paying attention* with your students. Show them the advantages of

good attention skills in terms of finishing work more quickly and receiving more study time.

7. Teach children how to pay attention using self-monitoring.

Behavior Interventions for Students with ADHD

The behavior interventions described in Chapter 16 are also appropriate for students with ADHD. Du Paul and Stover (2003, pp. 145–147) suggest considering the following issues when designing behaviorally based interventions for classroom problems related to ADHD:

1. A thorough assessment of the specific presenting problems, including functional assessment, should be conducted to guide the design and selection of intervention components (e.g., target behaviors and their function(s), instructional strategy, motivational program).

2. Children diagnosed with ADHD typically require more frequent and specific feedback than their classmates to optimize their performance. As such, initial phases of interventions aimed at ADHD-related problems should incorporate contingencies that can be delivered in a relatively continuous manner. Schedules of reinforcement should be introduced gradually, as some laboratory-based evidence indicates that children with ADHD have more difficulty maintaining their behavior under intermittent reinforcement schedules than do their peers (Douglas, 1984). Related to the issue of timing of reinforcement, in one study (Rapport, Stover, Du Paul, Birmingham, & Tucker, 1985) children with ADHD tended to choose smaller, more immediate rewards over larger, delayed rewards contingent upon completion of academic work. These results were to emphasize the need to attend to the general notion that to be effective, contingencies need to be in place at the "point of performance."

3. Contingent positive reinforcement should be the primary component of a behaviorally based intervention program for problems related to ADHD. [See Chapter 16 for more on this topic.] But some evidence exists to suggest that exclusive reliance on reinforcement may distract the child from the task at hand. Alternatively, this concern may be ameliorated by the use of positive reinforcement (Abramowitz, O'Leary, & Rosen, 1987; Rosen, O'Leary, Joyce, Conway, & Pfiffner, 1984) and redirection of the child toward appropriate task behavior. The effectiveness of verbal reprimands and redirections can be enhanced through *specificity* of communication regarding the teacher's concerns and through *consistent delivery immediately* following the occurrence of problem behavior(s) (Pfiffner & O'Leary, 1993). Furthermore, treating children with dignity and respect requires that reprimands and redirection statements be made in a *brief, calm, and quiet* manner. As much as possible, reprimands should be delivered *privately* while making eye contact with the child.

4. When students' behavior during independent work periods is targeted for change, initial task instructions should involve no more than a few steps. The child then should be asked to repeat directions back to the teacher to demonstrate understanding. Similarly, student homework and related tasks/projects should be assigned one at a time, with more complex tasks broken into smaller units. In some cases, the overall amount of assigned work would be reduced for the child with ADHD. The length and complexity of the workload would be increased gradually as the child demonstrates successful independent completion of increasingly larger units. Repetitive material (e.g., reassigning erroneously completed worksheets) should be avoided. Alternatively, an assignment focused on the same skill or concept area could be substituted to avoid boredom and potential exacerbation of attention problems.

5. Academic products and performance (e.g., work completion and accuracy) are preferred as targets of intervention as compared with specific task-related behaviors (e.g., attention to task or staying in one's seat) for several reasons. First, this preference promotes teacher monitoring of important student outcomes. Second, this preference promotes attention to the organizational and academic skills (e.g., working with the appropriate materials for an assignment, soliciting formative feedback on initial task performance) necessary for independent learning and for completing academic assignments. Third, a focus on active academic responding does not violate the "dead man test for behavior" (i.e., desired behavior) articulated by Lindsley (1991). This "rule" stated that "if a dead boy could do it, it

Note: Reprinted with permission of The Guilford Press.

wasn't behavior" (Lindsley, 1991, p. 457). Employing treatment targets like "sitting still" and "not calling out" violates the dead man test. Finally, this preference for academic responding as a treatment target promotes a focus on behavior that is incompatible with inattentive and disruptive behavior, and as such may lead to multiple desired outcomes, including a reduction in disruptive behavior (Pfiffner & O'Leary, 1993).

6. Preferred activities (e.g., free-choice activity time, access to a classroom computer) should be used as reinforcers rather than tangible rewards (e.g., stickers and consumable items) whenever possible. Such contingencies may include making access to a preferred classroom activity contingent upon completion of an assignment in a less-preferred subject area (e.g., completion of a math worksheet leads to access to reading activities). Also in the reinforcement, the specific rewards or reinforcers employed should be varied or rotated as needed to prevent disinterest with them, and thus with programs (i.e., reinforcer satiation). Finally, rather than assuming that specific activities will be motivating for the child, reward "menus" should be developed through direct questioning of the child as to what she or he wants to learn or by observing her or his preferred activities.

7. To enhance the positive incentive value of classroom privileges, employ a "priming" procedure with the child prior to academic assignment periods (Rapport, 1987). "Priming" involves the teacher and student in reviewing a list of possible classroom privileges *prior* to beginning an academic work period wherein the student chooses which activity he or she would like to participate in following the work period.

8. The integrity or fidelity with which an intervention program is implemented must be monitored and evaluated (Gresham, 1989). Such monitoring can serve as the basis for making changes in program components, justifying additional resource needs, and/or developing and providing additional training material or coaching with those carrying out the procedures.

Instructional Strategies for Students with ADHD

Instructional strategies employed with students with learning disabilities described throughout this book are also appropriate for students with ADHD. Emotional controls, such as teacher proximity, preferential seating (with an appropriate attending model available), and the opportunity to work in different settings if desired, are beneficial. Some useful guidelines for classroom teachers are:

- Approach the ADHD child with an understanding of the underlying condition.
- Be aware of the child's limitations.
- It is difficult, but you should try to distinguish between behavior that is noncompliant (the child refuses to do something) and behavior that is the result of ADHD (the child can't do something). Treat these behaviors differently. Behaviors that a child can't do require instruction or development of a strategy for compensation. Behavior that is noncompliant requires disciplinary techniques designed to teach compliance and eliminate noncompliance, and removing a privilege or points or noncompliance.
- Interpret groups' test results cautiously. This child may have rushed through the test, answered impulsively, or have been distracted and not completed the test. Therefore, results may not be useful in determining skill levels for the ADHD child.
- Remember that medication is not a panacea. An ADHD child who has been placed on medication typically has strikingly improved behavior but often will not have acquired the same skills as other children. Extra instruction may be necessary.
- Take advantage of the energy and spontaneity of the ADHD child to help eliminate potential difficulties. For instance, when planning on a class play, the ADHD child may be quite frustrated (and frustrating to you and classmates) if cast as the father who stands quietly and observes before saying his one line.
- Provide for close supervision during unstructured times like recess to help control risk-taking and eliminate potential injuries. Work with parents and other professionals.
- Ask parents for information about strategies that have been tried with their child in the past.
- Help parents locate resources for dealing with manifestations of ADHD outside of school such as training in child management skills.

- Involve parents in using management strategies such as daily checklists or assignment sheets to help with behavior and assignment completion.
- Use in-school resources. The school psychologist may be willing to observe the ADHD child to assist you in identifying specific behaviors or times when interventions would be helpful. Techniques that the school psychologist may be able to assist with include the think aloud program or verbal self-monitoring.
- Monitor changes in the child's behavior. If the ADHD student is taking medication, work with the parents and physicians in completing behavior checklists or keeping logs of behaviors to help ensure that medication is providing optimal benefits. Expect ADHD to be an ongoing condition and plan for this chronicity. Behavior management strategies are likely to be necessary on an ongoing basis throughout the elementary grades and often in middle school and high school. Strategies for elementary students require the teacher as manager. As the child gets older, he or she will need help in learning self-management strategies.

Ideas for Elementary Students
- Special seating near you or slightly apart from classmates may help reduce effects of distractibility.
- Provision of short assignments, or longer assignments broken down into shorter segments, may increase task completion.
- Pairing assignments with a checklist on the child's desk on which he or she can check off competed tasks may help with assignment completion. After showing the child how to make the checklist, provide blank checklists for the child to fill out each day.
- Extra reinforcement will probably be needed if the ADHD child is to learn and continue to follow classroom rules. Developing rule-governed behavior requires frequent reinforcement and clear statements of what behavior is being reinforced. Response cost strategies have proved to be effective with many ADHD children. Such strategies involve giving points for appropriate behaviors and having the child pay a fine (in points) for inappropriate behaviors. Response cost systems work best when the rules are very specific.

- Organization is particularly difficult for many ADHD children. Try using a checklist of what to take home from school each night. Divided notebooks can be useful if the student understands how to use them. Assist with organization of desk or locker space.

Ideas for Secondary Students
- Since organization often continues to be a problem, assist this student with organizational strategies. For example, help the student to learn how to use a divided notebook for different subject areas and check periodically to ensure that this system is being used.
- Have the student purchase a small assignment book and use it daily.
- Help the student learn to make and use checklists. For example, when several assignments need to be completed, have the student list them and check them off as they are competed. Similarly, a checklist of what to take home or bring back to school can be used.
- Plan long-term projects with the student using a calendar with specific dates on which tasks are to be completed. Check back periodically to see how the student is progressing.

Working with Parents of Students with ADHD

Intervention for students with ADHD typically includes parent training. Some schools provide behavioral training for parents, as do professional/parent advocacy groups. Collaborative strategies for working with parents are discussed elsewhere in this book. They are useful in working with parents of students with ADHD.

McNamara and McNamara (2000) list resources for parents: organizations/support groups and books. These will now be presented.

Organizations/Support Groups. Perhaps one of the most useful strategies for parents of children with ADHD is to meet with other parents who share their concerns. The support of others who have gone through similar experiences is very helpful. Moreover, parents who have "been in the trenches" can be of great assistance to parents who are just discovering that their child has ADD. The following is a list of support groups:

Attention Deficit Disorder Association
P.O. Box 972
Mentor, OH 44601
(800) 487-2282
Web site: http://www.adda.org

This organization provides referrals and information services. Parents can get the names of professionals in their area who serve the needs of individuals diagnosed with ADHD. They can also receive information regarding various aspects of ADHD from this organization.

Children with Attention Deficit Disorders
(CHADD)
8181 Professional Place
Suite 201
Landover, MD 20785
(301) 306-7070
(800) 233-4050
Web site: http://www.chadd.org

This organization has been in the forefront of efforts to provide appropriate services to children with ADHD and their families. There are numerous local chapters throughout the country where parents can find a supportive group of professionals and parents who are knowledgeable about all aspects of ADHD. Frequently, CHADD invites speakers who focus on a particular aspect of ADHD, and it is not unusual to find teachers attending these meetings so that they can be better informed. We urge parents to join this organization.

In addition to these organizations, some parents may find it useful to contact the LDA if they suspect that their child has a learning disability. This association provides useful information and referral services.

Learning Disabilities Association of America
(LDA)
4156 Library Road
Pittsburgh, PA 15234

(412) 341-8077
Web site: http://www.ldanatl.org

Books. Parents can also benefit from reading about ADHD. A sampling of helpful books is as follows:

- Barkely, R. A. *Attention deficit hyperactivity disorder: A handbook for diagnosis and treatment* (2nd ed.). New York: Guilford Press, 1998.
- Conner, C. K. *Feeding the brain.* New York: Plenum Press, 1989.
- Fowler, M. *Maybe you know my kid: A parent's guide to identifying, understanding, and helping your child with ADHD.* Secaucus, NJ: Carol Publishing Group, 1991.
- Goldstein, S., & Goldstein, M. *Hyperactivity—why won't my child pay attention?* New York: Wiley, 1993.
- Ingersoll, B. *Your hyperactive child: A parent's guide to coping with attention deficit disorders.* New York: Doubleday, 1988.
- Maghadam, H. *Attention deficit disorder: Hyperactivity revisited: A concise source of information for parents and teachers.* Calgary, Alberta, Canada: Detselig Enterprises, 1988.
- McNamara, B. E., & McNamara, F. J. *Keys to parenting a child with a learning disability.* Hauppauge, NY: Barron's, 1995.
- Parker, H. *The ADD hyperactivity workbook for parents, teachers and kids.* Plantation, FL: Impact, 1988.
- Silver, L. D. *The misunderstood child: Understanding and coping with your child's learning disability.* New York: Times Books, 1998.
- Wilens, T. E. *Straight talk about psychiatric medications for kids.* New York: Guilford Press, 1999.
- Wodrich, D. L. *ADHD: What every parent wants to know.* Baltimore: Paul H. Brookes, 1994.

Instructional Strategies for Memory

Swanson (1998, pp. 146–150) provides the following practical conceptual principles, based on research, that can be useful guidelines:

A. *Memory Strategies Serve Different Purposes*
    One analysis of the memory strategy research suggests [that] there is no single best strategy for students with LD. . . . A number of studies, for ex-

ample, have looked at enhancing performance by using advanced organizers, skimming, asking questions, taking notes, summarizing, and so on. But apart from the fact that students with LD have been exposed to various types of strategies, the question of which strategies are the most effective is not known. We know [that] in some situations, such as when remembering facts, the key word approach appears to be more effective than direct instruction models (Scruggs & Mastropieri, 1989). But, of course, the rank ordering of different strategies changes in reference to the different types of learning outcomes expected. For example, certain strategies are better suited to enhancing students' understanding of what they previously read, whereas other strategies are better suited to enhancing students' memory of words or facts. The point is that different strategies can effect different cognitive outcomes in a number of ways.

B. *Good Memory Strategies for Non-LD Students Are Not Good Strategies for LD Students and Vice Versa*

Strategies that enhance access to knowledge for normally developing students will not be well suited for all children with LD. For example, Wong and Jones (1982) trained LD and non-LD adolescents in a self-questioning strategy to monitor reading comprehension. Results indicated that although the strategy training benefited the adolescents with LD, it actually lowered the performance of non-LD adolescents. To illustrate this point further with children with LD, Swanson (1989) presented students with LD, mental retardation, giftedness, and average development [with] a series of tasks that involved base and elaborative sentences. Their task was to recall words embedded in a sentence. The results of the first experiment suggested that children with LD differ from the other groups in their ability to benefit from elaboration. It was assumed that the elaboration requirement placed excessive demands on the central processing strategies of children with LD when compared with the other ability groups. This finding was qualified in the next experiment and suggested that encoding difficulty must be taken into consideration when determining strategy effects, but the results

suggested that children with LD may require additional strategies for their performance to become comparable to that of their cohorts. In another study (Swanson, Cooney, & Overholser, 1988) college students with LD were asked to recall words in a sentence under semantic and imagery instructional conditions. The results suggested, contrary to existing literature, that readers with LD were better able to remember words in a sentence during instructional conditions that induced semantic processing. In contrast, non-LD readers favored imagery processing over semantic processing conditions. In sum these results suggest that strategies that are effective for non-LD students may be less effective for students with LD.

C. *Effective Memory Strategies Do Not Necessarily Eliminate Processing Differences*

It appears logical that if children with LD use a strategy that allows them to process information efficiently, then improvement in performance is due to the strategies affecting the same processes as they do in non-LD students. The assumption has emanated primarily from studies that have imposed organization on seemingly unorganized material. For example, considerable evidence indicates that readers with LD do not process the organizational features of information in the same manner as non-LD students (Swanson, 1986). For example, Swanson and Rathgeber (1986) found in categorization tasks that readers with LD can retrieve information without interrelating superordinate, subordinate, and coordinate classes of information, as the non-LD children do. Thus, children with LD can learn to process information in an organizational sense without knowing the meaning of the material. The point is that simply because children with LD are sensitized to [the] internal structure of material via some strategy (e.g., by cognitive strategies that require the sorting of material), it does not mean they will make use of the material in a manner consistent with what was intended from the instructional strategy.

D. *The Strategies Taught Are Not Necessarily the Ones Used*

The previous principle suggests that during intervention different processes may be activated that are not necessarily the intent of the instructional intervention. It is also likely that students with LD use different strategies on tasks in which they seem to have little difficulty, and these tasks will likely be overlooked by the teacher for possible intervention. It is commonly assumed that although students with LD may have isolated memory deficits (verbal domain) and require general learning strategies to compensate for these processing deficits, their processing of information is comparable with that of their normal counterparts on tasks with which they have little trouble. Several authors suggest, however, that there are a number of alternative ways for achieving successful performance (Pressley, 1994), and some indirect evidence indicates that the LD may use qualitatively different mental operations (Shankweiler et al., 1979) and processing routes (e.g., Swanson, 1988) from their non-LD counterparts.

E. *Memory Strategies in Relation to a Student's Knowledge Base and Capacity*

One important variable that has been overlooked in the LD intervention literature is the notion of processing constraints (Swanson et al., 1996). Memory capacity seems to increase with development, with a number of factors potentially contributing to the overall effect. It appears that short-term memory capacity increases with age (Case, Kurland, & Goldberg, 1982). The number of component processes increases the speed with development, with faster processes generally consuming less effort than slow processes, and thus the same amount of capacity can seem greater (i.e., there is a functional increase of capacity with increasing efficiency of processing). The older children are likely to have more and more organized prior knowledge that can reduce the total number of chunks of information that is processed and decrease the amount of effort to retrieve information from long-term memory. Because of these developmental relationships, as well as the constraints that provide the development, this could play a role in strategy effectiveness. To test this possibility, Pressley, Cariglia-Bull, and Schneider (1987) studied children's ability to execute a capacity-demanding imagery representation strategy for the learning of sentences. Children in the experimental condition of these experiments represented a series of highly concrete sentences (for example, the angry bird shouted at the white dog, the turkey pecked the coat). They were asked to imagine the meanings of these sentences. Control condition participants were given no instruction. Further, children benefited from imagery instruction (there was an imagery versus control difference on the memory posttest). However, performance depended on the child's functional short-term memory capacity, as reflected by individual differences in performance on classic memory span tasks. That is, the imagery versus control difference in performance was only detected when functional short-term memory was relatively high.

F. *Comparable Memory Strategy May Not Eliminate Performance Differences*

Several studies have indicated that residual differences remain between ability groups, even when ability groups are instructed and/or prevented from strategy use (Gelzheiser et al., 1987). For example, in a study by Gelzheiser et al. (1987), LD and non-LD children were compared on their ability to use organizational strategies. After instruction in organizational strategies, the LD and non-LD children were compared on their abilities to recall information on a posttest. The results indicated that LD children were comparable in strategy use to non-LD children but were deficient in overall performance. In another study, Swanson (1983) found that the recall of a group with LD did not improve from baseline level when trained with rehearsal strategies. They recalled less than normal achieving peers, although the groups were comparable in the various types of strategy used. The results support the notion that groups of children with different learning histories may continue to learn differently when the groups are equated in terms of strategy use.

G. *Memory Strategies Taught Do Not Necessarily Become Transformed into Expert Strategies*

Children who become experts at certain tasks often have learned simple strategies and, through practice, discover ways to modify them into more efficient and powerful procedures (Schneider, 1993). In particular, the proficient learner uses higher-order rules to eliminate unnecessary or redundant steps to hold increasing amounts of information. The child who is LD, in contrast, may learn most of the skills related to performing an academic task and perform appropriately on that task by carefully and systematically following prescribed rules or strategies. Although children with LD can be taught strategies, some studies suggest that the difference between LD (experts in this case) and non-LD children is that the latter have modified such strategies to become more efficient (Swanson & Cooney, 1985). It is plausible that the child with LD remains a novice in learning new information because he or she fails to transform memory strategies into more efficient forms (see Swanson & Rhine, 1985).

H. *Strategy Instruction Must Operate on the Law of Parsimony*

A "number of multiple-component packages" of strategy instruction have been suggested to improve the functioning of children with LD. These components have usually encompassed some of the following: skimming, imagining, drawing, elaborating, paraphrasing, using mnemonics, accessing prior knowledge, reviewing, orienting to critical features, and so on. No doubt there are some positive aspects to these strategy packages.

1. These programs are an advance over some of the studies that are seen in the LD literature as rather simple of "quick-fix" strategies (e.g., rehearsal or categorization to improve performances.

2. These programs promote a common skill and have a certain metacognitive embellishment about them.

3. The best of these programs involved (a) teaching a few strategies well rather than superficially, (b) teaching students to monitor their performance, (c) teaching students when and where to use the strategy to enhance generalization, (d) teaching strategies as an integrated part of an existing curriculum, and (e) teaching that includes a great deal of supervised student practice and feedback.

The difficulty of such packages, however, at least in terms of theory, is that little is known about which components best predict student performance, nor do they readily permit one to determine why the strategy worked. The multiple-component approaches that are typically found in a number of LD strategy intervention studies must be carefully contrasted with a component analysis approach that involves the systematic combination of instruction components known to have additive effects on performance. As stated by Pressley (1986, p. 140), good strategies are "composed of the sufficient and necessary processes for accomplishing their intended goal, consuming as few intellectual processes as necessary to do so."

Instructional Strategies for Information Processing

Lenz, Bulgren, and Hudson (1990), as cited in Mercer and Pullen (2005, pp. 291–292), characterize instructional strategies for "information processing sensitive instruction":

1. [Are] fashioned and differentially delivered based on the teacher's knowledge of the range of information-processing and communication abilities of students (Deshler, Alley, Warner, & Schumaker, 1981).

2. [Promote] student attention or reception of incoming information (Lenz, Alley, & Schumaker, 1987; Mayer, 1987).

3. [Promote] the activation of strategies that enable the student to access and integrate prior knowledge with to-be-learned information (Ausubel, 1960; Lenz et al., 1987).

4. [Promote] the activation of strategies that enable the student to build logical or structural connections between and among incoming ideas and ideas already in memory (Bulgren, Schumaker, & Deshler, 1988; Mayer, 1987).

5. [Promote] the active participation of the student in the learning process as a planner, implementer, and evaluator (Brown, 1978; Hughes, Schumaker, Deshler, & Mercer, 1993; Van Reusen, Bos, Schumaker, & Deshler, 1987).

6. [Instruct] the student [about] the "why, when, and where" aspects of information related to the use of knowledge (Brown, Day, & Jones, 1983; Lenz & Hughes, 1990).

7. [Inform] the student of progress, and provide appropriate feedback in a manner that improves learning (Kline, Schumaker, & Deshler, 1991; Palincsar & Brown, 1984).

8. [Lead] the student in the learning process through expert scaffolding and proleptic teaching (Deshler & Schumaker, 1988; Vygotsky, 1978).

9. [Take] advantage of the developmental and social contexts of leaning by gradually moving from adult guidance and modeling to peer and student guidance and modeling (Allington, 1984; Lenz, Schumaker, Deshler, & Beals, 1984; Palincsar & Brown, 1984; Vygotsky, 1978).

10. [Plan] for and promotes the acquisition and integration of semantic, procedural, and strategic knowledge throughout all phases and types of instruction (Mayer, 1987).

SUMMARY

This chapter has focused on the underlying psychological processes and their relationship to the field of learning disabilities. Early on in the field, this was a topic of major importance. Due to a series of negative research findings, it later lost its appeal. However, recent research has produced renewed interest in and reexamination of these processes. The processes of perception, memory, attention, and cognition were discussed, as well as ADHD. Due to its overlapping and comorbidity with learning disorders, ADHD is a disorder that teachers of students with learning disorders must recognize. Instructional strategies for all processes and ADHD were provided.

SPRINGBOARDS FOR REFLECTION AND DISCUSSION

1. Talk to a veteran teacher. As a new teacher, how much emphasis did he or she place on underlying psychological processes of learning? How did he or she evaluate these processes? Was this teacher trained in isolation?

2. Review the early literature or process teaching. Why do you think it was so popular?

3. Observe a student with ADHD in the classroom. What are some of the observable behaviors? What interventions are being employed?

4. Attend a meeting of a parent group for children with ADHD such as CHADD. What is your impression?

5. Review the work of Swanson and his colleagues on memory. How can you apply their findings in the classroom?

6. Speak to an adult with ADHD. What advice does he or she have for teachers?

Chapter 5

PREREFERRAL INTERVENTION STRATEGIES

CHAPTER OBJECTIVES

At the completion of this chapter you will:

- understand how the prereferral process works.
- be able to develop a referral form.
- conduct effective team meetings.
- develop prereferral instructional strategies.

Mr. Barrett was concerned about Angela's performance in reading and writing. Unlike most of his third-grade students, she struggled with sight words and lacked the fluency of most of her classmates. Her decoding skills were adequate, but her slow reading rate and frequent errors interfered with comprehension. She was a reluctant reader. Mr. Barrett was also concerned about Angela's unwillingness to write. He knew that her writing would be impacted by her poor reading skills, but not to this extent. A year ago, Mr. Barrett would have made a formal referral to the multidisciplinary team for an evaluation for possible classification as learning disabled. However, as of September, his school had instituted a prereferral process. The prereferral team (known as the instructional support team [IST] in his district) met on a weekly basis. Mr. Barrett had to give the IST information regarding Angela and then meet to discuss instructional strategies he could use prior to a formal referral for an evaluation. What would you do if you suspected one of your students of having a learning disability? Would you view the prereferral team as a stalling tactic to keep the special education rate down? Would you be intimidated by having to let your colleagues know that you were uncertain about how to teach this student? These are questions many teachers have when dealing with the issue of prereferral intervention. Many teachers and parents think they know when a child needs special education, and they truly believe that the child will be best served when so classified. This chapter will discuss options prior to formal referral and issues/concerns that need to be addressed if this is to become a viable option for classroom teachers with student who are displaying unexpected underachievement.

THE PREREFERRAL PROCESS

The prereferral process is illustrated in Figure 5-1. Initially, a classroom teacher identifies a student who displays unexpected underachievement—that is, less achievement than others in his or her class who are receiving the same instruction. In the past, this student may have been referred directly to the multidisciplinary team for a thorough evaluation. That approach has been criticized as one reason for the large increase in the number of students identified as having learning disabilities—in particular, culturally and linguistically diverse students in urban areas (McNamara, 1999). In the prereferral process, the teacher would make a referral to the prereferral team, which typically included the principal, the psychologist, a special education teacher, regular education teacher(s), and the teacher presenting the student. It might also include a social worker, an occupational therapist, a physical therapist, and/or a speech-language pathologist if needed. The team would schedule a meeting to discuss instructional strategies to be implemented in the regular education classroom. All results, successful and unsuccessful, would be documented. Additional strategies would be employed and additional team meetings scheduled. If the team reached a point where they had exhausted all

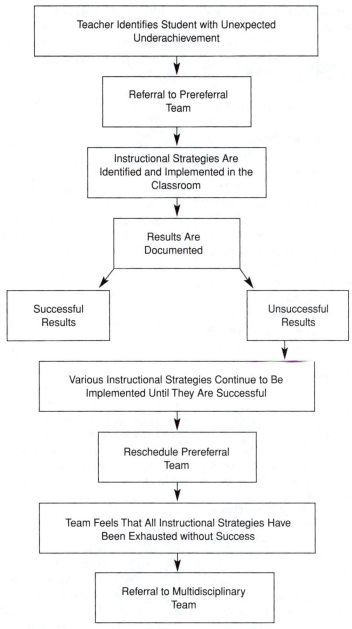

Teacher Identifies Student with Unexpected
Underachievement

↓

Referral to Prereferral
Team

↓

Instructional Strategies Are
Identified and Implemented in the
Classroom

↓

Results Are
Documented

↙   ↘

Successful
Results

Unsuccessful
Results

↓

Various Instructional Strategies Continue to Be
Implemented Until They Are Successful

↓

Reschedule Prereferral
Team

↓

Team Feels That All Instructional Strategies Have
Been Exhausted without Success

↓

Referral to Multidisciplinary
Team

FIGURE 5–1   The Prereferral Process

instructional strategies without success, they would make a referral to the multidisciplinary team.

PREREFERRAL TEAMS

Prereferral teams are discussed in Chapter 6. Their purpose is simple: to attempt to do everything possible prior to a formal referral. These teams can reduce the number of referrals for special education services, particularly for students from culturally and linguistically diverse backgrounds (Knotek, 2003).

After the inception of P.L. 94-142, the Education of All Handicapped Children's Act (EAHC) of 1975, schools were required to exhaust all instructional options prior to a referral to special education, but no prereferral teams were required. Clearly, this was not the case in most public schools, especially when the students were culturally and linguistically diverse. Even in IDEA 1997 the establishment of prereferral teams to ensure that everything possible was done prior to a referral to special education was not mandated. Buck, Polloway, Smith-Thomas, and Cook (2003) note that the prereferral process has been conceptually stable over time and that 86% of the states either require or recommend a prereferral process. They cite the following defining features (p. 350):

1. A process that is preventive (i.e., interventions are developed and implemented before a formal, special education evaluation).
2. A problem-solving approach that is team based (i.e., team members review data on a referred student, hypothesize causes to explain the student's difficulties, and develop strategies to remediate those difficulties).
3. An approach that is action-research oriented (i.e., a team develops specific interventions that the referring teacher(s) is expected to implement in his/her classroom [either with or without outside assistance] and then evaluate in terms of its effectiveness).
4. An intervention process that is centered upon the enhanced success of students and teachers within the general education setting and in the general education curriculum.

Buck et al. (2003) studied the implementation of prereferral practices across states and found that practices varied widely. However, if carried out effectively, prereferral practices have many potential benefits.

First, students receive assistance in their own classes prior to any consideration of specialized program placement. Second, school faculty potentially develop a professional, collaborative relationship which will enhance effective programs beyond concerns for pre-referral interventions. Third, when pre-referral intervention procedures are most effective, the number of inappropriate referrals to special education is reduced and consequently potential cost savings due to fewer inappropriate placements may occur. Finally, an effective program can enhance educational programs for all students and can create a more inclusive school environment. Thus the primary beneficiaries will be the children who have access to the modifications and accommodations that may derive from the pre-referral or child study process. (p. 358)

The utilization of prereferral intervention strategies has increased, suggesting that recognition of the referral, identification, and classification of students with special education needs are cumbersome and inaccurate. This is equally true for students who are mislabeled as having a learning disability (Pugach & Johnson, 1989). Prereferral intervention strategies are usually classified as (a) informal, school-based, problem-solving teams and (b) consultation between the special educator and the regular educator.

One early prereferral model was developed by Graden, Casey, and Christenson (1985), with six stages of intervention. The first four stages represent the actual prereferral, and the last two represent the traditional referral process to determine whether or not special education services are necessary. The model is as follows:

Stage 1:   *Request for Consultation*
The regular classroom teacher must request assistance with problem solving or intervention for a particular student. While it can be initiated on the building level or more formally through a district

committee, the former is favored. An ongoing relationship exists among all professionals (regular and special) rather than a more informal, building-level approach.

Stage 2: *Consultation*

During the actual consultation process, the classroom teacher and the consultant specify the reason for referral in objective, measurable terms. After this occurs, an action plan is formulated and evaluation measures are put in place. Interventions are implemented and evaluated.

Stage 3: *Observation*

Observation in the classroom is next. The observer (who may be a special educator, a psychologist, or a social worker) describes the curriculum, the tasks, and the demands placed on the student. He or she also observes the behavior of the teacher, the physical arrangement of the classroom, and the interactions of the student. The causes and consequences of the student's behavior are also noted. Based upon this observation, the appropriate parties meet and discuss the success of the interventions.

Stage 4: *Conference*

During the conference, a decision is made to continue or modify the intervention plan or refer the child for an evaluation to determine special education eligibility.

Stages 5 and 6: *Formal Referral and Formal Program Meeting*

For those students who are thought to need special education services, a referral and a formal program meeting are scheduled to discuss the findings. This occurs after significant interventions have been implemented in the regular classroom setting.

Ponte, Zins, and Graden (1988) note that if a prereferral process is to be implemented, a number of organizational factors need to be considered. These authors apply the principles developed by Maher and Bennett (1984) and Maher and Illback (1985). This framework is referred to as DURABLE (discussing, understanding, reinforcing, acquiring, building, learning, and evaluation).

This approach allows a school to make decisions regarding the effectiveness of a program and whether to modify or eliminate it. The authors note that the intervention chosen is linked to the needs of the school rather than imposed. This is critical. Each school must examine its needs using systematic needs assessment. Once the specific needs are evident, the appropriate prereferral interventions can be implemented.

INSTRUCTIONAL SUPPORT TEAM (IST)

The IST can also be effective in refining the referral process (Lochner, 2000). These teams are designed to:

- provide consultation to teachers to meet students' classroom needs
- provide a forum for effective home–school communication and problem solving
- provide a structured process to design student intervention and support plans

This requires a great deal of training for teachers and administrators. The focus is on what services can be provided in the regular classroom so that if a referral is eventually made, the teacher can be somewhat confidant that he or she has used all instructional interventions. A typical IST meeting has the following components:

1. Introducing the problem and the process
2. Statement from the referring teacher and parent
3. Group discussion with the referring teacher and parent
4. Brainstorming
5. Selecting strategies
6. Establishing an Instructional Support Plan (ISP)
7. Closing the meeting

Inherent in all prereferral models is collaboration. All interested parties (special educators, regular educators, administrators, support personnel, and parents) must come together in the interest of the student.

INSTRUCTIONAL STRATEGIES

Prereferral teams attempt to generate possible solutions for problems that can be implemented without a formal referral to the multidisciplinary team. Theoretically, schools are supposed to do all they can prior to an official referral. However, it is hard to define "all." There is a time in the prereferral process when the team of professionals decides that the student requires a full evaluation and a formal referral. During the prereferral process, the list of instructional strategies can be endless. There are books that list literally thousands of prereferral interventions. The difficulty is in linking the intervention with the specific needs of the student, as well as the ability of the teacher to implement the intervention and his or her comfort level with the intervention. For example, in the IST model, the classroom teacher is the final arbiter of what strategies will be implemented in the classroom. Therefore, if several behavioral techniques are suggested by the team, the teacher decides which ones he or she will try and then report back to the team. It should be noted that these interventions will also benefit other students in the class.

Figures 5-2 to 5-4 are examples of student referrals by a classroom teacher to a prereferral team and the instructional strategies generated during the brainstorming phase.

In all three of these cases, the presenting teacher decides what strategies to implement immediately, as well as those he or she might use later and those he or she does not feel comfortable using at this time. At the next IST meeting, the teacher will be responsible for providing evidence of whether or not the intervention is working. This typically consists of student work or data on behavioral concerns.

Note that most of the interventions are not so extraordinary that they cannot be carried out in the classroom, nor are they considered clinical methods unrelated to the classroom. Also, there is considerable overlap in the interventions suggested. This happens often. One of the major

benefits of the prereferral process is that it provides a collaborative forum for teachers to describe what works for them, and it provides support for the presenting teacher. It is a dynamic process, not a panacea. If it is effective, teachers will realize that there are ways to get help for their students other than classifying them as having a learning disability.

The final section of this chapter deals with best practices for prereferral teams.

BEST PRACTICES: THE IST MEETING

At 8:00 a.m. every Wednesday, the IST at Barnes Avenue School meets. The team consists of the principal, the psychologist, the literacy teacher, the school social worker, three regular classroom teachers, and one special education teacher. They often invite others to attend if needed, such as the occupational therapist or speech therapist. The meetings start promptly at 8:00. Five minutes are allocated for the presenting teacher to discuss his or her student. This may seem like a short period of time, but the team felt that nothing was being accomplished because they often spent too much time discussing the problem, leaving no time for the solution. All members of the team had access to all the referral information in the office. They tried to make copies, for example, of a Referral Form and distribute them to members, but a central location seemed more efficient (see Figure 5-5).

Once the 5 minutes were up, the timekeeper (this role rotated) indicated that it was time for brainstorming. The team used a freewheeling approach so that all parties could speak. No suggestion was thrown out or ridiculed. The scribe wrote all the ideas on a large sheet of Post-it paper so that everyone could see them. After 15 minutes, the team refined the list, made sure that the classroom teacher was comfortable with the instructional intervention discussed, and established a date for follow-up. In the beginning the process was very time-consuming, but now it seemed to run

Hudson Street Elementary School
Instructional Support Team

Name of Student: Maryanne Siles

Grade: 4   Sex: F   Teacher: Mr. Fiske

Date of Referral: 10/1/03

1. Describe the strengths of this student.

   Maryanne is a very enthusiastic student. She appears to take a genuine interest in the classroom. She is very eager to please her teachers.

2. Describe your primary concern and give examples of specific behaviors.

   She appears to be below grade level in the areas of reading and writing. She has very poor comprehension skills and has difficult formulating ideas to put into writing.

3. What classroom interventions have been attempted, how long have you used them, and how effective have these interventions been? If you discontinued using them, when and why?

   Has been recommended to attend extra help 2 days per week. Receives small-group guided reading instruction during reading time in class.

4. What services is the child receiving, if any?

   Remedial reading three times per week.

5. What do you hope to gain from this instructional support team meeting?

   Specific reading and writing strategies.

   During the brainstorming phase, the team generated the following list of interventions:
   - Reading partners
   - Read to younger students
   - Journal writing
   - Pen pal
   - Coordinate extra help personnel
   - Reward attempt at reading/writing
   - Use graphic organizers
   - Use a comprehension strategy such as SQ3R
   - High-interest/low-vocabulary books
   - Interest inventory
   - Utilize her good oral language skills
   - Language experience approach
   - Write and follow recipes
   - Provide a wide range of experiences
   - Contact parents to inquire about her interests

FIGURE 5–2

Hudson Street Elementary School
Instructional Support Team

Name of Student: Louis Mannes

Grade: 3   Sex: M   Teacher: Ms. Acosta

Date of Referral: 12-20-03

1. Describe the strengths of this student.

   Louis is a well-behaved student who puts forth good effort. He is quite verbal and enjoys partici-pating in class discussions. He gets along well with his peers.

2. Describe your primary concern and be specific about whether it is academic, social, behavioral, linguistic, motor, etc.

   Academic concerns—Louis has poor phonological awareness. His reading comprehension is also poor. His speech is characterized by misarticulations. He also needs to have directions repeated and/or restated.

3. What classroom interventions have been attempted, and what were the results?

   He attends extra help once a week and receives supportive reading and writing three times per week.

4. What services is the child receiving, if any?

   Remedial reading and writing support.

5. What do you hope to gain from this instructional support team meeting?

   Reading strategies

   Writing strategies

6. Does he need a speech-language screening?

   The following strategies were suggested:

   - Speech-language screening
   - Specific phonic instruction
   - High-interest/low-vocabulary book
   - Focus on oral language skills
   - Language experience approach
   - Reinforce effort
   - Interest inventory
   - Pen pal
   - Journal writing
   - Reduce complexity of language
   - Start with single-step demand/directions
   - Utilize task analysis
   - Coordinate extra help with reading and writing
   - Using a reading/writing buddy
   - Dictate his stories to parents and/or other students
   - Small-group instruction

FIGURE 5–3

Hudson Street Elementary School
Instructional Support Team

Name of Student: Abraham Siles

Grade: 4   Sex: M   Teacher: Ms. Faust

Date of Referral: 10-28-03

1. Describe the strengths of this student.

   Abraham is a respectful, well-liked boy. He is enthusiastic in the areas of science, social studies, and nonfiction reading. Math is an area of strength. He knows that focus and reading are difficult and has expressed a desire to do better.

2. Describe your primary concern and give examples of specific behaviors.

   Distractible—has great difficulty focusing during whole-class lessons and when directions are given. Often has difficulty completing assignments without repetition of directions or one-on-one help.

   Writing—difficulty using the planning page, beginning a new piece, and retaining ideas discussed during the one-on-one conference.

   Reading—lack of sight words, decoding difficulty.

3. What classroom interventions have been attempted, how long have you used them, and how effective have these interventions been? If you discontinued using them, when and why?

   Distractibility—close proximity to teacher, subtle redirection indicating when directions will be given, visual cues (chart).

   Writing—teacher modeling of web and writing piece, frequent writing conferences.

4. What services is the child receiving, if any?

   Remedial reading three times per week.

5. What do you hope to gain from this instructional support team meeting?

   New strategies to help him focus and remain on task.

   Suggestions for reluctant writers

   Instructional strategies generated for Abraham:

   - Use a divider to avoid distraction.
   - Place a schedule card on his desk.
   - reinforce all attending behaviors.
   - Use a contingency contract for paying attention.
   - Develop a list of rewards.
   - Contact parents to determine his interests/reinforcement.
   - Use math strengths to assist with reading.
   - Use lower-level texts.
   - Use a word wall and a personal dictionary.
   - Provide specific phonics instruction.
   - Employ a multisensory approach for sight words.
   - Place him near students who pay attention.
   - Provide a graphic organizer.
   - Provide a pen pal.
   - Write directions for younger students.
   - Pose specific questions prior to reading.
   - Perform frequent comprehension checks.
   - Develop an interest inventory.

FIGURE 5–4

Instructional Support Team Referral Form

Name of Student _____ Nick _____ Date _____ 12/20/97 _____

Date of Birth _____ 3/20/89 _____

Parent/Guardian Grade _____ Grade __8__

Phone (H) _____ (W) _____

Referred by _____ Classroom Teacher _____

Briefly describe this student's strengths (interpersonal, math, language, visual, kinesthetic, musical, others).

Nick is very bright, and had a great deal of background knowledge related to history and science. He has excellent vocabulary and a well-developed, dry sense of humor. Strong math skills, conscientious, cooperative most of the time; has a few class friends. Does much better with reading and writing on a one-to-one basis.

Briefly describe the academic, behavioral, or emotional difficulty this student is presently experiencing. Describe the conditions in which the problem exists.

Very poor speller despite daily practice, multisensory instruction, and reduced number of words. Struggles with the writing process and reading fluency. Stronger Silent-Reading Comprehension score near grade level when he reads high-interest material. Regularly disrupts class by trying to be funny with peers. Gives up and throws paper during spelling and writing classes.

The following is a list of possible interventions you may have used in the classroom:

Material modification	Rewards/consequences	Behavior contract
Peer instruction	Cooperative learning	Self-esteem activities
Different environment	Test modifications	Rewards/incentives
Individual instruction	Use of assistant/volunteer	Other (list below)

Expand: What works? What doesn't work?
Other: *Weekly teleconferences with mother. Daily follow-up at home for spelling.*

*Verbal contact with Vice Principal to go for math if he does well in spelling and doesn't ____ peers (tried for 2 weeks and he hasn't earned a walk yet!)

**Nick refuses to use the reduced word list. Does not like to write, but will give information and answer questions orally. Nick passed on spelling tests all year. Copy attached.

Have any of the following interventions been used to address this student's difficulty? If so, please check.

Parent Contact (circle):
Phone _____ Letter Conference Date(s) of Contact <u>9/20, 10/3, 10/14</u>

_____ Names of Others Involved

_____ Professional Consultation

_____ Observations

_____ Counseling

_____ Instructional Support

_____ Remediation

<u>Speech Therapist—student has difficulty with classroom noise; needs things repeated often</u>

FIGURE 5–5   Referral Form

Summary of Contacts:

Eight (8) discipline reports for throwing papers and pencils and disturbing class last month

ADDITIONAL INFORMATION
Previous Testing: Psych, speech, medical, education, OT/PT, outside evaluations, others(s)

Name	Date	Results
Hearing/Vision	_9/20/97_	_well (within normal limits)_
K-Screening	_6/94_	_failed_
Speech/Words	_10/95_	_distortions of "R" closed_

Work Samples   (please attach or bring with you to the first meeting).
What is the status of the home situation?
Supportive family

Describe the student's previous school experiences.

Has struggled with reading and spelling since Grade 1. Parents and he read daily at home.

How will you inform the parents(s) of the time, location, and structure of the IST meeting?
Phone call

What other individuals should be invited to the staffing (past or present)?
Speech therapist, classroom and special area teachers. Vice Principal

First Meeting Date _____   IST Meeting Location_____

FIGURE 5–5   _(Continued)_

efficiently. In $1^{1}/_{2}$ hours the team usually discussed three students. They felt that their colleagues were beginning to realize that this collaborative process was yielding results. The number of referrals to special education was reduced, and those that were made appeared to be more appropriate.

Prereferral Instructional Modifications

It may be useful to provide all teachers with specific instructional modifications that can be used throughout the prereferral process (Wagenberg, 2003). Simple suggestions that can be easily implemented are helpful to regular education teachers and make the prereferral process more efficient. See Table 5-1 for specific strategies.

IMPLEMENTATION

Levittown: How One District Utilized a Prereferral Team

A team approach was employed in a suburban school district that experienced many of the same problems as large urban school districts (Lochner & McNamara, 1989). A special education program began to represent a disproportionately large percentage of the school population. Consequently, this program was perceived as a panacea for any student who was not meeting expectations. Faculty and students alike were isolated from their regular education counterparts. These factors caused an unusually

TABLE 5–1   Teaching Modifications

If Student Has Difficulty	Try This
Becoming interested	• Tell stories related to people's lives • Provide concrete experiences • Read story or article aloud to stimulate interest • Seat student close to teacher
Getting started—give cue to begin work	• Give work in smaller amounts • Provide immediate feedback • Sequence work • Provide time suggestions • Check on progress • Peer or peer tutor
Paying attention to spoken word	• Give explanations in small, distinct steps • Provide written backup to oral directions • Have student repeat directions • Use buddies, tape directions • Shorten the listening time • Alternate spoken with written manipulative tasks • Look directly at student; place hand on student's shoulder
Following directions	• Use fewer words • Provide examples • Repeat • Have student repeat • Provide checklist • Use auditory and visual directions
Keeping track of materials or assignments	• Use notebook • Use large envelope for each subject • Keep extra assignment sheets for resource teacher and parents • Have student carry a mailbag • Write assignment on board • Give rewards for bringing supplies
Paying attention to printed word	• Select a text • Highlight • Underline, number • Keep desk clear of extras • Place desk facing wall or use carrel • Overhead transparency
Reading textbooks	• Use lower-level or adaptive text if available • Tape text • Shorten amount of reading required • Have students read aloud in small groups • Allow extra time for reading • Omit reading requirements • Put mail ideas on index cards • Use oral tests • Use a buddy or allow group work • Preteach vocabulary word • Give take-home tests • Use larger type

If Student Has Difficulty	Try This
Completing tasks on time	• Reduce amount to be accomplished • Allow more time • Write schedules • Provide checklists • Provide closure at points along the way
Expressing himself/herself verbally	• Accept alternate form of information: written report, artwork, exhibit, chart/graph, bulletin board, photos • Ask questions requiring short answers • Provide prompts • Give rules for class discussion • Teach students to ask questions in class • Question at the teaching level • Break student in gradually by speaking in smaller groups • Allow taped reports
Staying on task	• Reduce distraction • Increase reinforcements • Provide checklist • Reduce amount of work • Give time-out • Provide quiet alternatives for a short time
Learning by listening	• Provide visuals • Use flash cards • Have student close his or her eyes and visualize the information • Spell by visualizing the whole word • Teach use of acronyms • Give explanations in small, distinct steps • Remove extra words • Provide study guide
Working in groups	• Provide a partner • Provide a student with responsibility or a position of leadership • Provide more structure by defining tasks and listing steps
Working independently	• Assign tasks at the appropriate level • Be certain that the student can see an end to the task • Give precise directions • Reinforce often • Provide various types of work within the assignment
Understanding what is read	• Reduce the language level • Be more concrete • Reduce number of new ideas • Provide experiences for a frame of reference • Provide study guide • Give organizational help • Provide alternate media • Remove extra words ("Jane, please sit," not "Jane, would you please sit in your chair?") • Use the fill-in-the-blank technique

(continued)

TABLE 5–I Teaching Modifications (*continued*)

If Student Has Difficulty	Try This
Writing legibly	• Use formats low on writing: multiple-choice, fill-in, programmed • Use manipulatives • Have student type • Allow use of tape recorder • Use graph paper • Save papers for 2 weeks and then have students read what they wrote • Teach writing diligently
Spelling	• Dictate word; ask student to repeat it • Avoid traditional spelling lists • Teach short, easy words in context: *on* and *on,* right *on! on* account of • Have students make flash cards • Teach words by spelling patterns • Avoid penalizing for spelling errors • Hang words from ceiling during study time or post on board or walls for constant visual cues • Provide a tactile aid to spelling (letter of sandpaper, saltbox, etc.)
Understanding cause/effect: anticipating consequences	• Use concrete examples • Use real-life situations • Teach cause/effect directly: brainstorming, role playing, simulation • Have students use their imaginations
Seeing relationships	• Directly point out relationships • Draw arrows on worksheets or test to show that ideas are related • Teach directly relations of function, category, opposition, sequence • Provide direct practice • Provide headings or a partially filled-in chart for an example • Use a banner with symbols for ideas/events
Expressing himself/herself in writing	• Accept alternate forms of reporting: oral report, tape-recorded interview, taped interview, maps, photographic essay, panel discussion • Have student dictate work to someone else • Have student prepare only notes or outline on subject • Shorten amount required • Provide practice with story starters, open-ended stories
Drawing conclusions and making inferences	• Teach thinking skills directly • Draw a parallel to a situation that the student might have experienced in problem solving
Remembering	• Provide a checklist • Provide cues • Have student make notes to self • Teach memory skills • Teach use of acronyms and other mnemonic devices

high referral rate to the Committee on Special Education (the team employed for the multidisciplinary team in New York State). For example, during the 1986–1987 school year, over 15 cases per week, or over 600 for the year, were referred to the Committee on Special Education for possible special education placement.

An independent audit confirmed that the rate of referral and the level of service were higher than expected. Furthermore, because most of these students were not eligible for special education services, the regular education teachers were somewhat frustrated by the perceived lack of action on their referral. The students were still in their classes, and they still did not know what to do with them. This situation is not peculiar to this district. Reports in the professional literature note that special education is both costly and ineffective (Algozzine, Christenson, & Ysseldyke, 1982; Graden, Casey, & Christenson, 1985). To change this two-tier system of education, one for regular staff and one for special staff, a development program was created and implemented.

Glatthorn (1990, p. 62) identified six conditions that were necessary in supporting professional development:

1. There is strong district-level leadership; a district administrator or supervisor coordinates and monitors the entire program.
2. There is strong leadership at the school level; the principal exercises leadership in fostering norms of collegiality, modeling collaboration, and rewarding teacher cooperation.
3. There is a general climate of openness and trust between administrators and teachers.
4. The cooperative programs have a distinct focus and make use of a shared language.
5. The district provides the resources needed to initiate and sustain the cooperative program.
6. The school makes organizational changes needed to support collaboration; the school schedule enables the teachers to work together; staff assignment procedures facilitate cooperation.

This program met these conditions. Initially, the board of education and the superintendent of schools make a commitment to provide resources to examine the problem. The principal's support is another condition necessary for success, and this was secured. A superintendent's day conference was scheduled to address "The Needs of the Atypical Child." Teachers and administrators were included on the planning committee.

MAJOR COMPONENTS OF THE STAFF DEVELOPMENT PROGRAM

Consultant Services

A special education consultant, with expertise in learning disabilities, was selected to work with the assistant superintendent for administration and pupil personnel services. The consultant provided services to staff members in a nonevaluative manner. As noted above, it is critical that this be independent of the teacher evaluation process. The major purpose of the program was to provide technical support and training to all teachers regarding the needs of atypical learners. In addition, there was a desire to increase the interaction between regular and special educators. This was accomplished through the use of building-level teams.

Building-Level Teams

The use of building-level teams is not a new concept in education. Chalfant and Pysh (1989) note that many school districts utilize school-based support teams. Will (1986) suggests that such teams enhance the ability of regular educators to help students with learning problems. This concept is not new to the staff in the Levittown district. A *cadre* model has been employed in staff development in the areas of writing, reading, and thinking. This was an important consideration because of the diversity of elementary schools in Levittown. Building-level teams give the building staff a sense of ownership of the program and reflect specific needs, not global concerns.

Building-Level Team Members

Each building team included at least the following:

One regular education teacher
One special education teacher
One speech-language pathologist
One school psychologist

Membership on the team was voluntary, and although these were highly motivated staff members, an incentive program was also implemented. Each team member received two in-service credits for the first year of the project and one credit per year for each subsequent year. These credits could be applied to their salary increments. Team members also were allowed to attend workshops (substitute coverage for their classes was provided) and received consultant support. The major responsibilities of the cadre were:

1. To provide technical support and training to all teachers who were working with atypical children.
2. To make several presentations to their faculty.
3. To follow up with staff and administrators regarding problems, solutions, or additional needs.

In order to carry out these responsibilities, a needs assessment had to be developed.

BUILDING-LEVEL NEEDS ASSESSMENT

Each building-level team identified the needs of its colleagues. A consensus of 75% was reached, and the list of needs was prioritized. It was important for each team to be responsible for its own needs assessment. Thus, the assessment was not imposed on them by the central administration, and they were able to identify the concerns of their colleagues based on their day-to-day interaction.

PROGRAM IMPLEMENTATION

Initial Training

Each team was responsible for developing and implementing a presentation to their colleagues based upon the results of the needs assessment. Prior to the presentation, the entire group ($n = 40$) met with the consultant and the assistant superintendent for administration and pupil personnel services for a training session. They were given a wide variety of formats and had an opportunity to plan and receive feedback from the other building teams. For many team members, this was the first time they had ever made a presentation to their colleagues. Considerable effort went into allaying their anxiety, providing ample preparation time, and reinforcing their efforts.

The formats employed were as varied as the topics (see Figure 5-6). The entire faculty evaluated each session. The feedback was utilized in the development of the ongoing program throughout the school year.

Ongoing Training

Throughout the school year, building-level teams met to provide training for their colleagues. Two group meetings addressed the needs of the teams in their buildings.

A booklet was developed by the entire group, the consultant, and the assistant superintendent to provide a tangible product for all district staff members. The contents were as follows:

1. Special Education Categories
2. Effective Teaching Methods (Academic)
3. Effective Teaching Methods (Behavioral)

As each team develops yearly goals, the members continue to receive support and training via consultative services and group training sessions. And while the needs of each building continue to vary, they can all be subsumed under the major

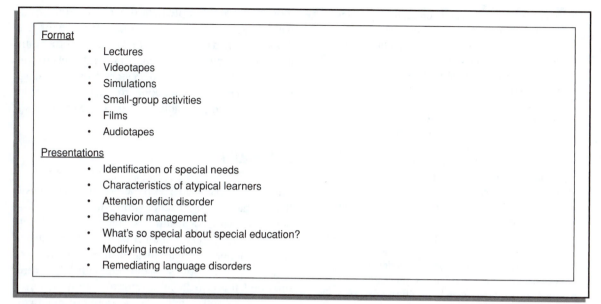

Format

- Lectures
- Videotapes
- Simulations
- Small-group activities
- Films
- Audiotapes

Presentations

- Identification of special needs
- Characteristics of atypical learners
- Attention deficit disorder
- Behavior management
- What's so special about special education?
- Modifying instructions
- Remediating language disorders

FIGURE 5–6   A Sample of Formats and Topics Employed in In-Service Programs

goal of the project: to provide all teachers with the skills necessary to teach atypical learners.

Impact

Anecdotal reports suggest that the staff development program described above was successful. Administrators and teachers appear to be very positive about the functioning of the teams. Regular and special educators, given opportunities for interaction, realized that they could solve many of their problems through collaboration. The quantifiable results of this partnership have also been impressive:

- The rate of referral to the Committee on Special Education dropped from 15 per week (over 600 per year) to 6 per week (240 per year).
- Enrollment in the special education program dropped from 1,125 to 901.
- Only one member asked to be removed from a team.
- An increasing number of staff members asked to join the building-level team.

EVALUATING THE PREREFERRAL

The prereferral process is time-consuming. Schools need to make sure that the process is productive and efficient. Clearly, teachers will not utilize the services of the team if they feel they are wasting their time, if they feel intimidated, or if they feel that the suggestions are not effective. Therefore, it is critical for the school faculty and staff to evaluate the effectiveness of the team. Salend (2005, p. 53) provides an excellent list of questions that can be employed to evaluate the school's prereferral system (p. 53):

- Are administrators, educators, and family members committed to implementing and promoting a pre-referral system?
- Are there criteria for the selection of educators to serve on the pre-referral support team?
- Does the pre-referral support team include educators who have a range of backgrounds, experiences, expertise, and training and who perform a variety of functions?

- Are family members and community agencies involved in the pre-referral process?
- Does the pre-referral support team have the resources and time to perform its activities?
- Is there a system to help teachers access the services of the pre-referral team?
- Do the forms and procedures employed in the pre-referral system facilitate the process?
- Do pre-referral support teams have adequate and reasonable procedures for determining the goals and types of pre-referral systems based on students' strengths; needs; educational, social, and medical history; language and cultural background, as well as the teacher's concerns and the learning environment?
- Does the pre-referral support team consider and suggest a range of reasonable instructional and family involvement strategies, curricular and classroom design adaptations, alternative assessment procedures, testing modifications, culturally relevant instructional and classroom management techniques, adaptive devices, teacher training and collaboration activities, and school-based and community-based supportive services to address the referral problems?
- Are pre-referral interventions suggested by the pre-referral support team implemented as intended and for a sufficient period of time?
- Does the pre-referral support team collect data to examine the effectiveness of the pre-referral interventions and the pre-referral process and to make revisions based on these data?
- How would you rate your school's pre-referral system? ( )Excellent ( )Good ( )Needs Improvement ( )Needs Much Improvement
- What are some goals and steps you could adapt to your school's pre-referral system?

Let's go back to Mr. Barrett. He attended the IST meeting and presented his concerns about Angela. All the team members had received copies of the referral prior to the meeting, so the majority of the meeting was spent brainstorming solutions. Over 20 solutions were listed, and Mr. Barrett selected 5 to implement immediately and 4 more if these were not effective; he would wait on the remainder. He was given a follow-up period (1 month), and a case manager was assigned to follow up with him. During the month, he would implement the interventions, evaluate Angela's progress, and collect samples of her work to bring back to the team. There may be a point in the future when a decision to refer Angela to the multidisciplinary team is necessary. However, there must be evidence that a concerted effort was made to do everything possible prior to the referral.

SUMMARY

This chapter has focused on the prereferral process. Rather than having teachers immediately judge students as having a learning disability, with the development and implementation of an IEP, prereferral allows teachers to engage in a collaborative process. Examples of practices associated with ISTs were provided. It is equally important to determine what constitutes good team practices; therefore, practices were provided for meetings, strategies, implementation, and evaluation. This is an exciting opportunity for teachers to learn from each other and to add to their repertoire of classroom interventions.

SPRINGBOARDS FOR REFLECTION AND DISCUSSION

1. Interview a regular education teacher regarding his or her perceptions of the prereferral process.
2. Interview a special education teacher regarding his or her perceptions of the prereferral process.
3. Speak to a parent in your local school district. Is he or she aware of the prereferral process? If so, does he or she consider it effective?
4. Attend a prereferral team meeting. What was your impression?
5. Are you in favor of providing team members with lists of instructional interventions or should they develop them as a team?
6. Do you think the prereferral process is a stalling tactic to reduce the number of referrals for special education services? Why or why not?

6 CHAPTER IDENTIFICATION OF STUDENTS WITH LEARNING DISABILITIES

CHAPTER OBJECTIVES

At the end of this chapter you will be able to:

- appreciate the complexity of identifying students with learning disabilities.
- know what to do if you suspect a student of having a learning disability.
- know the difference between traditional and nontraditional assessment.
- employ informal, nontraditional measures in your classroom.
- know the legal requirements for the identification of students with learning disabilities.

Wilson was referred by his parents and teacher because they were concerned about his school performance. When he was observed in his second-grade classroom, he sat in the back row. He tried to pay attention, but it was difficult; the classroom was small, yet filled with 35 students and one new teacher. This was particularly true when it came to reading instruction, especially when the teacher presented a phonics lesson.

Wilson's parents had come from Puerto Rico 4 years earlier and spoke very little English. His 10-year-old sister struggles in school but is passing. She attends an after-school reading program and is making good progress. Wilson is not. On a recent standardized achievement test, he scored very low. As he sits in the rear of the classroom, his teacher continues to provide instruction, but it is lost on Wilson. Some school personnel suspect that Wilson has a learning disability, although he is not a native speaker of English and his language community speaks and reads Spanish. The reading teacher feels that he has many of the characteristics of students with learning disabilities that cannot be explained by the fact that he is not a native speaker. However, most school personnel are convinced that he is a typical child raised in a non-English-speaking environment and that if he is given bilingual or ESL (English as a Second Language) instruction, he will be fine. Meanwhile, he is passing the time. His teacher struggles to find ways to make this a productive year for Wilson, But nothing seems to work.

It is difficult to identify a student with a learning disability. It's even more difficult with a child like Wilson.

Frequently, teachers refer students whom they suspect of having a learning disability when they are not native speakers of English. This was the case with Wilson. Some school personnel thought he might have a learning disability because he had many of the characteristics of students with such disabilities. You need to be very cautious because the characteristics of persons with disabilities and English language learners overlap.

Fradd and Weismantel (1989) note similarities in the characteristics of students with learning disabilities and English language learners in academic performance, language disorders, perceptual disorders, attention, memory and social emotional difficulties.

REFERRAL PROCESS

Classroom teachers are concerned when students do not perform well in school. Often they want to know if the reason for this unexpected underachievement is a learning disability. Students served in the specific learning disability category represent 50.5% of all students served under IDEA Part B during the 1999–2000 school year (23rd Annual Report to Congress, Table AA9).

A referral can be sent directly to the multidisciplinary team responsible for the classification of students with special educational needs. However, as indicated in Chapter 5, most school districts employ a prereferral process. Parents can refer their child directly to the multidisciplinary team.

PREREFERRAL TEAMS

Since the inception of P.L. 94-142, the Education of All Handicapped Children Act, teachers have been required to document what they did prior to referral. They must describe the interventions they used in their classrooms and other schoolwide interventions that were unsuccessful. Prereferral makes this process more formalized. Additionally, prereferral teams provide a collaborative forum for school personnel to problem-solve and assist each other before deciding that a full multidisciplinary evaluation is required. These teams are also called **teacher assistance teams, the prereferral intervention model, mainstreaming assistance team model, school-based consultation team model, problem-solving model, and instructional support teams** (Chalfant & Pysh, 1989; Chalfant, Pysh, & Moultrie, 1979; Elksnin & Elksnin, 1989; Fuchs & Fuchs, 1989; House, Zimmer, & McInerney, 1991; Krackendoffel, Robinson, Deshler, & Schumaker, 1992; Lockner, 2000). Regardless of the term used, they help refine the process of identifying a student with a learning disability. This is particularly important for students from culturally and linguistically diverse urban settings. Gottlieb, Gottlieb, and Trogone et al. (1991) documented the disproportionately large number of referrals of African American and Hispanic students compared to White students. The prereferral process appears to reduce these inappropriate referrals. (See Chapter 5 for more specific information.)

IDENTIFICATION PROCESS

When you read the guidelines for the identification of students with learning disabilities (see Figure 5-1), the process seems easy, but it is not. Determining the students' potential compared to their performance can be reduced to a formula, but is it useful? Exploring all the exclusions appears reasonable, but is it? The current identification procedures have been widely criticized (see Scruggs & Mastropieri, 2002), and a book has been written just on the identification of learning disabilities (Bradley et al., 2002). IDEA 2004 no longer requires the use of the achievement–intellectual ability discrepancy.

As noted in Draft Federal Regulation 6-10-05:

§300.307 Specific Learning Disabilities

a. General. A State must adopt, consistent with §300.309, criteria for determining whether a child has a specific learning disability as defined in §300.8. In addition, the criteria adopted by the State—

   1. May prohibit the use of a severe discrepancy between intellectual ability and achievement for determining whether a child has a specific learning disability as defined in §300.8;
   2. May not require the use of a severe discrepancy between intellectual ability and achievement for determining whether a child has a specific learning disability as defined in §300.8;
   3. Must permit the use of a process that determines if the child responds to scientific, research-based intervention as part of the evaluation procedures described in §300.304; and
   4. May permit the use of other alternative research-based procedures for determining whether a child has a specific learning disability as defined in §200.8.

b. Consistency with State Criteria. A public agency must use the State criteria adopted pursuant to paragraph (a) of this section in determining whether a child has a specific learning disability.

   The determination of whether a child suspected of having a specific learning disability is made by the child's parents and the group. The groups consists of:

   1. The child's regular teacher; or
   2. If the child does not have a regular teacher, a regular classroom teacher qualified to teach a child of his or her age; or
   3. For a child of less than school age, an individual qualified by the SEA to teach a child of his or her age; and

4. At least one person qualified to conduct individual diagnostic examinations of children, such as a school psychologist, speech-language pathologist, or remedial reading teacher.

The group must:

1. Conduct, as appropriate, individual diagnostic assessments in the areas of speech and language, academic achievement, intellectual development, and social-emotional development;
2. Interpret assessment and intervention data, and apply critical analysis to those data;
3. Develop appropriate educational and transitional recommendations based on the assessment data; and
4. Deliver and monitor specifically designed instruction and services to meet the needs of a child with a specific learning disability; and

b. Includes—(1) A special education teacher; (2) (i) The child's general education teacher; or (ii) If the child does not have a general education teacher, a general education teacher qualified to teach a child of the child's age; and
c. Other professionals, if appropriate, such as a school psychologist, reading teacher, or educational therapist.

§300.309 Determining the Existence

a. The group described in §300.308 may determine that a child has a specific learning disability if—

1. The child does not achieve commensurate with the child's age in one or more of the following areas, when provided with learning experiences appropriate for the child's age:

   (i) Oral expression
   (ii) Listening comprehension
   (iii) Written expression
   (iv) Basic reading skill
   (v) Reading fluency skills
   (vi) Reading comprehension
   (vii) Mathematics calculation
   (viii) Mathematics problem solving

2. (1) The child fails to achieve a rate of learning to make sufficient progress to meet State-approved results in one or more of the are as identified in paragraph (a)(1) of this section when assessed with a response to scientific, research-based intervention process; or

   (ii) the child exhibits a pattern of strengths and weaknesses in performance, achievement, or both, or a pattern of strengths and weaknesses in performance, achievement, or both, relative to intellectual development, that is determined by the team to be relevant to the identification of specific learning disability, using appropriate assessments consistent with §§300.304 and 300.305; and

3. The group determines that its findings under paragraphs (a)(1) and (2) of this section are not primarily the result of—

   (i) A visual, hearing, or motor disability;
   (ii) Mental retardation;
   (iii) Emotional disturbance;
   (iv) Cultural factors; or
   (v) Environmental or economic disadvantage.

b. For a child suspected of having a specific learning disability, the group must consider, as part of the valuation described in §§300.304 through 300.306, data that demonstrated that—

1. Prior to, or as part of the referral process, the child was provided appropriate high-quality, research-based instruction in regular education settings, consistent with sections 1111(b) (8) (D) and (E) of the ESEA, including that the instruction was delivered by qualified personnel; and
2. Data-Based documentation of repeated assessment of achievement at reasonable intervals, reflecting formal assessment of student progress during instruction, was provided to the child's parents.

c. If the child has not made adequate progress after an appropriate period of time, during which the conditions in paragraphs (b)(1) and (2) of this section have been implemented, a referral for an evaluation to determine if the child needs special education and related services must be made.

d. Once the child is referred for an evaluation to determine if the child needs special education and related services, the timelines described in §300.301 and 300.303 must be adhered to, unless extended by mutual written agreement of the child's parents and a group of qualified professionals, as described in §300.308.

§300.310 Observation

a. At least one member of the group described in §300.308 other than the child's current teacher, who is trained in observation, shall observe the child, and the learning environment, including the regular classroom setting, to document academic performance and behavior in the areas of difficulty.

b. In the case of a child of less than school age or out of school, a group member must observe the child in an environment appropriate for a child of that age. (Authority: 20 U.S.C.1221e-3; 1401 [30]; 1414[b][6])

§300.311 Written Report

a. For a child suspected of having a specific learning disability, the evaluation report and the documentation of the determination of eligibility, as required by §300.306 (a) (2), must include a statement of—

1. Whether the child has a specific learning disability;

2. The basis for making the determination, including an assurance that the determination has been made in accordance with §300.306 (c)(1);

3. The relevant behavior, if any, noted during the observation of the child and the relationship of that behavior to the child's academic functioning;

4. The educationally relevant medical findings, if any;

5. Whether the child does not achieve commensurate with the child's age;

6. Whether there are strengths and weaknesses in performance or achievement or both, relative to intellectual development in one or more of the areas described in §3003.309 (a) that require special education and related services; and

7. The instructional strategies used and the student-centered data collected if a response to a scientific, research-based intervention process, as described in §300.309 was implemented.

b. Each group member shall certify in writing whether the report reflects his or her conclusion. If it does not reflect his or her conclusion, the group member must submit a separate statement presenting his or her conclusions. (Authority: 20 U.S.C.1221e-3; 1401[303];1414[b][6])

PARENTS' RIGHT TO REQUEST AN EVALUATION

Parents have a right to request an evaluation if they think their child needs special education or related services. If the request is refused, the school district must notify the parents in writing. It is preferred that schools and parents collaborate to assist students by utilizing the prereferral procedures of the school. Teachers should not attempt to circumvent the process by suggesting that parents bypass the prereferral team. Rather, if they work together, a reasonable plan can be developed to make a decision about the presence (or absence) of a learning disability.

PROBLEMS WITH THE DISCREPANCY FORMULA

The process from referral to classification is in flux, with organizations and individuals calling for an overhaul. This must begin with the referral process. It is no longer acceptable to rely on the IQ-achievement discrepancy, underlying process disorders, and the exclusion clause. The emphasis must be on a dynamic process that provides for early screening and remediation and an appreciation of the student's culture, language, and race.

Project Forum at the National Association of State Directors of Special Education (Schrag, 2000) conducted a survey of the 50 states and the District of Columbia on the use of the discrepancy formula and other grades for determining the eligibility of students with learning disabilities. They concluded:

• The use of the discrepancy formula, as a method of documenting a severe discrepancy for identifying the presence of a learning disability and for the purposes of special education eligibility determinations, is outdated and ill advised. Specifically, there is a need for procedures that focus on how the student is performing in the classroom, in the general curriculum, and in district and statewide assessments.

- Regression and other discrepancy formulae are statistical methods designed only for obtaining consistency and have no value in determining or understanding students' needs, since standardized intelligence and cognitive measures utilized in determining serve discrepancy are not generally correlated to the student's curriculum and to improving teaching and learning.
- Rigid use of LD discrepancy formulae/approaches takes away the decision-making responsibility from the assessment team regarding special education eligibility. (p. 6)

A special issue of the *Journal of Learning Disabilities* (Siegel, 2003) focused on the use of IQ scores in the diagnosis of learning disabilities. Jimenez, Siegel, and Rodrigo Lopez (2003) and Share and Silva (2003) suggest that their research does not support the use of a discrepancy formula based on the IQ score in the diagnosis of a learning disability. Others (Jimenez et al., 2003; Stage, Abbot, Jenkins, & Berninger, 2003) indicate that IQ is not a powerful predictor of a student's ability to benefit from remediation. The editor of the *Journal of Learning Disabilities* (Siegel, 2003) strongly states that "in the interests of providing remedial help for all children and adults who have a learning disability, we should abandon the concept of I.Q. and turn our efforts toward early identification, early intervention and remediation" (p. 3).

Fletcher, et al. (2002) reviewed the research on the classification of learning disabilities and note that the IQ-achievement discrepancy is the most controversial component of the definition. They conclude, "thus, consistent with the call of many researchers, the viability of the I.Q.-discrepancy classification hypothesis must be questioned" (p. 205). They suggest that the concept of IQ currently used is no longer useful. It has more to do with compliance with federal legislation than with providing high-quality instruction that is scientifically verified. They suggest eliminating the use of IQ in defining learning disabilities. IQ tests do not measure aptitude for learning or a student's response to intervention.

IDEA 2004 reflects this thinking and no longer requires the documentation of a discrepancy.

However, as noted in Chapter 2, this change will not occur overnight. A number of models will be developed, implemented, and evaluated before a consensus develops. One approach recommended by the Learning Disability Roundtable (2002, Exhibit A, pp. 18–19) is a multitiered collaborative problem-solving approach. The major components are as follows:

A multi-tiered, collaborate problem-solving approach which initiates early intervention, trial and coaching, progress monitoring and inter-disciplinary evaluation was named as a promising alternative to current practices by the Learning Disability Roundtable (2002). The major components of this approach will be:

- Decisions about a student's specific instructional needs are based primarily on a student's lack of responsiveness to effective instruction. This means that a first step toward identifying students who might need special education services is to determine whether the instructional environment is adequately individualized, structured and supportive to facilitate learning for all capable students.
- Targeted interventions' are implemented with fidelity, and data are collected on student performance. The effects of interventions are monitored and decisions about types (and intensity) of ongoing instruction and support are made for individual students at the classroom level.
- Students' progress is carefully documented within clear timelines, and response to instruction (RTI) provides additional validation of students' specific instructional needs, as well as informs decisions about how each student could best be served by special and regular education and related services personnel.
- Instructional interventions are formulated and implemented to ensure that students have access to general education curricula, and to provide support needed for mastery of literacy, learning strategies and social skills critical for school success.
- Students in need of special education services are provided relevant instruction and support, with ongoing collaboration among regular and special education and related service personnel.

- Students exit special education services as soon as objective data indicate that they have made sufficient progress to achieve independently in the general education classroom without special education services. The decision to end special education services does not mean that the student no longer has a disability or that a decision to re-enter the system could not be made at a later date. The option to retain, exit or re-enter students would be made on an individual basis and be reflected in an IEP or transitional IEP process.

RESPONSE TO INSTRUCTION

The problem-solving approach advocated by the Learning Disability Roundtable (2002) is the notion of evaluating a student's response to instruction (RTI). This had been proposed as an alternative to the failed discrepancy model. Vaughn and Fuchs (2003), in a special series in *Learning Disabilities Research and Practice* (3[3]), discuss the model. It is divided into three Phases:

Phase I   Initially, the rate of growth for all students is assessed to determine the effectiveness of instruction.
Phase II   During this phase, students who are performing dramatically below their classmates are identified.
Phase III   The student's response to adaptation in the classroom is measured.

Vaughn and Fuchs state:

This model has been termed "a three-tiered prevention model" with primary intervention consisting of a general education program; secondary intervention involving the fixed duration, intensive, standard protocol trial; and tertiary invention synonymous with special education. (p. 139)

The major benefits of this RTI model are:

- Identifying individuals at risk rather than by deficit.
- Identifying and treating students with learning disabilities early.

- Reducing bias in the identification process for learning disabilities.
- Connecting identification assessment with instructional planning and progress monitoring.

Clearly, the model is in the early stages of development. Vaughn and Fuchs (2003) identify some of the potential problems:

- In an RTI model, are learning disabilities real?
- Do we have validated intervention models and measures to ensure instruction validity?
- Is an inadequate response to instruction a defensible endpoint in the identification process?
- How intensively should **instruction** be defined in an RTI model for learning disabilities identification?
- Are there adequately trained personnel to implement an RTI model?
- When should due process be initiated?

RTI is currently the most popular alternative to the discrepancy formula in determining eligibility for the classification of learning disabilities (see the special series of the *Journal Learning Disabilities, 38*[6], November/December [2005] on Research Topics in Responsiveness to Intervention). In this special series, a number of issues related to the viability and implementation of this model are discussed, as well as alternative modes. For example, Mastropieri and Scruggs (2005, p. 529) propose the following:

- Create change in general education so that "RTI-type" first- and second-tier reading programs are implemented in general education. That is, all students are assured of evidence-based instruction (although variability in response to student and teacher characteristics is accepted). Further, supplemental procedures are in place for students who fail to demonstrate adequate progress, for any reason. Students who are referred to special education, then, have already been assured very high quality general education treatments. Such procedures should guard against overidentification in two ways: First, "teaching disabilities" as a cause of LD will be eliminated, since all students will have received high-quality instruction. Second, school personnel will be less likely to refer students to special education because other services simply are not available (MacMillian, Gresham, & Bocian, 1996; MacMillan, Gresham, & Bocian, 1998). Such a requirement can help enforce strict criteria for LD identification. Because the first- and second-tier services are entirely within the domain of general education and appropriate to the scope of general education, services should come from general education budgets.

- All students identified as having LD will demonstrate very low achievement in one or more significant areas of school functioning, and this level of functioning will be documented from more than one record, possibly including teacher reports, evidence of student classroom performance, and standardized test scores.
- All students identified as having LD will meet exclusionary criteria with respect to sensory and motor functioning; social-emotional functioning; or economic, environmental, or cultural disadvantage.
- All students will demonstrate a discrepancy (e.g., 1, 1.5, or 2 standard deviations) between IQ and achievement. Schools and state and federal educational authorities can determine the best criteria, or whether these must be standard across states.
- Early identification will be encouraged so that appropriate remedial services can be maximized. With appropriate general education services in effect, it can be determined for students at very early ages that general remedial services alone will not be sufficient to ensure their adequate school functioning. There will be little to be gained from adopting a "wait-to-fail" approach.
- The final decision is made by a team but must be supported by evidence. To the extent that all measures are vulnerable and all students unique, it is important that teams of professionals agree on the best decisions for individual students. However, such decisions must be supported to the greatest extent possible by reliable evidence.

As Reschly (2005) notes, the issue of eligibility decisions will not be resolved in the near future. There are other options, such as those proposed by Mastropieri and Scruggs (2005), that have strong advocates. Reschly states, "a consensus has not yet emerged and any resolution in the near future is likely to be controversial" (p. 515).

ASSESSMENT PRACTICES

Assessment models used to evaluate underachieving students typically consist of a fixed battery of standardized and informal assessment instruments or a battery of varied instruments, which may differ from student to student at the discretion of the assessor. No single battery of standardized or informal assessment instruments should be expected to completely describe the full range of any student's achievement or potential.

A number of standardized tests are frequently employed to identify students with learning disabilities. They will be discussed in Chapters 12, 13, 14 and 15, which deal with specific curriculum areas. Readers are encouraged to consult textbooks that focus exclusively on assessment for a more thorough analysis of standardized tests. You may be asked to assist in test selection, but usually not until you've been in the school for a while (see the next section for some thoughts on test selection).

PRACTICAL CONSIDERATIONS IN TEST SELECTION

Most new teachers have little to say about the types of tests used to identify students with learning disabilities. Typically, some districts use a fixed battery of standardized and informal assessment instruments. While these may differ from student to student, rarely will you have total discretion in selecting the tests or other procedures. Yet, you've learned from your coursework and textbooks that certain tests are good and others are not. Are you supposed to administer tests that you know lack reliability, validity, and standardization? Or complain to the Director of Special Education that the tests he recommends are out-of-date and not technically sound? This is a dilemma that many new teachers face. In the long term, you may become a member of a committee that evaluates a few assessment tools, and your input will be valued. Right now, the reasonable, sensible approach is to supplement the standardized test with more informal, nonstandardized measures discussed later in the chapter, such as portfolio assessment, authentic assessment, criterion-referenced tests, and curriculum-based measures.

Also, provide the evaluation team with observational reports, anecdotal records, interviews, and examples of the student's work. This will enable the team to make decisions based on a variety of assessment tools. And as you become a member of the team, your views on the assessment battery will be valued.

It is often argued that testing should not drive instruction. More importantly, testing should not drive assessment. Rather, tests and test-like procedures, in conjunction with other information on student achievement, should inform the assessment process.

Furthermore, any hypothesis about student achievement or ability that is generated from an educational assessment must be based on multiple forms of evidence of student performance (Chittenden, 1991). Standardized test results, performance data, and observational data from teachers, parents, and other informants must be gathered, and thoughtful decisions must allow for systematic collection of evidence over time and in a variety of settings. Also, even the most comprehensive assessment may not produce irrefutable evidence of specific learning disabilities. In such cases, continued observation, data collection, and carefully monitored instructional modification can be conducted. The following principles can be used to guide a thoughtful assessment of student performance that takes cultural and linguistic diversity into account.

GUIDING PRINCIPLES FOR A MODEL OF EDUCATIONAL ASSESSMENT

It is proposed that educational assessment be led by the following principles:

1. The purpose of the assessment must be clearly defined.
2. Diagnostic questions must guide the assessment.
3. Multiple forms of evidence of student performance must be gathered.
4. Evidence of achievement must be gathered over time and in a variety of contexts.
5. Evidence of student performance must be based on curriculum materials and experiences that are familiar to the student.
6. Evaluators must be able to accept lack of closure.

Clear Definition of the Purpose of the Assessment

A thorough educational assessment should not begin with routine standardized tests, but rather with a clear definition of the purpose of the assessment and its expected outcomes. The issues to be addressed in this initial phase include:

1. A description of the presenting problem by the person making the referral.
2. Specific diagnostic questions.
3. An outline of the assessment outcomes expected by the person making the referral and by others involved with the student.

Often the person making the referral may simply need to discuss the perceived academic problem with another person who knows the student's behavior, such as an educational evaluator, a parent, or another of the student's teachers. A focused discussion of what is perceived to be typical learning or behavior can result in a better understanding of the student's achievement and in the attempt to modify classroom instruction.

A clear understanding of the anticipated outcomes of an educational assessment is crucial. Is the assessment being conducted for classification, for design of instructional procedures, or for a change in placement? These issues need to be explicitly stated and made clear to all concerned so that the diagnostic questions can be appropriately framed.

Diagnostic Questions Guiding the Assessment

A model is proposed in which diagnostic questions are the basis of the educational assessment. Messick (1987) has proposed that assessment be conducted within three contexts:

1. The interpersonal student context
2. The sociocultural context in which the student functions or has functioned
3. The instructional context of the school.

Diagnostic Questions Regarding Student Context

In the assessment of specific learning disabilities, one critical question is posed: Is there sufficient information, from multiple forms of evidence, to conclude that perceived underachievement is the result of a pathological condition within the student that warrants a special educational classifications and placement?

Diagnostic Questions Regarding Sociocultural Context

Do cultural factors interfere with the student's ability to master the content as presented? Do cultural factors interfere with the referring person's ability to observe the full range of the student's ability and achievement? Do linguistic factors prevent the student from benefiting from the current instructional approach? Do linguistic factors prevent the student from demonstrating his or her ability and content mastery? Do socioeconomic factors interfere with the student's ability to master and demonstrate knowledge of the content in the current instructional setting?

Diagnostic Questions Regarding Instructional Context

Underachievement is a hallmark of specific learning disabilities. However, it is often difficult to determine if the underachievement of many urban students reflects lack of adequate instruction or a student-specific information processing problem. Vaughn and Fuchs (2003) discuss the need to assess the instructional environment to ensure that all students are learning.

Gathering Multiple Forms of Evidence of Students' Performance. Student-specific diagnostic questions should drive the assessment, along with various forms of evidence of the student's ability and achievement. These questions can then be answered. The conclusions about general ability and mastery of content should not be based on one test performance on a single assessment format. Nor should they be based on the observations of a single informant.

Leung (1996) suggests that those responsible for the assessment of culturally and linguistically diverse students employ six "quality" indicators:

- Examination of the opportunity to learn
- Involvement of parents or caretakers
- Use of only trained interpreters
- Nonreliance on psychometric tests
- Full use of a Multidisciplinary Team
- Use of informal clinical judgment

Leung (1996) encourages evaluators to examine multiple forms of evidence. Otherwise, they will likely miss a significant part of what a student knows. Leung cautions against using data collection procedures that go according to plan. We need to be suspicious of an evaluation that is ordinary with a population that is extraordinary.

Multiple forms of evidence in a variety of contexts, consisting of traditional standardized tests, performance assessments and portfolios, parent/teacher observations, and interviews, are necessary (Chittenden, 1991).

Gathering Evidence of Achievement Over Time and in a Variety of Contexts. A major concern in educational assessment is the speed with which this complicated task is expected to be accomplished. In fact, the rush to classify students, which has led to an increase in the number of ill-trained educational evaluators, is based more on a desire to avoid litigation resulting from being found out of compliance with state and local regulations than on theoretically and ethically sound assessment practices. While very real pressures are placed on school districts, it is also true that significant numbers of students are classified in special education categories because the bureaucratic and fiscal constraints of the educational system require classification in order to receive even the most minor support services.

The assessment of a typical learner in an urban area may, in some cases, require a longitudinal assessment of the student's demonstrated ability and achievement in which various interventions are interwoven. As Leung (1996) notes, slowing down the process can be invaluable. In such cases, diagnostic teaching may be necessary to provide a more informative picture of the ways in which a specific student represents knowledge in the context of his or her own experiences. Given the controversy surrounding the theoretical and operational definitions of specific learning disabilities, the most appropriate course of action might well be careful documentation of the student's learning of new information over a span of time, in a variety of contexts, and under varying conditions.

Basing Evidence of Student Performance on Curriculum Materials and Experiences That Are Familiar to the Student. When the purpose of an assessment is to decide whether or not to label the student, it is especially important that the assessment of academic achievement be curriculum-based. That is, the assessment of academic achievement should be based on curriculum content that was taught to the student and on experiences that are familiar to the student. Large-scale achievement testing rests on the assumption that a common core of information is taught to all students at the same time. However, it is becoming increasingly clear that many urban communities include children who have temporary residences, such as shelters for the homeless or

the battered, and who may have been unable to follow a consistent academic curriculum because they moved from one residence and school to another. The inability to ensure a match between material tested and material taught weakens the validity of the interpretation of test results.

Accepting Lack of Closure. As stated previously, accurately identifying children with specific learning disabilities, especially in culturally and linguistically diverse settings, is a complicated task that should not be held to the constraints of a traditional assessment. The multiple forms of evidence discussed above, and the suggested longitudinal nature of the assessment process, are based on the realization that situations will arise in which it is simply not clear that the student's underachievement is a result of inborn processing deficits. In fact, when issues of language, culture, and experience arise, the assessment can result in confusion about the existence of a specific learning disability. In such cases, the assessment process could go on, and data should continue to be collected from a variety of sources and in a variety of contexts.

Evaluation, the process of describing student behavior and determining the level of student performance or the stage of development, should be thoughtful and reflective. Too often it becomes simply the administration of standardized tests and interpretation of the scores. As a result, there are numerous criticisms of these tests.

ASSESSING THE CLASSROOM

One way to evaluate instruction in the regular education classroom is to assess the classroom. Here are some areas to consider (Cohen & Spenciner, 2003, pp. 109, 110–111):

1. *Materials*
   - variety

     Do students have access to a variety of materials?

- format

  Is the format of the materials appropriate?

2. *Manipulatives*
   - availability and appropriateness

     Are manipulatives available?
     Are manipulatives appropriate?

3. *Learning Activities*
   - instructional method

     Does the teacher use a variety of instructional methods?
     Does the teacher use effective, scientifically based methods and materials?
   - opportunities to make choices

     Does the classroom teacher provide students opportunities to make choices during learning activities?
   - opportunities to share ideas

     Are student comments and questions respected and encouraged?

4. *Instructional Demands*
   - clear instructions for completing the assignments

     Does the teacher provide clear instructions and check for student understanding before students begin learning activities and assignments?
   - assignments that are appropriate in difficulty and in length

     Are students assigned work that is appropriate in difficulty and length?
   - learning activities and assignments that are relevant to the students

     Do students perceive that the work is useful?
     Can students use a variety of materials?

5. *Modification*
   - changes in furniture, equipment, or materials

     Is there easy and convenient access to furniture and equipment?
     Can students use the materials or is there a need for accommodations or modifications?

6. *Grouping*
   - grouping of students

     Do students complete some work independently?
     Can students work with a peer?
     Do students have opportunities to work cooperatively with others?

7. *Instruction*
   - adjustments

     Are the instructional strategies appropriate or is there a need for revision?
     Is there a variety of instructional methods in use?
   - pace of instruction

     Is the pace of instruction delivery appropriate?
   - adequate levels of assistance

     Does the teacher (or teaching assistant) provide prompts and other types of assistance on an as-needed basis to students?
     Is assistance faded as soon as possible?

8. *Expectations*
   - demands placed on students

     Are the teacher's expectations appropriate?

9. *Student Involvement*
   - teacher support

     Does the teacher encourage student involvement?
     Is the student actively involved in learning activities?
     Does the student participate in classroom discussions?
   - peer support

     Do other students interact with the student?
     Does the student interact with other students?

10. *Assessments*
    - tools

      Does the teacher use a variety of assessment approaches in assessing student instructional needs and progress?
    - format

      If appropriate, does the teacher implement alternative formats?

- feedback

  Does the teacher give students feedback and suggestions for improvement?

11. *Curriculum*

    - curriculum reform and standards

      Does the curriculum reflect recent reform, standards, and contemporary views?

12. *Schedule*

    - predictability of the daily schedule

      Does the classroom teacher follow a regular schedule?
      Is the schedule posted for students to see?
      Is there a minimum of interruptions?

13. *Transitions*

    - preparation and follow-through

      Does the teacher prepare students for the transition from one activity to another?
      Does the teacher provide time for students to transition?

CLASSROOM-BASED ASSESSMENT

Performance Assessments and Portfolios

In response to growing dissatisfaction with traditional standardized multiple-choice formats, national interest in performance-based assessments is developing. These alternative assessments consist of such activities and materials as open-ended responses, portfolios, and performances. In general, these instruments are highly contextualized; that is, items are embedded in a context that is familiar to the student. Some researchers have used the term *authentic assessments*. Pike and Salend (1995) compare traditional and authentic assessment procedures.

Traditional Assessment

Traditionally, educational decisions are based on assessment data collected from teacher-administered, norm-referenced, standardized tests (Salend, 1994). Norm-referenced testing provides information that allows comparison of the student's performance to norms based on the scores of other students. However, while norm-referenced testing is often employed to determine eligibility for special education services, it provides no specific information for planning, implementing, and evaluating a student's educational program. Norm-referenced test scores tend to be static, reflecting only one score on a particular day under certain conditions. They do not reveal a student's attempts to determine correct answers, nor do they acknowledge the student's effort.

Authentic Assessment

Authentic assessment refers to a variety of informal and formal student-centered strategies for collecting and recording information about students. The strategies attempt to facilitate student learning by linking assessment and instruction. Authentic assessment procedures emphasize both the process and products of learning and place value on input from teachers and students (Anthony, Johnson, Mickelson, & Preece, 1991). Teachers who effectively use authentic assessment practices continuously observe and interact with their students to discover not only what the students know, but also how they learn. For authentic assessment to be meaningful for students and teachers, it should be based on the following principles:

- Assessment should be linked to what students are actually learning and what they might be learning.
- Assessment should be viewed as a continuous and cumulative process.
- Assessment should be conducted throughout the school day and across the curriculum.
- Assessment results should be based on data from a variety of assessment strategies.
- Assessment should occur during real learning experiences.
- Assessment should involve collaboration of students and teachers.

- Assessment findings should be easily communicated to students, parents, professionals, administrators, and other decision makers. (Pike, Compain, & Mumper, 1994)

Effective authentic assessment strategies involve students in the assessment process and make them the focus of all evaluation activities. Salend (1983, p. 20) found that students' performance levels, as measured via self-assessment procedures, were superior to the performance levels determined by a multidisciplinary planning team using standardized assessment instruments. Information from teachers, parents, and the students themselves can be included in an ongoing process of instruction, performance, and reflection. However, the increasing national infatuation with performance assessments, especially portfolios, should not be interpreted as a solution to the problems of assessing minority students. In fact, these assessments may require a more thorough understanding of the content and the desired student outcomes than conventional standardized measures.

Portfolio Assessment

Wesson and King (1996) suggest that portfolios have many advantages. Portfolio assessment is a formative assessment that allows both teachers and students to monitor students' progress over the course of the year. Teachers can thus make timely adjustments in instructional methods.

Portfolios provide a method for students to assess and reflect on their growth. Typically, standardized assessment tests are administered at the beginning and end of the school year to provide benchmarks of learning. This approach has little value for special educators. They are concerned about monitoring progress as the year unfolds.

Portfolio assessment structures the process of allowing students to assume ownership of their learning, which promotes internal control. This approach encourages students to become invested in their learning by empowering them.

The portfolio model emphasizes the breadth and scope of learning. Thus, it is a more sensitive model for assessing learning than is a model focusing on a narrow set of skills.

Yet, the potential application of this model in the special education classroom has problems. The greatest one is time. Teachers must restructure their time to schedule conferences. During conferences, materials must be collected and shared with peers, reflected on, and evaluated.

- The criteria for judging materials need specification and involvement of the student. Clearly, the teacher is the guide in developing the standards for evaluating the student's products, but this should be done in collaboration with the student. Teacher education in specifying these standards is necessary if portfolios are to be used to their full potential.
- Teachers must employ a recordkeeping system that is time-efficient and meaningful. This is challenging given the already existing demands on the special educator's time. Classroom guides for reading and writing instruction in general education would be an excellent starting point to get tips on establishing criteria and recordkeeping systems that might be applied to exceptional education (Farr & Tone, 1994; Tierney, Carter, & Desai, 1991).
- The methodology to encourage reflection needs to be specified in advance so that the student can reflect meaningfully on his or her growth. In assisting the student with this process, the teacher's role is best conceptualized as collaboration and consultation. The teacher must feel comfortable with getting the student to talk about his or her progress rather than with the traditional role of describing and passing judgments on student work without student input.

Though special educators are trained to value student-centered learning, they also face a challenge in using this model with general educators who may feel more comfortable with a teacher-centered form of assessment. Thus, for special educators working closely with general educators, adopting this developmental perspective to assessment will be an ongoing challenge requiring strong in-service and collaborative efforts. Guidelines for developing and using portfolios (Wesson & King, 1996, pp. 47–48) are as follows:

1. *Both the teacher and the student help compose the portfolio.* The student's ideas about what to include are important, because the portfolio is a chronicle of learning from the learner's and teacher's points of view. However, the teacher may require some additional ideas about items that contribute to an understanding of the student's progress. Thus, the contents are a combination of items selected by the teacher and the student.

2. *The portfolio is a selective collection relating to the school or district instructional goals for the grade.* Not every piece of writing should go into it. If no specific goals are available, then the teacher should develop specific goals. In special education, the individualized education program (IEP) is already in place; therefore, the selection of items to be placed in the portfolio is based on the IEP. Only goal-relevant information needs to be included. Another criterion for selection is the degree to which the item helps the teacher and student make instructional decisions.

3. *The portfolio should be multifaceted and include many different types of data.* It is impossible to represent a student's growth with only one kind of measure; multiple sources of information should be used.

4. *The portfolio should be organized by areas and time.* For example, in a literacy portfolio, reading-related items may be in one section and put in chronological order to show progress. The written-language data could be in the nest section and also be in a time series order. An alternative organizational scheme would be to place items that deal with the same thematic unit within a section. For a thematic unit on bears, that section of the portfolio may contain a list of sources used to research bears, rough drafts of the report, and the final copy, as well as bear stories the student read, an audiotape of the student reading a selection from a chosen book, bear poems written by the students, and a videotape for the Three Bears play put on by the class. There is no one way to organize the portfolio, and the decision of how to organize should be systematic and deliberate on the part of the teacher and students as they discuss the possibilities and decide on a rationale for choosing a specific organizational scheme.

5. *Portfolios should be accessible to both teachers and students so that the information they contain may be used and updated frequently.* Teachers may want to develop a time-line so that at the end of every unit or report card period, every student's portfolio will be reviewed and items added and deleted. Without a specified time-line, some children's portfolios may remain stagnant and become merely a record-keeping system, as opposed to a line to instruction. An alternative is to update and check one portfolio daily and, thereby, schedule reviews at regular intervals (about monthly) for each student.

PARENT–TEACHER OBSERVATION AND INTERVIEW

Student Ability Conference

Since no single observer can describe the complete range of an individual's ability and achievement, the assessment process includes a dialogue among teachers, parents, and, whenever possible, the student. The model of a student ability conference with an open discussion of the student's performance in a specific domain or set of domain is discussed from various perspectives. This conference provides an opportunity to explore strategies to identify and enhance the student's range of talents, as well as to isolate academic areas that may require alternative instructional approaches. In addition, the student ability conference allows teachers and parents to form an educational partnership. This conference is similar to the prereferral meeting or teacher

Student's name: Naomi R

Teacher: Mrs. Dunkin Date: June 22, 1993

Parents: Mr. & Mrs. R

Address: 2401 West Main Street, Sayville, New York 11782

Home phone: (516) 374-9001 Work phone: 374-2108

Date of Birth: October 11, 1996

Members Present:

Mrs. R., Parent	Dr. Barone, Psychologist
Ms. Dunkin, Teacher	Mr. Jones, Art Teacher
Naomi, Student	Ms. Maldora, Nurse
Ms. Abrams, Social Worker	Dr. Alegro, Principal

Summary

Mrs. R. reports that Naomi is a responsible child at home, assisting with her siblings and very cooperative. School personnel report the same. Mr. Jones, the art teacher, believes that Naomi has exceptional talent in art and that this should be pursued through an enrichment program. Dr. Barone, the school psychologist, agrees and notes that her visual-motor skills are superior, but he is concerned about her reading skills. Mrs. R. is also concerned about this, as is Ms. Dunkin, her teacher. Naomi also feels uncomfortable reading in class and doesn't understand why she can't read. It was agreed that Ms. Abrams, the school social worker, would meet with Naomi and the reading teacher to conduct a brief reading evaluation and then schedule another student ability conference in 2 weeks to discuss the findings.

FIGURE 6–1 Student Ability Conference

assistance team meeting discussed previously, the difference being the addition of the student (when appropriate) and parents. All parties can develop a plan that can be monitored (see Figure 6–1).

Criticism of Standardized Tests

There is great dissatisfaction with the use of standardized tests in the classification of students with learning disabilities.

Misleading information	Traditional test findings provide a limited view of student learning. Choate and Evans (1992) note that many classroom skills are not assessed by these tests, which sample a broad range of skills. Test results can mislead people to think that the score is an absolute value rather than merely an indicator. Furthermore, test scores do not explain the approach students take when responding to test items. Some students give wrong answers for reasons unrelated to their knowledge (e.g., test anxiety, feeling sick or sleepy, effects of medications, or difficulty marking answer sheets). Thus, using these tests to make decisions about students' futures (e.g., if they will pass reading) may result in incorrect decisions. A good (valid) test has good (accurate) predictive validity; many standardized, norm-referenced tests do not.
Unfairness	Many of the traditional tests are unfair to certain populations, particularly some students with learning disabilities (Choate, Enright, Miller, Poteet, & Rakes, 1987). They are biased in the

(continued)

	sense that the language usage, cultural examples, and learning styles or skills required to successfully complete test items do not reflect those of persons with limited English proficiency, low incomes, minority or cultural group membership, and males. Some tests tend to favor middle- to upper-class White boys (Neil & Medina, 1989)
Distraction	Test results often are used as measures of accountability—for example, in teaching reading objectives and goals and as yardsticks for comparing schools to determine which is "better" (i.e., has higher average scores). When these factors are emphasized, attention is distracted from conditions that may contribute to low average scores—overcrowded classrooms, lack of adequate instructional material, administrative focus on test scores rather than on acquiring knowledge, high-level thinking, and so on.
Quality control	Testing is a big business in America. The taxpayer cost of state and local testing is approaching $1 billion a year. Students at some grade levels take as many as 12 comprehensive tests in a single year (Moses, 1990). However, there is no authority to guarantee regulations or quality control, although recent demands for alternative assessment may eventually result in quality control.
Expense	Traditional testing is expensive in terms of material costs and time (administering, scoring, posting results). The money set aside for traditional testing in a school budget might better be allocated to other assessment approaches that are less expensive, more time-efficient, and less biased, and that produce results with more meaning for educational decisions.
Use of results	Standardized tests too often are used unfairly to shut Americans out of education and employment opportunities (Moses, 1990). In an interview with Kirst (1991), Lorrie Shepard pointed out that when tests drive instruction, the curriculum often covers only what is on the test. Teaching to the test—at least when it is a standardized multiple-choice test—restricts the curriculum to test items that are factual, concrete, and isolated from a broader, better-integrated curriculum. Hanson (1993) characterizes tests as gatekeepers, allowing only some individuals to pass through. He suggests that test scores can redefine an individual both in his or her eyes and in the eyes of others.
Sending the wrong message to students	Traditional tests foster a one-right-answer mentality, limiting students' thinking processes. Although some questions do have only one correct answer, others (e.g., causes of the Civil War) do not (Hambleton & Murphy, 1992, (pp. 213–214).

Grossman (1996, p. 282) cited additional criticisms of standardized assessments applied to students with culturally and linguistically diverse backgrounds.

- Standardized assessment procedures do not accurately or validly describe how students function in the present, nor do they predict how students will function in the future.
- They ask "Do you know what I know?" rather than "What is it that you know?"
- The data collected with standardized instruments are typically collected in non-classroom situations under unusual circumstances by unfamiliar assessors, and therefore do not reflect how students function in real life classrooms with real life teachers.

- Percentile ranking, grade-level placements, and other norms provided by standardized tests are not realistic because national norms are not necessarily true for a given school district, school, or class. The content of courses taught at the seventh-grade level in a predominantly middle-class suburban school may be very different than the course content in a school serving predominantly poor urban students. Thus, students who score at the seventh-grade level on a nationally normed reading test may actually be functioning much lower than a middle-class neighborhood suburban school and much higher than the typical seventh-grade student in some other school districts.
- Standardized assessment procedures are not easily adapted to students' contextual, cultural, and linguistic characteristics.

- They measure different attributes with different groups of students. When used with limited-English-proficient, non-European American and poor students, they measure what students have been exposed to, how fast they can work without making careless mistakes, how motivated they are to succeed and do their best, how well they can adapt to the particular format of the procedure, how they respond to pressure, and so on, not their achievement, learning potential, earning disabilities, or whatever else they may measure when used with European American middle-class students who are English proficient and speak standard English.
- They require all students to fit a preconceived mold. Despite the lip service we pay to the myriad ways in which individuals differ, and claim to celebrate this variety, our practices speak otherwise. In fact it is performance on these tests—with their narrow and rigid definition both of when children should be able to perform particular skills and how they should be able to exhibit their knowledge—that determines whether we see children as okay or not. In the process we damage all children—we devalue the variety of strengths they bring them to school. All differences become handicaps.

In rebuttal, the Council of America Psychological Associations as cited in Grossman, 1996, p. 283, states:

Good psychological decisions require good evidence, and some of the most useful and reliable evidence comes from well-designed and properly interpreted standardized tests. . . . Yet for a variety of reasons, some valid and some not, testing has been the constant target of attack, joined in often by political figures or by the popular media. Testing continues to play an informative role in psychological decisions, for example in counseling practice and educational guidance, yet the science and profession of psychology are damaged by lopsided attacks, which often go without correction, comment or rebuttal. Now, therefore, the Council of the American Psychological Association asserts the following:

1. Standardized testing, competently administered and evaluated, is a valuable tool in individual, educational, and personnel decision-making.

2. Abuses of testing, through unwarranted labeling or interpretation, are to be avoided, as are abuses of any valuable tool.

The problem is that the traditional standardized tests used to assess learning disabilities often have shortcomings. Some questions raised by the use of traditional norm-referenced, standardized tests with diverse populations include:

- Does the test or a subtest of it answer the diagnostic questions of the assessment team?
- Are the student's education a experiences represented by the normative population?
- How will the student's results on the standardized test be used?
- What inferences about the student's ability and achievement will be drawn from the score on the standardized test?

CURRICULUM-BASED ASSESSMENT

Ysseldyke and Algozzine (1995) note the value of curriculum-based assessment. This assessment, when conducted properly, can be an important tool for teachers and diagnostic specialists in a number of ways (see From Research to Practice: How to Develop a Curriculum-Based Assessment). According to Ysseldyke and Algozzine, these are the benefits of curriculum-based assessment:

- *Analysis of the learning environment.* By careful examination of the learning environment, curriculum-based assessment helps to identify pitfalls that may be interfering with the student's learning. Such assessment isolates problems with the instructional materials, with the manner of presentation (such as lecture or workbook), and with the grouping of students in the classroom.
- *Analysis of task-approach strategies.* By focusing on the student's task-approach strategies, curriculum-based assessment helps teachers identify basic learning skills that the student may need to develop.
- *Examination of student's products.* Through systematic examination of a student's work

samples, curriculum-based assessment can spot particular error patterns.

- *Controlling and arranging student tasks.* By manipulating the ways in which materials are presented and the specific tasks that students are asked to perform, the curriculum-based assessment procedure helps teachers determine which approaches are most productive. (p. 296)

Choate, Bennett, Enright, Miller, Poteet, and Rakes (1987) list several reasons for using curriculum-based assessment:

FROM RESEARCH TO PRACTICE: DEVELOPING A CURRICULUM-BASED ASSESSMENT

Fuchs, Fuchs, and Speece (2002) suggest that curriculum-based measurement, a type of curriculum-based assessment, allows the evaluation team to measure the performance of a student in relation to that of his or her peers and to measure his or her rate of learning. This has been referred to as a *dual discrepancy.* Cohen and Spenciner (2003, pp. 148, 149) suggest the following steps in developing curriculum-based measures:

Step 1: *Identify the Purpose(s).*
Use the instrument to determine eligibility or entry into a curriculum, to develop the goals for intervention, or to evaluate the student's progress in the curriculum. Sometimes, one instrument can serve multiple purposes. For example, teachers can use the CBA instrument to develop goals and to evaluate the student's progress.

Step 2: *Analyze the Curriculum.*
Determine what the curriculum teaches. Determine the specific tasks that the student should be learning.

Step 3: *Develop Performance Objectives.*
Determine if a student has demonstrated progress in the curriculum. Specify behaviors that the student must demonstrate in order to indicate progress in the curriculum.

Step 4: *Develop the Assessment Procedures.*
In this step, develop specific test items that correspond with the performance objectives. The teacher can develop different types of items: for example, observing the student or requesting that the student perform specific actions or specific academic tasks, demonstrate particular behaviors, or answer particular questions. Make sure to delineate the scoring procedures. You will have to specify how you will determine how well the student performs. Considerations about reliability and validity are important. The CBA instrument must be valid. It must have a close correspondence with the curriculum.

Step 5: *Implement the Assessment Procedures.*
Once the assessment procedures have been developed, you can collect information. How you decide to record and keep track of the information will be important. The way in which teachers assess students must be consistent each time. Recording sheets will be helpful in keeping track of the information you collect. Piloting, or trying out, the CBA items before actual implementation is a good idea. Although a great deal of thought has gone into the development and construction of the items, it is always good practice to try out the items before using them to assess students. You should administer CBA items according to the procedures that have been developed.

Step 6: *Organize the Information.*
Summarize the information that you have collected. Tables, graphs, or charts can be useful.

Step 7: *Interpret and Integrate the Results.*
Integrate the CBA information with information from standardized tests, observations, anecdotal records, and other forms of assessment. This is the point in the assessment process where instruction and assessment link. The decision-making process continues as educators, along with the team, decide where, when, and how instruction should proceed.

Pemberton (2003, p. 18) provides an example. It complies with the procedural requirements of P. L. 94-142 and IDEA for assessing students in need of special education.

- It is efficient.
- It is a valid, reliable basis for making decisions.

- It can be used to make different kinds of decisions (for example, screening, program effectiveness).
- It increases student's achievement.
- It helps teachers decide what to teach.

A number of classroom-based assessments are provided in Chapters 12 to 15.

IMPLICATIONS FOR TEACHERS

Since the development of the category of learning disabilities, one of the key components of the operational definition has been the discrepancy between intelligence and achievement. IDEA 2004 no longer requires this mandate. This represents a radical shift in the way students with learning disabilities are identified.

Clearly, this change has major implications for teachers. How will students be identified? What will teachers' role be in the assessment process? Ongoing research must be conducted on effective methods of identification. There is considerable interest in the RTI approach. As the evidence is accumulated, we will be able to make informed decisions. And yet, every day, schools are referring, assessing, and classifying students with learning disabilities—with all the problems associated with assessment and identification. Your school psychologist may still administer tests of intellectual ability and academic achievement in order to establish a discrepancy. You may be required to observe the student in class and provide specific information for informal classroom-based measures (see the chapters on specific disabilities). You may have to fill out a rating scale and provide information on specific behaviors (see Chapter 16). Through formal and informal measures, you will be involved in a process that will attempt to determine if a student is performing at a level markedly different from that of his or he peers and if he or she has been provided with proven teaching interventions.

SUMMARY

Determining eligibility for a classification of learning disability is a complex process. It should be a collaborative decision made by a problem-solving team. Before that decision is made, you must consider:

- Legal requirements
- Parental concerns
- Prereferral strategies
- Selection of assessment tools
- Measurement of student performance

This chapter has focused on the new regulations for determining eligibility, as well as practical guiding principles of assessment that you should employ. Classroom-based assessments were also discussed.

Remember Wilson? Does he have a learning disability? It would be easy to say "no," attributing his poor performance to a language difference, but much more examination is needed before a decision can be made. How well does he do compared to other students in his class? What is his rate of learning? Has he received high-quality instruction? What prereferral interventions have been employed? Are his culture and language being considered throughout the process? Only when these issues are determined can we answer the question "Does Wilson have a learning disability?"

SPRINGBOARDS FOR REFLECTION AND DISCUSSION

1. What kinds of tests does your local school district use and why?
2. What are the pros and cons of classifying a student with a learning disability?
3. What would you suggest to parents who wanted their child evaluated?
4. Reflect on the problems encountered by Wilson's parents. They want what is best for him but are not sure what this is. Should he

be classified as having a learning disability? What kinds of services should be available to him? What could you say to his parents?

5. Why do you think the achievement–performance discrepancy formula has been so widely used despite its criticism?

6. Consider the ethical dilemma below. What would you do? It should be clear by now that the identification of students with learning disabilities is not an exact science.

However, there are situations in which it is clear that a student does not have a learning disability, yet the evaluation team so classifies her because that is the only way, in their school, to get appropriate services for this student. This becomes an ethical dilemma. Do you classify the student as having a learning disability knowing that she doesn't? Do you reject the classification of learning disability knowing that she will not get any services? There is no easy answer to these questions. What is clear is that schools need to provide carefully constructed educational interventions to all students in need. Yet, more and more schools simply do not have the funds for personnel and material. Some at-risk students have to fail badly to become eligible for services. Some have attributed the large number of students classified as having learning disabilities to this situation. Hopefully, with the NCLB law and more efficient and effective prereferral practices in place, these decisions will not have to be made.

CHAPTER 7
COLLABORATION WITH COLLEAGUES, FAMILIES, AND THE COMMUNITY

CHAPTER OBJECTIVES

At the end of this chapter you will be able to:

- understand the need to collaborate.
- employ specific collaborative strategies.
- understand the various coteaching approaches.
- develop competencies to enable you to work with families.
- understand the impact of a learning disability on the family and on the students in the community.

Mr. Marett and Ms. Gordon had worked in the same high school for over 20 years but had never worked together. They were well respected in their areas of expertise (his, social studies; hers, special education) and were friendly, collegial professionals. When their school district wanted to implement a coteaching model on the secondary school level, they asked for volunteers, who were gently coaxed by the administration to be in the forefront of this new approach. These highly respected professionals seized this opportunity to reenergize their teaching. They spent a few weeks with other colleagues and consultants exploring various coteaching models, learning strategies, and collaborative approaches. When the new school year began, they planned their lessons together during a common planning period. They employed a variety of techniques in their classroom, and it was apparent from Day 1 that they were equal partners in the process. They were sure of this, and they made it clear to their students. Through collaboration, consultation, and training, they honed their skills and became shin-

ing examples of how this process can work. They were not alone. Other colleagues shared their enthusiasm and, before long, decided to try this approach. Now, over 50 pairs of teachers are involved in coteaching. They say that they benefit from the expertise and camaraderie of their coteacher. They enjoy having another professional in the classroom and, most important, their students have benefited from this arrangement.

How would you feel about sharing your classroom? Would you prefer working alone? Do you think you will have a choice when applying for a teaching position? How difficult is coteaching? Clearly, it isn't for everybody, but prospective teachers who can work with others and embrace the collaborative model are strong candidates for teaching positions, as coteaching is a widely used, inclusive model. One cannot work in a school today without being willing and able to function in a collaborative environment. This chapter is divided into three sections. The first deals with colleagues, the second focuses on families, and the final one discusses manifestations of learning disabilities in the home and the community.

COLLABORATION

The role of the special educator has changed. The number of self-contained classes has declined drastically, and the number of students with learning disabilities who are being taught in regular education classes (80% of their day) has doubled in

the last decade (23rd Annual Report to Congress, 2001, Table AB8).

It is unusual for a teacher of students with learning disabilities to work alone. They are involved in building-level, prereferral, and multidisciplinary teams, and they probably will be coteaching for part of the school day. Klinger and Vaughn (2002) cite the need to train prospective learning disability specialists in collaboration and consultation due to the shift in their roles and responsibilities. Other researchers emphasize the need for collaborative practice (Mastropieri, Scruggs, Graetz, Norlad, Garchizi, & MuDuffie, 2005; Salend, 2005; Weiss & Lloyd, 2003).

What Is Collaboration?

Friend and Cook (2003) define interpersonal collaboration as "a style for direct interaction between at least two coequal partners voluntarily engaged in shared decision making as they work toward a common goal" (p. 5). They go on to say that coteaching is a style, a way of interacting, the nature of the relationship. This definition helps to clarify the term because **coteaching** has been used to describe many different activities in schools.

CHARACTERISTICS OF COLLABORATION

There is a consensus on the characteristics of collaboration. McLeskey and Waldron (2002), Weiss and Lloyd (2003), and Friend and Cook (2003) cite these defining characteristics of collaboration:

- Collaboration is voluntary.
- Collaboration requires parity among participants.
- Collaboration is based on mutual goals.
- Collaboration depends on shared responsibility for participation in decision making.
- Individuals who collaborate share resources.
- Individuals who collaborate share accountability for actions.

Each of these characteristics will now be discussed.

Collaboration Is Voluntary

Collaboration works best when school personnel participate in the collaboration process. They view this as valuable and believe that if they share ideas, expertise, and beliefs, students will benefit. They enjoy working on teams, like to share ideas,

and thrive on interpersonal contact. And yet, in many small school districts, it is difficult to carry out state and federal mandates, such as developing prereferral teams, solely on a volunteer basis. There are teachers and support staff who should be on the team or coteach. Therefore, waiting for volunteers may not be the best approach. Certain "volunteers" may need to be selected—those whom everyone agrees are critical for the success of the team. This does not suggest that the process should be closed; it merely recognizes that in small school districts, volunteers may need to be encouraged. Some school districts provide incentives for volunteers, such as credits, training, or extra pay. In certain school districts, most frequently coteachers are not volunteers but rather nontenured personnel. Too often, teams are overloaded with nontenured staff members who feel (rightly or wrongly) that they cannot refuse to collaborate if they want to receive tenure. Most teachers recognize that collaboration is here to stay and appreciate its benefits, but they may have too many other professional responsibilities. Therefore, while voluntary collaboration is a goal, it may not always be possible.

Collaboration Requires Parity Among Professionals

Effective collaborative teams value the input of all members. Good coteachers value each other's expertise. Without parity, it is difficult to function as a team. Parity does not mean that everyone has the same competencies. It merely means that all team members participate, and their expertise and opinions are valued. No one member has more power than the other. Obviously, schools are hierarchical. The principal is in charge. There are veteran teachers with seniority and new, nontenured teachers. Yet, for a collaborative team to function, all members must see each other as equal. The principal is just one member of the team when they are discussing options for a student.

If the principal overrides team decisions or does not allow adequate input from all members, the team will not be able to function effectively. With certain administrative structures and personalities, this may be a serious impediment.

Collaboration Is Based on Mutual Goals

This does not suggest that team members will always share the same goals. It does means that they are clear on the goal of the team. How that goal will be reached will vary, but the mission should be clear. For example, all members of the prereferral team should agree that the primary purpose of the team is to ensure that everything has been done for a student prior to a referral. Some members may view the team as a stalling tactic, postponing the inevitable classification. Others may view it as another mandate that will hurt their students and "keep the numbers down." And still others may view it as a worthwhile process. This team will not be able to function because the members' goals are so disparate. There may be disagreement on the specifics of the prereferral plan, but if the overall goal of the team is not mutually agreed upon, collaboration will not be possible.

Collaboration Depends on Shared Responsibility for Participation in Decision Making

Shared responsibility does not mean equal responsibility. In coteaching teams on the secondary school level, the content area specialist may do most of the content-area instruction. The special education teacher may be responsible for identifying those students who are not grasping the content and providing alternative approaches. This may not always work out to an equal division of labor, yet it is shared. The prereferral team may decide that a behavior plan needs to be developed for a particular student. Not every member of the team can do this, but all can participate on some level and share in the decision-making process. Over time, if roles appear to be dramatically unequal, teams need to reevaluate the way members participate, deliberate, and make decisions.

Individuals Who Collaborate Share Resources

For collaboration to succeed, all parties must share their resources. Therefore, if the speech pathologist has materials appropriate for a third grader who is being discussed by the prereferral team, they should be shared. If a social studies teacher has workbooks that are helpful in preparing for the state assessments, then these should be shared. Fortunately, most school personnel are more than willing to share their ideas and resources. If they are not, they are not good candidates for a collaborative project.

Individuals Who Collaborate Share Accountability for Actions

Sometime in your school career, you have worked on a group project, and felt that you did most of the work and that others were not responsible. This can happen in collaborative arrangements.

A coteacher says that he will call a parent and forgets to do so. A meeting is scheduled for 9 a.m. and someone forgot to reserve the room. It is up to the other members to function as a team and assume the responsibilities of the weak member. Hopefully, over time, responsibilities will balance out. If not, it will be necessary to reconsider the composition of the team.

Certain characteristics emerge over time. Initially, it may be difficult to get staff members to participate. Over time, they begin to trust one another, enjoy working together, and develop a sense of community. Finally, the collaboration reaches a point where other staff members become interested. When they see the benefits of collaboration and the increased satisfaction of their colleagues, they want to be included.

TEAMS

You will probably be asked to join a team in your school or district—the multidisciplinary team, the IEP team, or a prereferral and/or coteaching team. Effective collaborative teams have certain characteristics, regardless of what they are called. Thomas, Correa, and Morsink (1995) list the following 10 (p. 74):

1. *Legitimacy and autonomy.* Effective teams have recognized and supported functions and are free to operate independently.
2. *Purpose and objectives.* Effective teams have identified goals and work together sharing information and expertise to achieve these goals. The team members have a common set of norms and values that guide the team's functioning.
3. *Competencies of team members and clarity of their roles.* The members of effective teams are skilled not only in their own disciplines but also in collaborative problem solving, communication, and cultural diversity.
4. *Role release and role transitions.* Effective teams consist of members who can share their expertise with others, implement programs, use strategies from other disciplines, learn from others, and seek assistance and feedback
5. *Awareness of the individuality of others.* Effective teams consist of members who recognize and accept the perspectives, skill and experiences of others.
6. *Process of team building.* Effective teams are committed to the process of working together and functioning as a team. Conflicts between team members are resolved through problem solving, communication, and negotiation.
7. *Attention of factors that affect team functioning.* Effective teams use cooperative goals structures, create a supportive communication climate, share roles, and reach decisions through consensus.
8. *Leadership styles.* Effective teams rotate leadership responsibilities. Leaders are expected to solicit all points of view and involve all members in the decision-making process.
9. *Implementation procedures.* Effective teams consider a variety of factors when designing and implementing interventions.
10. *Commitment to common goals.* Effective teams are committed to collaborative goals and problem-solving techniques.

Multidisciplinary Teams

A key component of P.L. 94-142, the Education of All Handicapped Children Act, was the establishment of a multidisciplinary team to identify, evaluate, and place students. Prior to its enactment in 1975, it was not unusual for decisions regarding eligibility and placement to be made unilaterally, often by the school psychologist. This team had different names in different states—for example, the Committee on Special Education (CSE) in New York and the Student Study Team (SST) in California. This team is usually comprised of a regular education teacher, a psychologist, a special education teacher, a parent of a child with a disability who resides in the school district, and an administrator. Other professionals, such as an occupational therapist, a literacy specialist (also called a **reading teacher**), or other personnel deemed appropriate may also participate on the team. Various disciplines are requested to ensure that a number of perspectives are presented and that the decision is not made by one or a few individuals.

The IEP Team

Once a student is classified as having a learning disability, the IEP team must develop the IEP. The composition of the team is dictated by IDEA:

> IDEA provides guidelines for the composition of multidisciplinary teams. The term *individualized education program team* or *IEP team* means a group of individuals composed of—
>
> (i) the parents of a child with a disability;
> (ii) at least one regular education teacher of such child (if the child is, or may be, participating in the regular education environment):
> (iii) at least one special educator, or where appropriate, at least one special education provider of such child;
> (iv) a representative of the local education agency who—
>   a. is qualified to provide, or supervise the provision of, specially designed instruction to meet the unique needs of children with disabilities:

b. is knowledgeable about the general curriculum; and

c. is knowledgeable about the availability of resources of the local education agency;

(v) an individual who can interpret the instructional implications of evaluation results:

(vi) at the discretion of the parent or agency, other individuals who have knowledge or special expertise regarding the child, including related services personnel as appropriate; and

(vii) whenever appropriate, the child with a disability. IDEA-2004 no longer require short term objectives and benchmarks; annual goals still must be measurable.

An example of an IEP is presented in Table 7–1. There is no universally accepted form; therefore your school will differ from the one shown.

Developing Culturally Competent Teams

It is important that teams address issues related to a culturally and linguistically diverse student population. Schensul (1995), as cited in Craig, Hull, Haggart, and Perez-Selles (2000), suggests that cultural competence requires the following:

- A capacity for cultural self-assessment.
- The ability to understand one's own socio-cultural context.
- A willingness to ensure that these are good reasons or explanations for differences among groups.

It is critical that teams become culturally competent in order to meet the needs of diverse student populations. See the next section for questions that will guide your team in this process.

Research to Practice: Questions That Guide Culturally Competent Teams. Craig et al. (2000, p. 10) generated the following series of questions that can guide teacher assistance teams in becoming more culturally competent. These questions are appropriate for all types of pre-referral teams.

Questions About Cultural Context

1. What do we know about this student's linguistic, ethnic, and cultural background?

2. How would this child's family explain the student's behavior which is in question?

3. Do we notice the same or similar behaviors in other students with similar cultural backgrounds?

4. Is there any indication that the student's behavior has a cultural explanation?

Questions About Classroom Rules/Expectations

1. In what ways are students expected to respond to questions and directions?

2. In what ways are students expected to behave toward authority?

Questions About Classroom Practices

1. In what ways is the teacher using flexible grouping?

2. In what ways is the teacher compacting curriculum?

3. In what ways is the teacher promoting interdependence?

4. In what ways is the teacher differentiating instruction?

5. In what ways is the teacher celebrating diversity?

Questions to Promote Culturally Competent Recommendations

1. Are there rules, expectations, and response behaviors that need to be explicitly taught to this student?

2. Are there classroom practices that need to be added, refined, or eliminated to more effectively support this student?

3. Do we need more information about this student's background and socio-cultural context before we make recommendations for classroom adaptation?

COLLABORATIVE TEAMS

Remember Mr. Marett and Ms. Gordon (see Personal Perspectives: Reflection on Coteaching From a High School Team)? They had worked in the same school for a number of years but had never worked together. For this relationship to work, they had to get to know each other as teachers. An effective way to do this is to respond to questions on specific

TABLE 7–I Individualized Education Plan

I.D. #: _____ CSE Date: _____

Background/Current Placement

Student's Name: _____ D.O.B.: _____ G.A.: _____

Parent's Name: _____

Address: _____

Telephone: (H) _____ (W) _____ (C) _____

Student's Dominant Language: _____ Home Language: _____

Current School: _____ Grade: _____

Program: _____

CSE Recommendations

Nature of meeting: _____ Initial _____ Annual review _____ Triennial _____

Other Review: _____

Classification: _____

Placement: (specify) _____

Program:

_____ Related Services _____ Resource Room _____ Special Class

Other: _____

Class size: _____ Carnegie credits to date: _____

Specialized transportation: _____

Specialized equipment: _____

Twelve-month program: _____ Yes _____ No (site): _____

Regular phys. ed. program: _____ Yes _____ No

Adaptive phys. ed.: _____ Yes _____ No

Foreign language waiver: _____ Yes _____ No

Other waivers: _____

Transitional/Declassification Support: _____

Test Modifications

_____ None _____ Extended time _____ Special location

___ Use of calculator ___ Questions/directions ___ Braille/large type

___ Dictation of answers (use of tape recorder, word processor, or other)

_____ No penalty for spelling except on spelling tests

_____ Other:

Description of Educational Services

Percentage of day mainstreamed: _____

Percentage of day in special services: _____

Svcs/Class/Res. Rm.	Amount per Day	Days per Week	Person Responsible

Name: _____

Present Level of Educational Performance/Function Levels

Area	Name of Test	Date	Level
Reading-dec.			
Reading comp.			
Mathematics			
Written language			

(continued)

TABLE 7–I   Individualized Education Plan (*continued*)

Area	Name of Test	Date	Level
Spelling			
Other			
Other			

Classroom functioning/Least restrictive environment statement:
Learning Characteristics
Cognitive functioning: _____

Learning style: Modality strengths & weaknesses _____
Recommended strategies _____
Management Needs

_____ Classroom behavior does not interfere with instruction
_____ Classroom behavior may interfere with instruction
_____ Aggressive, self-abusive, withdrawn, or other behaviors
         requiring highly intensive supervision
_____ Severe impairment requiring habitation, treatment, and intensive monitoring
Comments: _____

Name _____
Social Development
Vision:
___Normal __Needs corrective lenses __Vision impairment ___Blind
Hearing:
___Normal _____ Mild loss _____ Hearing impairment _____Deaf
Current medications/treatments: _____
Special Alerts/Comments: _____
Educational Plan
Date of initial classification: _____
Projected date to begin this plan: _____
Current plan runs from _____ to _____
Projected date of review: _____
Evaluation Criteria: _____

Annual Goals	Short-Term Objectives

Committee on Special Educational Attendance
Committee members: Others in attendance:
Chairperson: _____   Teacher(s): _____
Psychologist: _____   Reading teachers: _____
Physician (if requested): _____ Parents: _____
Parent member: _____   Student: _____
L.D. specialist: _____   Others: _____
Speech/lang. pathologist: _____
Counselor: _____

Topic	Questions
Philosophy and Beliefs	What are our overriding philosophies about the roles of teachers and teaching and about students and learning? How do our instructional beliefs affect our instructional practice?
Parity Signals	How will we convey to students and others (e.g., teachers, parents) that we are equals in the classroom? How can we ensure a sense of parity during instruction?
Classroom Routines	What are the instructional routines for the classroom? What are the organizational routines for the classroom?
Discipline	What is acceptable and unacceptable student behavior? Who is to intervene at what point in students' behavior? What are the rewards and consequences used in the classroom?
Feedback	What is the best way to give each other feedback? How will we ensure that both positive and negative issues are raised?
Noise	What noise level are we comfortable with in the classroom?
Pet Peeves	What aspects of teaching and classroom life does each of us feel strongly about? How can we identify our pet peeves so as to avoid them?

FIGURE 7–1   Topics/Questions for Coteachers

Source: From Friend, Marilyn and Cook, L. *Interactions: Collaboration Skills for School Professionals,* 4/e. Published by Allyn and Bacon, Boston, MA. Copyright © 2002 by Pearson Education. Reprinted by permission of the publisher.

topics related to the coteaching relationship. Friend and Cook (2002) provide a useful set of questions to explore these important concerns. These should be addressed before the school year starts or very early in the year. It is also helpful to address these topics periodically throughout the school year, perhaps quarterly. The topics and questions are listed in Figure 7–2.

Personal Perspectivies: Reflections on Coteaching from a High School Team.   Mr. Marett and Ms. Gordon found coteaching very satisfying. Remember, these were two very competent teachers when they worked alone; they did not need help. Yet, the opportunity to work in a blended classroom containing both students with special educational needs and their peers without disabilities has made them even more competent. Some of their thoughts on coteaching are these:

"Having a partner makes you a better teacher."
"Gives you another perspective."

"All students benefited."
"Renewed respect and support for administration" (critical for success).
"Student behavior improves."
"Two expert educators teaching the class. What can be bad?"
"Training of teachers and commitment of district is the key to success."

On a more concrete level, one teacher who never liked to call parents and did not feed particularly effective when doing it. It was helpful that the coteacher didn't mind doing it and was better at it.

The most frequently cited coteaching approaches are described below (Friend & Cook, 2003; Rice & Zigmond, 2000; Weiss & Lloyd, 2002).

One Teach, One Observe

In this arrangement, one teacher is responsible for providing instruction, while the coteacher observes a particular student or group of students for specific reasons. For example, a math class in a middle school utilized this approach because the teachers could not figure out where a particular student broke down in writing specific equations. This method can also be utilized when there is a question about note-taking skills or attending behaviors.

One Teach, One Drift

One teacher circulates around the classroom assisting students, checking work, making sure that they understand the lesson, and so on. The coteacher is responsible for the overall lesson. In a kindergarten class one teacher might explain how to make a mask, using a variety of materials, while her coteacher moves about the room to make sure that all students are following the directions.

Station Teaching

Typically, the class is divided into three or four work "stations." The students move from station to station and complete the task. If there are three stations and two teachers, one station may call for independent work. In a middle school English class on poetry, one group utilized the computer to research a poet, another group read poems from various poets, and still another group wrote their own poems. In a high school English class, the students were assigned to five groups. Each group went to a station where members had to respond to specific questions about a book they were reading. They wrote their responses using a colored marker and evaluated the responses of other groups. At 10-minute intervals they moved to another station. Both teachers moved to various stations to comment on the work, respond to questions, and reinforce the group's effort and behavior.

Parallel Teaching

The coteacher divides the class in half, and each teacher teaches the same lesson. This reduces the class size and enables the teachers to assess students throughout the lesson. It also provides more opportunities for individual attention and reinforcement. It can be used in math classes, where complex problems with multiple directions are introduced. By dividing the class, the teachers can identify problems and use various methods to meet the needs of the smaller group.

Alternate Teaching

This arrangement allows one teacher to provide different instructions to a smaller group. It is useful when teachers need to reinforce a previous lesson, teach prerequisite skills, or provide for practice. If the teacher realizes that all the students who need these interventions have learning disabilities, the grouping strategies should be reconsidered.

Team Teaching

In this free-flowing approach, both teachers are responsible for instruction at the same time. They may alternate parts of the lesson, but neither one has the primary role. One may move around the room and interject a comment about a particular procedure. The two teachers mesh together, function as one, and begin to complete each other's sentences. When team teaching works well, there is a chemistry that makes learning exciting. However, there are potential problems when both teachers feel compelled to teach. There may simply be too much adult talk, and many students may find it distracting and difficult to focus on what is relevant and what is not.

How Do You Decide Which Coteaching Approach to Use?

A lot depends on the personalities and teaching styles of the coteachers. However, it seems reasonable to try different approaches, depending upon the grade and the subject taught. Trying different approaches also avoids the problem of getting into a rut and using the same approach repeatedly. In addition, it helps to ensure parity, as each coteacher is seen in a variety of roles.

WHAT DOES THE RESEARCH SAY ABOUT COTEACHING?

A review of the very limited research reported by the Division for Learning Disabilities and the Division for Research of the Council for Exceptional Children (2001) concluded that the research on student achievement is limited. The research base is inadequate, and continued research is needed. The authors note that much has been written on how to do coteaching, but there is little unequivocal evidence to support this practice. Mastropieri et al. (2005) examined coteaching in content areas, employing a case study approach. They found that "the relationship between the co-teachers is a major critical component influencing the success or failure of the inclusion of students with disabilities" (p. 260). So, what should you do if you are asked to coteach? Many schools are utilizing this type of team and report satisfaction among teachers. Perhaps a reasonable solution might be to conduct your own research. One district is currently examining student outcomes, as well as teachers', students', and parents' perceptions of the coteaching model in inclusive settings. By evaluating all aspects of the program, they may be able to make sound decisions on whether the time, effort, and money put into the program can be supported by results.

COLLABORATING WITH FAMILIES

Remember Wilson (see Chapter 4)? Wilson's family was remarkably cooperative with the university-based clinic that he attended and that his sister had attended in the past. He never missed a session, and if his mother could not bring him (by subway and bus), his sister did. Whatever the tutor recommended, the family did. This was not the case with his school; the teachers rarely had time for Wilson's family. The meeting times conflicted with his parents' work schedules, and no accommodations were made. His IEP was handwritten in English (their native language is Spanish), and was so jargon-laden and illegible that they couldn't understand it, regardless of the language. Notes were sent home (in English), and when Wilson's sister tried to get clarification, school personnel would not speak with her, only with Wilson's parents. Over the years the contacts became less frequent, and it was clear to Wilson's family that while the school may have cared about him, they didn't care about them. And Wilson's family is not alone.

Many families feel that there is no connection between them and the school. As you read the following comments from families, consider how you would feel and what you could do to make the relationship more collaborative.

- "Would it kill her to smile? Every meeting I attend, she sits there with this stern facial expression that makes everything seem so ominous."
- "Can't they find some adult chairs in the school? I know it sounds crazy, but I'm convinced they want you to be so uncomfortable that you can't wait to leave the meeting."
- "I was once told by a psychologist that I was just the mother; what did I know? At first I thought he was joking, but soon realized he wasn't. I never spoke to him again and requested another psychologist for my daughter."
- "I was given fifteen minutes to discuss my child's psychological, academic, and social progress in school. Fifteen minutes! They've got to be kidding. I need more time, more meetings, more contact. I feel so left out of his education."
- "I tape-record all of my school meetings so that I don't forget or misinterpret anything when I discuss it with my husband. Well, the last meeting, the principal brought a tape recorder, placed it on the table, and said, 'If you are going to tape the meeting so am I.' Why was she so threatened by this? I just don't get it."
- "It seems every time we have a meeting, they forget to get an interpreter. I'm tired of them grabbing someone, anyone, who works in the school, to translate for her. This is very hard, very personal, and I don't know who these people are."

The professional literature (Bauer & Shea, 2003; Kroth & Edge, 1997; Overton, 2005; Turnbull & Turnbull, 2001) provides ample support for the benefits of working collaboratively with parents and families. The collaborative process enables schools and families to utilize all available resources to achieve desired outcomes. Students benefit because all interested parties work together on their behalf. There has been a shift away from contacts solely with parent to broaden the support by including students' extended families. As the student population becomes increasingly diverse, we need to be able to collaborate in a variety of ways to include all family members who support the student. The following section discusses this new paradigm shift.

COLLABORATION WITH FAMILIES, NOT JUST PARENTS

The League of School Reaching Out (Davies, 1991; Edge & Franken, 1996) suggests expanding parent involvement to include other family members. The rationale is:

1. For many children, the term *family* includes more than parents; the latter is too narrow to describe the reality. Today, the child's primary family may consist of grandparents, aunts and uncles, or other persons.
2. Involvement goes beyond parents and families to include all social and community agencies that serve children. Urban families experiencing stress because they are having economic difficulties, struggling to find housing, or encountering barriers of language, culture, and social customs need assistance and support.
3. The new legal definitions do not require family members to come to school. Services and activities can take place in neighborhood settings and at home.
4. The new legal definitions include persons who lack English language proficiency, self-confidence, or the energy or time to take part

in traditional parent involvement activities, as well as those who fear schools because of cultural norms or negative school-related experiences.
5. The new legal definitions focus on families instead of on the agendas of teachers and administrators. They extend beyond purely academic functions to all contributions of families to their children's education.
6. The new legal definitions emphasize the inherent strengths of families instead of the old "deficit" perception of the traumas, troubles, and pathologies of urban families.

Guiding Principles for Parenting Programs

Teachers need to understand the needs of parents and develop collaborative relationships. Davis, Kroth, James, and Van Curen (1991, p. 2) established the following principles for developing programs to meet the needs of families:

1. Families are not a homogeneous group; therefore, services and programs should be individualized based on families' needs and preferences, and a variety of types and levels of activities should be provided (Kroth & Otteni, 1985).
2. "Parents have to be recognized as the special educators, the true experts on their children; and professional people—teachers, pediatricians, psychologists, and others—have to learn to be consultants" (Hobbs, 1978).
3. All families and children have strengths.
4. Most parents do care and do want to help their children; however, sometimes they lack the skills. These skills are teachable.
5. Lack of involvement may not reflect a lack of caring or concern, but rather overriding primary family needs that take first priority.
6. A variety of legitimate family forums can promote healthy child and family development.
7. Accepting and respecting diverse cultural, ethnic, and racial heritages, lifestyles, and values is essential.

8. Family involvement is critical across the years of childhood and adolescence.
9. Family involvement is not a separate, distinct component; it is integrated throughout the entire special education services system.
10. Successful family involvement is a long-term process. Program development takes time, commitment, and extensive work.

Culturally and Linguistically Diverse Families

Teachers must be able to collaborate with the families of all of their students. Classrooms are diverse, and teachers need to increase their own cross-cultural competence. One of the first things you as a teacher may want to do is become more aware of your own cultural perceptions.

Lynch and Hanson (1998), cited in Turnbull and Turnbull (2001) (p. 65), suggest a number of ways in which you can enhance your own cultural competence:

- Learn about the families in the community served. What cultural groups are represented? Where are they from? When did they arrive? How closely knit is the community? What language(s) is spoken? What are the cultural practices associated with child rearing? What cultural beliefs surround health and healing, disability, and causation? Who are the community leaders and/or spiritual leaders, and what are their roles in advising and counseling families?
- Work with cultural mediators or guides for the families' cultures to learn more about the extent of cultural identification within the community at large and the situational aspects of this identification and regional variations.
- Learn and use words and forms of greeting in the families' languages if families are English-language learners: ensure that trained interpreters are present for assessments and meetings with family members.

- Allow additional time to work with interpreters to determine families' concerns, priorities, and resourses, and to determine the next steps in the process. Remember that rapport building may take considerable time but that it is critical to effective intervention.
- Recognize that some families may be surprised by the extent of parent–professional collaboration that is expected in intervention programs in the United States. Do not expect every family to be comfortable with such a high degree of involvement. However, never assume that they do not want involvement and are not involved from their own perspective. Likewise, do not assume that they will become involved or will feel comfortable doing so.
- Use as few written forms as possible with families who are English-language learners or non-English speaking. If forms are used, be sure that they are available in the family's language. Rely on the interpreter, your observations, and your own instincts and knowledge to know when to proceed and when to wait for the family to signal the readiness to move to the next step.
- Recognize the power differentials that many families experience between agency representatives and themselves; be aware of the larger sociopolitical climate that is influencing families' decision making.

There is a danger in formulating stereotypic notions of "African American" or "Hispanic" or "Asian" or "Native American" families. No prototypical family represents each group. Rather, teachers need to appreciate the unique needs of a wide variety of families who do not share their language or culture. This notion of *cultural reciprocity* (Kalyanpur & Harry, 1999) allows teachers to appreciate belief systems that may differ from their own. It enables them to listen to the families' stories and appreciate their perceptive. Turnbull and Turnbull (2001) provide a few suggestions for developing an "Adapted Posture of Cultural Reciprocity" (p. 66):

1. Learn about the family's strengths, needs and expectations that evolve from the "family story." Also find out the priorities and preferences for their child's educational program—IEP, placement, related services, extracurricular activities, and so on. Seek to understand and honor the cultural values and priorities as you establish a reliable alliance with them.

2. Converse with the family about the assumptions that underlie the cultural values and priorities. Seek to find out about their rationales.

3. As you reflect on their priorities and preferences, identify any disagreements or alternative perspectives that you or other professionals have, as compared to those of the family, associated with providing educational supports and services to the student and/or family. Identify the cultural values that are embedded in your underlying interpretation or the interpretation of other professionals. Identify how the family's views differ from your own.

4. Acknowledge and give explicit respect to any cultural differences identified, and fully explain the cultural basis of your professional assumptions or the assumptions of other professionals.

5. For discussion and collaboration, determine the most effective way of adapting your professional interpretations to the family's value system.

COMMUNICATING WITH FAMILIES

Teachers are in the advice-giving business. They are used to solving problems and identifying solutions. However, communicating with families requires more. One skill that is necessary for successful communication is listening. Bauer and Shea (2003, pp. 154–155) suggest six skill areas of active listening that teachers should attend to:

1. Hear the message
   - Concentrate on what the speaker is saying
   - Take control of the listening environment, minimizing distractions and having everything you need at hand
   - Be ready when the speaker begins—pay attention from the first word

   - Look like a listener—sit up, look at the speaker, and nonverbally communicate that you are interested

Example: A student's father has come by and asks to talk with you after school. You face the parent, inviting him to begin. The area is quiet and private. You are sitting up, nodding, and looking at the parent.

2. Work at understanding the message
   - Put your ego aside, paying attention to what the individual is saying rather than formulating your response
   - Monitor your behavior
   - Don't interrupt—it stops the speaker's flow of thought and makes it harder to follow the message

Example: Parent states, "This is the worst year my son has ever had in school." Rather than responding, you nod and wait for him to continue.

3. Remember the message
   - Repeat the content back to the speaker
   - Remain calm—it's hard to remember what is said if you are angry or stressed

Example: You respond, "This has been a difficult year?" and look at the speaker encouragingly.

4. Interpret the message
   - Keep the speaker's background, goals, and role in mind
   - Think about the speaker's nonverbal communication
   - Watch for the relationship between verbal and nonverbal cues
   - Attend to the speaker's voice
   - Identify the level of communication: Is the speaker stating fact or opinion? Is the speaker communicating feelings?

Example: You recognize that the father must be truly upset because this is the first time he has ever come to school. You notice that he is agitated and holding a note in his hand. His voice is trembling, and he has to stop to gather himself.

5. Evaluate the message
   - Think about the speaker's credibility
   - Try to follow the speaker's line of reasoning
   - Consider the speaker's evidence or lack of evidence

Example: The father states that he never knows what's going on with his son. He tries to talk to the child's mother but doesn't seem to get any answers. He received a letter indicating that his son did not pass the proficiency test and didn't even know he was taking the test.

6. Respond to the message
   - Reflect the speaker's message, paraphrasing to check understanding
   - Provide perception checks
   - Continue a supportive listening climate
   - Be physically alert, maintaining eye contact, but minimize gestures and random movements

Example: You reflect back to the parent: "You're concerned that you hadn't received earlier information about the test." "You were unaware that your son was taking the test."

FORMAL MEETINGS

Many meetings can be characterized as formal meetings, such as those required by law (IEP, multidisciplinary team) or district policy (parent-teacher conferences, open school night). By contrast, there are times when the teacher calls a family regarding a child's progress, or has a chance meeting on the street, in a mall, or at a baseball game. These informal meetings also provide an opportunity to share and collaborate. In both cases, the teacher must be well prepared.

The IEP Conference

The purpose of the IEP conference is to incorporate parents' ideas into the student's educational program and to discuss with parents the teacher's focus for the year. The special education teacher would be wise to consult with, or have present, regular classroom teachers who are involved with the student. Much can be done prior to, during, and after the conference to make parents feel that they are productive members of the team.

Before the Conference. Before developing or updating the IEP, the teacher should schedule a group-parent meeting. IDEA 2004 allows for updating and making minor changes without having a formal meeting if the family agrees. The major purpose of such a meeting is to explain the purpose of the IEP and to inform parents of their legal rights. The meeting can also acquaint the parents with the format used by the school district. Letting parents know the rationale for the conference and the delivery of services provided for in the IEP will help establish lines of communication. Often parents sign the IEP signifying their approval of the program, only to find that they are not receiving appropriate related services provided for by law. Obviously, this does little to build a trusting relationship between the home and the school. Being clear, precise, and honest with parents will increase their ability to help carry out the educational plan. It will also help allay any anxieties they may have regarding the parent-teacher conference.

For parents to offer meaningful input to the IEP, they must have time to formulate their ideas. Coming to a meeting and being asked for suggestions cannot be considered "meaningful input." Teachers should send a letter to parents (see Figure 7–2) at least 2 weeks prior to the conference requesting their ideas about the student's educational program and including a stamped, addressed envelope. This lets them know that their input is important and will be considered by the teacher. If parents do not respond to the letter, a phone call can be made in an attempt to get this important information.

During the Conference. Teachers must do everything possible to make parents realize that they are a vital component of their child's or adolescent's education. One way to do this is to hold the meeting in a room other than the classroom. Classrooms are often filled with distracting stimuli, and rarely with enough room for a table and comfortable chairs. If the meeting must be in a classroom, the teacher should never sit behind the desk. This arrangement creates a physical, and perhaps psychological, barrier between the teacher and the parents. In addition, if *any* student's work is displayed, *all* students' work should be displayed. A circular table is preferred because no one is at the head and is therefore perceived as most

Student: _____

Teacher: _____

Date: _____

On (date) we will meet to develop or update the individual educational plan for your child. Any ideas, thoughts, and concerns you have regarding the educational program for the year will be greatly appreciated. Feel free to use additional paper if necessary. Looking forward to seeing you.

Signed: _____

FIGURE 7–2   Parent Information Form

important or most powerful. If possible, refreshments should be available to reinforce the message that the teacher is pleased to have the opportunity to plan this program with the parents.

After the Conference.   A follow-up phone call or letter to the family can help establish a collaborative relationship. It provides feedback and allows the teacher to clarify any issues and respond to parents' concerns.

INFORMAL MEETINGS

Informal meetings are important to families and are a valuable way to communicate. If you meet a parent in the hallway at the end of the day, or at a school or social event like a baseball game, it is necessary to establish clear parameters without being offensive. You may want to keep the conversation lighthearted and defer discussing substantive matters until your records are available. Parents will appreciate your need to provide them with specific information and the importance of being prepared for the meeting. There are times when you will run into a parent on the street or in the local mall. Again, it is fine to be friendly and sociable while considering issues of confidentiality. You need to be clear about not sharing information that is best reserved for a different setting. Finally, phone calls are an important way for some

families to communicate with schools. Turnbull and Turnbull (2001, p. 190) adapted some excellent suggestions for the Parent Center of the Albuquerque Public School (1995) when using the telephone:

- Treat every message (incoming or outgoing) as an important call.
- Always identify yourself as you place a call or answer one. When you return, thank the caller for waiting. (On long-distance calls, make every effort to avoid putting a parent on "hold.")
- Always offer the caller or person being called your help or assistance.
- Allow time for parents to ask you their questions.
- Return all calls promptly; the exception, of course, is if you are involved in the classroom with students.
- Give definite information and offer positive information.
- Avoid the use of vague statements that may force the caller to dig for information. Vague statements are irritating and waste time.
- As the conversation ends, thank the caller before you say goodbye.

USING TECHNOLOGY TO COLLABORATE

One of the most widely used forms of technology is the Internet. Many schools have access to it, as do public libraries and families. However, not all families can afford a computer, and not all families are computer literate. They may not feel comfortable sharing that information with you. And while the Internet is one more way of collaborating, it may not be accessible to a variety of families for many reasons. Some schools provide home assistance to students and their families via the Internet, and there are innumerable sites dealing with children with disabilities (see http://www.ldonline.org and http://www.ld.org). Teachers must be careful not to exclude families who can't, won't or don't want to utilize technology to enhance collaboration.

A helpful low-tech method to collaborate with parents is the use of videos. Many teachers send home videotapes that model appropriate instruction in order to assist the family. Others model a particular behavioral intervention to provide consistency in behavior at home and at school. The same caution noted for computers applies here: some families may not have access to a VCR and require other ways to collaborate.

MANIFESTATIONS OF LEARNING DISABILITIES IN THE HOME AND COMMUNITY

Learning disabilities do not disappear at 3:00 p.m. or on weekends. Every aspect of the child's or adolescent's life can be affected by a learning disability. Simple routines, such as those of meals, bedtime, and homework, can cause problems at home for the entire family. The list of possible difficulties is endless. Teachers need to be cognizant of the ways in which specific learning disabilities manifest themselves in the home and community.

Considers Michael's family. There are three boys between the ages of 5 and 11, Michael being the oldest. His parents live in an upper-middle-class suburban community where academic success is highly regarded. Michael was diagnosed with a learning disability at 7 years of age. His oral language skills are above average, as is his intellectual level, but his ability to read is significantly below

expectations. His parents have tried a variety of approaches outside of school, and he is making small gains in school. Yet, the gap is widening. Michael's parents told his teacher that they are less concerned with his performance in school than when he is out of school, especially at family functions. A trip to the local restaurant can cause anxiety. Once, when Michael's grandmother accompanied them, she asked him to read the menu. Although she was well aware of his reading problem, she found it incomprehensible that this bright, verbal boy couldn't read. He fumbled, began to turn red, perspired, and finally cried. His mother became angry at her mother and they all left the restaurant in a huff, screaming at each other without having eaten. Michael's mother wonders if they will ever be able to go to a local restaurant like a normal family, or to a family party, and not worry about Michael's being embarrassed, or saying the wrong thing, or dealing with the realization that Michael's younger brother can read better than him. She does not know what to do. In her mind, school is the least of Michael's problems.

How can you help Michael's family? Are there times when you can become too involved? What community resources are available to you and Michael's family?

SUMMARY

This chapter has focused on collaboration in a variety of settings. It is no longer possible for teachers of students with learning disabilities to work in isolation. To succeed, they need to develop collaborative relationships with their colleagues and with the parents and other family members of their students. This chapter has also discussed the various teams teachers may join, as well as ways to appreciate and assist the families of students both in and out of school. A learning disability is not just a school-related disorder; it impacts the home and the community. This knowledge will make teachers more effective and enable their students to have a full, rich, rewarding life in and out of school.

SPRINGBOARDS FOR REFLECTION AND DISCUSSION

1. Do you prefer working alone or with others? What are some changes that you must make to be a good team member?
2. How do you feel about coteaching? Would you mind having a colleague in your classroom? In your journal, reflect on how you feel about this relationship and what you would need to make it effective.
3. Attend a special education parent-teacher association meeting to become aware of the needs of parents.
4. If you are in a field placement, ask if you can attend a parent-teacher conference, an IEP meting, or a multidisciplinary team meeting. How would you feel if you were related to the student being discussed? What would you like to tell the team members about yourself? What would you like to know about them? How will you communicate with each other?

5. Attend a social, religious, or cultural function of a racial/ethnic group other than your own. What were you impressions? How did you feel? How could this experience help you as a teacher?
6. Attend an extracurricular activity at school (e.g., a basketball game, a chess club meeting) in which your student is involved. Is it apparent that your student has a learning disability? How could you help?
7. Interview an adult with a learning disability to see how it has impacted this individual's life, job, and family.
8. Complete the chart below for students on your class. One example (Memory) is provided. In the "Disability" column, write down the areas in which the student has difficulty. Then write down how this difficulty manifests itself in the "School," the "Home," and the "Community" columns. This can be helpful in a parent-teacher conference. It should be an ongoing process, with you adding to the list as the concerns become apparent.

STUDENT'S NAME_____

Learning Disabilities in the School, Home, and Community

Disability	School	Home	Community
Memory	Forgets assignment Forgets homework Poor comprehension Poor test grades	Forgets to take dog out Doesn't remember birthdays Is always late Doesn't call back friends	Can't follow rules of game Doesn't remember when the Scout meeting was Is always late for games

RESOURCES FOR PARENTS

Effective teachers of students with learning disabilities recognize that parents benefit from contact with other parents and with organizations. Schwab Learning (http://www.schwablearning.org) provides the following list of organizations that parents can contact for additional information and support:

- The International Dyslexia Association (IDA)—an international organization offering information and referral and other services for people with dyslexia and related difficulties in learning to read and write.
  www.interdys.org
  (410) 296-0232
  (800) ABCD123 (toll free)
- Learning Disabilities Association of America (LDA)—a parent-driven national organization offering support groups and information to help families dealing with learning disabilities.
  www.LDAAmerica.org
  (888) 575-7373 (toll free)
  (212) 545-7510
- National Center for Learning Disabilities (NCLD)—a national organization that develops and delivers research-based programs for teachers and parents, shapes public policy and maintains an online database of learning disabilities resources.
  www.ncld.org
  (888) 575-7373 (toll free)
  (212) 545-7510
- Schwab Learning—an online guide to the landscape of learning disabilities, developed by the Charles and Helen Scwab Foundation especially for parents of children who are newly identified with a learning disability.
  www.schwablearning.org
  (800) 655-2410
- Council for Learning Disabilities (CLD)—an international organization that promotes new research and effective ways to teach people with learning disabilities.
  www.cldinternational.org.
  (913) 492-8755
- Division for Learning Disabilities (DLD)—an international group of teachers, university professors and researchers who work to improve education for people with learning disabilities. DLD is part of The Council for Exceptional Children.
  www.dldcec.org
  (888) 232-7733 (toll free)

Another very good resource on the World Wide Web is www.ldonline.org.

8 CHAPTER EDUCATIONAL PLACEMENTS

CHAPTER OBJECTIVES

At the end of this chapter you will be able to:

- identify the trends in placement decisions for students with learning disabilities.
- understand the rationale for educational placements.
- identify the reasons for inclusion.
- understand the major components of an inclusive program.
- identify the reasons for the development of the resource room.
- understand the major components of the resource room model.

The majority of students with learning disabilities spend 80% of their school day in regular education classrooms alongside their peers without disabilities. This was not always the case. Early programs during the 1960s and 1970s placed students with learning disabilities in self-contained classrooms with other students with learning disabilities and a special education teacher. During the 1970s, there was a shift toward the resource room model with the emphasis on the least restrictive environment in P.L. 94–142, the Education of All Handicapped Children Act of 1975. This act, and the emphasis on inclusion, have changed the way services for students with disabilities are provided in schools. The shift since the 1990s has been dramatic.

What do you think is the best placement for students with learning disabilities? As a teacher of these students, you may have to wear many "hats." Do you think it would be difficult to be a resource room teacher and provide push services in a regular classroom rather than in the resource room (referred to as **push-in**)? How would you feel about being in a coteaching arrangement and spending your entire day in a regular classroom? These are real concerns of teachers in the field as a variety of educational placements are explored by school districts trying to meet the needs of students and comply with federal and state mandates regarding the least restrictive environment.

This chapter discusses the rationale for this shift and describes a variety of educational placements for students with learning disabilities.

LEAST RESTRICTIVE ENVIRONMENT

Students are required by law to be placed in the least restrictive environment. Educational Placements move from most restrictive to least restrictive on a continuum. Many years ago, Deno (1970) developed the following cascade of services for students with special educational needs:

Restrictiveness of Educational Placement

10. Hospital or Institution
9. Homebound Instruction
8. Residential School
7. Special Day School
6. Full-time Special Education Classroom
5. Special Education Classroom with Part Time in General Education Classroom
4. General Education Classroom Placement with Resource Room Assistance
3. General Education Classroom Placement with Itinerant Teacher
2. General Education Classroom Placement with Collaboration Teacher Assistance
1. General Education Classroom Placement with Few or No Supportive Services

It is rare for students with learning disabilities to be placed in environments 6 through 10. The Twenty-Second Annual Report to Congress from the U.S. Department of Education (2000) indicated that most students with learning disabilities spend their school day in regular education classes, either full-time (44%) or part-time (39% receive resource room services). Only 16% of all students with learning disabilities are in self-contained classes. This represents a dramatic shift since 1990, when 17% of these students were placed in regular classrooms, 59% in the resource room, and 21% in separate classes. As a teacher of students with learning disabilities, you will most likely work in an inclusive setting or resource room—or perhaps in a combination of placements. It is less likely that you will teach in a self-contained class of students with learning disabilities.

MAINSTREAMING AND THE LEAST RESTRICTIVE ENROLLMENT

In the past, the term **mainstreaming** was employed when a student with learning disabilities was educated alongside his or her peers without such disabilities. There is great variability in the procedures associated with mainstreaming, and with the increasing popularity of **inclusion**, the former term is used less often. Neither mainstreaming nor inclusion is mentioned in federal or state mandates. The term that is employed and that has guided these practices is **least restrictive environment** (LRE).

In a training package on the IDEA amendments of 1975, developed by the Office of Special Education Programs, the National Information Center for Children and Youth with Disabilities (NICHCY) and the Federal Resource Center for Special Education (1997) discuss the LRE. This is the environment where the student can receive an appropriate education designed to meet his or her special educational needs while still being educated with peers without disabilities to the maximum extent possible. Depending on the student's individual needs, the LRE could be the regular classroom, with or without supplementary aids and services; a pull-out program for part of the day, with the remainder of the day being spent in the regular classroom or in activities with students

who do not have disabilities; a special education class in the student's neighborhood school; or even a separate school specializing in certain types of disabilities. Thus, one student's LRE may be very different from that of another student. The determining factor is the student's needs. When deciding upon the LRE, the multidisciplinary team must consider the following:

- Is the placement based on the student's identified strengths and needs?
- Does the decision consider whether the student could achieve any of his or her IEP goals in a general education class, including special classes, with the use of supplementary aids and services?
- Does the decision consider whether modification of the curriculum could enable the student to meet any of his or her goals in general education classes?
- Does the decision consider all options on the continuum from special to regular education?
- Does the recommendation consider opportunities for the student to participate with students without disabilities in nonacademic and extracurricular activities?
- Does the recommendation consider potential harmful effects of removal from the general education setting or on the quality of services that the student needs?
- Does the recommendation consider proximity to the student's home?

For the majority of students with learning disabilities, the LRE is the regular classroom setting. IDEA 2004 continues to emphasize the importance of the LRE. Let's take Aaron as an example.

When Aaron was 3 years old, he was classified as a "student with special needs," due to a language-based disorder, and attended a private school for preschoolers with special educational needs. When he was screened for kindergarten, he continued to exhibit receptive and expressive language problems. His parents assumed he would be placed in a self-contained class, but the recommended placement was an inclusive kindergarten class. There are two teachers in Aaron's class, and they employ a variety of coteaching approaches (see Chapter 7). Frequently, they use the station teaching approach and make sure that Aaron is integrated into a group with learners on all levels. So far he is doing remarkably well, exceeding his IEP goals. Three times a week, a speech-language pathologist comes into the classroom and conducts a "language lesson" with the entire class. Once a week, she meets with Aaron's teachers to discuss ways they can facilitate his language production. All of them are optimistic that he will continue to make good progress in his inclusive class. At some point in the future, he may be able to function in the LRE of a regular classroom with one teacher and resource room support.

INCLUSION

The emphasis on the LRE has increased inclusionary practices for students with learning disabilities (see Best Practices: In Inclusion, One Size Does Not Fit All).

Early advocates of inclusion (Biklin & Zollers, 1986; Garner & Lipsky, 1987; Will, 1986) recommended totally integrated programs for students with special educational needs. As was the case in the past in the field of learning disabilities, this recommendation was based more on public policy than research findings. A number of studies (Hocutt, 1996; Holloway, 2001; Manset & Semmel, 1997; Murawski & Swanson, 2002; Rea, McLaughlin, & Walther-Thomas, 2002; Waldren & McLeskey, 1998) produced equivocal findings. Essentially, they found that some placements were effective and others were not. No one service delivery model was more effective than others. As Zigmond (2003) notes, "research does not support the superiority of any one service delivery model over another" (p. 120). What does matter is what goes on in those settings. The time on task and the type of instruction (explicit and intense) are more important than the location. At this time, additional research is needed on student outcomes, not specific delivery models. We need to accumulate evidence that will enable placement decisions based on what works best for an individual student with learning disabilities. Where does this leave you? As a teacher of students with learning disabilities, you will most likely spend most of your career in an inclusive setting. What matters is what you do in that setting. Your job will be to meet the needs of your students whether you are a coteacher providing push-in services in the regular classroom and/or providing services in the resource room. The quality of instruction in those placements is more important than the placement itself.

PRINCIPLES OF INCLUSION

Inclusion means many things to many people. Full inclusion means that a student with learning disabilities is in a regular classroom full time, and all services are provided in that classroom at the student's current grade level. Salend (2001) states that inclusion is designed to change schools in such a way that the needs of all students can be met, not just those who are classified as requiring special education. Inclusion is a philosophy that encourages and appreciates diversity in our schools. Salend lists the four following principles of effective inclusion (pp. 8–9):

Diversity

Effective inclusion improves the educational system for all students by placing them together in general education classrooms regardless of their learning ability, race, linguistic ability, economic status, gender, learning style, ethnicity, cultural background, religion, family structure, and sexual orientation. Inclusionary schools welcome, acknowledge, affirm, and celebrate the value of *all* learners by educating them together in high-quality, age-appropriate general education classrooms in their neighborhood schools. *All students* have opportunities to earn and play together, and participate in educational, social, and recreational activities. These inclusionary practices, which promote acceptance, equity, and collaboration, are responsive to individual needs and embrace diversity.

Individual Needs

Effective inclusion involves sensitivity to and acceptance of individual needs and differences. Educators cannot teach students without taking into account the factors that shape their students and make them unique. Forces such as disability, race, linguistic background, gender, and economic status interact and affect academic performance and socialization; therefore, educators, students, and family members must be sensitive to individual needs and differences. In inclusive classrooms, *all students* are valued as individuals capable of learning and contributing to society. They are taught to appreciate diversity and to value and learn from each other's similarities and differences.

Reflective Practice

Effective inclusion requires reflective educators to modify their attitudes, teaching and classroom management practices, and curricula to accommodate individual needs. In inclusive classrooms, teachers are reflective practitioners who are flexible, responsive, and aware of students' needs. They think critically about their values and beliefs and routinely examine their own practices for self-improvement and to ensure that *all students'* needs are met. Educators individualize education and differentiate instruction for all students in terms of assessment, techniques, curriculum accessibility, teaching strategies technology, physical design adaptations, and a wide array of related services based on their needs. Students are given a multiple and multimodality curriculum, as well as challenging educational and social experiences that are consistent with their abilities and needs.

Collaboration

Effective inclusion is a group effort; it involves collaboration among educators, other professionals, students, families, and community agencies. The support and services that students need are provided in the general education classroom. People work cooperatively and reflectively, sharing resources, responsibilities, skills, decisions, and advocacy for the student's benefit. School districts provide support, training, time, and resources to restructure their programs to support individuals in working collaboratively to address student's needs.

To succeed, inclusion requires a great deal of collaboration (see Chapter 7). This process cannot occur without planning and input from all contributors.

The Wisconsin Education Association Council (1996) recommends the following when moving toward an inclusive approach:

1. A continuum of placements, supports and services should be made available for all students, but always assume that every student's first placement is in regular education.
2. All placement decisions should be based on a well-developed IEP with an emphasis on the needs of the child, her/his peers and the reasonable provision of services.
3. Top-down mandated full inclusion is inappropriate. Neither federal nor state law requires full inclusion.
4. Before any new programs are developed, the building staff must agree on a clearly articulated philosophy of education (and education ethic). Teachers and support staff must be fully involved in the decision-making, planning and evaluation processes for individual students and building-wide programs.
5. Extensive staff development must be made available as part of every teacher's and paraprofessional's workday. Areas of emphasis include:
   - Emphasis on higher-order thinking skills
   - Integrated curricula
   - Interdisciplinary teaching
   - Multicultural curricula
   - Life-centered curricula
6. Work toward unifying the special education and regular education systems. For instance, separate evaluators and evaluation systems are counterproductive. There should be one system.
7. Ensure that sufficient licensed practitioners are employed to address the social, emotional, and cognitive needs of all students. In inclusive settings, reduced class sizes and/or increased numbers of teachers in the classroom are necessary.
8. Appeal processes must be developed that allow teachers to challenge the implementation of IEPs and placements that they determine to be inappropriate for a child.
9. Involve parents and students as partners in the decision-making process.
10. When developing programs, consider multiple teaching/learning approaches like team teaching, co-teaching, peer partners, cooperative learning, heterogeneous grouping, study team planning, parallel teaching, station teaching, etc.

The Wisconsin Education Association Council (1996) concluded that it is critical that any district

or school considering more inclusive practices take the time necessary to plan effectively. Attention to special education students and staff alone is only half a strategy. Planning should involve all stakeholders in researching, discussing, and examining the entire educational program. Real inclusion involves restructuring of a school's entire program and requires constant assessment of practices and results. (See Salend, 2005, and Lewis and Doorlag, 2006, for ways to evaluate the effectiveness of your program.)

Best Practices: In Inclusion, One Size Does Not Fit All. What is the best model for inclusion? Currently, there is no research to support one best approach, and most programs are developed and implemented based on local needs and financial considerations. It seems obvious, for example, that having two teachers in the same classroom all day is ideal. However, this is not financially viable for many school districts because it would require hiring additional staff. Schools need to consider the number of students in inclusive settings and the continuum of services that need to be available; this is required by law. Also, the size of the district will dictate the type of program. Large districts have more flexibility in deploying staff and determining educational placement. Most school districts approach the inclusive process in a slow, thoughtful manner. Once a decision regarding placement is made, they have a variety of options. However, for the student with learning disabilities, this usually means resource room placement. When an elementary school student is placed in an inclusive setting, he or she may have two certified teachers (one special educator, one regular educator) all day long. The teachers receive extensive training in collaboration and instructional strategies. On the middle and high school levels, a student may be in one or two inclusive classes and the remainder of the day in a self-contained class. These students also receive instruction from two teachers (a content area specialist and a special education teacher).

RESOURCE ROOM

Almost 40% of students with learning disabilities receive support in the resource room. School districts may also provide services similar to those in the resource room but employ another name such as **skills center** or **study skills**. Many times these services support the inclusive classroom and allow the district to provide services without the restriction on class size mandated for the resource room. For many, the resource room model is synonymous with services for students with learning disabilities.

Definition

The resource room is a classroom where students come for part of their instructional day to receive special education services. However, it is more than a physical space. It is a concept that calls attention to the fact that students with learning disabilities can benefit from regular classroom placement. A special education student placed in a resource room program still has considerable time (over 50%) in the regular classroom. Although most states have guidelines on the amount of time to be spent in the resource room, the important point is not the specified time, but rather the idea that this placement is significantly different from the special education self-contained class. In the self-contained class, the student spends most of the day with and receives primary instruction from the special education teacher. By contrast, the student with learning disabilities who is placed in a resource room spends no more than half of the day there and receives supplemental instruction from the special education teacher. Primary instruction takes place in the regular classroom.

The resource room teacher provides the student with strategies to succeed in the regular classroom. This arrangement represents a markedly different way of providing services to students with learning disabilities and has produced some confusion for special and regular educators alike (McNamara, 1989).

Rationale

Although many attribute the popularity of the resource room to the mainstreaming movement, its origins appear to have a stronger base. Early proponents of the resource room model pointed to the increasing uneasiness with self-contained special classes for educable mentally retarded students. Dunn (1968), in his now classic article, questioned the justification of placing students with mild disabilities (including those with learning disabilities) in self-contained classes. He was not alone in his concern. Readers interested in investigating the many issues can peruse the large literature on the efficacy of self-contained special education classes (see Dunn, 1968; Johnson, 1962; MacMillan, 1971; Pertsh, 1936; Shattuck, 1946; Van Etten & Adamson, 1973). Essentially, the placement of students in self-contained classes could not be supported by empirical evidence.

If the self-contained classroom was no longer viewed as an acceptable alternative to regular education for students with learning disabilities, how could special education services be provided to them? What appeared necessary was a service delivery model that allowed students to be educated with their peers without disabilities to the maximum extent possible, and at the same time to receive special education in areas of need. This led to the development and implementation of the resource room model.

There is little doubt that resource room programs gained impetus from the mainstreaming movement and the placement of students in the LRE. However, it is important to be aware that special education resource room programs were developed on the basis of instructional need, not as a result of legislative or administrative dictates.

THE ROLE OF THE RESOURCE ROOM TEACHER

There is widespread agreement in the professional literature on the role of the special education resource room teacher. Wiederholt, Hammill, and Brown (1983) divide the responsibilities of the job into three major categories: assessment, teaching, and consulting. Others employ a wide variety of administrative structures to discuss similar role functions. For example, Jenkins and Mayhall (1976) differentiate between indirect and direct services. The former focus on identification of the academic and behavioral skills that must be taught, development and monitoring of the intervention plan, and ongoing communication with the regular classroom teacher. The latter are the services provided to the student. Reger (1973), one of the earliest proponents of the resource room model, believes that special education resource room teachers must provide regular classroom teachers with appropriate models for teaching the student with special needs. They do this through consultation and formal in-service training. The current demand for more thorough staff development programs provides the resource room teacher with ample opportunities for consultation and training. As others have noted (Cienion, 1968; Hallerick, 1969; McNamara, 1989; Sabatino, 1972), these functions are in addition to the assessment and teaching responsibilities.

The role of the special education resource room teacher is more complex than is often realized. Reger (1972) has elevated the role to that of an expert and notes that to be an effective practitioner, one must understand the major functions included in this role. Clearly, these functions will vary from one school district to another. However, it is evident that evaluation of the educational problem, development and implementation of the intervention plan, and ongoing communication with regular educators are major components of the role, regardless of the setting. Reiter (1986) examined resource room teachers' perception of their role. The findings were consistent with those of other investigators. The role has three components: educational evaluation implementing and evaluating the intervention plan, and communicating with regular classroom teachers. The next three sections provide an overview of these components.

Conducting Educational Evaluations

Resource room teachers, along with school psychologists, are typically responsible for evaluating the academic and behavioral skills of students who are placed in the resource room or who may be placed there in the future. Hammill and Bartel (1971) note that schools evaluate students for three reasons: classification, placement, and planning an educational program. The last reason is of critical importance to the resource room teacher. By definition, children attending the resource room spend most of their school day in a regular classroom. Therefore, the assessment should be related to the curriculum: basic skills on the elementary level and content areas on the middle and secondary levels. Frequently, a disproportionate amount of time is engaged in "diagnoses for identification versus diagnoses for teaching" (Hallahan & Kauffman, 1976). The former is characterized as formal standardized testing, usually administered by a professional other than the teacher and outside of the classroom. This testing typically satisfies the administrative requirements of the school district but often fails to provide the teacher with adequate information to develop an educational program. This is where diagnosis for teaching comes in. It usually consists of criterion-referenced tests administered by the teacher in the low-structure, natural setting of the classroom and is directly related to the development of an intervention plan.

Generally speaking, the approach advocated here is the development of an intervention plan that remediates the student's weaknesses, focusing on his or her strengths (Lerner, 2006; Johnson & Myklebust, 1967; Smith, 2004). The methodology employed should be similar to that used in the regular classroom. The goals of instruction should be identical to those of the student's regular classroom teacher and are directly related to the development of an intervention plan.

If resource room teachers are to develop intervention plans based on sound psychoeducational principles, the selection of assessment tools must consider the student's educational setting. In addition to being guided by general considerations regarding assessment, resource room teachers need to consider this question: Are the procedures employed sensible and reasonable for the student's class and school? Typically, this analysis relies heavily on criterion-referenced tests and behavioral assessment techniques (see Chapters 12 to 16).

Implementing and Evaluating the Intervention Plan

Typically, the highest percentage of a resource room teacher's time is spent on direct instruction. The number of methods and materials used in special education settings is growing rapidly. The resource room teacher must keep abreast of them and must be skilled in evaluating their effectiveness. More importantly, the resource room teacher must develop a theory of instruction. Resource room teachers are constantly involved in making decisions about the needs of their students. Do students benefit from tutoring sessions in the resource room? Should one prepare them for the test on Friday? Should one remediate their basic skills? Should one provide them with strategies that will enable them to learn more effectively?

The teacher must be prepared to make these decisions based on a conceptual framework of the purpose of a resource room. Without such a framework, decisions will be based on the needs of the moment, with little thought to the overall operation of the program.

Communicating with Regular Classroom Teachers

Since students placed in the resource room spend the majority of the school day with regular educators, those responsible for special education must establish a cooperative working relationship with these teachers. If the academic and behavioral skills taught in the resource room are to transfer to the regular classroom, the regular educator must play a meaningful role in the process. The concept of teacher consultation is viewed as the key to a successful resource room program (see Chapter 7 for a discussion of collaborative strategies).

The resource room teacher should also develop a brochure to be presented to other staff members during the first week of school. This will allow them to become familiar with the objectives of the resource room.

In addition to academic and behavioral reporting systems, regularly scheduled face-to-face consultation will greatly enhance the cooperation between regular and special educations. Contacts with regular classroom teachers must be approached with the same rigor as contacts with students.

The Physical Setting

The physical condition of the resource room can impact student behavior—both academic and social. The size and location of the room are important in developing the resource room program. How these factors are considered can either hinder or facilitate student performance.

Size. A resource room should be as large as a typical regular education classroom. There may be situations in which the room is smaller, but given the equipment needed, it is difficult to justify a reduction in size. At the very least, the teacher needs enough space to conduct both small-group and individual lessons, provide a "quiet space" for students, store materials and student data, and have access to electrical outlets for audiovisual equipment. When the room is too small, students often interfere with each other, especially those who have difficulty attending to tasks. It is unreasonable to ask a student who has an attention deficit to remain on task in the face of so many blatant distractions. This is not to suggest that a stimulus-free environment is warranted; however, too much may be going on in close physical proximity for this student to remain on task. Adequate space allows the student to at least be available for learning.

Location. A few years ago, a local high school conducted a resource room program in a prefabricated module outside the school. Students attending this program had to leave the main building and walk a short distance to receive special education services. This isolated setting kept those in the program from being integrated with the rest of the students. The resource room students may have felt stigmatized, students without disabilities were ignorant of the program, and the resource room teacher was cut off from her regular education colleagues. This is an extreme example of the implications of resource room location. However, it is still not unusual to have resource rooms located in isolated, underutilized, or inappropriate sections of a school building.

When deciding where to locate the resource room, one must consider the students' grades and the organization of the building. Elementary school students may be placed in a particular wing or on a particular floor. Logically, the resource room should be located there. If the resource room serves both elementary and intermediate school students, then a location central to both groups is sensible. At the junior and senior high school levels, there may be more than one resource room. Once again, they should be located close to the students being served. This reduces the travel time from the regular to the special education setting and, most importantly, increases opportunities for interaction between regular and special education personnel. One high school resource room teacher asked to have her room located next to the teachers' lounge, enabling her to converse and consult with many regular classroom teachers. The resource room program must be perceived as an integral part of the school. The proper location will help to reinforce this concept.

Scheduling

Resource room teachers frequently feel pulled in many directions. Nowhere is this more evident than in scheduling. Schedules must be developed so that they conform to the administrative structure of the building, meet students' needs, do not interfere with the activities of regular classroom teachers, and allow the resource room teacher to comply with state regulations on student–teacher ratios. Clearly, this is not a simple task. The school's principal must be involved in scheduling, and resource room teachers must have enough time to consult with their regular education colleagues. Some schools have instituted a common period, or x period, prior to the start of the school day, to allow for this type of communication. Too often, however, teachers are left to find time themselves. This problem only reinforces the belief that ongoing communication is not a valued practice in the school.

Once the schedule is established so that regular and special education teachers can communicate with one another, individual students must be scheduled for the resource room program. On the elementary level, it is vital to do this in cooperation with the regular classroom teacher. The resource room teacher should set up a meeting in which both teachers can determine the most reasonable time for the student to come to the resource room. Both teachers need to consider the student's strengths and weaknesses, what he or she would be missing in the regular classroom during a difficult transition period, how the student feels about the part of the day spent in the resource room, and so forth. Obviously, there will be times when compromises must be made. However, if scheduling decisions are renegotiated every marking period, they are easier for all concerned parties to accept.

On the secondary school level there is much more flexibility, and the resource room teacher must consult with guidance personnel to assist in scheduling. Frequently, students on this level attend the resource room during an elective period. Sometimes parents opt to eliminate certain subjects, such as a foreign language, and students attend the resource room during that period. Parents and teachers should consider if a student needs a particular course for graduation, postsecondary planning, or employment. Scheduling is complex, and there are no easy answers. However, when flexibility and reason prevail, most problems can be worked out.

All these issues point to the fact that there is no typical day for a resource room teacher. Sample schedules and responsibilities may be misleading because the variation is so wide. In a survey of over 20 schedules and responsibilities conducted by the author, all of the teachers interviewed reported lopsided assignments—for example, with one student during period 1, two during period 2, and five for the next two periods.

In this same survey, all teachers had one period per day to consult with their regular education colleagues, and a few had two. One problem was that their available period did not always coincide with that of the regular classroom teacher. Therefore, a great deal of consultation occurred before and after school, during lunch, or haphazardly throughout the day. One school had a period prior to the beginning of the school day for this purpose, and it was extremely effective.

All teachers noted that they had frequent "walk-ins"—students who came by to take a test or needed a pass or needed help in a wide variety of subjects. It was also not unusual to have a classroom teacher stop by during a class period with a specific concern regarding a resource room teacher.

CONSULTANT TEACHER MODEL

Consultant teachers are special education teachers who provide instruction to students (also called **direct services**) or consult with regular education teachers (**indirect services**). In many cases, consultant teachers provide a combination of services that frequently overlap with those of the resource room teacher. They may work with a small group of students on specific reading skills and consult with the classroom teacher on effective management techniques. The following is from the New York State United Teachers Information bulletin 990038, *Consultant Teacher Services* (2000):

1. As defined in Sections 200.1(m) and 200.6(d) of the Regulations, consultant teacher services means direct and/or indirect services provided to a student with a disability who attends general education classes and/or such student's general education teachers. General

education classes includes career and technical education.

- Direct consultant teacher services means specially designed individualized or group instruction provided by a certified special education teacher to a student with a disability to aid such student to benefit from the student's general education classes.
- Indirect consultant teacher services means consultation provided by a certified special education teacher to general education teacher(s) to assist them in adjusting the learning environment and/or modifying their instructional methods to meet the individual needs of a student with a disability who attends their classes.

2. According to Section 200.4 of the Regulations, if the student has been determined to be eligible for consultant teacher services, the Committee on Special Education must indicate in the student's IEP the general education classes in which the student is to receive consultant teacher services, as well as the amount of time that consultant teacher services will be provided to the student.

3. When consultant teacher services are specified in the IEP, the general education teachers of the student for whom the service will be provided must be given the opportunity to participate in the instructional planning process with the consultant teacher to discuss objectives, and to determine the methods and schedules for the service 200.4 (e).

4. Under 200.6 of the Regulations, the total number of students with disabilities who can be assigned to a full-time consultant teacher must not exceed twenty. Other instructional assignments may not be given to a full-time consultant teacher. Section 200.6(d)(3) of the Regulations allows a school district to request a variance from the State Education Department concerning the maximum student load of twenty students with disabilities. Local leaders who need more information regarding variances should consult NYSUT Information

Bulletin Education Variances and the Part 200 Regulations #990006.

5. Each student requiring consultant teacher services must receive a minimum of two hours of direct and/or indirect services each week (200.6 {d}).

6. An individual providing consultant teacher services must be a certified special education teacher. The State Education Department has interpreted this to include all special education teachers certified under Section 80-2.6 of the Regulations of the Commissioner of Education, including teachers of the speech and hearing handicapped. In addition, under 200.6 (b) of the Regulations, a certified reading teacher (Section 80-2.7 of the Regulations) may provide "specially designed reading instruction" as a consultant teacher service.

STUDENT PERCEPTIONS OF EDUCATIONAL PLACEMENTS

How do students feel about their placement? Vaughn and Klinger (1998) synthesized eight studies from 1987 to 1996 that examined students' perceptions of instructional settings. Overall they found that (a) most of them preferred services outside the regular classroom for part of the day; (b) they liked the resource room; (c) they enjoyed inclusion because it helped them make friends; (d) they valued support services in the regular education setting; and (e) they did not know how they were placed in the special education setting. And while the students' perceptions of their placement are important, they do not address the effectiveness of that placement. It can be helpful to know why they like some programs more than others, or their understanding of their disability and how they were placed. One student thought he was in the resource room because he had failed a test and believed that if he passed another test he would "get out." Students' perceptions and feelings about their placement may impact their performance. However, at this time, we simply do not know the relationship between them.

COMBINATION OF APPROACHES

It is not unusual for a student with learning disabilities to be provided with both pull-out services (resource room) and push-in services (consultant teacher) in an inclusionary approach. (See Implications for Teachers: Combination of Approaches.) As a teacher of students with learning disabilities, you will need to be flexible, providing services based on the needs of your students and being guided by their IEPs. And while the LRE must be provided, this does not mean that all students with learning disabilities will be placed in regular education classes. Thomas and Rapport (1998), in their article on the legal basis for the LRE, state:

> It is our view that if state education agencies or local school districts were to maintain segregated placements that effectively met the academic needs of children with disabilities, but were not least restrictive, such a practice would violate the IDEA and not qualify as "appropriate placement." Similarly, however, if state educational agencies or local school districts were to mandate full inclusion for all children with disabilities, without a determination of each individual child's needs and ability to participate in a regular education environment, such a practice, on its face, would also violate the IDEA. (p. 77)

This is an exciting time to be a teacher of students with learning disabilities. You may find yourself juggling roles throughout the day. And if you move from one district to another, you may find different service delivery models for the same types of students. You will need to keep abreast of the professional literature, as well as changes in the law that govern your practice.

Implications for Teachers: Combination of Approaches. Every morning, Mr. Andrews starts his day in the first-grade inclusive class working with his coteacher. There are 23 students, including 6 with learning disabilities. They spend their entire school day in the classroom, but he doesn't. At 10 o'clock he runs down to his resource room,

and he and his para-educator teach five third-grade students with learning disabilities for 45 minutes. They spend the remainder of their time in their regular classroom. After a preparation period, he coteaches for about an hour in a second-grade classroom. After lunch he returns to that classroom for a short time, then is off to his resource room for the remaining 2 hours of the school day.

In his role as a resource room teacher, Mr. Andrews consults with regular classroom teachers regarding the areas of need that he must to focus on in the resource room. He also shares ideas and techniques that can be employed in the regular education classrooms.

In the beginning, he could not keep track of the students' needs and felt he could not consult with regular classroom teachers frequently enough. Scheduling students for the resource room is difficult enough, but it is even worse when one is there only part of the day. By midyear, there was some order to the class. And while Mr. Andrews believes that this is best for the students, there are days when he longs for last year, when he taught in a self-contained classroom all day long.

Wearing many hats is something special educators do. This is not to say that it is easy or desirable. There may be more efficient and effective ways to utilize your time. Mr. Andrews feels it is hard to shift from coteaching in the inclusive classroom to providing supplemental instruction in the resource room. However, given the size of his school and the needs of his students, this situation will not change. His life would be a lot easier, he thinks, if the district would only hire one or two more teachers. However, he realizes that this will not happen soon.

SUMMARY

There has been a dramatic shift in the educational placements for students with learning disabilities. In the late 1960s and early 1970s, most of these students were in self-contained classes with a special education teacher who provided all the instruction. The most recent data indicate that the majority of students are now being educated in regular education classrooms, either full-time or part-time. In the late 1980s, the resource room was the fastest-growing educational placement, serving over 50% of students classified with mild learning disabilities. This is no longer the case; inclusionary approaches are now on the rise. This chapter has discussed these trends, focusing on the most frequently employed placements for students with learning disabilities: the inclusive classroom and the resource room.

SPRINGBOARDS FOR REFLECTION AND DISCUSSION

1. Visit a school for students with learning disabilities. Reflect on the need for such a placement. Is it based on academic performance or behavior? Why do you think parents would opt for such a placement? Is the local school district paying the tuition? Is there a difference in the quality of instruction?

2. Visit a local school. What placement options are available for students with learning disabilities? Which one is used most often?

3. Interview a resource room teacher on the elementary level and one on the secondary level. What are the differences in their instructional practices?

4. Interview an experienced special education teacher. What is his or her opinion of the various placement options? Has this opinion changed over the years? What has influenced this opinion?

5. Speak to students with learning disabilities who are receiving a variety of services. Which do they like and why? If they had a choice, which one would they prefer?

6. Observe a few inclusive classrooms and list their strengths and the concerns they raise. How are they the same? How are they different?

7. Do you think there are situations in which the self-contained classroom would be the LRE for a student with learning disabilities? Why?

8. Interview regular classroom teachers. What is their perception of inclusion?

CHAPTER 9

PRESCHOOL STUDENTS WITH LEARNING DISABILITIES

CHAPTER OBJECTIVES

At the end of this chapter you will:

- understand the complexities of diagnosing preschoolers with learning disabilities.
- know the early warning signs of a learning disability.
- be aware of screening devices employed to assess preschoolers with learning disabilities.
- be aware of the comprehensive developmental assessment procedures employed with this population.
- learn about various interventions for preschoolers with learning disabilities.

Discussing early childhood (preschool) learning disabilities is a problem for a number of reasons. Learning disabilities are primarily school-related disorders, and despite efforts at early identification, relatively few students are classified as having a learning disability prior to age 9 (U.S. Office of Education, 2002). Therefore, there is a very limited research base on which to draw when discussing best practices. However, some of you will be working with preschoolers with special needs; with preschoolers who have been described as having learning disabilities; or with students who are at risk for learning disabilities. Today there is an increased emphasis on early identification, especially of those who are at risk for reading failure. It is hoped that research will continue in an attempt to provide empirically validated identification, assessment, and instructional practices for these young learners.

Benjamin was born prematurely (8 months' gestation) with a very low birth weight of 2 lb 10 oz. He was a late talker, was motorically slower than most children his age, and had difficulty with writing, coloring, and using utensils to eat. At age 3 he was identified as having developmental delay and will attend a preschool program for students with special educational needs. Do you think he has a learning disability? Do you think he will be so classified when he enters kindergarten?

Paige was born after a full-term pregnancy. Her parents report that all of her milestones have been age appropriate, and she is an alert, attentive child with a good attention span. On the preschool screening test she had difficulty with letter- and word-naming tasks, and shows little interest in books and reading. What are the chances that Paige has a learning disability? Her parents were shocked by the results of her screening test and plan to find a tutor.

And finally, Sarah. There is no indication that Sarah has any difficulty with academic tasks, but she has poor impulse control and does not get along with the other 4-year-olds in her play group. Her parents are concerned but have been reassured that everything is normal. Could Sarah have a learning disability?

The three children described above may or may not be eligible for classification as having a learning disability when they reach school age. It would appear that Benjamin is at risk, but we cannot be sure. Paige and Sarah may or may not meet the criteria for a learning disability. This is the problem with preschool children with learning disabilities. It is difficult to identify such children in this age group for a host of reasons. This chapter will discuss these reasons, as well as the characteristics of preschoolers with learning disabilities, assessment procedures, and interventions. All of these issues will be discussed in the context of complex legal and practical issues that confront those who work with children in this age group.

CHARACTERISTICS OF PRESCHOOLERS AT RISK FOR LEARNING DISABILITIES

Practical Concerns

Do Benjamin, Paige, and Sarah have learning disabilities? Are they at risk for learning disabilities or are they normally developing preschoolers? In discussing the characteristics and identification of preschool children with learning disabilities, there are no simple answers. As Smith (2004) notes, "identifying a preschooler as learning disabled is just a calculated guess, because we don't really know whether, once the child reaches school age, a discrepancy between intellectual abilities and achievement will develop" (p. 38). Shapiro, Church, and Lewis (2002) also point out that a learning disability is usually identified after the child enters elementary school. In fact, data indicate that relatively few 6-, 7-, and 8-year-olds receive services for learning disabilities. Therefore, we are on shaky ground when we discuss who these students are, what they look like, and how we can identify them. The following further complicate issues the process:

- Laws governing preschoolers (3–5 years of age) do not require a specific classification such as learning disability. Rather, such children are classified as developmentally delayed.
- Learning disabilities have traditionally been defined as academic disorders.
- The more severe the disability, the more likely the child will be identified.
- The more severe the disability, the more services are available.
- The **exclusionary clause** in the definition of learning disabilities negates the presence of one of the strongest predictors of school failure—poverty.
- Issues and concerns related to students from culturally and linguistically diverse urban areas compound the complexity of the identification process.

Each of these factors will be discussed more fully below.

Laws Governing Preschoolers with Special Needs

According to Part B of IDEA 2004, states can identify preschoolers as having a developmental delay. Smith, Strain, Sandall, Snyder, McLean, Broudy-Ramsey, and Sumi (2002), in a review of the research literature on early childhood special education from 1991 to 2001, recommend that researchers employ the IDEA classification system because the studies rarely include information on the disability. For example, Part B provides for a free, appropriate public education for preschoolers aged 3 to 5 who have a developmental delay in at least one of five areas—physical, cognitive, communication, social or emotional, or adaptive development. Suppose more than one area is affected? One child could be identified with low cognitive development, and another child attending the same program could have a social development delay. Who has a learning disability and who does not? We simply cannot tell from most studies.

The law also allows multidisciplinary teams to decide if they will use an IEP or a IFSP (Individualized Family Service Plan). The IFSP is mandated for birth through 2 years of age (this age group is governed by Part C of IDEA 1997 and IDEA 2004). If the team employs the IFSP, the transition to elementary school may be more complicated since the plan is geared to family rather than school involvement. Also, identification of a student with learning disabilities prior to age 2 (early intervention) is highly unlikely.

Learning Disabilities Has Traditionally Been Defined as an Academic Disorder

While many have called for the inclusion of social and emotional factors in the definition of learning disabilities, the latter are still classified primarily as academic disorders. The most frequent referral occurs when a regular classroom teacher observes unexpected underachievement in a students—referred to as the **wait and fail** model. School personnel are usually reluctant to initiate a referral early in the child's academic career, preferring to wait and see how the student progresses. During the preschool years, this reluctance is heightened. Students may receive interventions for other concerns, but we do not know if they have a learning disability.

The More Severe the Disability, the More Likely the Child Will Be Identified

A child with a minor articulation problem will probably not be noticed, but one who is still not speaking at age 2 will. A child who has a few temper tantrums will probably be viewed as a typical preschooler who will outgrow them, but a child who is aggressive toward others and the self will be of concern. Generally speaking, the more observable the disability or disorder, the more likely parents or preschool teachers will seek help. The child who has minor problems that may result in their classification as learning disabilities upon entering elementary school may go undetected. Alternatively, those minor problems may not be an indication of a learning disability. (See Assessment later in this chapter.)

The More Severe the Disability, the More Services Are Available

Historically, services have been provided to those students whose disabilities were clearly observable and severe (Gallagher, 2000). Programs for students who are mentally retarded and for those with physical, visual, and hearing disorders have been available for preschoolers since the mid-1960s. Exactly how many children of preschool age have learning disabilities is difficult to ascertain. However, during the elementary school years, the incidence increases dramatically.

The Exclusionary Clause in the Federal Government's Definition of Learning Disabilities Negates the Presence of One of the Greatest Predicators of School Failure

Children who are born into poverty are at risk for school failure (see Donovan & Cross, 2002), yet "economic deprivation" is one of the factors excluded when identifying children with learning disabilities. When studies are cited that highlight the overwhelming benefits of early intervention programs (American Academy of Pediatrics, 2001; Guralnick, 1997; Lerner, Lowenthal, & Egan, 2003), they include poor children. Upon entering school, will these students be eligible for classification as having learning disabilities?

Issues Related to Students from Culturally and Linguistically Diverse Urban Areas Complicate the Process

For many of these students, the issues may be related to their culture and/or language rather than a specific learning disability (see Chapter 4). Whether these students are included in the preschool special education population also complicates the discussion of exactly who these preschool students with learning disabilities are and what instructional practices are effective for them.

PREDICATORS OF LEARNING DISABILITIES IN EARLY CHILDHOOD

Much has been written about predictors of school failure (see Torgesen, 2004). Who is at risk? How can they be identified? What are their strengths and weaknesses? This literature typically does not begin until kindergarten and focuses primarily on reading disorders. For the majority of students who will eventually be so classified, the learning disability will be due to difficulty with reading. However, this does not mean that all students who have reading disorders have learning disabilities. It is impossible to distinguish those with learning disabilities from those who are at risk for reading failure. According to Shapiro et al. (2002), early indicators of learning disabilities include difficulty with social interaction, impulse control, and motor skills. Scarborough (1990, 1998) indicates that the most important predictor is difficulty with semantics and syntax. It should be noted that Scarborough's work involved students who were at risk for reading disorders. Perhaps the most reasonable way to address this topic is to look at the characteristics of students with learning disabilities. If preschoolers have such problems in several areas, they should be considered at risk for learning disabilities and evaluated.

Characteristics of Learning Disabilities During the Preschool Years

Motor Problems. Students with learning disabilities may have poor fine and gross motor skills. Early leaders in the field focused on these concerns. Smith (2004) notes that many of the early studies of motor (and perceptual) problems by Frostig, Kephart, and Johnson and Myklebust serve as excellent guides for the instruction of preschoolers with potential learning disabilities. Fine motor tasks that may alert teachers to future learning disabilities are difficulty holding eating utensils, crayons, and pencils; playing with puzzles, blocks, or beads; or coloring or copying shapes or objects. Gross motor difficulty may include a delay in achieving motor milestones such as crawling, walking, hopping, skipping, and jumping. Children may lack coordination in playground activities, sports, or other physical activities. They may be slightly awkward, bumping into objects and knocking things over.

Perceptual Deficits. Some preschoolers may have difficulty interpreting information from the environment. Students with learning disabilities have been noted to have difficulty with auditory and/or visual perceptual tasks. Most of the literature has focused on reading, so, it is difficult to say with certainty what perceptual deficits would be apparent in the 3 to 5 age range. A great deal has been written about early predictors of reading disorders (see Chapter 13), and perceptual skills deficits have been noted, especially in phonemic awareness. Some children with potential learning disabilities may have difficulty with nursery rhymes or rhyme in general, frequent confusion of similar-sounding words, and difficulty tracking words.

Attention Deficits. Approximately one third of students with learning disabilities may have ADHD. Others may have difficulty attending to tasks, limited attention spans, and/or an inability to distinguish between relevant and irrelevant information, but these problems may not be severe enough to be diagnosed as ADHD. As a group, preschoolers have difficulty sitting, attending for long periods of time, and staying on task. However, if these problems occur in all settings and are noted by many adults, they may be indicators of future difficulty in school. They may indicate ADHD, a learning disability, or a combination of both.

Memory Disorders. Another characteristic of students with learning disabilities is difficulty with tasks that require memory. Memory is a complicated process (see Chapter 4). This fact, coupled with the limited memory repertoire of preschoolers, complicates the predictive process. How can you assess the memory function of a 3- to 5-year-old when it varies so frequently? Obviously, if the child has significant difficulty remembering the names of common objects, family members, daily routines, or frequently visited places, this is a matter of concern and may be a precursor of learning disabilities. Some preschoolers may not have adequate attending skills, so their memory skills will appear poor. Clearly, there is considerable overlap.

Does the 3-year-old child who cannot remember nursery rhymes have a memory disorder? Does she lack the perceptual ability to perceive the words correctly? Does she lack the attending skills necessary to focus and remember? Is she interested in other things? Or is she a normally developing child? In many cases, only time will tell.

Language Disorders.   Many students with learning disabilities have language-based disorders. Preschoolers who have difficulties with receptive language such as understanding sounds, words, or sentences, or with expressive language abilities such as naming common objects, syntax, and limited length of utterances, may have a learning disability. They may also have a language disorder or they may be experiencing the typical variability of a preschooler. They may not have reached their language milestones within an appropriate time frame. They may be reluctant to speak, and/or they may appear not to understand the world around them. They may have already demonstrated disorders in the form, content, and use of language (see Chapter 12).

Social Perceptual Disorders.   There is considerable debate in the field of learning disabilities regarding social perceptual disorders. In assessing preschoolers, this issue is even more complicated (see Chapter 16). The preschooler who has difficulty making friends, never gets invited to birthday parties, and/or says the wrong thing at the wrong time may or may not have a learning disability. However, if these problems persist, they need to be addressed regardless of the etiology.

Other Early Warning Signs.   The most common indicator of a learning disability in the preschool years is difficulty with language (for more information, go to http://www.ldonline.org). Specifically, preschoolers who talk late have difficulty pronouncing words, slow vocabulary growth, and trouble with rhyming activities. These children may also have trouble remembering specific bits of information, such as the day of the week, numbers, and the alphabet. They may be distracted, restless,

and have trouble focusing. They also may have trouble interacting with their peers because they cannot communicate.

If preschoolers exhibit difficulty in the areas noted above and are markedly different from their age-group peers, they need further evaluation. The following section discusses the assessment process from the initial screening to a more thorough analysis.

ASSESSMENT

Professionals and parents must exercise extreme caution when assessing preschool children. The range of normal development at this age level is broad, and many assessment devices, especially standardized tests, lack sufficient validity and reliability. This does not mean that we should merely wait until the child enters school. However, we need to be cautious and humble regarding our ability to identify preschoolers with learning disabilities. Through judicious data collection and assessment, coupled with input from a variety of professionals and family members, a reasonable decision can be made when the child enters kindergarten. Cohen and Spenciner (2003) divided the assessment process for this age group into two categories: (a) screening and (b) comprehensive developmental assessment. The purpose of screening is to cast a wide net in order to identify those students who have a disability or are at risk for a disability. Parents or medical doctors may identify a delay or disorder and suggest that the child be screened. Screening procedures are typically very broad and quick, and should not be thought of as a complete assessment. Their only purpose is to identify those students who need more through evaluation. Due to these limitations, it is not surprising that screening procedures may identify students who do not have disabilities and miss those who do. Ongoing, frequent screening will help reduce these errors. Cohen and Spenciner (2003, pp. 314–315) provide a table of selected screening instruments.

Comprehensive Developmental Assessment

If it appears that the child may have a learning disability, a more comprehensive assessment is necessary. This assessment should cover a variety of areas and include many professionals in order to ascertain whether or not the child has a developmental delay. The following table (9–2) on selected developmental assessment instruments is provided by Cohen and Spenciner (2003, pp. 322–326).

In addition to these instruments, practitioners are encouraged to use a variety of informal assessment procedures, such as observation, checklists and rating scales, criterion referenced tests, and authentic assessment.

The preschooler at risk for a learning disability or suspected of having a learning disability needs early intervention. A specific intervention plan needs to be developed based on the child's needs. During the early school years, the diagnostic process may reveal a disability other than a learning disability. The only thing that is certain when identifying preschoolers with learning disabilities is the uncertainty. Professionals must be able to deal with this uncertainty while at the same time meeting the needs of the student.

EARLY CHILDHOOD INTERVENTIONS

The Committee on Minority Representation in Special Education (Donovan & Cross, 2002) reviewed the literature on research-based early intervention and concluded that there is "ample theoretical and empirical support to justify launching systematic prevention efforts" (p. 163). The effects of poverty cannot be overstated. It is consistently implicated in a number of factors that contribute to school failure and place a child at risk at an early age (Brooks-Gunn & Duncan, 1997; Donovan & Cross, 2002; Park, Turnbull, & Turnbull, 2002; Salend, 2005). Teachers of students with learning disabilities who teach in poverty-stricken areas,

both urban and rural, need to be cognizant of this factor (see Chapter 3 for more specific information).

Students with developmental delays must be provided with a free, appropriate public education. Most programs are noncategorical; that is, they include students with a range of disabilities. Therefore, as noted above, whether they provide services for students with learning disabilities is not easily determined. Moreover, it is difficult to decide what methods are valued for specific disabilities. Nationally recognized programs such as Head Start and the High/Scope Perry Preschool programs provide services for students who are developmentally delayed or at risk. However, these children may be living in poverty and/or eligible for classification in the 12 IDEA categories other than learning disabilities. Does this matter? Some say that it does not; rather, we need to provide services based on need, not label. And yet, if we want to validate practices for students with learning disabilities, we may not be able to do so. Therefore, what should govern our practice? Smith et al. (2002) state that from a variety of theories on early childhood special education and early intervention, "an implicit theory of practice" (p. 170) has emerged. They propose the following tenets for such a theory (p. 166):

- Families and homes are primary nurturing contexts.
- Strengthening relationships is an essential feature.
- Children learn through acting and observing their environment.
- Adults mediate a child's experience to promote learning.
- Children's participation in more developmentally advanced settings is necessary for successful and independent participation in those settings.
- Early intervention/early childhood special education practice is individually and dynamically goal oriented.
- Transitions across programs are enhanced by a developmentally investigative adult.
- Families and programs are influenced by the broader context.

This theory of practice is based on all students with special educational needs, not just those with learning disabilities. Bowman, Donovan, and Burns

TABLE 9-1 Selected Screening Instruments

Instrument	Areas Assessed	Age Range	Reliability	Validity	Norms	Time to Administer
AGS *Early Screening Profiles* (Harrison et al., 1990)	Cognitive/language self-help/social, articulation survey, behavior survey, motor profile, home survey, and health history survey	2 years to 6 years 11 months	Internal consistency mean .85; test-retest range .78 to .89; interrater mean .92	Numerous studies support concurrent, predictive, and construct validity	1,149 children from 26 states and the District Columbia stratified by geographic region, race, age gender, socioeconomic status, and enrollment of school district	15 minutes to 30 minutes for children; 10 minutes to 15 minutes for teacher and parent questionnaires
Ages & Stages Questionnaires (ASQ) (Bricker & Squires, 1999)	Communication, gross motor, fine motor, problem solving, and personal-social	4 months to 60 months	Adequate	Adequate	2,008 children	10 minutes to 20 minutes
Brigance Preschool Screen (Brigance, 1998)	11 skill areas	2 years, 9 months to 5 years	None reported	None reported	Criterion-referenced test	12 minutes to 15 minutes
Denver Developmental Screen, Test II (DDST II) (Frankenburg et al., 1990)	Gross motor, language, fine motor acaptive, and personal-social	Birth through 5 years, 11 months	Limited information reported	Limited information reported	2,096 children stratified by maternal education, residence, and ethnicity	5 minutes to 10 minutes
Developmental Indicator for the Assessment of Learning-Third Edition (Dial-3) (Mardell-Czudnowski & Goldenberg, 1998)	Motor skills, conceptual abilities, and language skills	3 years through 6 years, 11 months	Test-retest reliability .84 to .88; internal consistency adequate	Evidence of validity is adequate	1,560 English-speaking and 650 Spanish-speaking children stratified by age, gender, geographic area, race or ethnic group, and parent education level	30 minutes

(continued)

TABLE 9–1 Selected Screening Instruments (*continued*)

Instrument	Areas Assessed	Age Range	Reliability	Validity	Norms	Time to Administer
Early Screening Inventory-Revised (ESI-R) (Meisels, Wiske, Marsden, & Henderson, 1997)	Visual-motor/ adaptive, language and cognition, and gross motor	ESI-P (3 years to 4 years, 6 months) ESI-K (4 years, 6 months to 6 years	Interrater .99 Test-retest .98 Interrater .98 Test-retest .87	Limited information Limited	997 children 5,034 children	15 minutes to 20 minutes
First STEP (Miller, 1992)	Cognitive, communication, motor, social-emotional, and adaptive	2 years, 9 months to 6 years, 2 months	Test-retest reliability coefficients range from .85 to .92; interrater reliability from .77 to .96	Adequate concurrent validity	1,433 stratified by gender, geographic region, and race/ethnicity based on 1988 U.S. Census	15 minutes

Source: From Cohen, L. G., & Loraine Spenciner. *Assessment of Children and Youth with Special Needs,* 2/e. Published by Allyn and Bacon, Boston, MA. Copyright © 2003 by Pearson Education. Reprinted by permission of the publisher.

TABLE 9–2 Developmental Assessment Instruments

Instrument	Areas	Age Range	Type	Reliability	Validity
Assessment, Evaluation and Programming System (AEPS) for Infants and Children: Vol.1, AEPS Measurement for Birth to Three Years (Bricker, 1993)	Fine motor, gross motor, adaptive cognitive, social-communication, and social	Birth to 3 years	Criterion-referenced instrument for planning, monitoring, and evaluating a child's progress	Adequate	Teachers and other early intervention providers should examine materials to make a decision for individual programs
Assessment Evaluation and Programming System (AEPS) for Infants and Children: Vol. 3. AEPS Measurement for Three to Six Years (Bricker & Pretti-Fronteczak, 1996)	Fine motor, gross motor, adaptive cognitive, social-communication, and social	3 years through 6 years	Criterion-referenced instrument for planning, monitoring, and evaluating a child's progress	Adequate	Teachers should examine materials to make decisions for individual programs
Bayley Scales of Infant Development II (Bayley, 1993)	Mental scale and motor scale	1 year through 3 years, 6 months	Normal-referenced: 1,700 children participated: stratification based on 1988 U.S census	Adequate	Adequate
Boehm Test of Basic Concepts, Third Edition Preschool (Boehm 3 Preschool) (Boehm, 2001)	Easic relational concepts	3 years through 5 years, 11 months	Norm-referenced: over 1,600 children, stratified by gender, race/ethnicity, region and parent education level according to the U.S. current population survey, October 1998: school enrollment supplemental file, U.S. Bureau of Census	Adequate	Adequate

Test	Concepts Measured	Age Range	Standardization	Reliability	Validity
Boehm Test of Basic Concepts, Third Edition-Preschool Spanish Edition (Boehm 3 Preschool) (Boehm, 2001)	Basic relational concepts	3 years through 5 years, 11 months	Norm-referenced: over 400 Spanish-speaking children, stratified by gender, race/ethnicity, region, and parent education level. The sample under-represented the northeastern region and over-represented the southern and western regions.	Adequate	Additional
Boehm Test of Basic Concepts, Third Edition (Boehm-3) (Boehm, 2000)	Basic relational concepts	Kindergarten through grade 2	Norm-referenced: over 10,000 children stratified by race/ethnicity and region according to the U.S current population survey, October 1998: School Enrollment Supplement File, U.S Bureau of Census and socio-economic level of the school district	Adequate	Adequate
Boehm Test of Basic Concepts, Third Edition Spanish Edition (Boehm-3) (Boehm, 2000)	Basic relational concepts	Kindergarten through grade 2	Norm-referenced: Over 1,600 children stratified by region and socioeconomic level of the school district; there is a lack of representation from the northeastern region	Internal consistency is adequate; test-retest ranges from .78 to .80	Additional validity studies are needed
Braken Basic Concept Scale Revised (Bracken, 1998)	Receptive knowledge of concepts including: color, direction/position, letters, self-social, sizes, awareness, texture/materials, comparisons, quantity, shapes, time/sequence, and numbers/counting	2 years, 6 months to 7 years, 11 months	Norm-referenced	Internal consistency ranges from .78 to .98 for the subtests and .96 to .99 for the total test; test-retest for the total test is .94	The manual presents evidence for content, concurrent, and predictive validity

(continued)

TABLE 9-2 Developmental Assesment Instruments (*continued*)

Instrument	Areas	Age Range	Type	Reliability	Validity
BRIGANCE Inventory of Early Development Revised (Brigance, 1991)	Pre-ambulatory, gross motor, fine motor, adaptive, speech and language, general knowledge and comprehension, social-emotional, reading readiness, basic reading, writing, and math	Birth to 7 years	Criterion-referenced norms developed from a literature review	Not reported	Not reported
Carolina Curriculum for Preschoolers with Special Needs (Johnson-Martin, Attermeier, & Hacker, 1990)	Cognition, communication, social, adaptive, fine motor, and gross motor	3 years to 5 years	Criterion-referenced	Not reported	Teachers should review materials to make decisions for individual programs
Developmental Assessment of Young Children (Voress & Maddox, 1998)	Cognition, communication, social-emotional, physical, and adaptive	Birth through 5 years, 11 months	Norm-referenced: 1,269 children in 27 states participated; comparison of percentages to the *Statistical Abstract of the U.S.* (1996)	Adequate	Adequate
Hawaii Early Learning Profile (HELP) for Preschoolers (VORT, 1995)	Cognitive, language, gross motor, fine motor, social, and self-help	3 years to 6 years	Curriculum-based	Descriptions and guidelines in the manual are designed to promote consistency	Teachers should review materials to make decisions for individual programs
Infant-Preschool Play Assessment Scale (Flagler, 1996)	Cognitive, communication, sensorimotor, fine motor gross motor, and social-emotional skills	Birth through 5 years	Criterion-referenced	Not reported	Teachers should review materials to make decision for individual program

Instrument	Areas Assessed	Age Range	Standardization/Norms	Reliability	Validity
Kaufman Survey of Early Academic and Language Skills (K-SEALS) (Kaufman, 1993)	Expressive language, receptive language, number, letter, and word skills	3 years through 6 years	Norm-referenced: 1,000 children from 28 states stratified by geographic regions, race, age, gender, socioeconomic status, and enrollment of school district	Adequate	Adequate
Mullen Scales of Early Learning (Mullen, 1995)	Gross motor, visual reception, fine motor, receptive language, and expressive language	Birth through 5 years, 9 months	Norm-referenced: 1,849 children from 4 geographic regions stratified by age, gender, race/ethnicity, father's occupation, and urban/rural	Adequate for younger age groups	Evidence of construct validity is presented
System to Plan Early Childhood Sevices (SPECS) (Bagnato & Neisworth, 1990)	Communication, sensorimotor, physical, self-regulation, cognition, and self/social	2 years to 6 years	System that links assessment of the child to program planning, development of the individualized plan, and evaluation	Adequate test-retest	Teachers should examine materials and make decisions regarding individual programs
Vineland Social-Emotional Early Childhood Scales (SEEC) (Sparrow, Balla, & Cicchetti, 1998)	Social-emotional functioning: paying attention, entering into intentional social interactions, understanding expressions of emotion, constructing and observing relationships, and developing self-regulation behaviors	Birth through 5 years, 11 months	Norm-referenced: norms were derived from normative data of the Vineland Adaptive Behavior Scales (ABS), expanded (items from the ABS were used to construct the SEEC)	Adequate	Adequate

Source: From Cohen, L. G. & Loraine Spenciner. Assessment of Children and Youth with Special Needs, 2/e. Published by Allyn and Bacon, Boston, MA. Copyright © by Pearson Education. Reprinted by permission of the publisher.

(2001), in their review of the research on preschoolers' education, suggest that the principles that guide high-quality programming for any preschooler are relevant and necessary for students with learning disabilities. They identify four program features that should be emphasized:

1. Communication skills
2. Social and emotional skills
3. Attention to individual differences
4. Emphasis on parent participation

Other researchers (Lerner et al., 2003; Salend, 2005; Smith, 2004) note the same focus for preschoolers. Students are taught communication skills, social skills, attending ability, and processing and motor skills. Collaboration with families is critical, and typically preschool personnel assist parents in obtaining the services and supports necessary to foster their child's development. How this is carried out is illustrated (Lerner et al., 2003, p. 120) by an example of a typical school day of a preschooler with learning disabilities with objectives that cover all the areas described above.

Specific interventions will vary, and we simply don't know what works and for whom during this critical time period. Bender (2004) notes that "even if the identification issues were resolved, the effectiveness of instruction has not been demonstrated for these children" (p. 402).

THE TYPICAL SCHOOL DAY OF PRESCHOOLERS WITH LEARNING DISABILITIES

The typical school day for the 4.7% of 3- to 5-year-olds classified as having a developmental delay varies. Most of them, 53% according to the U.S. Office of Education (2000), are educated in inclusive settings. Whether they have learning disabilities is impossible to know, given the current identification process. Some argue that because such a high percentage of school-age children are classified as having learning disabilities, the preschool population must be similar. However, we simply do not know.

Lerner et al. (2003) note that the typical preschool day includes a variety of learning centers, music, and movement activities that enable students to use and practice communication, socialization, fine and gross motor, cognitive, and adaptive skills.

An example of one school district's program follows.

Practical Considerations: One School District's Preschool Program. The Bellmore, New York, Union Free School District operates a 10-month self-contained special education preschool program which serves 3- to 4-year-old children (Famularo, 2005). The program is based on a multidisciplinary team approach. The teachers, speech therapists, psychologist, and occupational and physical therapists work closely together to plan and implement a program that addresses each child's IEP goals. There is a strong emphasis on language development. Hence, in addition to providing IEP services, the speech therapist team teaches classroom lessons on a weekly basis. The psychologist serves as both a direct service provider and a consultant to the staff concerning the classroom environment, behavioral/social issues, and character education. The psychologist also offers parent workshops.

The preschool program is child-centered. Its purpose is to promote and develop expressive language skills, communication and pragmatic skills, receptive language skills, socialization skills, self-confidence, independence, risk-taking abilities, sensorimotor integration skills, prereadiness skills, and multi-cultural and environmental awareness. Children are exposed to and taught developmentally appropriate skills in these areas. Incorporated in the school day are music, art, physical education, and library visits.

The program's location within a public school allows for integration of the students, wherever and whenever appropriate, with their regular education peers.

The preschool program consists of four sections of half-day special education classes. One section is comprised of 3-year-old children and has a student/staff ratio of up to 12:1:1. The remaining three sections are comprised of 4-year-old children and also have a student/staff ratio of up to 12:1:1, where six children are classified and six children are nonclassified students identified as at risk. This design allows for the integration of classified and nonclassified students. The preschool serves 48 students. Students in the younger class turn 3 by December 1 of the calendar year of their attendance. All students are classified as "preschoolers with a disability." Related services provided by the program include speech-language therapy, occupational therapy, physical therapy, educational counseling, and parent counseling.

SUMMARY

There is little research on the characteristics of, identification of, and intervention for preschoolers with learning disabilities. This is due to a number of factors, especially the language of IDEA 1997 and the recently reauthorized IDEA 2004 classification system, which does not require the specific diagnostic category of learning disabilities until the child reaches school age. Therefore, it is difficult, if not impossible, to differentiate preschoolers with learning disabilities from those with other developmental delays. Given this background, this chapter has provided assessment tools and various interventions employed with these young learners.

SPRINGBOARDS FOR REFLECTION AND DISCUSSION

1. Observe a typical preschool. Do you see students who may have a learning disability? How do they differ from other students?
2. Observe a program for preschoolers with special educational needs. What is the range of academic and social behaviors? Can you differentiate those with learning disabilities from other students? If yes, how?
3. Find out what kind of screening your local school district employs. Is it valid and reliable? Why did they decide to use it?
4. Interview a preschool teacher of students with learning disabilities. How does he or she assess their progress and determine what interventions to use?
5. What signs would you look for in a 4-year-old child whose parents were concerned about his or her progress in preschool?
6. What are the pros and cons of classifying a preschool student with learning disabilities?
7. Speak to the parents of a preschooler with a learning disability. When did they first notice a problem? How did they get help? Are they pleased with the school program?
8. Why do you think we know so little about the effectiveness of instructional programs for preschoolers with learning disabilities?

MIDDLE SCHOOL AND HIGH SCHOOL STUDENTS WITH LEARNING DISABILITIES

CHAPTER 10

CHAPTER OBJECTIVES

At the completion of the chapter you will understand:

- the nature of adolescence.
- the characteristics of adolescents with learning disabilities.
- issues related to high-stakes testing and standards.
- the relationship between juvenile delinquency and learning disabilities.
- the collaboration between special educators and content area teachers.

In the early 1970s, the author attended a workshop of the International Council for Exceptional Children (CEC) in New York City. As a teacher of middle school students with learning disabilities, he wanted to attend as many workshops on middle and secondary special education as possible. There was little professional literature on the topic in both journals and textbooks, and he was excited about the prospect of learning what other teachers were doing. How did they balance the academic and social-emotional needs of their students? How much emphasis should be placed on basic skill acquisition versus content area instruction? A perusal of the conference offerings was extremely disappointing. There were literally hundreds of workshops, but fewer than a handful dealt with middle and high school students and even fewer with adolescents with learning disabilities. There was a belief that with proper remedial efforts, learning disabilities could be "cured" by the time these students entered high school. Since then, the topic of adolescents with learning disabilities has grown enormously. Much more is known about middle and high school students in general, there is a large body of empirical evidence to support specific interventions, and there are various ways to deliver services to these students. This chapter focuses on those changes that have occurred over the last 30 years. It addresses the academic, social-emotional, and behavioral needs of middle and high school students with learning disabilities and discusses issues/concerns that are unique to this population, including high-stakes testing, the link between juvenile delinquency and learning disabilities, learning strategies, and collaborative models.

TRANSITION FROM MIDDLE TO HIGH SCHOOL

Everyone thought that the transition from middle to high school would be difficult for Meghan. Her middle school utilized a team approach, and all of her teachers were aware of her learning disability. Most classes employed some type of group work, and she always could rely on a peer in her group. The activities were differentiated, she had accommodations for testing, and her homework was modified. What she liked most was the feeling of being a member of a team; all the members knew each other, and they seemed to appreciate that, in spite of her learning disability, she had many strengths.

Meghan thought high school would be different—more students, bigger classes, and teachers who didn't know that she had a learning disability. She was concerned about reading. She could decode words, but comprehending what she read always posed a problem. She worried that the books would be too hard and that there would be too much to read. She was also concerned that the amount of work would be overwhelming. Then there was the social side—making friends, going to special events, eating lunch. It was just too much.

When September arrived, Meghan was anxious about the new school year. However, after a few days, most of her fears were allayed. Her guidance counselor had already met with all of her teachers, giving them a profile identifying her strengths and needs. Her resource room teacher worked closely with her content area teachers, and most classes were cotaught. This was not what she expected. She pictured the teacher standing up in front of the class lecturing for 45 minutes. That hardly ever happened. Usually a "Do Now" list, based on homework, was posted. Then the teacher introduced the lesson, and the class broke up into small groups. Both teachers circulated around the classroom assisting students. They always provided a strategy for dealing with the content information. If Meghan had difficulty, she could always go to the resource room for additional help.

For many middle school students with learning disabilities, the transition to high school is not what they anticipate. Moreover, many elementary and middle school teachers are not aware of the scope of services on the middle and high school levels and reinforce the notion that these are large, impersonal institutions. It is not easy to meet the needs of middle and high school students with learning disabilities, especially if they are performing significantly below their peers. How would you organize your class to provide a variety of instructional approaches? How do you grade students? When you are collaborating with regular education colleagues, when do you plan? How do you divide up responsibilities? Do you teach content or strategies? These concerns must be considered if you are to be an effective teacher of middle and high school students with learning disabilities.

ADOLESCENCE: A TIME OF TRANSITION

As students move from elementary to middle to high school, they experience a shift in focus and a change in expectations. Obviously, there are also more personal transitions related to their physical, emotional, and social status. It appears that many researchers have overstated the negative aspects of this stage of development, so much so that many teachers of students with learning disabilities do not feel comfortable working with this age group. In actuality, most students progress through adolescence unscathed, as do their teachers. It has been estimated that only 20% of adolescents experience significant difficulties (Smith, 2003). To be sure, their reactions to specific situations may be extreme, but to characterize adolescents as filled with anxiety and negativism is wrong. The great majority of them go to school, perform well, have healthy interactions with their peers, families, and teachers, and become productive adult members of society. For students with learning disabilities, there may be other concerns. As they move through the school years, their disability may manifest itself in different ways. This, coupled with growing social-emotional demands, increases the probability of behavioral difficulties. However, the picture is not all pessimistic. A large body of empirical evidence supports the use of specific approaches for these students that was not available earlier in the field of learning disabilities. Much more is now known about teaching these students. The challenge is to translate research into classroom practice.

CHARACTERISTICS OF ADOLESCENTS WITH LEARNING DISABILITIES

One of the major issues related to students with learning disabilities is school failure. Mercer and Pullen (2005) discuss five major deficit areas for adolescents with learning disabilities: academic, cognitive, metacognitive, social interactions, and motivation.

Academic Deficits

On almost any academic measure, secondary students with learning disabilities perform at a lower level than their peers without disabilities. Their deficits are persistent and continue to interfere with academic success. Shaywitz (2003) notes that the gap widens for students with dyslexia as they enter secondary school, and other researchers (Deshler, Ellis, & Lenz, 1996; Reith & Polsgrove, 1994) report similar findings.

Cognitive and Metacognitive Deficits

Mercer (1997) notes that the ability to reflect on one's thinking process or cognitive strategies appears to be impaired in students with learning disabilities. They are inactive learners, may not understand task demands, and utilize ineffective and inefficient strategies. They tend not to think about their thinking and are less reflective than their peers without learning disabilities.

Social Interactive Deficits

Hazel and Schumaker (1988), as reported in Mercer (1997), note that students with learning disabilities (a) tend to use unacceptable behaviors in social situations, (b) are less able than their peers to solve social problems and predict the consequences of their social behaviors, (c) misinterpret social cues, (d) fail to adjust to the characteristics of their listeners, and (e) fail to take into account the thoughts and feelings of other people. In a recent review of the literature on the social skills of adolescents with learning disabilities, Court and Gwan (2003) noted a connection between learning disabilities and the acquisition of social skills. The authors differentiate between verbal and nonverbal learning disabilities and suggest that the former are more responsive to social skills training.

Motivation Deficits

Not surprisingly, adolescents who experience school failure are less likely to want to go to school, to be motivated to do well when they do attend, and to establish a plan for school completion and post-secondary options. Mercer (1997) cites a number of studies indicating that these students are not motivated to learn. As a teacher of middle and high school students with learning disabilities, this may be your biggest hurdle. Many of your students may not see the relationship between the work they do daily and success in school or in life.

In summary, the deficits of middle and high school students with learning disabilities are complex. They interact in such a way that it is not easy to isolate particular deficits. What is necessary is an intervention plan that addresses all of these students' needs.

THE LINK BETWEEN JUVENILE DELINQUENCY AND LEARNING DISABILITIES

For many years there has been discussion in the professional literature (Block, 2000; Dowling, 1991; Murray, 1976) and in conferences on the link between juvenile delinquency and learning disabilities. While all researchers have found that this relationship is not causal—that is, learning disabilities do not cause delinquency—it is also clear that it must be addressed. Brier (1989) notes that 30% to 50% of students with learning disabilities become delinquent. It has been suggested that the nature of learning disabilities, such as attentional, academic, language, social perception, and self-esteem deficiencies, interact with other factors and predispose some adolescents to delinquency. Brier (1994) assessed the effect of interventions on the recidivism rate of adolescents with learning disabilities who committed nonviolent crimes and who received psychosocial, educational, and vocational interventions. The results were encouraging; recidivism rates were significantly reduced for those who completed the program.

Three major hypotheses have been posited to explain this relationship (see also Figure 10–1):

1. *Academic failure.* Poor school performance leads to a negative self-concept, causing students to drop out of school and get involved with other delinquents.

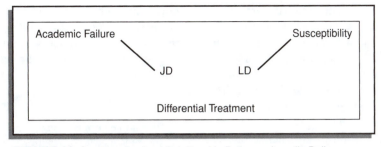

FIGURE 10–1 Hypothesized Relationship Between Juvenile Delinquency (JD) and Learning Disabilities (LD)

2. *Susceptibility.* The nature of learning disabilities places these students more at risk for antisocial behavior.
3. *Differential treatment.* Students with learning disabilities are more likely to get caught when they engage in delinquent behavior.

Malmgren, Abbot, and Hawkins (1999) suggest that there are many methodological flaws in the literature. They question the relationship between learning disabilities and delinquency and suggest that when one controls for gender, ethnicity, and socioeconomic status, there is no direct relationship between them. While it may seem obvious that a student who does poorly in school and drops out is more likely to get involved in marginal groups, much more research is needed on this relationship.

INCREASED DEMANDS ON ADOLESCENTS WITH LEARNING DISABILITIES

School reforms such as IDEA 2004 and NCLB have led to an increase in standards, competency tests (also referred to as **high-stakes testing**), and inclusion of students with learning disabilities in regular classrooms. Most middle and high school students with learning disabilities spend most of their time in regular education classes alongside their peers without disabilities. These increased demands make success in school much more difficult.

Mercer and Pullen (2005) note that the following academic demands are placed on middle and high school students with learning disabilities:

- Gaining information from written material
- Gaining information from lectures
- Demonstrating knowledge through tests
- Expressing information in writing
- Working independently with little feedback
- Demonstrating a broad set of cognitive and metacogitative strategies
- Interacting appropriately
- Demonstrating motivation to learn (pp. 161–163)

When you look at this list of academic demands, you can imagine the difficulties your students with learning disabilities will have. For example, they may have trouble attending to lectures, and those with a written language disorder will be at a marked disadvantage in a class where the teacher relies heavily on essay exams. Most adolescents with learning disabilities may not be motivated to learn, given their history of school failure (see Chapter 16 for additional information). For example, Jessie, a 10th grader with a learning disability, has spent her entire school career in self-contained (in elementary school) or inclusive classes (in middle school). Her high school program is somewhat varied. She is in a self-contained earth science class taught by a special education teacher who is also certified in science. She is in an inclusive class with two teachers for math, English, and social studies. And she is mainstreamed for art, music, and physical education. Throughout the day, she experiences many failures. She has a difficult time keeping up with the reading demands and tends to give up. If you walked into her class, you would see her with her head on the desk, appearing to be uninterested. However, she is simply overwhelmed.

Vocational and employment demands may also pose problems for your students as they enter the workforce. The transition from an environment that provides a great deal of support to one that values independent work behaviors can be troubling. Couple this shift with specific disabilities in literacy and math, and you can see why these demands may be overwhelming for your students.

HIGH-STAKES TESTING

In addition to these demands, most states have statewide assessment procedures. Twenty-three states require the student to pass an exit exam or competency exam in order to graduate (and there are no accommodations for these tests). This widespread use of one test to demonstrate competence poses particular problems for adolescents with learning disabilities. The NRC published a report on high-stakes testing of special education students (Heubert & Hauser, 1999). They had two recommendations:

1. To increase such students' participation in large-scale assessments, in part so that school systems can be held accountable for their educational progress, and
2. To test each such student in a manner that provides appropriate accommodation for the effect of a disability or of limited English proficiency or the subject matter being tested, while maintaining the validity and comparability of test results among all students. (p. 16)

This appears to be difficult, and many states are grappling with alternative forms of assessment. The National Center for Learning Disabilities (2002)

notes that alternative assessments are more likely to be available for students with severe disabilities than for those with learning disabilities, and they have developed the following policy recommendations (pp. 1–3):

Test Validity and Reporting
Students with disabilities are usually not included in the sample population used in test development, nor are students with disabilities, when included, given appropriate accommodations. This results in a lack of test validity and the development of assessments that are, in fact, assessing the student's disability, not his or her ability. Assessments should be designed and validated so as to ensure that the normative sample includes students with disabilities using appropriate accommodations. Testing results should report both aggregated and disaggregated data and should be reported at the state, district, and school level. Data should be used to determine the effects of high stakes assessment on students with LD.

Access to Accommodations
Students with learning disabilities must be provided the same accommodations on the assessments that they have used during their educational careers. Decisions about the accommodations to be provided on assessments are the sole responsibility of those involved in the formulation of the student's Individualized Education Program (IEP) or Section 504 Plan, generally a team consisting of the student, his or her parents, and appropriate school personnel. Such decisions should not be limited by any predetermined list of accommodations formulated at the district or state level. Accommodations should not be labeled as "standard" or "non-standard." The test results of students with learning disabilities who participate in an assessment with accommodations should count for whatever purposes the assessment system has been validated and the scores of these students should not be "flagged" in any way that will have a stigmatizing effect.

Alternate Assessment
Most students with LD do not require a different set of standards, but they do require both instruction and assessments that are better suited to their unique needs. Just as these students require differentiated instructional approaches in order to learn the same material as their non-disabled peers, they

should have access to a meaningful alternate assessment system that is based on the same standards as the regular assessment. Alternate assessments should allow students with learning disabilities to demonstrate their knowledge, rather than the effects of their disabilities.

Parent and Student Involvement

Parents and students should be given clear and accurate information about the assessment system, accommodations, alternate assessments, and appeals. The short- and long-term effects of non-participation should be fully discussed with parents and students to ensure a complete understanding of the consequences of any large-scale assessment system.

Political and Administrative Considerations

Considerations, such as how the inclusion of students with LD in high stakes assessments will affect reporting of scores of schools and districts, must not be allowed to override the rights and needs of students with learning disabilities nor adversely affect the benefits of the students once included.

Use of Test Scores

In designing and implementing remediation options for students failing or performing poorly, educators and administrators must protect the rights and needs of students with learning disabilities.

Limit on Use of High Stakes Tests

Multiple measures of student performance should be utilized in the assessment systems, and no one measure or test score should determine the educational future of students.

INCLUSION AND THE ADOLESCENT WITH LEARNING DISABILITIES

As has been noted frequently in this book, most students with learning disabilities are being educated in regular education classrooms. On the secondary level, this poses a problem because most content area teachers are not licensed or certified in special education, and many special educators are not licensed or certified in the content areas. In addition, the current realities of secondary schools listed below impact teachers who are trying to

provide appropriate instruction for middle and high school students with learning disabilities (Bulgren & Lenz, 1996):

- Pressure to cover large amounts of content
- Complexity of content-area textbooks
- Significant academic diversity
- Limited opportunities for academic interactions
- Instruction geared to achieving students
- Limited time for planning and teaching
- Limited opportunities for collegial study, planning or teaching

Inclusive practices on the secondary level usually involve some type of coteaching. (See Chapter 7 for a discussion of coteaching and various models.) Coteaching is much more than two educators teaching in the same classroom. It takes time, planning, and reflection. Unless there is adequate collaboration (see Chapter 7), students will not succeed. Whether you are a coteacher or a resource room teacher, there must be adequate communication between you and the regular classroom teacher. The next section discusses ways of providing students with learning disabilities access to the regular education curriculum.

ACCESS TO THE REGULAR EDUCATION CURRICULUM

Middle and high school students must be provided with access to the regular education curriculum. King-Sears (2001) suggests three steps for gaining access: analyzing the curriculum to become familiar with it; enhancing areas of the curriculum that are weak; and considering ways to adapt and modify the curriculum for students with disabilities. Other approaches that were developed for all students, not just those with learning disabilities, also provide guidance for teachers of students with learning disabilities. Two that will be discussed are differentiated instruction and universal design.

Differentiated Instruction

Tomlinson and Eidson (2003) recommend a variety of differentiated practices that enable teachers to meet the needs of diverse students, including those with learning disabilities. Teachers should differentiate the content, the process, the product, the effect, and the learning environment based on the needs of all students (see Tomlinson, 2002, 2003, for additional information). Salend (2005, pp. 337–338) provides the following questions teachers should address when differentiating instruction in their classrooms:

- What are the themes, goals, and objectives of the lesson/activity?
- What teaching materials and arrangement will be used in the lesson/activity?
- When, where, and how long will this lesson/activity occur?
- Will students be able to participate in this lesson/activity in the same ways as their classmates?
- What supports, learning strategies, instructional accommodations and/or instructional technology/assistive devices are needed to help students participate fully?
- How can the curriculum be supplemented or changed to address the different learning needs of students?
- How can the lesson/activity be differentiated to reflect students' learning styles, language, culture, experiences, behavioral needs, interests, talents, strengths, challenges, and IEPs?
- How can the lesson/activity be differentiated in terms of the type and amount of work, teaching materials used, grouping patterns, assistance needed, pace and time, and the products produced?
- Can the student participate in the activity but work on other skills or work with others on an activity that has different goals?
- How can the lesson/activity be differentiated to motivate and engage students and provide them with choices?
- What materials will be needed to engage students in the lesson/activity?
- How can the classroom environment be differentiated to engage students in the lesson/activity?

- How can student mastery of the content of the lesson/activity be assessed?

Universal Design

The term **universal design** was initially used in product design and architecture. The aim was to design products and environments that were usable by as many people as possible (The Center for Universal Design, 1997). It has also been applied to educational settings (Salend, 2005; Scott, McGuire, & Shaw, 2003) and refers to providing a flexible curriculum and materials so that all students can learn. The curriculum and materials are useful, appealing, and safe for all students; they are flexible and provide choices for students; they are simple and easy to use; they clearly communicate essential information to all students; they utilize multiple formats; their use requires a minimum of physical effort; and they are accessible by all students, regardless of their size, posture, or level of mobility. These principles of universal design provide greater access to the regular education curricular and allow for greater differentiation of instruction.

Kame'enui, Carnine, Dixon, Simmons, and Coyne (2002, p. 9) present six principles of effective instructional tools that provide access to the curriculum for all students:

Big Ideas
Highly selected concepts, principles, rules, strategies, or heuristics that facilitate the most efficient and broadest acquisition of knowledge.

Conspicuous Strategies
Sequences of teaching events and teacher actions that make explicit the steps in learning. They are made conspicuous by the use of visual maps or models, verbal directions, full and clear explanations, etc.

Mediated Scaffolding
Temporary support for students to learn new material. Scaffolding is faded over time.

Strategic Integration
Meaningful consideration and sequencing of instruction in ways that show the commonalities and differences between old and new knowledge.

Primed Background Knowledge

Related knowledge placed effectively in sequence, that students must already possess, in order to learn new knowledge.

Judicious Review

Sequence and schedule of opportunities learners have to apply and develop facility with new knowledge. The review must be adequate, distributed, cumulative, and varied.

Teachers of students with learning disabilities in middle and high school can increase access to the regular education curriculum by employing the principles instructional design cited above (see Kame'emui et al., 2002, for more specific strategies to accommodate diverse learners). These principles, as well as the principles of differentiated instruction and universal design, are not specific to students with learning disabilities; however, they have applicability in inclusive classrooms.

PROVIDING APPROPRIATE INSTRUCTION

As students with learning disabilities progress through middle school and high school, the gap between their performance and that of their peers without disabilities widens and becomes more obvious. Some instructional approaches and/or materials are not age appropriate and may have been used before your students entered middle or high school. Deshler and his colleagues at the University of Kansas have been helpful in addressing the needs of this age group and their teachers. Deshler and Putnam (1996, pp. 4–6) present six factors that are basic to quality programming for middle and high school students with learning disabilities:

1. Adolescence is one of the most difficult and challenging of all developmental stages.
2. Quality programming decisions for adolescents with learning disabilities must be based on an understanding of the exact nature of the difficulty(ies) with which they contend.
3. Adolescents must be involved in all aspects of planning and implementing their instruc-

tional programs including assessment; program specification; goal setting; monitoring and evaluation; and program modification.
4. How teachers define their role in relation to the adolescent with learning disabilities greatly affects the nature and quality of the at-risk student's education.
5. What teachers teach to adolescents with learning disabilities will have a profound influence on the extent to which these students become independent learners and performers.
6. How teachers teach strategies to adolescents with learning disabilities is paramount.

As a teacher of adolescents with learning disabilities, it is clear that what and how you teach is critical to their success. Deshler and his colleagues at the University of Kansas have developed numerous empirically based strategies to assist you. These strategies will now be discussed.

Learning Strategies

The University of Kansas Center for Research on Learning (previously known as the Institute for Research in Learning Disabilities) has been at the forefront in the area of learning disabilities on the secondary level. Since the mid-1970s, it has provided high-quality, empirically based interactions using a learning strategy model. This model teaches students methods to acquire, organize, remember, and retrieve information, focusing on how to learn, how to behave, and how to do well both academically and socially. The aim is that through instruction in specific strategies, students will become introspective, independent learners who will develop efficient and effective problem-solving skills. Deshler and Lenz (1989), as cited in Deshler and Putnam (1996, p. 23), suggest that as a teacher of middle and high school students with learning disabilities, you should develop the following three areas for effective instruction:

1. A range of general strategies that can be applied to all content areas, as well as specific strategies for learning targeted content, must be identified (e.g., strategies for learning content

and strategies for learning social studies content). The teacher must know the strategies that are most related to success, must understand their critical features, and must be able to articulate them in meaningful ways to students. These strategies may relate to student motivation, social interactions, or academic performance.

2. The teacher must know how to present information in a way that will induce students to learn when students do not have effective and efficient strategies for acquiring information. This means that the acquisition and generalization of strategies for learning content requires explicit instruction that is both intensive and extensive to ensure that the time spent teaching strategies to help students learn is not wasted.

3. The environment in which learning and instruction take place must facilitate and enhance strategic learning, performance, and competence across all educational settings and interactions.

Critical Features of Learning Strategies Approach

Ellis and Lenz (1987, p. 27) identified three critical features of learning strategies: content, design, and usefulness. Specific characteristics of each will now be presented.

Content
- Lead to a specific and successful outcome.
- Are sequenced in a manner that leads to an efficient approach to the task.
- Cue students to use specific cognitive strategies.
- Cue students to use meta-cognition, that is how an individual seek and uses feedback from themselves [sic] as a task is being completed.
- Cue the students to select and use appropriate procedures, skills, or rules.
- Cue the student to take some type of overt action.
- Can be performed by the student in a limited amount of time.
- Are essential and do not include unnecessary steps or explanations.

Design
- Use a remembering system.
- Use simple and brief wording.
- Begin with "action words."
- Use seven or fewer steps.
- Use words that are uncomplicated and familiar to students.

Usefulness
- Address a common but important existing problem that students are encountering in their settings.
- Address demands that are encountered frequently over an extended time.
- Can be applied across a variety of settings, situations, and contexts.

All three features must be incorporated into the teaching of learning strategies. Clearly, to succeed, this requires time, effort, and collaboration on the part of regular education and special education teachers.

Instructional Principles

There are several important instructional principles in the learning strategies approach:

- Teach prerequisite skills.
- Teach regularly and with intensity.
- Emphasize and reinforce personal effort.
- Teach to mastery.
- Integrate instruction so that students will learn how and when to use the strategy.
- Discuss and demonstrate cognitive processes.
- Emphasize generalization.

These principles must be employed throughout instruction in the learning strategies approach. Identify the prerequisite skills your students need in order to use the strategy; then teach them. Never assume that they have these skills. This is a difficult approach to implement (Bender, 2005). You must use it regularly and with intensity, including the students in the process. Their personal commitment and effort should be reinforced. Once the students learn the strategy (mastery), you must integrate it so that they will know not only how to use it, but also when. This will increase the probability of transfer of learning (generalization). Middle and high school students with learning disabilities need to become active partners in the learning process. Model and discuss the strategy with them and demonstrate specific cognitive processes (i.e., attention, memory, metacognition). Finally, emphasize ways in which they can employ the strategy in a variety of settings across content areas (King-Sears & Mooney, 2004) to enable them to generalize. The stages of implementation, described below, provide more specific instructions.

IMPLEMENTING THE MODEL

There are eight stages in implementing the learning strategies model (Ellis & Lenz, 1996, p. 38):

1. Pretest and Make Commitments
2. Describe the Strategy
3. Model the Strategy
4. Verbal Elaboration and Rehearsal of the Strategy
5. Controlled Practice and Feedback
6. Advanced Practice and Feedback
7. Confirm Acquisition and Make Generalization Commitments
8. Generalization

Each stage is presented in Table 10-1.

A practical example of how one teacher, Ms. Washington, utilized a particular strategy (PREP) with her students, was provided by Salend (2005, p. 256):

Ms. Washington has noticed that several of her students are not prepared for class physically and mentally. She observes the students closely for several days to determine which skills and strategies they use successfully and which ones they seem to lack. She then meets with the students to talk about her concerns and how their current approaches are affecting thief performance. Though initially reluctant, the students indicate that they aren't pleased with their classroom performance and would like to do better.

She discusses a learning strategy called PREP and explains how it might help them. PREP involves four stages:

Prepare materials
- Get the notebook, study guide, pencil, and textbook ready for class.
- Mark difficult-to-understand parts of notes, the study guide, and textbook.

Review what you know
- Read notes, study guide and textbook cues.
- Relate cues to what you already know about the topic.
- List at least three things you already know about the topic.

Establish a positive mind set
- Tell yourself to learn.
- Suppress put-downs.
- Make a positive statement.

Pinpoint goals
- Decide what you want to find out.
- Note participation goals. (Ellis, 1989, p. 36)

After reviewing the strategy and briefly explaining each stop, Ms. Washington asks the students to decide if they are willing to make a commitment to learning this strategy. One student says, "No," and Ms. Washington tells her that she does not have to learn it, but if she changes her mind she can learn it at another time. The other students indicate that they are willing go try to learn the strategy. To increase their motivation and reinforce their commitment, Ms. Washington has the students set goals.

Ms. Washington begins by modeling and demonstrating the strategy by verbalizing and "thinking out loud" so that students can experience the thinking processes they will need when using the strategy. She models the procedure several times, using a variety of materials from the class, and reviews how she uses the PREP acronym to remember the steps in the strategy. Students discuss how the PREP strategy compares with their current approaches to learning, as well as the overt and the covert behaviors necessary to implement the strategy.

Next, Ms. Washington has the students attempt to learn the steps of the strategy. She divides them into teams and has each team rehearse and memorize the strategy and its proper sequence. To help some

TABLE 10–1   Stages in Implementing the Learning Strategies Model

Stage 1: Pretest and make commitments	To succeed, middle and high school students with learning disabilities need to participate actively in the learning process. The major purpose of the initial stage of strategy instruction is to motivate them to commit to the approach. They need to know why this approach is effective, how it will help them succeed, and how other students have successfully used it. Additionally, this is the point where teachers can assess the entry-level performance of each student in order to establish responsible goals.
Stage 2: Describe the strategy	Students must understand the rationale for the new approach. They need to know exactly how it will help them in all subject areas, as well as its relevance to out-of-school activities. At this stage, they will be given information on the processes involved in learning and how to apply them. Throughout this stage, students will actively participate in discussions of the effectiveness of the approach compared to other approaches they have used in the past. Most middle and high school students with learning disabilities recognize that most of their efforts have not been successful, and it is critical for them to understand why this approach has a higher probability of success.
Stage 3: Model the strategy	This involves much more than describing an approach. The teacher actually demonstrates a strategy and utilizes language similar to that students may employ when they self-talk and problem-solve. Gradually, the students will become involved in some of the steps and then in all of them. Start with easy material and encourage students to think out loud, reinforcing their efforts. This is difficult for many students with learning disabilities, who tend to be passive learners. You may need to use a great deal of reinforcement at this stage.
Stage 4: Verbal elaboration and rehearsal of the strategy	Students need to describe the strategy in their own words and discuss the goals. Why use it? When? Where? Once they can discuss it, they must rehearse the stages through memorization. Again, start slowly with easy material. It is critical that students succeed at each step. Give them feedback that encourages them to try the approach. If they don't accept it, it will not succeed.
Stage 5: Controlled practice and feedback	At this stage, students are discovering how to use the learning strategy without the typical pressures and demands of the curriculum. The material should be at a level commensurate with their ability and the task demands, requiring few or no higher-level thinking skills. Students are not to be challenged at this stage. Careful selection of material will allow them to gain confidence and gradually take control of the strategy. The teacher reviews the strategy, provides guided practice through modeling, and gradually encourages the students to work independently.
Stage 6: Advanced practice and feedback	Once again the teacher reviews the strategy, provides guided practice, and moves the students toward independence. However, at this stage, the teacher is giving the students materials that approximate the real world of the classroom. Teachers need to provide a variety of materials, both well designed and poorly designed, so that students gain control over the typical materials they will encounter in school.

Stage 7: Confirm acquisition and make generalization commitments	Deshler, et al. (1996) note that this is the stage where many teachers fall short. They fail to promote generalization. Students must recognize the need to apply the strategy across content areas and settings. They need to demonstrate mastery of the strategy and employ it. They must recognize why it is important to do so (success vs. failure in school) and know that they will be supported by special and regular educators.
Stage 8: Generalization	Students need to know when to use the strategy, how to remember it, practice using it, receive feedback regarding their performance, adopt the strategy, and incorporate it into their problem-solving approach if they are to generalize. This will not happen by chance. This stage is highly dependent on the collaboration between regular and special educators. On the secondary level, students with learning disabilities will most likely be taught in regular classrooms by regular educators with little or no training in learning disabilities. It is critical that special educators collaborate with them if students are to succeed. And nowhere is this more important than when the teacher is utilizing a learning strategy approach and wants to generalize learning.

students learn the strategy, she gives them cue cards. As students memorize the stops, Mr. Washington gives them cue cards containing less information. When the students can give the steps in the correct sequence, Ms. Washington has them apply the strategy with materials from the classroom. Students work in cooperative learning groups to practice the strategy and receive feedback from their peers. Ms. Washington circulates around the room, observes students using the strategy and provides feedback. She encourages the students to concentrate on becoming skilled in using the strategy and not to be concerned about the accuracy of the content. As students become adept in using the strategy, Ms. Washington gives them other material so that they can apply the strategy in many different situations. When students are able to do this, Ms. Washington gives them a test to check their mastery of the material.

Once students master the strategy. Ms. Washington encourages them to use it in her class. She observes them to see if they are employing the strategy and keeps records of their academic performance. Periodically, Ms. Washington reviews the strategy procedures. She cues students to use the strategy through verbal reminders, cue cards, listing the strategy on the board, and reviewing its components. Because the strategy has greatly improved the students' performance, Ms. Washington is working with some of the other teachers to help students use them in their classrooms.

EXAMPLES OF LEARNING STRATEGIES

Below are a five learning strategies that are effective in content areas: PARTS, SNIPS, DEFENDS, PIRATES, and ANSWER. (PARTS) is used for perusing textbooks (Ellis, 1996, p. 86):

Perform goal setting
    Clarify why you are analyzing the chapter parts.
    Identify a goal related to this reason.
    Make a positive self-statement.
Analyze little parts (title, headings, visuals, and words)
    Explain the information indicated by the part.
    Predict what the section under the part is about.
    Tie the parts together.
Review the big parts (introduction and summary)
    Search for signal words that indicate main ideas.
    Decide what the author thinks is important.
    Relate new information to what you already know.
    Paraphrase the main message.

Think of questions you hope will be answered
　　Check questions provided by the chapter.
　　Formulate your own questions.
State relationships
　　How does the chapter relate to the unit?
　　How does the chapter relate to what you already
　　　know?

Analyzing Visual Aids

Too often adolescents with learning disabilities who have difficulty reading ignore visual aids. These aids enable them to obtain information from textbooks even though they are difficult for them to read. Ellis (1996, p. 91) presents the (SNIPS) strategy for analyzing visual aids.

Start with questions and predictions
　　Question to clarify why you are analyzing the
　　　visual.
　　Question to find out what is important to under-
　　　stand and remember about the visual.
　　If you can't think of your own question, let the
　　　type of visual be a signal for a good question.
　　Picture = What is it a picture of? Is it something
　　　important to remember?
　　Graph/Chart = What is being compared? How?
　　Map = What key areas are important to see?
　　　Why are they key areas?
　　Timeline = Shows the history of what? From
　　　when to when?

Using what you already know about the information in the visual, predict what you think the visual will be about.

Note what you can learn from the hints
Look for hints that signal answers to your questions, and then identify what they tell you.

　　Title says the visual is about . . .
　　Print says . . .
　　Lines are used to show . . .
　　Color is used as decoration? Or to show . . .
　　Other hints indicate . . .?

Identify what is important
　　What is the main idea that should be remem-
　　　bered about the visual?

What are some important facts that can be iden-
　　tified from the visual? Which facts should be
　　remembered?
Plug it into the chapter
　　Think about what the chapter is about.
　　How does the visual relate to the chapter?
　　How does the visual relate to what this section
　　　of the chapter is about?
See if you can explain the visual to someone
　　Find someone to who you can explain the
　　　visual (explain it to yourself if nobody else is
　　　available).
　　Tell what you think the visual is about and how
　　　you think it relates to what the chapter is
　　　about.
　　Identify what you think are the best hints on the
　　　visuals and tell why they are good hints.

Written Language

Ellis and Colvert (1996, p. 174) developed the DEFENDS strategy. Its major components are as follows: **D**ecide on the goals. **E**stimate main ideas and details. **F**igure the order. **E**xpress these right away. **N**ote your main idea right away. **D**rive it home in the last sentence. **S**earch for errors.

Test-Taking Strategies

Many adolescents with learning disabilities are poor test takers. They may know the information but have difficulty responding to tests. Two strategies that have been effective are PIRATES, for objective tests, and ANSWER, for essay tests (Deshler et al., 1996).

In the PIRATES strategy students **P**repare to succeed. **I**nspect the instructions. **R**ead. **A**nswer or abandon. **T**urn back. **E**stimate. **S**urvey.

The ANSWER strategy is used for essay tests and students should **A**nalyze. **N**otice requirements. **S**et up and outline. **W**ork in the details of the response. **E**ngineer your response. **R**eview. (See Deshler et al., 1996 for a more detailed description of these strategies).

Reading in the Content Area

The SCROL strategy assists students with content area, textbooks by helping them use text headings (Grant, 1993, p. 484):

S— Survey the headings and subheadings.

C— Connect the subheadings by writing key words that link them with illustrations. You can also connect them with illustrations and/or graphic organizers.

R— Read the text and write the headings.

O— Outline the main ideas and details to support the headings from memory.

L— Look to see how accurate you are and modify if necessary.

SUMMARY

Teaching adolescents with learning disabilities requires a change in focus from the elementary grades. These students must meet the demands of a difficult curriculum and exit assessments in order to receive a diploma. Teachers must be able to provide high-quality instruction that enables their students to generalize across the curriculum. This chapter has focused on the nature of adolescents, the relationship between juvenile delinquency and learning disabilities, and the impact of inclusion. Finally, to meet the new curriculum demands, differentiated instruction, universal design, and the learning strategies approach were discussed.

SPRINGBOARDS FOR REFLECTION AND DISCUSSION

1. Interview a teacher of adolescents with learning disabilities. How does he or she view the role of the secondary versus the elementary teacher?
2. Observe a high school and an elementary resource room. How do they differ? How are they the same?
3. Observe adolescents with learning disabilities in a classroom. How does the content area teacher meet their needs?
4. Observe a content area class that is cotaught. What coteaching approach is used? When do the teachers plan? How effective is the program?
5. Speak to a high school student with a learning disability. How does he or she deal with the disability in high school? How is this different from the student's coping strategy in elementary school?
6. Interview a parent of an adolescent with learning disabilities. What are some of the issues that emerge during the secondary years?
7. Observe a secondary self-contained classroom. What content is being presented? How much contact do the students have with mainstream education? Where do they go after high school?

TRANSITION PLANNING AND ADULTS WITH LEARNING DISABILITES

CHAPTER

CHAPTER OBJECTIVES

At the end of this chapter you will:

- understand the need to study adults with learning disabilities.
- become aware of post–high school options.
- know about laws affecting adult students with learning disabilities.
- learn about college and vocational programs for students with learning disabilities.

In the spring of 1985, Louis was 37 years old when he called the Learning Disabilities Clinic at an urban university. He did so after much prompting by his brothers, who were both medical doctors. Louis never did well in school and dropped out at the first chance at 16 years of age. He held a number of jobs in the construction trade and made a decent living. He rarely read and, fortunately, his job did not require many academic skills. However, when it did involve tasks such as simple multiplication or reading directions, he became agitated and often verbally attacked the person asking him a question or requesting a response. His major concerns at this point in his life were social-emotional issues. He had been divorced twice, was often aggressive (both verbally and physically) with coworkers, and had difficulty managing daily tasks such as keeping a checking account, paying bills on time, and reading menus. Louis always thought that he was "stupid" or "mentally retarded." It wasn't until his brothers suggested he might have a learning disability that (with much prompting) he decided to call the clinic. His goals were simple: he wanted to be able to read a book, and he wanted to know if he had a learning disability. A thorough evaluation confirmed the diagnosis of learning disability. Louis is not alone. Many people in their 30s and 40s went to school at a time when learning disabilities were not readily identified, and they struggled. Fortunately for Louis, his family was able to provide him with employment. And yet, he struggled daily because of his inability to read, compute, and write on even the most basic level. Moreover, he struggled with the emotional overlay that often accompanies a learning disability.

Contrast Louis's plight to that of Miriam, who was diagnosed with a learning disability in Grade 2, and received resource room services throughout her school years. A transitional plan was developed at age 16, and she attended a college program for students with learning disabilities. She went on to receive a graduate degree in education and is currently a special education teacher. Clearly, adults with learning disabilities do not fall into such neat dichotomies. They are a heterogeneous group with a variety of strengths, weaknesses, and coping strategies. What is clear is that learning disabilities do not disappear; they persist throughout life (Gerber, 2003).

Students who were classified as having learning disabilities in the 1970s and 1980s are now in their 20s and 30s. They are the first generation to have been provided with strong federal legislation (P. L. 94-142, the Education of All Handicapped Children Act of 1975) that ensured them a free, appropriate public education. They attended schools at a time when programs for students with learning disabilities proliferated and the number of students classified increased exponentially. Some went on to college, others went on to postsecondary vocational programs, and still others sought full-time employment after high school. Louis was too old to benefit from educators' awareness of the nature and needs of students with learning disabilities, whereas Miriam was in the right place at the right time (and the right school!). There are many persons along that continuum. This chapter focuses on their transition from high school and on adults with learning disabilities. What can be done for Louis at this point in his life? (See the next section.) Why is Miriam so successful? What services were available for her? What protections are in place to ensure that adults with learning disabilities are provided with the social, emotional, and career opportunities they deserve? And perhaps the most important question: Why is it important for teachers of students with learning disabilities to learn about adults with learning disabilities?

Practical Considerations: Louis, an Adult Whose Learning Disabilities Were Not Properly Addressed

If Louis were just 20 years younger, this would be a different story. He attended school in the 1960s, and in his district, if you had difficulty in school, you were viewed as mentally retarded or emotionally disturbed. Louis was neither, but he had a great deal of trouble in school. He was given minimal remedial help, placed in classes for slower students, and pushed through school until he was 16 and decided (with his parents' consent) to drop out. He held a series of low-paying jobs and finally, through family ties, was able to find work in the construction trade. His academic deficiencies appeared periodically but did not pose a threat to his job. His personal life was another story. He relied on specific people in stores and banks to assist him with his financial transactions, but when they left he was lost. He had

difficulty socially because he did everything possible to hide his disability but inevitable got caught. He blamed his two divorces on his anger related to his lack of academic skills and his wives' frustration with his unwillingness to seek help. It wasn't until his second divorce, difficulty on the job, and his brothers' prompting that he sought an evaluation. Both brothers were medical doctors and learned about the Learning Disability Clinic through a colleague. They felt he needed assistance to better understand the nature of his problem. During the initial interview, Louis was asked why he wanted an evaluation at this point in his life. He stated, "to find out if I'm mentally retarded or just stupid." It was sad that these thoughts lingered and he had no answers. It was optimistic that he was able to address them in order to stop his downward spiral.

A thorough psychoeducational evaluation indicated that the diagnosis of learning disability was appropriate. However, there were also several social-emotional issues that had to be addressed. The recommendations included reading instruction and therapy. In little more than a year, Louis was better able to control his anger, deal with his disability more effectively, and read newspapers and magazines. One of his short-term goals was to finish a book, something he had never done. He was on his way to reaching that goal.

REASONS FOR STUDYING ADULTS WITH LEARNING DISABILITIES

As a classroom teacher or an administrator, you may wonder why it is important to study adults with learning disabilities. Perhaps the most important reason is to become more reflective about your own teaching. Adults with learning disabilities have stories to tell about their own school experiences—what worked and what didn't, what they would have liked teachers to do, how they struggled, how they solved problems, and so on (see the next section)—and while this is not nec-

essarily research based, it is still valuable information that can be useful to teachers of all students with learning disabilities. Even a perusal of the professional literature on the topic indicates that for many adults with learning disabilities, life is a struggle despite the interventions they received in elementary and secondary school.

Best Practices: Listening to Adults with Learning Disabilities. There is a limited number of first-person accounts of learning disabilities, but this literature is growing. In *Meeting the Challenge of Learning Disabilities in Adulthood*, Hoffman (2000) presents cogent interviews with 13 adults with learning disabilities on topics varying from day-to-day life to spirituality. These interviews are presented in the context of characteristics of learning disabilities and provide wonderful insights for all teachers. Rodis, Garrod, and Boscardin edited *Learning Disabilities and Life Stories* (2001), a series of autobiographical essays by college students with learning disabilities. As the editors state, "while it can be tremendously helpful to read an 'experts' view on learning disabilities, such experts are outsiders; they have not, in most cases, lived the things they write about" (p. xi). Ferri, Connor, Solis, Valle, and Volpitta (2005) studied a unique group—teachers with learning disabilities—examining how these individuals constructed their own meaning of learning disabilities. Four teachers were interviewed (three special education teachers and one student teacher). Each was paired with a researcher and met for three 60- to 90-minute interviews. The researchers started with a life story narrative and based future interview questions on their detailed analysis of the initial interviews. What emerged was a thought provoking description of what it is like to live with a learning disability. The authors believe "that a discourse of LD grounded in lived experience and narrative has the potential to transform our thinking and our practice" (p. 75). Some of the teachers interviewed had very negative views of their elementary and secondary school years. While these accounts may not be easy to read, it is important that they be considered when developing and implementing academic and behavioral interventions

for students at any age. For secondary school teachers of students with learning disabilities the implications are clear. More collaboration is needed between high school and postsecondary educators, and vocational and technical options must be expanded. Also, collaboration with parents of students with learning disabilities will be enhanced if teachers view learning disabilities across the life span and not merely at their own grade level. Adults with learning disabilities provide a rich source of data, both qualitative and quantitative, that needs to be explored more thoroughly. Our understanding of the transition from high school to adulthood is "tentative at best" (Bender, 2004, p. 372) because of the lack of rigorous research designs.

LIFE BEYOND HIGH SCHOOL

The tongue-in-cheek ad shown in Figure 11–1 appeared in the *National Center for Learning Disabilities Newsletter* (February 2005). Horowitz (2005, p. 1) discusses the challenges faced by students, parents, and teachers during the transition process. He poses four reasonable questions that, if answered, would greatly facilitate the process:

- Which students are best suited for a competitive college experience, and which would do better with an introductory pre-college work or work-study experience?
- What accommodations are likely to enable particular students to succeed in competitive work or academic settings and how should these

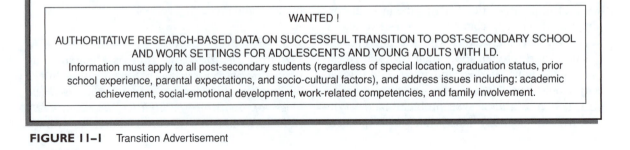

WANTED !

AUTHORITATIVE RESEARCH-BASED DATA ON SUCCESSFUL TRANSITION TO POST-SECONDARY SCHOOL AND WORK SETTINGS FOR ADOLESCENTS AND YOUNG ADULTS WITH LD.
Information must apply to all post-secondary students (regardless of special location, graduation status, prior school experience, parental expectations, and socio-cultural factors), and address issues including: academic achievement, social-emotional development, work-related competencies, and family involvement.

FIGURE 11–1 Transition Advertisement

students go about disclosing their LD and assuring their rights to these entitlements?

- What activities need to take place during a student's middle and high school career to build the self-confidence and self-advocacy skills that are essential to post-secondary success?
- What particular supports (including technology) are most likely to succeed in providing students the help they need in critical areas such as goal setting, time management, note taking, and seeking assistance?

Unfortunately, at this time we cannot answer all of these questions based on research (go to http://www.ldonline.org and click on "February 2005 Newsletter, Research Roundup"). The professional literature focuses mainly on college programs. Yet, as Horowitz (2005) notes, we cannot distinguish between students who would benefit from a college program and those who would not. The majority of students with learning disabilities will enter the workforce (NLT52, 2005), but there is little research evidence to guide practice. The National Longititudial Transition Study-2 (NLTS2) does provide some useful information on the postschool experience of youth with disabilities (Wagner, Newman, Cameto, Garza, & Levine, 2005, p. ES-6). Their findings regarding those with learning disabilities or other health impairments (OHI) are as follows:

- About three-fourths of out-of-school youth with learning disabilities or other health impairments have completed high school, almost all of those with a regular diploma.
- More than three-fourths have been engaged in school, work, or preparation for work since leaving high school, and about 45% were currently employed at the time of the interview.
- About one-third were expected by their parents "definitely" to go on to postsecondary education after high school, and about that many have done so within 2 years of leaving high school. Two-year college is their typical pursuit.
- Youth with learning disabilities or other health impairments have experienced among the broadest changes in their leisure-time and friendship pursuits, with large reductions in passive leisure

activities (e.g., watching television or using a computer) and large increases in seeing friends often.
- Although these youth are among the most likely to be registered to vote (about 70%), they also have experienced the largest decline in participation in pro-social organized groups and volunteer activities.
- Youth in these categories are second only to youth with emotional disturbances in the likelihood of being involved with the criminal justice system, and those with other health impairments show the only significant increase in arrest rates in the 2 years between interviews.

INDIVIDUALIZED TRANSITION EDUCATIONAL PLAN (ITEP)

The development of the ITEP should consist of the following (Salend, 2005, p. 268): postschool activities including postsecondary education, vocational training, integrated employment, continuing and adult education, adult services, independent living, daily living skills, and community participation. The ITEP must be based on the individual student's needs, preferences, and interests.

In designing ITEPs, planning teams should use person-centered planning (Kohler & Field, 2003) and actively involve students in the process (Thomas, Rogan, & Baker, 2001). Person-centered planning involves students, family members, educators, and community agency personnel in developing an ITEP that focuses on the person's strengths and preferences. The goals are to improve the person's quality of life and increase life satisfaction (Menchetti & Garcia, 2003, in Salend, 2005, p. 268). The process should include the following:

- An assessment of students' career goals and interests, strengths, dreams, independence, social skills, hobbies, interpersonal relations, self-determination, decision-making skills, self-advocacy, and communication levels. Sax and Thoma (2002) and Neubert and Moon (2000) provide an overview of procedures that you can use to assess the transitional planning needs of students, and plan and evaluate transitional programs.

- An assessment of students' current and desired skill levels, interests, and challenges in making the transition to postsecondary education, employment, community participation, and/or adult living.
- An identification of transition placement and programs that match assessment data.
- An assessment of the new environment(s) to identify the physical, social, emotional, and cognitive skills necessary to perform effectively in the new setting.
- A list of the related services, functional supports, accommodations and assistive devices that can affect success in the new environment(s), as well as any potential barriers such as transportation problems.
- A statement of and timelines for the goals and objectives of the transitional program, including those related to student empowerment, self-determination, self-evaluation, and decision-making skills.
- A list of the academic, vocational, social, and adult living skills necessary to achieve the transition goals.
- A list of teaching strategies, approaches, materials, accommodations, and experiences, as well as the supportive and community-based services and supports necessary to achieve the stated goals of the transitional program.
- A description of the communication systems that will be used to share information among professionals, among community agencies, and between school and family members.
- A system for evaluating the success of the transition program on a regular basis (Benz, Lindstrom, & Yovanoff, 2000; Johnson, Stodden, Emanuel, Luecking & Mack, 2002; Johnson, Zorn, Kai Yung Tam, Lamontagne, & Johnson, 2003; Schwartz, Jacobson, & Holburn, 2000; Steere & Cavaiuolo, 2002).

IDEA 2004 TRANSITION REQUIREMENTS

Additionally, IDEA 2004 provides several changes concerning transition requirements (Cortiella, 2005). It states that transition services should focus on academic and functional achievement to facilitate the transition from school to postsecondary settings. These services must be based on students' strengths, preferences, and interests, and they must be results-oriented. IDEA 2004 also establishes a clear starting point for the process. The first IEP after the student's 16th birthday must include transition planning. It must include measurable postsecondary goals and a plan to reach these goals. Finally, schools must provide a "Summary of Performance," including the student's academic achievement, functional performance, and recommendations on how to assist the student. Cortiella believes that these new changes will "help increase collaboration and improve the individualization of transition policy" (p. 3). Cohen and Spenciner (2003) suggest questions that can guide the assessment of the transition process regarding employment, postsecondary education, community involvement, personal and social areas, and independent living (see pp. 463–465 for more specific information about the various assessment tools that can be employed to answer specific questions).

POSTSECONDARY EDUCATION PROBLEMS OF INDIVIDUALS WITH LEARNING DISABILITIES

The transition from high school to postsecondary education or employment is difficult for many students, but it can be extraordinarily difficult for those with learning disabilities. Learning disabilities do not disappear on completion of high school; they exist for life. Some students do remarkably well, others struggle, and still others deal unsuccessfully with their learning disabilities every day. Phillip Cohn (1998), a college student with learning disabilities, has written eloquently about his daily struggles, including the anxiety and stress he experienced in dealing with academic requirements and social situations outside the classroom. He states:

> For most students, college is a time of unprecedented academic and social development; however,

for students with learning disabilities (LD), it can be a nightmare. When these students enter college they are not only beginning an unexplored and unfamiliar way of life but embarking on a journey that threatens their established motivational drive, need for order, compensatory skills, and social relationships, it is no wonder that so many students with LD suffer from emotional and physiological problems at the college level. To reduce the anxiety and stress inherent in adapting to college, these students must understand that thoughts and attitudes, not external events, create their feelings. By recognizing their anxious feelings, somatic reactions to anxiety, specific thoughts in anxiety-provoking situations, and coping strategies, students with LD can change the way they think, feel and behave. (p. 514)

Most adults with learning disabilities do not go on to college and often lack the vocational skills to seek gainful employment. Yet, most of the research on adults with learning disabilities focuses on college students and college programs (Field, Price, & Patton, 2003). What about those students who do not have the ability or desire to attend college? What are their options? The majority of students with learning disabilities work after high school (Bender, 2004), but there are simply not enough vocational options for them. Field et al. pose a number of questions that "demand exploration" (p. 383). In addition to those adults who do not go to college, what about those who are incarcerated or receive adult basic education? What about adults with learning disabilities who are homeless or have chemical dependency or mental health issues? What about adults with learning disabilities who have children with learning disabilities? By focusing our research efforts disproportionately on the college-bound student with learning disabilities, we neglect these important concerns.

Schools need to collaborate with local employers and vocational counselors to provide meaningful transition services to all students with learning disabilities, not just those who want to enter college.

Although students with learning disabilities form a larger group than any other group with disabilities, they receive less attention to transition planning than students with more severe disabilities

(Janiga & Costenbader, 2002). Because learning disabilities are school-related disorders, these individuals outside of the school setting are relatively neglected. Sitlington (1996) found that everyday activities that most adults perform easily—daily chores, job and household responsibilities, relating to others—continue to pose problems for adults with learning disabilities. As Smith (2004) notes:

Social and emotional adjustment, more so than the learning disability itself, means the difference between success and failure in postsecondary education, on the job and in handling the important personal friends and community responsibilities of adulthood. (p. 298)

There are personal accounts of adults with learning disabilities who have been successful (go to http://www.ldonline.org and click on "Life Stories"), and the popular media typically portray famous individuals who have a learning disability. Phillip Cohn (1998) discusses the cognitive behavioral strategies that he employed to deal with the anxiety and stress due to his learning disability, and there are stories of successful college programs for students with these disabilities. Why was Miriam, discussed at the beginning of this chapter, so successful? What can we learn from her experiences?

Mercer and Pullen (2005, p. 194) examined studies and research reviews dealing with the post-school adjustment of young adults with learning disabilities. Their difficulties include underemployment, job dissatisfaction, dependent living arrangements, social skills problems, poor work habits, and poor job selection. Clearly, these young adults need support. To provide opportunities for success Mercer, and Pullen (2005, p. 196) recommend the following:

1. In assessment, include an examination of protective factors (e.g., communication skills, sense of personal control, proactive tendencies, self-understanding, goal orientation, problem-solving ability, and presence of family and community supports) and risk factors (e.g., severity of learning disabilities, poor relationships, low frustration level, dysfunctional family, and passive

learning style). This data provides the information necessary to identify an individual's most relevant strengths and weaknesses and plan accordingly (Spekman, Herman, & Vogel, 1993).

2. Develop strategies and techniques for helping individuals understand their learning disabilities and their respective strengths and weaknesses. Efforts should be made to help adults with learning disabilities feel good about themselves (Adelman & Vogel, 1993; Spekman et al., 1993).

3. Teach individuals ways to adapt to their learning disabilities. These entail the development of coping strategies and problem-solving techniques.

4. Encourage individuals to be proactive and take control of their lives through goal setting, goal directedness, persistence, and hard work. Teach students to participate in their own transition plans.

5. Teach individuals how to network and develop support systems (e.g., build relationships) and use supportive persons (such as teachers, employers, therapists, counselors, family members, and friends).

6. Provide each student with learning disabilities with a mentor during the secondary school years. The mentor should be someone who believes in the individual, helps the individual set realistic goals, and provides encouragement during difficult times (Spekman et al., 1993).

7. Provide students with learning disabilities with the assistance needed to meet the academic requirements in vocational education. Minskoff and DeMoss (1993) present the Trade-Related Academic Competence (TRAC) program as a viable alternative for teaching students with learning disabilities the academic skills needed across 26 vocational education areas.

8. Provide students in secondary school and beyond with guidance in selecting vocational courses and careers (Adelman & Vogel, 1993).

9. Provide ongoing assistance to help students improve their academic and interpersonal skills and their compensatory strategies (Adelman & Vogel, 1993).

10. Educate more employers about learning disabilities. Employers tend to be more sensitive to individuals with physical disabilities than to individuals with cognitive disabilities (Adelman & Vogel, 1993; Anderson, Kazmierski & Cronin, 1995).

Smith (2004, p. 293) summarizes the research on successful adults with learning disabilities:

Successful adults with learning disabilities surround themselves with supportive friends, family and mentors, learning to accept their experience with learning disabilities, take advantage of constructional approaches and take on challenges with confidence that odds can be overcome.

LAWS AFFECTING ADULTS WITH LEARNING DISABILITIES

Students with learning disabilities are no longer protected by IDEA 2004 once they obtain a high school diploma or reach 22 years of age. There are two laws that cover adults with disabilities, including learning disabilities: Section 504 of the Rehabilitation Act of 1973 and the Americans with Disabilities Act (ADA) of 1990. It is important for educators to know that these are not special education laws; they are civil rights mandates established to ensure equal access to the opportunities available to any qualified individual. Section 504 states that "no otherwised qualified individual" shall be discriminated against in any program that receives federal financial assistance. The ADA goes beyond schools to ensure that individuals with disabilities have access to accommodations in all areas of their lives. As Gregg and Scott (2000) note: "These federal laws provide general frameworks for defining disability and considering documentation needs that are quite different from the definitional and theoretical debate occurring in the fields of LD and ADHD" (p. 8). Court decisions will continue to help define these issues. The school should provide specific information to students to make them aware of their rights so that they can advocate for themselves. For information on information on accessing these laws, go to http://www.ldon.org/advocacy.

COLLEGE PROGRAMS FOR STUDENTS WITH DISABILITIES

The first college program for students with learning disabilities was established in 1970 at Curry College in Milton, Massachusetts. Since then there has been a rapid increase in such program, which now number over 1,000. From 1989 to 1998 there was a 173% increase in the number of students with learning disabilities enrolled in college (Lock & Layton, 2001). In a review of the literature on postsecondary education for these students, Mull, Sitlington, and Alper (2001) note that there has been a 10-fold increase in the number of such students attending college since 1997. This transition is not easy for any student, particularly one with a learning disability. Much of the support available in high school may not be present. This, coupled with the newfound freedom, flexible scheduling, and the need for self-advocacy can make this transition extremely difficult (see Practical Considerations: Transitional Resources).

What Are Colleges Required to Provide?

Legally, colleges are required under ADA and Section 504 (see Laws Affecting Adults with Learning Disabilities) to provide support for students with learning disabilities. They are not required to modify admissions standards, course content, or programs of study (Madaus, 2005), nor do they have to provide an actual "Learning Disabilities Program." In what has been described as "arguably the most important case ever litigated to a conclusion on behalf of students with learning disabilities" (Sparks & Javorsky, 1999, p. 287), *Elizabeth Guckenberger et al. v. Boston University et al.* (see the *Journal of Learning Disabilities, 32* [4], 1999, for a special series on the lawsuit), students with learning disabilities sued Boston University. They were arguing against the institution of new policies for students with learning disabilities. The areas of concern were reasonable accommodations, the quality of the psychoeducational evaluation, the requirement

for reevaluation every 3 years, and course substitutions. As is the case in many legal battles, both sides claimed victory. However, the result was that the university had to make reasonable accommodations for students with learning disabilities. In a U.S. Department of Education (2000) survey of postsecondary programs for students with learning disabilities, 98% were found to provide at least one support service (Janiga & Costenbader, 2002):

88% provided alternative test formats or extended time

77% provided tutors

69% provided readers, note takers, or scribes

62% provided assistance with class registration

55% provided books on tape

Practical Consideration: Transitional Resources. Madaus (2005, p. 36) provides three useful transitional resources:

The Heath Resource Center

- The HEATH Resource Center is the National Clearinghouse on Postsecondary Education for Individuals with Disabilities. Resource papers, an extensive resource directory and useful fact sheets are available at http://www.heath.gwu.edu. Available publications include *Creating Options: Financial Aid for Students with Disabilities 2003, Assistive Technology for Students with Learning Disabilities, and Students with Learning Disabilities in Postsecondary Education.* Contact the HEATH Resource Center, George Washington University, 2121 K Street NW, Suite 220, Washington, DC 20037; telephone: 1-800-544-3284; Web site: http://www.heath.gwu.edu

U.S. Department of Educaton, Office for Civil Rights

- The U.S. Department of Education, Office for Civil Rights Web site (http://www.ed.gov/ocr) offers valuable information for students in transition. Included on the site are reports and resources, including *Students with Disabilities Preparing for Postsecondary Education: Know Your Rights and Responsibilities* (July 2002). This publication presents answers to a series of common questions related to the rights and responsibilities of students with disabilities in postsecondary education.

Wisconsin Department of Public Instruction

- The Wisconsin Department of Public Instruction (http://www.dpi.state.wi.us) offers *Opening Doors to Postsecondary Education and Training: Planning for Life After High School* (September 2003). This handbook for students, school counselors, teachers, and parents includes such sections as "Planning and Preparing for Postsecondary Education," "Timeline for Planning," and "High School: What Classes Must I Take?" The handbook also contains a "Postsecondary Education Exploration Worksheet" and an appendix of documentation guidelines. The handbook is available at http://www.dpi.state.wi.us/een/pdf/tranopndrs.pdf.

One frequently studied accommodation is foreign language requirements. Sparks, Philips, and Javorsky (2002) examined whether there was sufficient evidence to support course substitution for a foreign language, citing a number of studies indicating that students with learning disabilities can substitute another course for the foreign language requirement. Moreover, published articles provide specific procedures for doing so. When 158 college students with learning disabilities who had been granted course substitution were examined, many of the assumptions regarding learning disabilities and foreign language were found to lack substantiation. The authors recommend that the student enroll in foreign language courses and be provided with any accommodations necessary.

Faculty Receptiveness to Accommodations

Some college students felt that their professors did not support accommodations (Lehmann, Davies, & Laurin, 2000), failing to understand the nature and needs of students with learning disabilities. Even when professors were willing to provide accommodations, many students did not feel comfortable approaching them. To receive services, college students need to themselves, identify and

many are reluctant or unable to do so. The consensus in the literature on college students with learning disabilities is that they need to engage in self-advocacy and self-determination activities (see Best Practices: A Course on Learning Disabilities for Students with Learning Disabilities at the end of the chapter).

Lock and Layton (2001) recommend that students meet frequently with their professors and develop a self-advocacy plan. Kling (2000) developed a research-based mnemonic device called ASSERT to enable students to disclose their problems and advocate for themselves:

Awareness of disability
State disability
State strengths and limitations
Evaluate problems and solutions
Role play solutions
Try it in the real setting

Kling (p. 69) provides a example of the application of ASSERT by a 21-year-old woman with a "severe learning disability":

Awareness of Disability:
I realized that I had a disability when I was diagnosed at about 7 or 8 years old. I became aware that I needed help with special education classes and teachers in school.

State Nature of Disability:
When I was younger, I was definitely not comfortable talking about my disability, but I am better now. . . . People would talk to me and tell me, there are others who are a lot worse off than you.

Strengths/Weaknesses:
I am aware that my weaknesses are in my fine motor skills. I needed occupational therapy and speech therapy [in school]. I have a bad temper, and I get frustrated. I am not protective of others' needs, but I protect my own rights. I am aware that I can do a lot more than I give myself credit for. My strengths are my reading and creative writing skills. I also am a hard worker, and I try hard to succeed.

Evaluate Problems:
I was told I did something wrong in a job a few years ago. Although I didn't do anything wrong, my speaking

up for myself didn't seem to help. I couldn't really talk my way out of it, and it caused me to lose my job. If I had problem-solved, I could have made it better. I try to sit down, relax and think about the problem before reacting. I sometimes get nervous.

Role Play:
I am trying to role-play with people I trust, especially, because I tend to get excited—and people may think that is overbearing.

Try It:
I have tried to self-advocate in situations. I think I am more successful than I used to be.

This young woman did not need to work on several steps—awareness, stating the nature of the disability, or stating her strengths and limitations—although she did need to be reminded to back off when she became too excited. She worked on the later steps of ASSERT, which involved evaluating problems and solutions (particularly thinking before reacting) and using role play. She was willing to jump into the last step, "Try it," but did not always think out the solution before doing do. As a result, self-advocacy did not always work as effectively as it could have. Other recommendations are provided below by Madaus and Shaw (2000 p. 86), to assist students with the transition to postsecondary education. Students should receive help in the following areas:

- Clarifying the exact nature of their disability by reviewing the diagnostic report with a special educator or psychologist;
- Learning about civil rights and the different responsibilities of high schools and colleges under Section 504 and the Americans with Disabilities Act;
- Actively participating in Section 504 meetings and suggesting goals that focus on study skills, time management, and test-taking strategies;
- Using accommodations and auxiliary aids in high school classes that are deemed appropriate based on a review of diagnostic data and possibly acceptable in postsecondary classes;
- Selecting classes (with parental input) that will provide academic preparation for postsecondary environments;

- Avoiding the temptation of "retreating" to lower track classes if college-bound; instead, select[ing] solid college prep courses;
- Being wary of course waivers and carefully considering that these choices could limit college options;
- Using supports and accommodations in math or foreign language classes rather than seeking a waiver of course substitution, if possible;
- Knowing how, when, and where to discuss and request needed accommodations;
- Advocating for an IEP/504 goal (in 11th and 12th grades) to complete a psychoeducational evaluation that meets postsecondary documentation guidelines;
- Finalizing arrangements for the SATs or ACTs with necessary accommodations (see Web sites for ACT [www.act.org] and College Board [www.collegeboard.org]);
- Taking advantage of opportunities that will foster self-determination and independence through increased responsibility at home and in school;
- Deciding whether or not to disclose the disability prior to admission.

Although the number of students with learning disabilities continues to grow, they still attend college at a lower rate than their peers without disabilities (Smith 2004). Moreover, even as programs continue to proliferate, there is very little evidence to suggest what is effective and what is not. Mull et al. (2001, pp. 106–107) provide the following list of specific implications based on their review of the literature on postsecondary programs:

- Students need to be prepared to determine which of the accommodations and supports used at the secondary level will be needed at the postsecondary level, and to access these and other supports and accommodations needed.
- Students need to be trained in the use of the increasing number of assistive technology devices.
- Secondary teachers need to be aware of the demands of postsecondary education environments so [that] they can work with the student to acquire the skills, supports and accommodations to be successful in these environments.
- As a field, we need to deal with the issue of documentation of disability, which is required of students to access the accommodations and

support services they need at the postsecondary level. This is a particular concern since many secondary programs are moving away from specific disability labels and formal psychological testing.

- More emphasis needs to be placed on the training of staff at the postsecondary level to work with individuals with disabilities. This is particularly true for those who are providing direct services to these students. The AHEAD (Association of Higher Education and Disability) standards are a good start in this area.
- Finally, research needs to focus on evaluation of the effectiveness of specific support services and accommodations for students with disabilities at the postsecondary level. Research questions might include the following:
- Are the postsecondary accommodations and supports that are typically offered effective?
- Are the accommodations and supports that are effective at the secondary level equally effective ad the postsecondary level?

VOCATIONAL PROGRAMS

Research on postsecondary options for students with learning disabilities has focused primarily on college students (Field et al., 2003). The Learning Disabilities Association of America (2005) (see http://www.idanatl.org) provides information on vocational-technical schools and programs. There are private and public programs that allow these students to pursue a variety of career options. Two-year colleges also provide many programs (Stern, 2002).

Students with learning disabilities are underrepresented in vocational programs. There appears to be no collaboration and coordination between vocational and special educators to prepare students with learning disabilities for the world of work (Bender, 2004). Mellard and Lancaster (2003) recommend that community resources such as vocational rehabilitation programs, the Social Security Administration's Adult Education department, the Centers for Independent Living, as well as technical schools and community colleges, be utilized in planning the transitions.

SELF-DETERMINATION

In a review of the literature on self-determination and advocacy, Malian and Nevin (2003) found that self-determination is a predictor of the successful transition to adulthood. Field, Sarver, and Shaw (2003) believe it is critical for success in postsecondary education programs for students with learning disabilities. Regardless of the postsecondary option, it is an important component of the student's education. What is self-determination? Field, Martin, Miller, Ward, and Wehmeyer (1998, p. 2) define it as

> a combination of skills, knowledge, and beliefs that enable a person to engage in goal-directed, self-regulated, autonomous behavior. An understanding of one's strengths and limitations, together with a belief of oneself as capable and effective, is essential to self-determination. When acting on the basis of these skills and attitudes, individuals have greater ability to take control of their lives and assume the role of successful adults in our society.

Students who are self-determined assess their own strengths, weaknesses, needs, and preferences. This appears to be somewhat difficult for students with learning disabilities (Hoffman 2003). In your classroom, you can promote self-determination by teaching students to:

- set personal goals
- solve problems that act as barriers to achieving these goals
- make appropriate choices based on a personal preferences and interests
- participate in discussions that impact the quality of their lives
- advocate for themselves
- create action plans to achieve goals
- self-regulate and manage day-to-day routines

By teaching students and reinforcing their efforts to take command of their learning and their lives, you help them to become more autonomous (Agran, King-Sears, Wehmeyer, & Copeland, 2003). Allow them to make choices, promote the use of problem-solving skills, provide ample feedback, allow them to evaluate their choices and their work, and examine the consequences. This should be an ongoing process. The development of the transition plan provides an excellent opportunity to ask whether students are engaged in practices that lead to self-determination and self-advocacy. This is crucial for all students, regardless of their postsecondary plans. It will better prepare them to make informed choices about their future.

THE WORLD OF WORK

The transition from school to work can be difficult. There is very little information on the problems adults with learning disabilities encounter on the job, but it doesn't take much imagination to think of the many things that can go wrong on a typical workday.

This is not intended to portray a bleak picture, simply to be realistic. Some authors provide inspiring accounts of adults with learning disabilities. Shaywitz (2003), for example, describes adults with dyslexia who have succeeded against great odds. There are also accounts of famous people with learning disabilities who have done remarkably well in their particular field. These success stories may well be illuminating and inspiring, but they may also raise false hopes and lead to disappointment. There appears to be a high risk of job dissatisfaction among adults with learning disabilities (Witte, Philips, & Kakela, 1998). Stern (2002, p. 18) states that young adults with learning disabilities need to explain how their functional limitations might impact their transition to work. Some questions that can aid in this process are:

- Do you learn most effectively by reading, listening, demonstration, hands-on experience or some combination of these?
- How does your LD affect your reading?
- How many times do you have to read information before you understand it?
- Is it difficult for you to take notes on what your read?

- How does your LD affect your writing?
- Is it easier for you to write using a computer?
- Is it difficult for you to put your thoughts onto paper?
- Would it be easier to verbalize your papers into a tape recorder before writing them?
- Do you have difficulty in understanding verbal instructions and information?
- How many instructions can you remember at once?
- Do you usually need to have new information repeated over a period of time before you can retain it?
- Does it help to practice a task while someone is watching and giving you immediate feedback?
- Are you easily distracted?
- Do you learn best in a quiet environment?
- Do you have difficulty concentrating?
- What kinds of tasks are easiest to focus on?
- What classroom accommodations have you used in the past? Have they been effective?
- Have you had difficulties in past jobs? If yes, describe what was difficult.
- Are there any work situations or tasks you tend to avoid?
- Do you anticipate that you will need any job accommodations?
- Have you used accommodations in the past? If yes, please describe them.
- What kind of boss helps you perform at your best?
- Do you prefer frequent feedback on how you are doing?
- Do you need a quiet workplace?
- Do you work best in an environment that is orderly and structured?

Adults with learning disabilities are protected in the workforce under ADA and Section 504. Price and Gerber (2001) examined employers' experiences with employees with learning disabilities since the inception of ADA. These results were compared to those reported in a study by Gerber (1992). Price and Gerber wanted to know how much progress had been made. They found that employers were willing to assist their employees with learning disabilities, provided that those employees identified themselves and employers were provided with up-to-date information. Their findings indicate that employers need information and training regarding learning disabilities if the spirit of the law is to be upheld. They note that it is not clear who will educate employers. College graduates with learning disabilities tend to earn lower salaries than their counterparts without disabilities (Dickinson & Verbeek, 2002). However, according to the authors, this wage gap cannot be explained solely on the basis of discrimination. They also note that adults with learning disabilities fear job discrimination. This may be why so few of them report their disability to their employer. In one study (Madaus, Folley, McGuire, & Ruban, 2002), only 30% disclosed their disability due to fear of discrimination, even though 90% of the respondents said that their learning disability affected their work. Unlike Price and Gerber (2001), Madaus et al. (2002) found that 87% of their sample earned competitive wages in a range of fields and were satisfied with their jobs. Clearly, much more research is needed on the employment status of adults with learning disabilities. We need to go beyond the testimonials of celebrities to develop a research base in order to better understand the problems, issues, and concerns of this population and ways to provide effective and efficient solutions based on evidence. Perhaps then the "Wanted" advertisement by Horowitz (2005) will be more realistic.

SUCCESSFUL ADULTS WITH LEARNING DISABILITIES

What are the predictors of 'success' for individuals with learning disabilities? Raskind, Goldberg, Higgins, and Herman (2006) conducted a 20-year study to answer this question. At the time of the follow-up, the subjects were between the ages of 28 and 35. The authors discovered six attributes of success:

- Self-awareness
- Proactivity
- Perseverance

- Goal setting
- Presence and use of an effective support system
- Emotional stability

In general, successful adults with learning disabilities were aware of their disability, knew their strengths and weaknesses, and often described themselves as having a learning disabilities. They were actively involved in many activities and set reasonable goals. They readily accepted support from a wide variety of individuals ranging from family members and friends to professionals, and they developed effective ways of dealing with stressful situations. Finally, they were optimistic.

The implications for teachers of students with learning disabilities are clear. Schools need to instill those characteristics that lead to success, from early planning that focuses on self-awareness and goal setting to an ongoing effort to identify and utilize a broad support system. The majority of these students will not go on to college, and other postsecondary school options must be examined much more thoroughly. Research is needed on vocational programs and the world of work so that students will be aware of their options and which ones have a higher probability of success.

SUMMARY

This chapter has focused on the transition to postsecondary school options for adults with learning disabilities. The laws governing adults (versus those concerning school special education) were explained. Vocational, college, and work issues were discussed, and examples of effective programs were provided. If students are to succeed after high school, much more collaboration is needed in this crucial transition. Much more research must be undertaken, focusing especially on students with learning disabilities who will not go to college. Currently, little is known about options for adults with learning disabilities other than college.

SPRINGBOARDS FOR REFLECTION AND DISCUSSION

1. Interview adults with learning disabilities. What advice would they give to you as a teacher? What advice would they give to students with learning disabilities in elementary school? In high school?

2. Does your college have a program for students with learning disabilities? If it does, speak to the director. How are the students selected? What services are provided? What is the rate of graduation? Does the program follow up on graduates in the workplace?

3. Interview the parents of a high school student with a learning disability. What are their plans for the student's future? How is the students involved? What are parents' concerns or worries?

4. Speak to a guidance counselor at your local high school. What kind of transition planning does he or she do with students with learning disabilities? When does it start? Is self-determination included throughout this process?

5. Speak to a college student with a learning disability. What is college like for him or her—successes, failures, struggles? What kinds of support are available?

6. Respond to the four questions posed by Horowitz (2005). How would you gather information that would enable you to begin this process?

CHAPTER 12
SPOKEN LANGUAGE DISORDERS

CHAPTER OBJECTIVES

At the end of this chapter you will:

- understand theories of normal language development.
- know the characteristics of students with spoken language disorders.
- understand the need for both formal and informal assessment of spoken language disorders.
- be able to implement interventions for students with spoken language disorders.
- understand the issues related to students who are culturally and linguistically diverse.

Kathy was 7 years old when she was diagnosed with a learning disability. Her parents reported that she "understood everything" but could not express herself. On the first day of school, Kathy smiled and said nothing. Over time she tried to express herself, but her speech was unintelligible. Essentially, everything she said sounded like "ha ha" or "ba uh," and she changed the emphasis from the first to the second sound and vice versa. Kathy was a remarkably compliant child who appeared to understand the world around her but could not code her ideas in intelligent language. Her teacher consulted with the speech-language pathologist, attended workshops, and asked experts, all to no avail. Her language disorder was severe, and no one seemed to know what to do. What would you have done? Should you try to guess what her babbling means? Should you give her what you think she needs? Should you insist on more precise articulation? Kathy is an extreme example of a student with a learning disability who has a spoken language disorder, but she is not alone.

Tommy, age 12, was initially diagnosed as mentally retarded due to his poor expressive language. Tommy understood the world around him and had many friends but said very little that was understandable. He called his mother "mama" and his father "dada." Those were the only words that listeners could understand. Tommy received intensive speech and language therapy, both in and out of school. His parents were relentless in trying to convince the school district that he had average intellectual ability and should be classified as having a learning disability. Finally, they were able to find a psychologist who administered a nonverbal IQ test. Tommy scored in the average range. His classification was changed, and he was placed in a self-contained class for students with learning disabilities. Unlike Kathy, Tommy was very frustrated if he was not understood—which, unfortunately, was most of the time. He used a crude gestural system, but it was generally not effective. Unlike Kathy, Tommy made progress through the collaborative efforts of his teacher, his speech-language pathologist, and his family.

Jimmy was a bright, athletic seventh-grade student with a learning disability. His receptive vocabulary appeared age-appropriate, but when he spoke he had a hard time finding the right word. Sometimes he described the shape or the color or even make a sound associated with it. More often, he became frustrated and stopped talking.

There is a wide range of spoken language disorders among students with learning disabilities. Some are very subtle and go undetected but manifest themselves in reading and writing disorders.

How will you know? What assessment procedures could be employed? What interventions are successful with this wide range of disorders? How will you collaborate with the speech-language pathologist? This chapter provides information that will enable you to answer these questions.

NORMAL LANGUAGE DEVELOPMENT

Bloom (1988, p. 2) defined **language** as a "code whereby ideas about the world are expressed through a conventional system of arbitrary signals for communication." Bloom and Lahey (1978) and Lahey (1988) identified three major components of language: form, content, and use. The **form** of a language is the sounds, the meaning units, and the ways in which the meaning units are combined. This can also be described as **phonology, morphology,** and **syntactics.** The **content** of language is the meaning, also referred to as **semantics.** Finally, the *use* of language is how we speak and how we employ language in social situations. This is also called **pragmatics.**

In order to be competent in language learning, students must integrate the components of form, content, and use. Bloom and Lahey (1978) and Lahey (1988), in their seminal work on language development, provide the Venn diagram below as an illustration of this integration. It is the intersection of the diagram, the integration, that describes language competence.

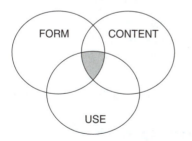

COMPONENTS OF LANGUAGE

Phonology

Phonology is the study of the rules that govern sounds and their combinations (Bernstein, 2002).

A **phoneme** is the smallest unit of speech that signals a different meaning. For example, a student should be able to hear the difference between the words *mat* and *fat*. The phonemes /m/ and /f/ are different and signal different words. There has been considerable research (see Chapter 13) suggesting that students with learning disabilities may lack this ability.

Morphology

Morphology is the study of word formations. A **morpheme** is the smallest linguistic unit that signals meaning. For example, the /s/ sound can signal the plural form at the end of a word or the possessive form when used with the apostrophe. The /s/ signals a change in meaning.

Syntax

Syntax refers to the rules that govern the language. It is the grammar of the language. Many students with learning disabilities lack knowledge of syntax, which has a profound impact on their reading and writing ability.

Semantics

Semantics involves understanding the use of words (Bernstein, 2002). Multiple word meanings, figurative language, and idiomatic language may pose problems for students with learning disabilities who have limited receptive language abilities and experiences. They have difficulty in social situations because they may not understand jokes or nonliteral languages (e.g., "Do I have to stand on my head to get you to understand this?").

Pragmatics

The final component of language is **pragmatics**, also referred to as **use**. It is why we speak, and it fulfills the social function of language. Understanding what to say and how to say it requires a great deal of information about the topic and the person to whom you are speaking. For example, you may report an event to your teacher in different

TABLE 12–1 Components of Language

Component	Definition	Receptive Level	Expressive Level
Phonology	The sound system of a language and the linguistic rules that govern the sound combinations	Discrimination of speech sounds	Articulation of speech sounds
Morphology	The linguistic rule that governs the structure of words and the construction or word forms from the basic elements of meaning	Understanding of grammatical structure of words	Use of grammar in words
Syntax	The linguistic rule system governing the order and combination of words to form sentences, and the relationships among the elements within a sentence	Understanding of phrases and sentences	Use of grammar in phrases and sentences
Semantics	The psycholinguistic system that patterns the content of an utterance, intent, and meanings of words and sentences	Understanding of word meanings and word relationships	Use of word meanings and word relationships
Pragmatics	The sociolinguistic system that patterns the use of language in communication, which may be expressed motorically, vocally, or verbally	Understanding of language cues	Use of language in context

language than you would to your friend. For students with language-learning disabilities, this component may be the most difficult because it requires them to generalize the skills they may have learned in a more therapeutic setting. This is why collaboration between teachers and speech-language pathologists is critical.

The skills taught in the clinical setting must be transferred to the classroom and other real-life settings. Mercer and Pullen (2005, p. 362) provide a simple table that summarizes the five components of language discussed above (see Table 12–1).

THEORIES OF LANGUAGE DEVELOPMENT

How do children learn how to understand and use language? Bloom and Lahey (1978) and Lahey (1988) suggest that knowledge of normal language development provides the best information about the ways in which the student with language

disorder will learn language. Yet, there is no universally accepted theory of language learning. It is generally agreed that there are four major approaches (Bernstein, 2002):

1. Behavioral
2. Psycholinguistic/syntactic
3. Semantic/cognitive
4. Pragmatic

Each approach will be briefly described below.

Behavioral Approach

Behaviorists believe that children learn language because it is reinforced. B. F. Skinner proposed this approach in his book *Verbal Behavior* (1957), presenting empirical evidence suggesting that children learn language from significant adults in their environment who provide models of language acquisition. Children model adult responses, practice these responses, and receive reinforcement for their utterances.

Psycholinguistic/Syntactic Approach

The leading proponent of this approach was Chomsky (1957, 1965), who believed that all children have an innate ability to learn language. This contrasts with the behaviorist approach, which suggests that language acquisition is a learned behavior.

Semantic/Cognitive Approach

Bloom (1970) is the leading proponent of this approach. Based on extensive observational studies, she proposed that children's utterances are expressed before they know anything about syntax. These utterances are based on their cognitive skills. Children talk about what they know, their experiences of the world around them, and how things function and interact.

Pragmatic Approach

In this approach, language is viewed within the context of social development. Children's social interactions provide them with the framework for language development. This approach suggests that children will talk only if there is a reason to do so.

Your theory of how children develop language will impact the way in which you assess language and develop interventions. (For more specific information on the limitations, contributions, and additional references for each approach, see Bernstein, 2002.)

CHARACTERISTICS OF STUDENTS WITH SPOKEN LANGUAGE DISORDERS

In their seminal work on learning disabilities, Johnson and Myklebust (1968) discussed disorders of auditory language, dividing them into auditory receptive and auditory expressive categories. Their work was based on empirical evidence and rich clinical observations.

Disorders of Auditory Receptive Language

Some students have difficulty understanding the spoken word. Their hearing acuity is normal, and their degree of difficulty varies. These students may also have a disorder referred to as **receptive aphasia,** which clearly affects their oral and written expression. A dictum of language development is that "input precedes output." Therefore, if students have difficulty comprehending spoken language, they will have difficulty expressing himself. This will also impact their ability to read and write. These students will have difficulty with phonetic awareness. Typically, they cannot discriminate differences in sounds and words and, cannot rhyme or blend sounds into words.

Disorders of Auditory Expressive Language

The three major disorders of expressive language are (a) reauditorization, (b) apraxia, and (c) defective syntax. Reauditorization is also referred to as **word retrieval** or **word finding.** Students know the word but cannot recall it for spontaneous usage. Students such as Jimmy, introduced at the beginning of the chapter, who are apraxic, cannot form the motor patterns necessary for speech. Both Kathy and Tommy, the other students discussed at the beginning of the chapter, were diagnosed as having apraxia. Finally, students with defective syntax have difficulty with word order, complete sentences, verb tense, and other grammatical forms.

Wiig and Semel (1984) conducted clinical research on large numbers of students with learning disabilities. They identified deficits in word knowledge, word and sentence formation, and word finding. These are similar to the deficits noted by Johnson and Myklebust (1967), with minor variations. When Wiig and Semel (1984, p. 5) asked students to complete the phrase "Jack, King and _____," their responses indicated deficits in word knowledge. Some of their responses are as follows:

1. Jack, King, and Princess.
2. Jack, King, and Mike.

3. Jack, King, and mother.
4. Jack, King, and Crown Prince.
5. Jack, King, and Jill.
6. Jack, King, and candle.
7. Jack, King, and Knight.
8. There are fifty-two cards in a deck. You have clubs, spades, hearts, and diamonds. And aces, and Jack, King, and Queen.

In their studies on word and sentence formation, Wiig and Semel (1984, p. 9) asked students a simple question: "Tell me what you saw on television last night." Here is the response from a middle school student with a learning disability:

1. There was this boy who was going to the doctor's.
2. He was taking drugs and he needed a good drug.
3. And when he went to the doctor, he took the good drug.
4. And then he went home and he started taking the bad drug.
5. He took needles and pills and everything.
6. Then the needles made him feel tired and made his stomach feel so painful.
7. Then he started on pills.
8. And he took a pill one at a time and each one hurt worse and worse.
9. And then he went to the doctor's 'cause his knee was turning all red and blue.
10. The doctor said it's 'cause of the pills.
11. Then the doctor gave him another medicine and he went and still took 'em.
12. And about two weeks later he was dead.

Students who have deficits in word finding often describe the function of an object, the sound it makes, or its color, shape, and so on. These students know the word for the object; they simply cannot recall it for spontaneous usage. When asked to describe how to make a peanut butter and jelly sandwich, a student with a learning disability gave the following directions (Wiig & Semel, 1984, p. 11):

You take bread.
You put the stuff, you know, the red stuff, on the bread.
And then you put the peanut butter on it.
And then you put it together.

And then you cut it with the . . . the sharp knife.
And it's done.

The language deficits described above will impact these students' ability to become proficient readers and writers (Catts & Kamki, 1999; Leong, 1999; Smith, 2004). And while Bloom and Lahey (1978) and Lahey (1988) do not employ a specific disability approach to language development and language disorders, they state that students with learning disabilities will most likely have difficulty with the interaction of the form, content, and use of language rather than a specific disorder in one of these three components.

BEHAVIORS ASSOCIATED WITH SPOKEN LANGUAGE DISORDERS

Students with language-learning disabilities may display behaviors related to the inability to understand and use spoken language. These disabilities may manifest themselves in a variety of behaviors. Table 12–2, compiled by Mercer and Pullen (2005, p. 368), lists these behaviors and provides an example of each (p. 429).

ASSESSMENT OF SPOKEN LANGUAGE DISORDERS

The assessment of students with learning disabilities who may have spoken-language disorders requires collaboration with the speech-language pathologist. Teachers of students with learning disabilities cannot do this on their own.

The roles and responsibilities of the school-based speech-language pathologist are varied. The America Speech-Language-Hearing Association (1999) provides guidelines in a number of areas. Wolf Nelson (2002, p. 313) cites those applicable to the assessment and evaluation processes:

Assessment: Forming an assessment plan, collecting data, using interview and observation strategies to understand the problem from the perspectives of

TABLE 12–2 Behaviors Associated with Language-Learning Disabilities

Characteristic Behavior	Example
Poor peer relations	Frequently plays alone
Poor adjustment to change	Becomes upset or confused when routine is altered
Perseveration	Persists in performing a task when not necessary
Poor emotional control	Becomes angry or cries easily
Easily frustrated	Stamps foot or sulks when asked to perform a task
Decreased initiation of communication	Sits quietly rather than requesting to have needs met
Excessive need to touch	Frequently hugs and touches others
Hyperactivity	Has difficulty sitting or standing without excessive movement
Variable performance	Performs well on a task and later appears unable to duplicate performance
Poor task persistence	Has difficulty completing tasks once initiated
Immaturity	Behaves like a younger child
Reduced vocabulary	Lacks understanding and use of object labels
Delayed responses	Needs additional time to understand simple directions
Behavior inappropriate to situation	Laughs and talks excessively to self
Difficulty recalling words (dysnomia)	Knows a particular word but is unable to recall it when needed
Impulsive	Acts or responds quickly without thinking
Difficulty following simple directions	Persists in standing when told to sit unless gestural cues are provided

participants, and using valid standardized and non-standardized assessment procedures to gain insights about the dimension of the problem.

Evaluation: Interpreting assessment data regarding the child's strengths, needs and emerging abilities; using the data to make diagnostic decisions about whether the child has a disorder and whether it affects educational performance; forming preliminary recommendations about how to respond to the area of concern.

Collaboration is crucial in selecting assessment procedures, administering and scoring formal standardized tests, and interpreting the findings. As a teacher of students with learning disabilities, you must rely on the special training of the speech-language pathologist. And as more students are being taught in inclusive classrooms, the speech-language pathologist will more likely be providing services in the classroom for part of the school day. This will be discussed further in the General Interventions section of this chapter.

Informal Assessment

A naturalistic, low-structure **language sample** is an excellent way to obtain evidence of a language-learning disability. This can be employed by parents at home (with appropriate training) and in school during those times when the student is in a natural environment—the lunchroom, during recess, and/or during a time in the **classroom** when students are engaged in a free activity. Lahey (1988) notes that this should include a language history, current language behaviors (FORM, CONTENT, and USE), a descriptor of nonlinguistic behaviors and a descriptor of the environment.

Bloom and Lahey (1978) and Lahey (1988) provide detailed information on how to carry out a plan for using a language sample. This is best accomplished in consultation and/or collaboration with a speech-language pathologist.

Standardized Assessment Procedures

There are times when you may need to assess oral language using a standardized test. Once again, this is best done in collaboration with a speech-language pathologist. Table 12-3, from Cohen and Spenciner (2003, pp. 259–262), lists tests commonly employed to assess oral language.

TABLE 12–3 Standardized Instruments of Oral Language

Instrument	Age Range	Type	Areas Assessed	Comments Regarding Technical Adequacy
Brigance Inventory of Early Development-Revised (Brigance, 1991)	Birth through 7 years	Criterion-referenced	Speech and language, including receptive language, gestures, vocalizations, expressive language, sentence length, and auditory memory	Skill sequences and associated grade levels were developed by a review of the literature.
Brigance Diagnostic Comprehensive Inventory of Basic Skill-Revised (Brigance, 1999)	5 years through 15 years	Criterion-referenced	Speech, including syntax and fluency, expressive language, articulation, and speech quality; listening skills, including auditory memory, and receptive language	Skill sequences and associated grade levels were developed by a review of the literature.
Clinical Evaluation of Language Fundamentals-3 (CELF-3) (Semel, Wiig, & Secord, 1996)	6 years through 21 years	Norm-referenced	Receptive and expressive language, morphology, syntax, semantics, and memory	Adequate.
Comprehensive Receptive and Expressive Vocabulary Test-Second Edition (CREVT-2) (Wallace & Hammill, 2002)	4 years through adulthood	Norm-referenced	Expressive and receptive language	Adequate.
Expressive Vocabulary Test (EVT) (Williams, 1997)	2 years, 5 months through 90+ years	Norm-referenced	Expressive vocabulary and language retrieval	Pictures contain a good balance of gender and ethnic representations. Adequate reliability and validity.
Expressive One-Word Picture Vocabulary-2000 Edition (EOWPVT-2000) (Brownell, 2000), English and Spanish forms*	2 years through 18 years	Norm-referenced	Expressive language	Limited information regarding norming sample.
Oral and Written Language Scales (OWLS) (Carrow-Woolfolk, 1996)	3 years through 21 years	Norm-referenced	Vocabulary, syntax, pragmatics, and higher-order thinking	Internal and test-retest reliability is weak for some age groups. **Comments**

Test	Age Range	Type	Area	Comments
Peabody Picture Vocabulary Test-Third Edition (PPVT-III) (Dunn & Dunn, 1997)	2 years, 5 months through 90+ years	Norm-referenced	Receptive language	During test development, items were reviewed for bias and cultural sensitivity. Adequate reliability and validity.
Prueba del Desarrollo Inicial del Lenguaje (Hresko, Reid, & Hammill, 1982)*	3 years through 7 years	Norm-referenced; norming sample consisted of 549 Spanish-speaking children from Mexico, Puerto Rico, and the U.S.	Receptive language for Spanish-speaking children and adolescents	This test is a direct translation of the Peabody Picture Vocabulary Test-R (Dunn & Dunn, 1981). Adequate.
Preschool Language Scale-3 (PLS-3) (Zimmerman, Strime, & Pond, 1992)	Birth through 6 years, 11 months	Norm-referenced	Auditory comprehension, expressive language	Adequate.
Test of Adolescent and Adult & Language-Third Edition (TOAL-3) (Hammill, Brown, Larsen, & Wiederholt, 1994)	12 years through 24 years, 11 months	Norm-referenced	Expressive and receptive language, syntax, semantics, and phonology, reading and writing	Adequate for measuring components of oral language.
Test of Early Language Development-Third Edition (TELD-3) (Hresko, Reid, & Hammill, 1999)	2 years through 7 years	Norm-referenced	Expressive and receptive language, syntax and semantics	Adequate.
Test of Language Development: Third Edition (TOLD-P:3) (Newcomer & Hammill, 1997)	4 years through 8 years	Norm-referenced	Expressive and receptive language, syntax, semantics, and phonology	Adequate.
Test of Language Development-Intermediate: Third Edition (TOLD-I:3) (Hammill & Newcomer, 1997)	8 years, 6 months through 12 years	Norm-referenced	Expressive and receptive language, syntax, semantics, and phonology	Adequate.
Test of Pragmatic Language (Phelps-Terasaki & Phelps-Gunn, 1992)	5 years through 13 years	Norm-referenced	Pragmatic language	Additional information concerning reliability and validity would be helpful.

(continued)

TABLE 12-3 Standardized Instruments of Oral Language (*continued*)

Instrument	Age Range	Type	Areas Assessed	Comments Regarding Technical Adequacy
Woodcock Language Proficiency Battery-Revised English Form (Woodcock, 1991)	2 years through adulthood	Norm-referenced	Auditory memory, expressive and receptive language, verbal analogies, reading and written language	Adequate.
Woodcock Language Proficiency Battery-Spanish Form (Woodcock & Munoz-Sandoval, 1995)*	2 years through adulthood	Norm-referenced; norming sample of Spanish version included individuals from Argentena, Costa Rica, Mexico, Peru, Puerto Rico, Spain, and several locations within the United States	Auditory memory, expressive and receptive language, verbal analogies, reading and written language	Spanish version is an adaptation, not a direct translation, of the English form.
Woodcock-Munoz Language Survey, Normative Update, English and Spanish Forms (Woodcock & Munoz-Sandoval, 2001)	4 years through adulthood	Norm-referenced; the normative update is based on the norming population of the Woodcock Johnson III (over 8,000 individuals); original norming sample of Spanish version included individuals from Argentina, Costa Rica, Mexico, Peru, Puerto Rico, Spain, and several locations within the United States	Oral language including picture vocabulary and verbal analogies, reading (letter–word identification) and writing (spelling, punctuation, capitalization, and word usage)	A screening test. Spanish version is an adaptation, not a direct translation, of the English form.

*The Spanish form is available.

Source: From Cohen, L. G. and Loraine Spenciner. *Assessment of Children and Youth with Special Needs*, 2/e. Published by Allyn and Bacon, Boston, MA. Copyright © 2003 by Pearson Education. Reprinted by permission of the publisher.

CONSIDERATIONS FOR CULTURALLY AND LINGUISTICALLY DIVERSE STUDENTS

All teachers of students with learning disabilities must be cognizant of the issues related to disproportionality (Artiles & Trent, 1994; Donvan & Cross, 2002; Gottlieb, Alter, & Gottlieb, 1994; McNamara, 1998; Quality Education for Minorities Project, 1990). Too often there is a rush to identify students as having a learning disability when in fact they are typically developing second-language learners (see Implications for Teachers: Second-Language Learners or Students with Learning Disabilities). Or they may be from culturally and linguistically diverse urban settings or living in poor urban or rural communities. All of these factors need to be considered when evaluating students' language ability. Burnett (2000) suggests the following guidelines:

- Gather information to determine whether the difficulties stem from language or cultural differences, from a lack of opportunity to learn, or from a disability as part of a pre-referral and intervention process.
- Include interpreters, bilingual educators, and an individual who is familiar with the student's culture and language as members of the IEP team.
- Assess the student's language dominance and proficiency to determine which language to use in the assessment process for special education services, if the student's home language is other than English.
- Select non-biased, appropriate instruments along with other sources of information (observation, interviews) from a variety of environments (school, home, community) to produce a multidimensional assessment.

Implications for Teachers: Second-Language Learners or Students with Learning Disabilities. Too often second-language learners are misdiagnosed as having learning disabilities (McNamara, 1998). As a teacher of students with learning disabilities, you need to be cognizant of the stages of language development among your students who are not native speakers of English. This will enable you to accumulate additional evidence when asking the question: "Is her language difficulty a result of second language learning or is it a language learning disability?" Salend (2005, p. 125) lists the following six stages:

1. *Pre-production or Silent Period.* Students focus on processing and comprehending what they hear but avoid verbal stimuli, context clues, [and] key words and use listening strategies to understand meaning, and often communicate through pointing and physical gestures. They may benefit from classroom activities that allow them to respond by imitating, drawing, pointing, and matching.
2. *Telegraphic or Early Production Period.* Students begin to use two- or three-word sentences, and show limited comprehension. They have a receptive vocabulary level of approximately 1,000 words and an expressive level that typically includes approximately 100 words. They may benefit from classroom activities that employ language they can understand, require them to name and group objects, and call for responses to simple questions.
3. *Inter-language Intermediate Fluency Period.* Students speak in longer phrases and start to use complete sentences. They often mix basic phrases and sentences in both languages. They may benefit from classroom activities that encourage them to experiment with language and develop and expand their vocabularies.
4. *Extension and Expansion Period.* Students expand on their basic sentences and extend their language abilities to employ synonyms and synonymous expressions. They are developing good comprehension skills, employing more complex sentence structures, and making fewer errors when speaking. They may benefit from classroom literacy activities and instruction in vocabulary and grammar.
5. *Enrichment Period.* Students are taught learning strategies to assist them in making the transition to the new language.
6. *Independent Learning Period.* Students begin to work on activities at various levels of difficulty with heterogeneous groups.

Social-Cultural Context of Spoken Language Disorders

Language cannot be assessed in a vacuum. It is necessary to become aware of those factors that contribute to or interfere with normal language acquisition. One way to do this is to employ the following questions developed by Salend (2005, pp. 127–128) for this purpose:

Length of Residence in the United States
- How long and for what periods of time has the student resided in the United States?
- What were the conditions and events associated with the student's migration?
- If the student was born in the United States, what has been the student's exposure to English?

Students may have limited or interrupted exposure to English and the U.S. culture, resulting in poor vocabulary and slow naming speed and affecting their cultural adjustment. Trauma experienced during migration or family separations as a result of migration can be psychological barriers that affect learning. Being born and raised in the United States does not guarantee that students have developed English skills and have had significant exposure to English and U.S. culture.

School Attendance Patterns
- How long has the student been in school?
- What is the student's attendance pattern? Have there been any disruptions in school? Students may fail to acquire language skills because of failure to attend school on a regular basis.

School Instructional History
- How many years of schooling did the student complete in the native country?
- What language(s) were used to guide instruction in the native country?
- What types of classroom has the student attended (bilingual education, English as a second language, general education, speech/language therapy services, special education)?
- What has been the language of instruction in these classes?
- What is the student's level of proficiency in reading, writing, and speaking in the native language?
- What strategies and instructional materials have been successful?

- What were the outcomes of these educational placements?
- What language does the student prefer to use in informal situations with adults?

Students may not have had access to appropriate instruction and curricula, resulting in problems in language acquisition, reading, and mathematics.

Cultural Background
- How does the student's cultural background affect second language acquisition?
- Has the student had sufficient time to adjust to the new culture?
- What is the student's acculturation level?
- What is the student's attitude toward school?

Since culture and language are inextricably linked, lack of progress in learning a second language can be due to cultural and communication differences and/or lack of exposure to the new culture. For example, some cultures rely on the use of body language in communication as a substitute for verbal communication. Various cultures also have different perspectives on color, time, gender, distance, and space that affect language.

Performance in Comparison to Peers
- Does the student's language skill, learning rate, and learning style differ from those of other students from similar experiential, cultural, and linguistic backgrounds?
- Does the student interact with peers in the primary language and/or English?
- Does the student experience difficulty following directions, understanding language, and expressing thoughts in the primary language? In the second language? The student's performance can be compared to that of students who have similar traits rather than to that of students whose experiences in learning a second language are very different.

Home Life
- What language(s) or dialects(s) are spoken at home by each of the family members?
- When did the student start to speak?
- Is the student's performance at home different from that of siblings?
- What language(s) or dialect(s) are spoken in the family's community?

- Is a distinction made among the uses of the primary language or dialect and English? If so, how is that distinction made? (For example, the non-English language is used at home, but children speak English when playing with peers.)
- What are the attitudes of the family and the community toward English and bilingual education?
- In what language(s) does the family watch television, listen to the radio, and read newspapers, books, and magazines?
- What is the student's language preference in the home and community?
- To what extent does the family interact with the dominant culture and in what ways?

Important information concerning the student's language proficiency, dominance, and preference can be obtained by soliciting information from family members. Similarly, the student's acquisition of language can be enhanced by involving family members.

GENERAL INTERVENTIONS

Once a thorough assessment has been performed in collaboration with the speech-language pathologist, and one that is sensitive to the diverse backgrounds of students, you are ready to develop an intervention plan. This section of the chapter will discuss general strategies for language comprehension and production, followed by specific language interventions for disorders frequently experienced by student with learning disabilities.

Most services are provided in inclusive settings, although there may be situations in which the speech-language pathologist recommends a pull-out. In either situation, collaboration is crucial. Explicit interventions, such as those cited in this section, should be implemented in a collaborative manner.

Language Comprehension

The following strategies may improve listening skills and increase the comprehension of students with language problems (Mercer & Mercer, 2005, pp. 263–264):

- If the student frequently has difficulty following directions or understanding information of increased complexity, establish eye contact and maintain attention prior to presenting information. Cue the student to listen by using silent pauses or instructions to listen to or look at the teacher. This helps to establish a mental set for listening.
- Ask the student to repeat or paraphrase directions or instructions to the teacher or a peer to ensure comprehension.
- To facilitate listening, arrange classroom seating to limit distractions from doorways and windows and to maximize the use of visual aids.
- When introducing a new concept or skill, use vocabulary that is familiar to the student and explain new vocabulary words by using familiar terms.
- Present new concepts in as many modalities as possible (e.g., auditory, visual, and kinesthetic), and use gestures to augment verbal presentations (Bos & Vaughn, 1998).
- To increase understanding of the relationship between semantic role and word order, encourage young children to act out sentences (e.g., "Mommy kiss baby") or manipulate objects and talk about their movement (Connell, 1986).
- Explain to students that listening is an active process that requires them to behave in specific ways, and teach them to identify specific behaviors associated with good listening (e.g., look, think about what is said, and repeat to yourself). Model effective listening skills by being attentive to students.
- Use introductory statements (such as "These are the main points" or "Before we begin") to provide an organizational framework and help students prepare for a task.
- Be sensitive to the students' linguistic sophistication and adjust the rate and complexity of instructional language accordingly. Use structurally simple and relatively short sentences of not more than five to ten words and limit the number of new and unfamiliar vocabulary words presented in a single lesson to five or less (Wiig & Semel, 1984).
- Teach specific memory strategies (e.g., visual imagery, clustering and grouping information, and

forming associations) to help students organize, categorize, and store new information for later retrieval.

- To enhance students' recall and memorization of new vocabulary, use the keyword method, in which familiar words are associated with each new concept or word (Mastropieri, Scruggs, & Fulk, 1990).
- Engage adolescents in concrete problem-solving activities to identify those who have difficulty thinking symbolically or using reasoning in nonsymbolic events (Moses, Klein, & Altman, 1990).

Language Production

The following strategies from Mercer and Mercer (2005, pp. 263–264) focus on improving the production or expressive skills of students with language problems:

- Expect students to speak occasionally in incomplete sentences because this is normal for discourse.
- Regardless of the effectiveness of a student's communication, convey that the message is important. React first to the content of a student's message because it is most important in the communication process, and then correct the syntax error.
- When attempting to expand a young child's utterances, provide one or two additional words to the child's spontaneous utterance for the child to repeat rather than impose adult structures that are difficult to imitate. Explain that the reason for the expansion of the utterance is not to correct what the youngster is saying but to give a more complex way of expressing thought (Bos & Vaughn, 1998).
- Teach language in various natural settings (e.g., classroom, cafeteria, and playground) rather than only in isolated groups. Also, teach language skills in connection with other curriculum content (Wiig & Semel, 1984).
- Act as a good language model, and ask students to imitate what they hear. Imitation is frequently a good measure of language skills because students tend to imitate only the forms they know and not necessarily what they hear.

- Use structured language programs that provide adequate opportunities to practice a new skill as well as interactive activities for applying the skill to relevant contexts (Bos & Vaughn, 1998).
- Comment or elaborate on students' ideas to demonstrate how more information can be expressed and how concepts can be associated.
- Use activities such as role playing and charades to improve a student's use of language in different contexts and to enhance the ability to recognize the importance of nonverbal skills such as eye contact, facial expressions, and gestures. Also, model and reinforce appropriate turn-taking in conversations.

SPECIFIC INTERVENTIONS

Word Finding

Specific interventions for word finding (also referred to as **Reauditorization**) are presented by Johnson and Myklebust (1967, pp. 119–123). Teachers of students with word finding problems should provide meaningful auditory stimulation, organize input, facilitate recall, employ rapid naming drills and teach self monitoring skills.

Sentence Formation

Wiig and Semel (1984, pp. 122–123) provide the following principles for correcting disorders in sentence formation:

Principle 1. Follow normal language development
Principle 2. Use familiar words
Principle 3. Limit sentence length
Principle 4. Use pictures
Principle 5. Illustrate unfamiliar words
Principle 6. Make sure the student knows the rule
Principle 7. Utilize familiar choices
Principle 8. Frequent practice

They recommend using transformation of sentences, scrambled sentences, sentence combining and expansion and a number of games that force students to play "reporter" and search for answers to questions.

Word Meaning

Principles for intervention for disorders of word meaning and word relationships are provided by Wiig and Semel, (1984, pp. 232–234):

Principle 1. Follow normal language development
Principle 2. Teach "typical" examples first
Principle 3. Proceed from general to specific
Principle 4. Proceed from simple to complex
Principle 5. Start with "positive" examples of antonyms
Principle 6. Limit Sentence length
Principle 7. Use pictures frequently
Principle 8. Emphasize critical components
Principle 9. Provide frequent practice
Principle 10. Use many examples
Principle 11. Utilize meaningful pragmatic tasks
Principle 12. Control vocabulary during generalization

Additional interventions for students who are having difficulty with word *meaning and word relationships are suggested by Thomas (2004, p. 159):*

1. **Dictionary Match-Up** (Multiple Meanings). Assemble pictures that represent words with more than one meaning. Print short dictionary definitions appropriate to students' reading level on 3″ × 5″ cards. Students will match the dictionary definition to the picture. Control the difficulty of this activity by varying the number of definitions and the number of pictures to be defined.

2. **Riddlemania** (Multiple Meanings). Present riddles to the students and have them explain the humor in each riddle.

3. **Word Search** (Figurative Language). Cultivate abstract thinking with lessons on choosing descriptive words. Begin with the concrete, and help the student to move on to more abstract conceptions. A hummingbird may be described as "green," "a blur of color," or "a tiny helicopter."

4. **Sense-Able Lessons** (Figurative Language). Use sensory experiences to stimulate students' use of descriptive language. Bring objects for seeing, tasting, feeling, hearing, and smelling, and compile a list of students' verbal reactions.

5. **Explain That** (Figurative Language). Discuss common idioms in class. Help students to discover the connection between the literal and figurative meanings.

   These examples can start the list:

   - She had two left feet. (Two left feet would cause one to be awkward.)
   - He was on pins and needles. (This would be an uncomfortable position which he would be eager to change.)
   - They were walking on eggs. (They were carefully trying to prevent a disagreeable situation.)

6. **Measure** (Space and Time Relationships). Measure objects in the classroom and make a bulletin board that tells that the door, for example, is 7 feet high, the desk is 3 feet wide, the dictionary is 8 inches by 10 inches, and the room is 8 yards long. State equivalents in feet and inches when applicable. Discuss how many miles it is from school to familiar places. The exercise will help students understand relative sizes and distances. Use the metric system only in areas where it is widely used.

7. **Calendar** (Space and Time Relationships). Provide sheets of paper marked in blocks for a calendar. Show students how to label the month, the days of the week, and the individual dates for that month. Then direct each student to choose personally important events for that month and write them on the spaces for the appropriate days. Events might include church, visit to friends, birthday party, spelling test, shopping, movie, piano lesson, scout meeting, or other activities. This should help students to learn to anticipate and prepare for coming events.

8. **Fables** (Cause/Effect Relationships). Read fables or stories with strong morals to the group; discuss the outcome of each. Help students to remember the events that caused the story ending.

9. **Because** (Cause/Effect Relationships). Suggest causes to the students and ask them to imagine possible effects. You might begin with these causes:

   The wind blew hard.
   The shoes were too small.
   He drove fast.
   The wood got wet.

TABLE 12–4 Summary of Language Disorders and Interventions

Language Disorder	Specific Interventions
Word finding	Meaningful auditory stimulation
	Organization of input
	Facilitation of recall
	Rapid naming
	Self-monitoring
	Continued usage
	Word association
	Conceptual categorization
Word meaning (semantics)	Follow normal developmental sequence
	Examples should be in the "best" context
	Go from general to specific meanings
	Go from simple to complex meanings
	Limit sentence length
	Utilize potential components
	Use many examples
	Extend range of application
	Multiple meanings
	Figurative language
	Space/time relationships
	Cause/effort relationships
Sentence formation (syntax)	Follow normal developmental sequence
	Utilize highly familiar sentences
	Limit sentence length
	Provide pictorial representations
	Provide ample examples
	Reception prior to expression
	Sentence transformation
	Use "W" questions

She took him a cake.

The price of oil went up.

Table 12–4 provides a quick reference to the type of language disorder and specific interventions you can employ.

APPLICATION OF TECHNOLOGY

Your school district may use specific oral language computer-based programs to teach oral language skills, or your students' parents may purchase these programs to be used at home. As a teacher of students with learning disabilities, you need to be aware of them. Consult with the speech-language pathologist in your school, as well as the National Educational Technology Standards for Students (http://www.iste.org/standards/iste.html.) As this is a rapidly growing area, you should be aware of the current research on the effectiveness of these programs. Two programs that focus on phonological awareness skills are EAROBICS (http://www.cogcom.com) and FAST FORWARD (http://www.scientificlearning.com.) Ongoing research is necessary to demonstrate their effectiveness.

INCLUSIONARY PRACTICES

There are a number of settings in which language interventions can take place. Some students will work with the speech-language pathologist in a separate setting (pull-out), while others may receive services in their classrooms (push-in). Some students with language disorders may receive services indirectly from the classroom teacher (consultation). Finally, others will receive interventions in an inclusive classroom (collaborative consultation). Weiss (2002) notes the benefits and drawbacks of the various models. All of the models have both benefits and drawbacks, however the collaborative consultations model appears to be the most beneficial and reinforces mutual responsibility for the student.

Practical Considerations: Working with the Speech-Language Pathologist. Michael receives speech therapy, as a related service three times per week, as a pull-out. The speech-language pathologist sees him in her room for three, 1-hour periods on Monday, Wednesday, and Friday. And while you are aware of his IEP goal, you are not sure of exactly what happens in the "speech room," nor do you know what your role is in the classroom. What should you do? At the very least, you need to schedule a meeting with the pathologist to review these concerns and develop a reasonable way to communicate with each other. Due to the increase in inclusionary practices, more speech-language pathologists are providing services as push-ins, working in the classroom with the student and providing you with appropriate models to follow when the pathologist is not there. This takes time, effort, and training, but many teachers of students with learning disabilities find it much more favorable than a pull-out program. Moreover, they recognize that the speech-language pathologist can be a valuable source of information. In this chapter, a number of assessment tools and intervention practices are presented, but the best sources of information may well be speech-language pathologists. They are usually very well trained and have met stringent certification requirements. They will know the language needs of your students with learning disabilities and will be able to provide specific information regarding assessment and instruction. This is why establishing a collaborative

relationship is critical (see Chapter 7 for more information on collaboration).

In the inclusive setting, there will be a different relationship with the speech-language pathologist. You need to be aware of this shift in his or her role in order to maximize services for your students. The differences in this new role for the speech-language pathologist, summarized by Tiegerman-Farber (2003, p. 113), are as follows:

- The teacher and the speech-language pathologist will have a different working relationship, which affects individual and group learning: team teaching, consultation as well as direct intervention in the classroom.
- The speech-language pathologist will use instructional techniques to facilitate language for the child with a disability in a group setting.
- The child with a disability will have the opportunity to interact with typical peers in a variety of academic and social activities. This will change the structure and the organization of classroom learning.
- The physical classroom environment will be organized differently.
- Parents of children with and without disabilities will have more opportunities to meet, to socialize, and to learn from each other.
- The process for and content of learning will be based on a curriculum that includes language and communication goals.
- Children teaching children will become an important means of implementing the **curriculum.**

Tiegerman-Farber (2003) also notes that collaboration is critical (see Chapter 7) and that topics such as the physical environment, the composition of the class, specific needs of students, and strategies need to be addressed.

SUMMARY

This chapter has focused on a critical area of development—spoken language. For many students with learning disabilities, this is where the problems first appear. An overview of normal language development, including the major components and theories of language development, was presented, as well as the characteristics of students with spoken-language disorders, both receptive and expressive. It is critical to accurately assess the nature of the disorders of spoken language; therefore, informal and formal measures were provided. Specific interventions were presented, and collaboration with the speech-language pathologist was emphasized. Collaboration is crucial for the success of your students with spoken-language disorders, as most will be provided with these services in inclusive settings.

SPRINGBOARDS FOR REFLECTION AND DISCUSSION

1. Observe a typical 3-year-old and note how he or she uses language. Note the content and form of the language. What does the child talk about? How many words does he or she use per utterance? Is the utterance intelligible? Does the child appear to understand the surrounding environment?

2. Select a standardized test of language. What language components does it cover?

3. Observe a speech-language pathologist in a clinical setting and in an inclusive classroom. What are the similarities? What are the differences?

4. How would some of the language disorders described in this chapter manifest themselves in a reading disorder? In a written language disorder?

5. Interview a classroom teacher who works with a speech-language pathologist in an inclusive classroom. What are the advantages and disadvantages of this arrangement?

6. Interview a speech-language pathologist who works in an inclusive classroom. What are the advantages and disadvantages of this arrangement?

7. In what ways could you develop a collaborative relationship with the speech-language pathologist who is working with your students?

8. How could you ensure that the needs of your students with spoken language disorders can be met?

CHAPTER 13 READING DISORDERS

CHAPTER OBJECTIVES

At the end of this chapter you will be able to:

- understand the characteristics of students with reading disorders.
- become aware of ways to diagnose reading disorders.
- become aware of a variety of reading approaches used with students with learning disabilities.
- provide scientifically based reading interventions for your students.

You must be able to teach your students to read! As a teacher of students with learning disabilities, this may well be your greatest challenge. Most of your students will have reading problems, which will impact every aspect of their schoolwork and their lives outside of school. Consider Michael. He was in sixth grade, read considerably below grade level, and had already had a host of interventions, none of which were very successful. During the 2 years of working with Michael, his teacher decided that a language experience approach (see the Interventions section of this chapter) would be best for him. He improved, but the gap between him and his classmates continued to be wide. At home, his younger siblings (in Grades 2 and 4) were surpassing him in their ability to read. He did everything possible to avoid the printed word. His parents reported that he and his

brothers had grown further apart because as their academic achievements continued to grow, his remained stagnant. Frequently, he got into arguments related to homework that included any reading/writing assignment, often going to bed angry and to school angry. The emotional toll of his reading problems was worsening for Michael and his family. What would have happened if Michael had been diagnosed at an early age? Were there things his parents or teachers could have done to help him? Was a particular approach especially effective for him? Were all the key components in an effective reading program provided early in Michael's school career? What would you do? How would you evaluate his progress? What method would you employ? This chapter will address these concerns and others for students like Michael, who struggle daily with problems with the printed word.

TEACHING STUDENTS WITH READING DISORDERS

It has been estimated that approximately 80% of students with learning disabilities have reading disorders (Lyon, 1999; Shaywitz, 2003; Torgesen, 1998, 2005). Reading success is synonymous with school success. Conversely, students who are not efficient readers will have trouble in school. Moreover, reading disorders will have a direct effect on career choices and success as an adult. The impact of reading failure cannot be overstated (Shaywitz et al., 1999). As a teacher of students with learning

disabilities, you must be able to teach them to read. Often this will involve collaboration with reading specialists (literacy specialists), regular classroom teachers, and parents. However, it is critical to implement a reading program based on scientific evidence. This is no place for "beliefs."

DYSLEXIA VERSUS READING DISORDERS

Dyslexia is defined as a specific learning disability that is neurobiological in origin (Lyon, 2002, as cited in Shaywitz, 2003). "It is characterized by difficulties with accurate and/or fluent word recognition and by poor spelling and decoding abilities. These difficulties typically result from a deficit in the phonological component of language that is often unexpected in relation to other cognitive abilities and the provision of effective classroom instruction. Secondary consequences may include problems in reading comprehension and reduced reading experience that can impede the growth of vocabulary and background knowledge" (p. 132). Is it the same as a reading disorder? Some teachers may find it confusing because the terms **dyslexia** and **reading disorder** are used casually and interchangeably. For some, the term **dyslexia** signals a more severe reading disorder with neurological impairment. For others, it is used synonymously with **reading disorders.** The term employed is less important than a clear description of the student's reading problems and the type of intervention plan you develop.

Siegel (2003) discusses the issues surrounding the use of the terms. **Dyslexia** is a medical term, whereas **reading disorder** is an educational term. Although Siegel believes that they are synonymous, she prefers to use the term **reading disability** out of consideration for other professionals who find the term **dyslexia** "offensive" (p. 159). (In this book, the term **reading disorder** or **reading disability** will be used unless a cited author specifically uses the term **dyslexia.**)

CHARACTERISTICS OF DYSLEXTIA

Johnson and Myklebust (1967, pp. 174–179), in a classic textbook on learning disabilities, describe two types of dyslexia: visual and auditory. Based on their clinical observations and diagnostic findings, they cite the following characteristics of persons with visual dyslexia. They have visual discrimination problems, slow rate of perception, reversals, following sequences, and problems with visual memory, visual analysis and synthesis. Their drawings are inferior and they have difficulty following rules of games. Not surprisingly, they prefer auditory activities.

Students with auditory dyslexia have difficulty with auditory discrimination, auditory synthesis, auditory memory and auditory sequencing. They tend to prefer visual activities and perform below average on blending, syllabilization and rhyming tasks.

EARLY INDICATORS OF READING DISORDERS

There are early indicators of reading disabilities, and if they are not remediated, the student will fall further and further behind, so that the gap will never be closed. Shaywitz (2003, pp. 122–125) provides the following list of clues:

The earliest clues involve mostly spoken language. The very first clue to a language (and reading) problem may be delayed language. Once the child begins to speak, look for the following problems:

The Preschool Years
- Trouble learning common nursery rhymes, such as "Jack and Jill" and "Humpty Dumpty"
- A lack of appreciation of rhymes
- Mispronounced words; persistent baby talk
- Difficulty in learning (and remembering) names of letters
- Failure to know the letters in his own name

Kindergarten and First Grade
- Failure to understand that words come apart; for example, that *batboy* can be pulled apart into *bat* and *boy*, and, later on that the word *bat* can be broken down still further and sounded out as: "*b*""*aaaa*""*t*"
- Inability to learn to associate letters with sounds, such as being unable to connect the letter *b* with the "*b*" sound
- Reading errors that show no connection to the sounds of the letters; for example, the word *big* is read as *goat*
- The inability to read common one-syllable words or to sound out even the simplest of words, such as *mat, cat, hop, nap*
- Complaints about how hard reading is, or running and hiding when it is time to read
- A history of reading problems in parents or siblings

Indicators from Second Grade On
Problems in Speaking

- Mispronunciation of long, unfamiliar, or compli-cated words; the *fracturing* of words—leaving out parts of words or confusing the order of the parts of words; for example, *aluminum* becomes *amulium*. Speech that is not fluent—pausing or hesitating often when speaking, lots of *um's* during speech, no glibness.
- The use of imprecise language, such as vague references to *stuff* or *things* instead of the proper name of an object.
- Not being able to find the exact word, such as confusing words that sound alike: saying *tornado* instead of *volcano*, substituting *lotion* for *ocean*, or *humanity* for *humidity*.
- The need for time to summon an oral response or the inability to come up with a verbal response quickly when questioned.
- Difficulty in remembering isolated pieces of verbal information (rote memory)—trouble remembering dates, names, telephone numbers, random lists.

Problems in Reading

- Very slow progress in acquiring reading skills.
- The lack of a strategy to read new words.
- Trouble reading *unknown* (new, unfamiliar) words that must be sounded out; making wild stabs or guesses at reading a word; failure to systematically sound out words.
- The inability to read "small function" words such as *that, an, in.*
- Stumbling on reading multi-syllable words, or the failure to come close to sounding out the full word.
- Omitting parts of words when reading; the failure to decode parts within a word, as if someone had chewed a hole in the middle of the word, such as *conible* for *convertible*.
- A terrific fear of reading out loud; the avoidance of oral reading.
- Oral reading filled with substitutions, omissions, and mispronunciations.
- Oral reading that is choppy and labored, not smooth or fluent.
- Oral reading that lacks inflection and sounds like the reading of a foreign language.
- A reliance on context to discern the meaning of what is read.

- A better ability to understand words in *context* than to read *isolated* single words.
- Disproportionately poor performance on multiple choice tests.
- The inability to finish tests on time.
- The substitution of words with the same meaning for words in the text he can't pronounce, such as *car* for *automobile*.
- Disastrous spelling, with words not resembling true spelling; some spellings may be missed by spell check.
- Trouble reading mathematics word problems.
- Reading that is very slow and tiring.
- Homework that never seems to end, or with parents often recruited as readers.
- Messy handwriting despite what may be an excellent facility at word processing—nimble fingers.
- Extreme difficulty learning a foreign language.
- A lack of enjoyment in reading, and the avoidance of reading books or even a sentence.
- The avoidance of reading for pleasure, which seems too exhausting.
- Reading whose accuracy improves over time, though it continues to lack fluency and is laborious.
- Lowered self-esteem, with pain that is not always visible to others.
- A history of reading, spelling, and foreign language problems in family members.

In addition to observations made in the class-room and clinic, there is neuropsychological evidence of reading disabilities (Cutting & Denckla, 2004; Galaburda, 2005; Shaywitz, 2003; Shaywitz & Shaywitz, 2003). Using functional magnetic resonance imagining, investigators have mapped neural pathways in good and poor readers. Good readers had a consistent pattern of strong activation in the back of the brain and less activation in the front. Poor readers, by contrast, typically displayed a pattern of underactivation in the back of the brain. This exciting line of research may lead to promising ways to evaluate the effectiveness of various interventions based on specific brain patterns. (More information on the neurological causes of learning disability is presented in Chapter 3.)

ASSESSMENT OF READING DISORDERS

It is critical to assess the nature of the reading disability in order to develop a reasonable, sensible, scientifically based intervention plan. Once you formulate the assessment questions (also called **diagnostic questions**), you can begin to develop an assessment plan. Rhodes and Shanklin (1993), as cited in Cohen and Spenciner (2003, pp. 197–198), list the following 12 principles of literacy assessment:

1. *Assess authentic reading and writing.* When students read and write they must know the letters and their associated sounds (grapho-phonics), understand the meaning of language (semantics), and grasp the flow of the language (syntax).
2. *Assess reading and writing in various contexts.* An understanding of students' reading and writing abilities must consider the contexts in which reading and writing occur. Contexts relate to the types of reading materials, the purpose of the reading, and strategies in use.
3. *Assess the literacy environment, instruction, and students.* Reading and writing assessment must consider the environments in which reading occurs, the types of instruction in use, and the characteristics of students.
4. *Assess processes and products of reading.* The assessment of reading processes and students' products can provide a comprehensive understanding of students' abilities.
5. *Analyze error patterns.* The understanding of patterns of errors in reading and writing can help improve student performance. Errors in reading include miscues, omissions, substitutions, additions, repetitions, self-corrections, and pauses.
6. *Include the assessment of background knowledge.* Experience, prior learning, and background knowledge influence reading and writing performance.
7. *Consider developmental patterns in reading and writing.* Knowledge of typical developmental patterns in reading and writing can

contribute to our understanding of reading and writing abilities.
8. *Use sound principles of assessment.* Use sound principles or standards when assessing students. These standards apply to reliability, validity, observation, and scoring.
9. *Use triangulation.* Triangulation means that conclusions about student performance derive from multiple (here, at least three) sources of information. Rhodes and Shanklin advise caution when drawing conclusions about students when using only one source of information.
10. *Include students, parents, teachers, and other school personnel in the assessment process.* The involvement of students, parents, and other educators in the assessment process provides for the inclusion of multiple perspectives.
11. *Assessment activities should be ongoing.* Assessment activities should occur frequently and routinely. In this way, assessment activities integrate into and inform instruction.
12. *Record, analyze, and use assessment information.* Assessment information is effective only when it is in use. Record assessment data frequently, analyze it, and use it on a routine basis to guide instruction.

Standardized Tests of Reading

Typically, students will be evaluated using standardized tests and informal measures of reading. There are more standardized tests of reading than in any other curriculum area. Some of the more frequently used tests are listed in Table 13–1 (Cohen & Spenciner, 2003, p. 199).

Cohen and Spenciner (2003) advise educators to use caution when assessing reading skills through standardized measures. Contemporary views of literacy are not always reflected in these instruments, and teachers need to evaluate whether the tests reflect their reading curriculum. These tests are frequently biased against culturally and linguistically diverse and poor students. Cohen and Spenciner conclude their caution with the slogan "multiple, multiple, and frequent-use multiple approaches, multiple instruments and assess frequently" (p. 223).

TABLE 13-1   Standardized Tests of Reading

Test	Ages/Grades	Abilities
Gray Oral Reading Tests-4 (Wiederholt & Bryant, 2001)	Age 6 years through 18 years	Comprehension, oral reading skills
Nelson-Denny Reading Test (Brown, Fishco, & Hanna, 2000)	Grade 9 through college	Vocabulary, comprehension. reading rate
Standardized Reading Inventory-2 (Newcomer, 1999)	Pre-Primary through Grade 8	Oral reading, word recognition, comprehension
Stanford Diagnostic Reading Test 4 (Hartcourt Brace Educational Measurement, 1995)	Grades 1.5 through 13	Phonetic ability, vocabulary, comprehension
Test of Phonological Awareness (Torgesen & Bryant, 1994)	K through Grade 2	Awareness of individual sounds, words
Test of Reading Comprehension-3 (Brown, Hammill, & Wiederholt, 1995)	Ages 7 years to 17 years, 11 months	Vocabulary, syntactic similarities, comprehension, sentence sequencing
Woodcock Reading Mastery Tests-Revised Normative Update (Woodcock, McGrew, & Mather 1998)	K through adulthood	Visual-auditory learning, letter identification, word attack, word comprehension

Source: From Cohen, L. G. and Loraine Spenciner. *Assessment of Children and Youth with Special Needs.* Published by Allyn and Bacon, Boston, MA. Copyright © 2003 by Pearson Education. Reprinted by permission of the publisher.

Informal Measures

Most classroom teachers evaluate students' progress in reading on an ongoing basis. They may use teacher-made tests, informal reading inventories, published inventories, checklists, and the like.

Observing Reading Performance

An effective teacher of students with learning disabilities will observe student performance on a variety of reading tasks. Mercer and Mercer (2005, p. 300) provide questions you should consider:

- What is the student's attitude toward reading?
- What specific reading interest does the student have?
- Is the student making progress in reading?
- What strengths and weaknesses in reading does the student exhibit?
- During oral reading, does the student read word by word or with fluency?
- What kinds of errors does the student make consistently?

- What word analysis skills does the student use?
- Does the student use context clues to recognize words?
- Does the student have a good sight vocabulary?
- Does the student appear to pay attention to the meaning of the material when reading?

Assessment of Phonemic Awareness

Phonemic awareness has been linked to success in reading (Ehri, Nunes, Willows, Schuster, Yaghoub-Zadeh, & Shanahan, 2001; Lyon, 1995; Torgesen, 1999, 2000, 2005). The National Reading Panel (2002, p. 22) suggests the following ways in which a teacher can evaluate this ability in young children:

1. Phoneme isolation, which requires recognizing individual sounds in words. For example, "Tell me the first sound in *paste.*" (/p/)
2. Phoneme identity, which requires recognizing the common sound in different words. For example, "Tell me the sound that is the same in *bike, boy,* and *bell.*" (/b/)

3. Phoneme categorization, which requires recognizing the word with the odd sound in a sequence of three or four words. For example, "Which word does not belong? *bus, bun, rug*." (*rug*)
4. Phoneme blending, which requires listening to a sequence of separately spoken sounds and combining them to form a recognizable word. For example, "What word is /s/ /k/ /u/ /l/?" (*school*)
5. Phoneme segmentation, which requires breaking a word into its sounds by tapping out or counting the sounds or by pronouncing and positioning a marker for each sound. For example, "How many phonemes are there in *ship*?" (three: /s/ /I/ /p/)
6. Phoneme deletion, which requires recognizing what word remains when a specified phoneme is removed. For example, "What is *smile* without the /s/?" (*mile*)

Informal Reading Inventory (IRI)

An IRI provides useful information on a student's general reading level (Mercer & Pullen 2005; Salend, 2005). There are commercially available inventories, but the most useful ones are those you make up to be utilized in your classroom or school. Generally, you select a 100-word passage from your reading series or content textbook (50 words if the students are elementary readers, 200 if they are in middle or high school). To measure the student's comprehension of the passage, formulate a number of questions. These should vary from factual information provided in the passage to inferential information that will assess if the student can go beyond the facts. While you can compute a percentage score, it is probably more useful to get an overall sense of comprehension. It is difficult to ensure that all questions are equally difficult. If you

ask a child to retell the story, you can evaluate her overall ability to understand what she read. An IRI has three levels: independent, instructional, and frustration (see Table 13–2).

Mercer and Mercer (2005, p. 273) list the errors in commonly used marking systems (see Table 13–3).

Miscue Analysis

Miscue analysis helps you appreciate the process of reading. It is a qualitative analysis (Cavuto, 2003) that enables you to formulate hypotheses about why students make certain errors. Tucker and Bakken (2000, p. 17) provide an example:

A second grader [Brett] has read [the passage in Figure 13-1] orally, and the teacher has marked his "miscues" on the text. The numbers to the right of the miscues correspond to the following discussion:

Miscue 1 Substituted Black for Dark.
Brett retained the adjective slot with this meaningful substitution. He also showed some graphophonic (letter/sound relationship) awareness, as both words contain "a" and "k" along with similar letter configurations of the "b" for the "d." The meaning was not interrupted.

Miscue 2 Substituted Some for Smoke.
This miscue did not fit the sentence structure of the entire sentence but made some sentence structure acceptable with the last part of the sentence. Overall, the meaning was interrupted, but Brett showed use of the graphophonic system through the use of four of the five letters, as well as some sound similarity.

Miscue 3 Substituted Mr. for Mrs.
Brett retained the notion of a title, and the substitution was meaningful. The substitution definitely

TABLE 13–2 Informal Reading Inventory Levels

Levels of Reading	Decoding	Comprehension
Independent	98–100%	90–100%
Instructional	95%	75%
Frustration	Less than 90%	Less than 70%

TABLE 13-3 Informal Reading Inventory Errors in Marking Systems

Type of Error	Marking System	Example
Omissions	Circle the word or parts of the word omitted.	The boy went in (to) the (burning) building. down
Insertions	Use a caret to mark the place of insertion and write the added word or letters(s).	The children sat ^ at the table to eat lunch ^es
Substitutions	Cross out the word and write the substituted word above it.	realize Now I ~~recognize~~ your name.
Reversals	For letter reversals within a word, cross out the word and write the reversal word above it.	pot The ~~top~~ is lost.
	For reversals of words, draw a curved line going over, between, and under the reversed words.	Mary looked⌒often at the clock.
Repetitions	Draw a wavy line under the words which are repeated.	Everyone was cheering for me because I was a baseball hero.
Mispronunciations	Write the mispronounced word (indicating the student's pronunciation) over the correct word.	oc-top-us It was an octopus.
Hesitations	Use a slash to indicate improper hesitation	The/judge asked the jury/to leave the courtroom.
Aided words	Underline the word pronounced for the student.	The scared cat began to tremble.
Unobserved punctuation marks	Cross out the punctuation mark the student continued to read through.	Puppy saw the man He barked and barked.ˣ
Self-corrected errors	Write **sc** over the error notation	sc mouth This ~~mouth~~ is November.

Source: Mercer, Cecil D.; Mercer, Ann R., *Teaching Students with Learning Problems*, 7th edition, © 2005. Reprinted by permission of Pearson Education, Inc., Upper Saddle River, NJ.

showed strong letter/sound relationship. Some meaning was lost as the switch in gender occurred, although a question could be raised as to how much of an impact on the story the change in gender created.

Miscue 4 Substituted Mill's for Miller's.
Brett retained the name slot with a proper noun and even showed further language and graphic strength by putting the "'s" on the name. In the previous paragraph, the reader had substituted "Mills" for "Miller's." So, this miscue showed [that] the sense of language dictated the necessary attention to print. The miscue had high sound similarity, and meaning was not interrupted.

Miscue 5 Substituted On for No.
Brett first pronounced the word as "on" and then tried to correct the word to "no." Although the

sentence structure of the entire sentence was interrupted, reading the miscue from the beginning and stopping at "on" showed that some sentence structure was maintained. While perhaps minimum letter/sound relationship, the attempt to self-correct demonstrated that the reader probably knew that he wasn't making sense. Overall, the meaning was interrupted.

Miscue 6 Omission of the Period and Joining the Two Sentences Together.
Contrary to popular opinion about writing, "and" can begin a sentence. In this case, Brett showed appropriate sentence structure by eliminating the period and logically joining the two thoughts together. Meaning was certainly maintained.

Then he saw something bad. He saw dark ~~black~~ ①
~~some~~ ②
smoke coming out of the window of Mrs. ~~Mr.~~ ③
~~Mills~~ ④
Miller's house. Bob knew that no one was in ~~on~~ ⑤

the house to see the smoke. Bob called to his
~~and~~ ⑥   ~~she~~ ⑦
mother. He showed her the smoke. Then Bob

looked out the window. He kept looking at the
~~Mr.~~ ⑧   ~~Mills~~ ⑨
smoke coming out of Mrs. Miller's house.

FIGURE 13–1   Sample Informal Reading Inventory

Source: From "How Do Your Kids Do at Reading? And How Do You Assess Them?" by D. L. Tucker and J. P. Bakken, *Teaching Exceptional Children, 32,* July–August 2002, p. 17. Copyright 2002 by The Council for Exceptional Children. Reprinted with permission.

Miscue 7 Substituted She for Her.
Brett retained the appropriate pronoun slot, with the substitution being somewhat meaningful, rather than not knowing the sight words. Brett had just mentioned the word *mother,* which would make sense in that the pronoun substitution would be "she." Although the letters/sound relationship was high, the meaning was partly interrupted by the change in gender. The two remaining miscues in the paragraph are repeated miscues ("r", "m"), as Brett pronounced those same words with miscues 3 and 4, respectively. Brett was showing consistency in the use of miscues, particularly with ones that probably made sense to him as he was attempting to construct meaning.

INTERVENTIONS

Once you have identified the student's strengths and weaknesses, you can develop an intervention plan. Your instructional strategies should be based on evidence, not beliefs. The current body of evidence suggests specific methodology.

At the request of Congress, in 1997 the Director of the National Institute of Child Health and Human Development (NICHD), Dr. G. Reid Lyon, convened a national panel to assess the status of research-based knowledge, including the effectiveness of various reading approaches. They reviewed the empirical evidence to date (see NRP, 2000, for specific criteria). The National Reading Panel (NRP) issued a report in 2000 that has had a major impact on the implementation of specific programs.

The panel of 14 experts in the field of reading focused on the following topics:

- Alphabetics
- Fluency
- Comprehension
- Teacher education
- Computer technology

The following questions were developed to meet their charge (NRP, 2000, p. 3):

1. Does instruction in phonemic awareness improve reading? If so, how is this instruction best provided?

2. Does phonics instruction improve reading achievement? If so, how is this instruction best provided?
3. Does guided repeated oral reading instruction improve fluency and reading comprehension? If so, how is the instruction best provided?
4. Does vocabulary instruction improve reading achievement? If so, how is this instruction best provided?
5. Does comprehension strategy instruction improve reading? If so, how is this instruction best provided?
6. Do programs that increase the amount of children's independent reading improve reading achievement and motivation? If so, how is this instruction best provided?
7. Does teacher education influence how effective teachers are at teaching children to read? If so, how is this instruction best provided?

The answer to all of these questions was yes. While the panel had more research support in some areas than others, it was clear that direct, explicit instruction was critical to success. For example, phonics programs were more successful than nonphonics based programs, but within phonics programs, those using explicit, direct instruction were most effective. Students with learning disabilities have trouble deducing or inferring the information to be learned. This must be taught in a systematic, direct, fashion (Carnine, Silbert, & Kame'enui, 1997).

DIRECT INSTRUCTION IN READING

Direct instruction has been demonstrated to be extremely effective (Adams & Carmine, 2003; Adams & Englemann, 1996; Swanson, Lee, & Hoskyn, 1999). It is more than teacher-directed, intensive, and explicit instruction. It is defined by Adams and Carmine (2003, p. 404) as

> published curricula developed by Englemann and associates. Each curriculum usually contains one-half to 1 year school lessons. A distinctive feature of these curricula is that they have been field tested with students using a three-stage curriculum testing process.

The major characteristics of direct instruction programs are:

- teacher training
- brisk lessons
- assessment of students on a placement test
- maximum of 14 students in homogeneous groups
- 35- to 45-minute lessons
- scripted lessons
- specific correction procedures
- employs behavioral principles

There are two reading programs: Reading Mastery and Corrective Reading (Carnine et al., 1997). Reading Mastery, divided into six levels (I to VI), is a complete elementary reading program that teaches both decoding and comprehension. Students are placed on levels based on the results of a placement test. This highly structured, evidence-based method utilizes an intensive, explicit, phonics-based approach and teaches comprehension skills. Teachers follow a script and provide reinforcement throughout the instructional process. Corrective Reading is a remedial program for students from third grade to adulthood. As with Reading Mastery, they are placed on levels based on the results of a placement test (see http://www.sra4kids.com/productinfo/direct for additional information).

READING APPROACHES

Reading approaches can be broken down in a number of ways. Salend (2001) divides them into four major categories: (a) phonetic, (b) language experience, (c) whole word, and (d) whole language. He recognizes that some students may benefit from a specific approach but suggests that most students benefit from a balanced approach. While not a specific reading approach, phonemic awareness has been demonstrated to be a critical skill in reading; therefore, it will be discussed prior to the four approaches.

Phonemic Awareness

Phonemic awareness is the ability to focus on and manipulate phonemes (the smallest units of spoken language) in spoken words. A number of researchers (Torgesen, Wagner, Rashotte, Vellutino, Lyons) suggest that this ability may be the best predictor of reading success. Simmons, Gunn, Smith, and Kame'enui (1994), as cited in Mercer and Mercer (2001, p. 33), list five recommendations to enhance phonemic awareness instruction:

1. *Focus first on the auditory features of words.* When asking the student to blend the sounds of a word together or to identify the individual sounds in a word, instruction initially should occur without alphabetic symbols.
2. *Move from explicit, natural segments of language to the more implicit and complex.* Initial segmenting instruction should proceed from segmenting sentences into words, words into syllables, and syllables into phonemes.
3. *Use phonological properties and dimensions of words to enhance performance.* Task complexity can be controlled by initially selecting words with fewer phonemes and words in which consonant and vowel configurations can be distinguished easily (e.g., words with vowel-consonant or consonant patterns). Also, words with discrete phonemes (e.g., *rug*) are segmented more easily than those beginning and ending with consonant blends, and words that begin with continuous sounds (e.g., *sun, mat*) facilitate sound blending activities.
4. *Scaffold blending and segmenting through explicit modeling.* Strategies should be modeled by the teacher and practices over time to make the blending and segmenting processes obvious and explicit.
5. *Integrate letter–sound correspondence once learners are proficient with auditory tasks.* Blending and segmenting skills should be applied to realistic reading, writing, and spelling situations.

Phonetic Approaches

Salend (2001, p. 347) divided phonetic approaches into two types: (a) synthetic and (b) analytic. In the synthetic approach, students start from the part and move to the whole as follows:

1. Introduce letters and their names to students.
2. Teach students the sounds associated with each letter.
3. Give students opportunities to develop automaticity in grapheme–phoneme relationships.
4. Teach students how to blend sounds into words.
5. Offer activities that allow students to apply their skills to unknown words.

In the analytic approach, students are taught to analyze words, moving from the whole to the part:

1. Give students a list of words that have a common phonic element.
2. Question students about the similarities and differences in the look and sound of the words.
3. Help students determine the common phonetic patterns in the words.
4. Have students state the rule concerning the phonetic pattern.

The NRP (2000, pp. 2-103–2-104) noted several important ways in which phonetic programs may differ:

1. How many letter–sound relations are taught, how they are sequenced, whether phonics generalizations are taught as well (e.g., "When there are two vowels side by side, the long sound of the first one is heard and the second is usually silent."), whether special marks are added to letters to indicate their sounds, for example, curved or straight lines above vowels to mark them as short or long.
2. The size of the unit taught (i.e., graphemes and phonemes, or larger word segments called phonograms, for example, *-ing,* or *-ack,* which represent the rimes in many single-syllable words).
3. Whether the sounds associated with letters are pronounced in isolation (synthetic phonics) or only in the context of words (analytic phonics).
4. The amount and type of phonemic awareness that is taught, for example, blending or segmenting sounds orally in words.

5. Whether instruction is sequenced according to a hierarchical view of learning, with the steps regarded as a series of prerequisites (i.e., letters, then letter–sound relations, then words, then sentences) or whether multiple skills are learned together.
6. The pace of instruction.
7. The word reading operations that children are taught, for example, sounding out and blending letters, or using larger letter subunits to read words by analogy to known words.
8. The involvement of spelling instruction.
9. Whether learning activities include extensive oral drill-and-practice, reciting phonics rules, or filling out worksheets.
10. The type of vocabulary control provided in text (e.g., is the vocabulary limited mainly to words containing familiar letter-sound associations or are sight words introduced to help create a meaningful story?).
11. Whether phonics instruction is embedded in or segregated from the literacy curriculum.
12. The teaching approach, whether it involves direct instruction in which the teacher takes an active role and students passively respond, or whether a "constructivist" approach is used in which the children learn how the letter–sound system works through problem solving.
13. How interesting and motivating the instructional activities are for teachers and for students.

You should select the program that best meets the needs of your students. When teaching phonics following the guidelines provided by Steward and Cegelka (1995, pp. 298, 301–302) may be helpful:

- *Use lowercase letters for beginning instruction.*
- *Introduce most useful skills first.*
- *Introduce easy sounds and letters first.*
- *Introduce new letter-sound associations at a reasonable pace.*
- *Introduce vowels early, but teach consonants first.*
- *Emphasize the common sounds of letters first.*
- *Teach continuous sounds prior to stop sounds.*
- *Teach sound blending early.*
- *Introduce consonant blends.*

When students have mastered the ability to blend consonant-vowel-consonant words that start with continuous sounds (e.g., *fat*) and consonant-vowel-consonant words that start with stop sounds (e.g., *dig*), words beginning with consonant blends (e.g., *spot*) are introduced. Next, words ending with consonant blends (e.g., *sick*) are taught.
- *Introduce consonant digraphs.*
- *Introduce regular words prior to irregular ones.*
- *Read connected text that reinforces phonics patterns.*

Phonics instruction should never be considered the only teaching method. Students must be exposed to good, meaningful, and interesting literature. They need to develop a love of reading. Phonics instruction is not a total reading program. As the NRP notes, "phonics teaching" is a means to an end. You must also evaluate students' interest in reading and their ability to understand what they read.

Language Experience Approach

The language experience approach employs the student's own thoughts and words in the reading process. It is useful for students who have an adequate experiential background and expressive language (see Allen & Allen, 1982). This was the approach used with Michael, the sixth grader with learning disabilities introduced at the beginning of this chapter, who was struggling with reading. He received a great deal of systematic phonics instruction, but nothing seemed to click. His major difficulty concerned his inability to blend the parts of words, so *cat* was pronounced *cuh ah tuh*. No matter how hard he tried, he failed. His academic struggles were causing emotional and behavioral difficulties. What was apparent was his fund of knowledge and his excellent expressive language skills. Every morning Michael would dictate a story to his teacher. These stories were typed (prior to computer use in the classroom!), and Michael read them in the afternoon. Comprehension was increased because the story was his own words. His fund of words increased, and he was able to move on to easy books.

Whole Word Approaches

In these approaches, students are presented with new words (controlled vocabulary) in context (a sentence or paragraph). They decode the words using contextual cues rather than phonetic analysis. Salend (2001) notes that basal readers often employ this approach. They can also employ other decoding skills.

These readers introduce material in a gradual, logical sequence. Typically, there is a preprimer, a primer (K-1), and 1-1, 1-2, 2-1, 2-2, 3-1, 3-2, 4, 5, and 6 grade levels. A student text is provided, along with supplementary material and a teacher's edition. Students are prepared prior to reading; they then read, and discussion follows. For students with learning disabilities, these approaches are too broad and do not address their specific reading needs.

Whole Language Approach

In this reading approach, the emphasis is on reading for understanding rather than learning decoding skills in isolation. Some suggest that it is more of a philosophy than an approach. Initially, students are provided with meaningful, predictable texts. They use the familiar words to learn new words and also incorporate writing for early ages. The major components of a whole language program are described by Butler (n.d.), as cited in Salend (2001, pp. 350–353):

- *Reading Aloud to Students.* Read quality literature from a variety of genres to introduce them to the enjoyment and excitement of reading. Reading to students also allows you to model oral reading, promote vocabulary development and good reading habits, and offer background knowledge in such areas as story structure and content. When reading to students, you can introduce the selection by discussing the title and cover of the book and by asking students to make predictions about the book. You also can introduce the author and illustrator and talk with students about other books they have read by the author or on a similar topic or theme.

As you read to students, you can promote their interest and understanding by using animated expressions, displaying illustrations so that *all* students can see and react to them, relating the book to students' experiences, discussing the book in a lively, inviting and thought-provoking manner, and offering students a variety of learning activities (i.e., writing, drama, art) to respond to and express their feelings about the selection (Hoffman, Roser, & Battle, 1993).

- *Shared Book Reading.* You and your students sit close together and share in reading a variety of materials. You read a new or familiar story; students react to it through arts and crafts, drama, reading, or writing, and students then reread the story on their own. Big books with large print and pictures are particularly appropriate for shared book reading, as they allow you to display the words the students are reading.

- *Sustained Silent Reading.* During sustained silent reading, also referred to as *Drop Everything and Read (DEAR) time,* you, your students, and other members of the class read self-selected materials for an extended period of time. Typically, the rules for sustained silent reading are: (1) read silently, (2) do not interrupt others, and (3) do not change books.

- *Guided Reading.* Work with students in small groups to explore books and ideas. In addition, demonstrate reading strategies and help students learn how to use them. For example, you may demonstrate and discuss with students successful strategies for selecting a book, using context clues, or reading with a purpose.

An important component of guided reading is the *group reading conference,* a time when groups discuss books or selections that they have been reading independently. Structure the conference by asking open-ended questions that require students to think, express an opinion, and relate the selection to their own experiences. For example, you can use *literature circles or literature discussion groups,* small groups of students who work collaboratively to share their reactions to and discuss various aspects of books that all group members have decided to read (Goforth, 1998).

- *Literature Response Journals. Literature response journals* can be used as follow-up to sustained silent reading periods or literature discussion groups. In these journals, students describe their reactions to and thoughts about the material they have been reading, as well as any questions they have. Students also are encouraged to write about their opinions and emotional responses to the book, relate the book to their own experiences, and make predictions about the book and its characters. You can read students' journals and offer comments that encourage students to redirect, expand, and refocus their reactions and questions.

One type of literature response journal is the character study journal, in which students make entries related to an interesting character (Galda, Cullinan, & Strickland, 1997). While reading the selection, students react to and write about their character, including the character's dilemmas, feelings, and responses.

- *Individualized Reading.* Students learn to control their literacy by reading selections addressing their individual needs and teaching levels. They keep records of books read and their responses to these books and receive assistance from their teachers.
- *Language Experience.* Promote students' literacy by using students' language generated during both planned experiences organized by you and spontaneous experiences that happen during the day. Students' responses to these experiences are recorded and presented to them in a written format.
- *Children's Writing.* Students learn the writing process and write in a variety of genres....
- *Model Writing.* You model writing, providing students with the opportunity to observe composing and other elements of the writing process.
- *Opportunities for Sharing.* Students share their products with others through such activities as the writers' circle, the author's chair, or literature response groups....
- *Integrating Reading and Writing Throughout the Curriculum.* Give students opportunities to read and write across the curriculum. You also can use *thematic units*, which integrate reading, writing speaking, and listening to help students master content area material. When using thematic units, you typically structure and connect a series of reading, writing, and content area

learning activities based on a particular theme (Englert, Mariage, Garmon, & Tarrant, 1998). Lessons involving reading, writing, speaking, and listening related to the selected theme are then taught across the various content areas.

- *Whole Language Curricular Adaptations.* When using a whole language approach, you also can use a variety of teaching strategies and curricular adaptations. Some of these are discussed here.
- *Environmental Print.* Environmental print—that is, materials that are found in students' natural environments—can help students who are learning English read and give meaning to printed symbols. Environmental print can be used to promote literacy through role plays, journals, and copying. You also can establish learning centers that allow students to read magazines and newspapers written at different levels of difficulty as well as signs, labels, posters, calendars, advertisements, menus, and wall charts.
- *Story Telling.* Story telling can help students construct meaning from text, promote listening comprehension and vocabulary skills, and motivate students to read. While *all students* benefit from story telling, it is a particularly good teaching technique for students whose cultures have an oral tradition and for those who are learning a second language (Maldonado-Colon, 1991).
- *Picture Books.* You can motivate students to read and write through the use of *picture books*, short books that use pictures and illustrations to enhance the reader's understanding of the meaning and content of the story (Bligh, 1996). Picture books also can help students learn a wide range of reading strategies, such as prediction and using context and syntactical cues (Bligh, 1996).
- *Frames.* Frames outline important components of stories and provide cues to help students understand and write in a variety of genres. One effective frame is the *circle story*, which is developed by plotting a story's important components in a clockwise sequence on a circle diagram.
- *Story Grammars.* Story grammars are outlines of the way stories are organized. They often involve identifying and articulating a reading selection's main characters, storylines, conflicts, and ending (Dimino, Taylor, & Gersten, 1995). Story grammars motivate students to read and allow

students to expand on their experiences by generating stories.

- *Choral Reading.* Choral reading involves you and your students reading poems, predictable books, stories, and student-authored materials together (Englert et al., 1998). It can promote students' fluency, vocabulary development, diction, self-confidence, and motivation to read, and can help establish the relationship between oral and written language.
- *Drama.* Through drama, students can act out and retell stories through miming, gestures, role playing, and the use of props.
- *Recursive Encounters.* Students practice language and reading through repetition of themes, including recursive experience, so that they are repeatedly exposed to poems, songs, riddles, discussions, and stories. For example, repeated reading of a book or a selection can increase students' fluency and aid them in learning the rhythm, volume, tone, and language patterns of their second language.

READING COMPREHENSION

Understanding the printed word is the crux of reading. Without meaning, there is no reading. All reading programs include reading comprehension. For students with learning disabilities, reading comprehension can be problematic because it requires their active participation (Gersten & Baker, 1999). It relies heavily on previous experience and knowledge, and on active interaction with the material. Some strategies that are supported by scientific evidence are (NRP, 2000, p. 15):

1. *Comprehension Monitoring.* Students monitor their comprehension as they progress through the material.
2. *Cooperative Learning.* In cooperative groups (this is best done in an inclusive classroom) students learn and practice reading comprehension strategies.
3. *Graphic Organizers.* Students create ways to help them organize the information. These include webs, diagrams, outlines, etc. (See Inspiration, a computer-based program that can assist students in creating graphic organizers.)

4. *Answering Questions.* Teachers can help students focus on acquiring meaning by asking questions. Posing questions prior to reading can also assist them in comprehension of text.
5. *Generating Questions.* Asking these questions and working predictions increase active reading and interaction with the text.
6. *Story Structure.* Students are taught to understand the structure of stories and texts.
7. *Summarization.* This focuses the readers to think about what they read and integrate the ideas presented. Some students find it useful to write notes in the margin as they read, to assist them when they summarize.

TEACHING READING IN THE CONTENT AREAS

Content area (social studies, science, mathematics, and English) reading materials cause considerable difficulty for middle and high school students with learning disabilities. The shift from learning to read in the early grades to reading to learn is challenging, given the amount of material that must be read. If you are a teacher of middle and/or high school students with learning disabilities, you will most likely be in an inclusive classroom. You will be collaborating with the content area teacher to adapt and modify instruction, as well as teaching specific learning strategies (see Chapters 7 and 10 for more information).

Specific suggestions for content area reading are provided by Choate and Rakes (2004, p. 109):

1. *Term Topics.* Display a chart of major terms for a topic. Introduce and discuss each term, adding an explanatory phrase, 3 examples, and 3 non-examples to the chart. Then scramble information for student teams to match.

2. *Boxing Categories.* As new words are introduced and discussed, use boxes with key terms as category headings to help students see relationships and understand meanings. Always pronounce words and have students pronounce them. For review, present new terms in random order for students to organize under their headings.

3. *Word Sorts.*   Word sorts can be either closed or open. Give students a list of 8–16 content words to sort. In a closed sort, provide 2–3 categories under which to classify the words. For an open sort, have students sort the words according to their own categories. Before categorizing a word, students should state or find its meaning(s). Have students support their sorting with a defining sentence from the content book.

4. *Technical Matches.*   Using a bulletin board, post pictures of general areas of study, such as motion or government. Print technical terms on index cards and place them in a library pocket attached to the board. List 3–4 topical headings below the pictures. Have students pin the cards below the appropriate heading.

5. *Non-Technical Word Duals.*   List 3 non-technical words on the chalkboard. Beside each word, list 2 possible meanings. Have students read assigned sections of their text to determine which meaning of each term applies to the subject being studied, then substitute the chosen phrase for its matching word in a sentence in the text to verify their choices. Talk students through several examples, scramble the phrases for 3 additional words, and have students complete the activity independently.

6. *Vocabulary Cloze.*   As a review, present several sentences in which 1–2 technical terms have been omitted. Have students fill in the terms that make sense, referring to their texts as needed.

7. *Readability Accommodations.*   When the reading level of the content text greatly outdistances students' abilities, directly teach terms and then:

a. Use the textbook as reinforcement, not initial presentation, or offer a parallel text at an easier level; and/or
b. Provide extra assistance via study guides, story frames, teacher-highlighted text, advance organizers; and/or
c. Offer alternate methods for acquiring information via oral presentations, audiotapes, video tapes, captioned films, pictures, computer simulations, hands-on demonstrations, digital text with embedded assistance, other universal design procedures, [and] speech-to-print technology.

8. *Extra Practice.*   Develop Vocabulary Matches for several subjects; place the cards in file folders for students to use individually or in teams. Ask students to hunt for Non-technical Word Duals in a newspaper and to share with the class. For each subject, have students keep wordbooks of the words they learn, including page references to their texts for future study.

Neufeld (2006) suggests that the most reasonable way to view instruction in content area classes is to look at expert comprehenders, readers that employ effective strategies without prompting. The strategies are divided into two groups: (a) getting-ready-to-ready strategies and (b) during-and-after-reading strategies. Newfeld notes that teachers first "need to examine a strategy that is crucial to the effective use of all other strategies"—asking and answering questions. Those who comprehend content area texts are constantly asking questions about what they read. They are active readers. For students with learning disabilities this active reading process must be taught. Students need to ask the following questions:

- Why am I reading this text?
- How is it organized?
- What do I know about the topic?
- How is that related to this text?
- What is this chapter about?
- Do I "get it"?
- Is it unclear?
- Can I answer "W" questions?

In summary, Neufeld (2006, p. 310) recommends the following:

- Teach a few strategies.
- Teach students to use them with flexibility.
- Strategies are a means to an end.
- Provide ample practice.

APPLICATION OF TECHNOLOGY

There has been a proliferation of computer programs in the area of reading (Belson, 2003; Lewis, 1998). The NRP (2000) concluded that more research is needed in this area. Some programs that appear to be useful (Belson, 2003) are *Earobics* and *Fast Forward* (cited in Chapter 12). *Reading*

Blaster (Knowledge Adventure) focuses on spelling and sound–symbol correspondence, *The Living Books Series* (The Learning Company, www.broaderbund.com) provides CD-based "talking books" (see Lewis, 1998, for additional information on this type of program), and *READ 180* (The Scholastic Company), teacher.scholastic.com/read180/ provides a comprehensive reading program with multimedia text that offers background knowledge (used primarily with middle and high school students).

Graphic organizers are provided for students on *Inspiration* and *Kidspiration* (Inspiration Software, www.inspiration.com). It is important to note that these organizers are not used specifically by students with learning disabilities. They are for all students who are at risk for a reading disorder or who are having difficulty reading.

Some students may have such trouble reading that it is difficult, if not impossible, for them to get information from the printed page, especially textbooks. Your students can get free recordings from *Recording for the Blind and Dyslexic* (20 Roszel Road, Princeton, NJ 08540; http://www.rfbd.org). Three sources that "read" text aloud for students are the *Kurzweil Educational Systems* (http://www.Kurzweiledu.org), *Read Please,* and *Read Please Plus* (http://www.readplease.com). These can be of great assistance to students with learning disabilities on all levels, especially middle school through adulthood.

SPECIAL READING APPROACHES

The reading approaches described in this section are remedial in nature and are used for struggling readers. They have also been called **clinical approaches** because they are not typically used in regular classrooms.

Fernald Method

Many years ago, Grace Fernald (1943) developed a reading approach for students who had difficulty learning to read. Frequently, these were older students with a history of failure. Therefore, she employed many techniques (she referred to them as **positive reconditioning**) that sought to establish a positive relationship with reading. Her program was multisensory, utilizing the visual, auditory, kinesthetic, and tactile modalities (VAKT). This is a whole word approach based on the theory that students will learn through contextual clues and motivational procedures. There are four stages:

Stage 1

- A student-selected word is written on an index card, and the student traces the word.
- The student says the word (auditory) while tracing (tactile-kinesthetic).
- While the student is saying and tracing the words, he or she is seeing it (visual) and hearing it (auditory).
- When the student is ready, he or she writes the word.

Stage 2

- Tracing is no longer required, but the student must say and write the word.

Stage 3

- New words are learned through sight and through easy books.

Stage 4

- The student is ready to progress to other books by recognizing similarities in new words from his or her word bank.

This method, combined with a language experience approach, can be helpful for students with severe reading problems. They can dictate a story, and the words can be written on cards. The student can trace and say the words (Stage 1), and those words can then be placed in a word bank. Students who are unsure of a word can begin with the Stage 1 process. They never sound out the word.

Orton-Gillingham Approach

This is a multisensory approach that focuses on phonics instruction (Gillingham & Stillman, 1960). It is highly structured and requires a great deal of commitment from the teacher. It is recommended that you provide instruction in five weekly sessions for a minimum of 2 years. During that time, no other reading material should be used. This approach is more likely to be employed in a special school for students with learning disabilities than in a regular public school.

Consonants (white cards) and vowels (salmon-colored cards) are presented on drill cards and are introduced through a key word (*m* for *man*). The students are taught 10 letters (*a, b, f, h, i, j, k, m, p,* and *t*) and then taught to blend them. A procedure called Simultaneous Oral Spelling (SOS) is employed. The teacher says a word: then the student says it, moves the letters, and writes the letters while saying it. This approach integrates all of the language arts (reading, writing, and spelling) and focuses on a great deal of repetition and drill. In the past, it was criticized for being rigid and tedious, yet there are strong supporters who claim a great deal of success (see the International Dyslexia Association Web site: http://www.interdys.org).

Wilson Reading System

This is a complete program for teaching reading and spelling, including instruction in phonics awareness. Its major purpose is to teach students fluent decoding and encoding (spelling skills) to the level of mastery. Including 12 steps, it is direct, structured, cumulative, multisensory, and integrated. The company's Web site (http://www.wilsonlanguage.com) provides evidence of the program's effectiveness, including its inclusion in the National Institute for Writing's *Bridges to Practices*.

Reading Recovery (RR)

RR was designed for students who were having difficulty after their first year of reading instruction. Clay (1987) developed the program in New Zealand in an attempt to stop the cycle of reading failure. It is fairly popular in the United States, is offered in every state, and serves approximately 150,000 students per year (Practice Alerts 2002).

RR provides one-to-one instruction for 20 weeks. The program is supplemental; it does not take the place of classroom reading instruction. Students read authentic children's literature, and teachers continually analyze their progress. The books are introduced slowly, one at a time. The lesson consists of the teacher doing the following:

1. Listening to students read familiar works.
2. Making a running record of the reading.
3. Providing a brief lesson on letter identification plus word patterns.
4. Creating a brief story (usually one sentence).
5. Cutting the sentence up and having the student reassemble it.
6. Reading a new book.

Current research suggests that RR works for some students, but it is not a panacea. There are also questions regarding how well RR students maintain their gains. A report cited by the Commit an Exceptional Children (2001) notes that less than half of the children who entered the program achieved the goal of reading on the normal first-grade level by the end of Grade 1. One major advantage is that RR serves as a prereferral intervention for special education; unsuccessful students are often referred to special education placement.

As a teacher of students with learning disabilities, you will probably provide instruction in the regular classroom or the resource room. The next section presents an example of reading instruction involving collaborative teaching. Students with learning disabilities are included in the kindergarten classroom, and the two teachers plan and teach together.

Best Practices: Redefining Learning Disabilities in a Collaborative Classroom.   It was clear that the new kindergarten students were enthusiastic learners. The class was divided into four stations (see Station Teaching in Chapter 7), with six students per station. The first group worked at the Guided Reading

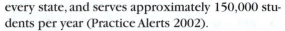

Station. The students were introduced to a new guided reading book and were engaged in learning prereading skills such as making predictions based on the cover of the book, title, author, and illustrations, tracking the text, and understanding it. Some students were further along in the reading process and were working on print knowledge. They were pointing to the first and last words, reading with meaning, and understanding the book. Ms. Groudas differentiated the activity and instruction, depending upon students' needs.

Her coteacher, Ms. Leace, was working with a group of students who were reading sentence strips. They consisted of simple, high-frequency words, and the students were excited as they read them correctly. Some students made up their own sentences from a word bank of index cards.

The third group of students worked with the paraprofessional. These students worked in pairs, matching upper- and lowercase letters. The final station was for students using independent words. These students were reading "their" words from their word boxes. They then wrote the words on a wipe board and used them in sentences. Not all students were able to do this.

Students (in groups) rotated from station to station until they completed all four. The teachers and the paraprofessional remained at the stations for the entire lesson. What was not clear from the observation of this lesson was the makeup of the class. This was an inclusive classroom. Of the 24 students, 6 had learning disabilities. Previously, these students would have been placed in a self-contained classroom. Clearly, there was a range of abilities. However, an observer would be hard pressed to identify those who were classified as having a learning disability.

These students were excited about and actively engaged in learning to read. Their teachers had developed classroom procedures and instructional practices to prevent failure. The students with learning disabilities did not see themselves as failures because successful reading experiences were built into their daily routine.

These students were benefiting from early identification and intervention in a collaborative classroom. Years ago, those with learning disabilities would have been placed in a self-contained classroom or a resource room. Now their learning needs were being met in a regular kindergarten with two teachers—a regular educator and a special educator—who, through extensive training and consultation, were able to plan effective interaction for all students. This has been the thrust of reconceptualization of learning disabilities. Students identified as having the potential for underachievement are given supplemental instruction in the regular classroom in small groups. If that practice is ineffective, they are given more specialized help.

Our practice needs to be governed by research. It is not sufficient to employ a particular reading approach because the teacher believes in its underlying philosophy. Students with learning disabilities need direct instruction that will enable them to read for meaning and pleasure. It should be provided by a teacher who understands the reading process, can evaluate the nature or the reading disorder, and can provide appropriate, evidence-based instruction.

SUMMARY

Identifying, assessing, and remediating reading disorders will occupy a great deal of your time as a teacher of students with learning disabilities. Whether you provide services in a resource room or a collaborative classroom (like Ms. Grudas and Ms. Leach), you will need to make sure that your students are receiving appropriate, scientifically based instruction. This chapter has discussed the nature of reading disorders, early warning signs, and characteristics. It has also provided ways to assess the nature of your students' reading problems and provide appropriate instruction. Finally, general and specialized approaches to reading were described.

SPRINGBOARDS FOR REFLECTION AND DISCUSSION

1. What is your philosophy of reading? This is a question many prospective teachers are asked on interviews. Begin to formulate your own philosophy, and rely on scientifically based evidence.
2. Interview the administrators responsible for literacy education in your school district. How do they select reading programs and materials? What are they currently using? How do they assess students' papers?
3. If possible, talk to an adult with a reading disorder. When did this person first realize that reading was difficult? What was his or her school experience like? How has it affected this individual's daily life?
4. Review current research in educational journals to keep abreast of the most recent finds.

5. See http://www.ldonline.org for valuable information on reading instruction.
5. How can you decide what method of reading instruction to use? When would you decide to move to a more specialized or remedial approach?
6. Observe a classroom where two teachers are collaborating on reading instruction. How does it differ from instruction provided by one teacher?
7. Observe a resource room. How does the instruction provided there differ from instruction provided by collaborative teachers?
8. Visit a school district that is using a specialized program such as RR or the Wilson Reading System. Why did they select that program? How are they assessing student progress? Does the program provide teacher training? What has been the response of the teachers?

CHAPTER 14
WRITTEN LANGUAGE DISORDERS

CHAPTER OBJECTIVES

At the end of this chapter you will be able to:

- understand the nature of handwriting disorders.
- assess and remediate handwriting disorders.
- understand the nature of spelling disorders.
- assess and remediate spelling disorders.
- understand the nature of written expression disorders.
- assess and remediate written expression disorders.

Tara hates her eighth-grade English class. Every day she has to copy notes from the board or from her teacher's lecture. She is reading below grade level, so the assignments are usually too difficult for her, and now, in the middle of the school year, it is clear that she is so far behind that she feels there is no way she can catch up. Modifications on her IEP allow her to use the computer to write, but it still takes a great deal of time. She is forever using the spell checker, and her writing samples are much shorter than those of most of her classmates. She never passes the weekly spelling tests, and her teacher is constantly criticizing her handwriting. Tara realizes that it is hard to understand, but there is little she can do to improve it. It was always bad, but she was told not to worry about handwriting and spelling—just get her ideas on paper. This is not easy. Her poor penmanship and inability to spell correctly directly impact her written expression. Other classes are hard, but English is torture! Tara goes to the resource room one period per day, but it is simply not enough. She uses the resource room to keep up with other subjects but hardly ever has the time to address her specific written language disability.

What would you do if you were Tara's resource room teacher? Would you attempt to improve her handwriting, spelling, and written expression or focus on only one problem? What should her English teacher do: Reduce the amount of written work? Attempt to improve her written language skills and utilize a word processor? And what does Tara do in all of her other classes when she is required to express her ideas in writing, take notes, write legibly, and spell correctly? This chapter will address these concerns and issues. Clearly, written expression is one of the most complex tasks for any student. It requires the integration of oral receptive language, oral expressive language, reading, and writing. It also demands good attending skills, good memory skills, good fine motor skills, and a fund of knowledge. It's little wonder that this area of the curriculum poses such problems for students with learning disabilities. This chapter is divided into three sections: handwriting, spelling, and written expression. Each section will discuss the characteristics of students with learning disabilities in each area, assessment procedures, and interventions that can be used in your classroom.

HANDWRITING

Characteristics

Students with learning disabilities frequently have difficulty with handwriting. They may have fine motor problems that interfere with their ability to hold a pencil or pen properly. They may have visual-perceptual motor difficulties that prevent them from copying and/or matching what they want to write with what they actually produce. Limited attention and memory may also interfere with their ability to produce legible writing. This is also a problem for adolescents and adults with learning disabilities as they struggle to fill out job applications and other forms. Figure 14-1 shows the handwriting of a middle school student with a learning disability who wrote in response to the prompt "Write down your experiences in middle school." The formation and size of the letters are not commensurate with this student's grade level. In addition to handwriting and spelling problems, this student has difficulty with written expression.

Johnson and Myklebust (1967) used the term **dysgraphia** to describe a specific disorder that results from difficulty with visual-motor integration. Persons with this disorder:

- cannot perceive a specific visual pattern
- may not be able to grasp a pencil properly
- cannot copy complex figures
- distort the sequence of handwriting movements

Students with learning disabilities write slowly and have uneven handwriting (Graham & Weintraub, 1996). Graham, Weintraub, and Berninger (2001) identified letters that posed the most difficulty for 300 beginning writers. About half of the problems were attributed to the letters *q, j, z, u, h,* and *k*. When they examined the products solely for illegibility, five letters accounted for more than half of the difficulties: *q, z, u, a,* and *j*. Students with learning disabilities also tend to write more slowly, less smoothly, more variably, and less legibly than their peers (Graham & Weintraub, 1996; Weintraub & Graham, 1998).

Assessment

Assessment should include a thorough analysis of how well the student copies and forms letters and numbers. Bain (1995, p. 82), as cited in Bain, Bailet, and Moats (2001), provides a useful handwriting survey (see Figure 14-2).

This survey provides specific information that will enable you to develop an intervention plan. Mercer and Mercer (2001, pp. 405–407) provide an excellent chart for the diagnosis of handwriting difficulties (see Table 14-1).

Interventions

There is considerable evidence to suggest that teaching handwriting is important (Graham & Harris, 2000). As a teacher of students with learning disabilities, you cannot assume that they will pick it up eventually or that it will come naturally through their writing. It must be taught because it will impact their written expressive language and slow them down, forcing them to focus on the information, and on spacing of letters, and reducing the quantity and quality of their written language products.

In a review of the literature on handwriting and spelling instruction for students with learning disabilities, Graham (1999) suggested the following principles of instruction:

1. It should be pleasant and interesting.
2. It must be explicit.
3. It must be integrated with reading and writing.
4. Both incidental ("caught") and explicit ("taught") instruction should be employed.

There has been discussion about what script should be taught to students with learning disabilities. And while there is no research to support the use of manuscript versus cursive writing, Graham (1999) recommends starting with traditional manuscript writing. Most students know how to form some letters, manuscript writing is easier to learn, it can be fast, and it may be more legible than cursive writing. Key components of an effective handwriting program include:

- naming letter names as they practice writing them
- modeling of letter production
- using visual clues, such as arrows for the direction of producing letters
- having students evaluate their own letter production.

All researchers agree that the posture, grasp of pen/pencil, and position of the paper are important. Many teachers use the Mnemonic 3P's to help students master the components of writing:

Kaff Assignment — not sure what teacher card means?

Dear Future Sixth Grader,

Write down your experience as a Candlewood Middle School student. Positive vs Negative

My experience in Candlewood is positive because they give me a choice of a lunch. Another positive is I like the projects. I wish I could bring another thing to school. A negative is having to wake up very early. One thing I like about Candlewood positive is it's stupendous and spectacular!

FIGURE 14–1 Handwriting Sample of a Middle School Student with a Learning Disability

Posture	Am I sitting straight in my chair?
	Are my feet on the floor? Are my arms on the table?

Pencil grip	Am I holding the pencil correctly?
	Are my thumb and index fingers in the right position?
	Is the pencil resting on my middle finger?
	Is the grip low enough?
	Is the grip too low?
	Is the grip too tight?

Paper position	Is it on an angle?
	Am I using my nonwriting hand to hold it down?
	Is it too far away?
	Is it too close?

Date _____

Student _____ Observer _____

Age _____   Grade _____   Handed: ☐ right ☐ left ☐ both ☐ undetermined

Teacher _____

Handwriting should be compared on the following activities to describe skills, and to identify the type of problem and the extent of any difficulty. Specific identification of problems will lead to a remedial plan.

Compare:
1. Write the lowercase alphabet: ☐ manuscript ☐ cursive ☐ both
2. Write the uppercase alphabet: ☐ manuscript ☐ cursive ☐ both
3. Write single words from dictation
4. Copy at near point.
5. Copy at far point.
6. Write creatively.
7. Takes notes.
8. Compare class work with writing tasks on this survey.

On task:

Pencil grip:	Position of anchor hand:
Pencil pressure:	Position of paper:
Organization of paper (L/R margins: placement of information; sequence of information)	
Letter formation:	Word formation:
Letter size:	Word size:
Letter slant:	Word slant:
Letter alignment:	Word alignment:
	Word spacing:

Additions: Omissions: Substitutions: Reversals:

Erasures: Speed & fluency:

Attitude toward handwriting:

Other:

FIGURE 14–2   Handwriting Survey

TABLE 14–1 Diagnostic Chart for Manuscript and Cursive Writing

Factor	Problem	Possible Cause	Remediation
Manuscript Writing			
Shape	Letters slanted	Paper slanted	Place paper straight and pull straight-line strokes toward center of body.
	Varies from standard	Improper mental image of letter	Have student write problem letters on chalkboard.
Size	Too large	Poor understanding of writing lines	Reteach size concept by pointing out purpose of each line on writing paper.
		Exaggerated arm movement	Reduce arm movement, especially on circle and part-circle letters.
		Improper mental image of letter	Have student write problem letters on chalkboard.
	Too small	Poor understanding of writing	Reteach size concept by pointing out purpose of each line on writing paper.
		Overemphasis on finger movement	Stress arm movement: check hand-pencil and arm-desk positions to be sure arm movement is possible.
		Improper mental image of letter	Have students write problem letters on chalkboard.
	Not uniform	Adjusting writing hand after each letter	Stress arm movement; move paper with nonwriting hand so writing hand can remain in proper writing position.
		Overemphasis on finger movement	Stress arm movement; check arm-desk and hand-pencil positions.
Space	Crowded letters in words	Poor understanding of space concepts	Reteach uniform spacing between letters (finger or pencil width).
	Too much space between letters	Improper lowercase letter size and shape	Review concepts of size and shape; provide appropriate corrections under size and shape.
Alignment	Letters not sitting on baseline	Improper letter formation	Evaluate work for letter shape; stress bringing straight-line strokes all the way down to baseline.
		Poor understanding of baseline concept	Review purpose of baseline on writing paper.
		Improper hand-pencil and paper-desk positions	Check positions to make sure student is able to reach baseline easily.
	Letters not consistent height	Poor understanding of size concept	Review concept of letter size in relationship to lines provided on on writing paper.
Line quality	Too heavy or too light	Improper writing Pressure	Review hand-pencil position; place wadded paper tissue on palm of writing hand to relax writing grip; demonstrate desired line quality.

Cursive Writing

Shape	Letters too oval	Overemphasis of arm movement and poor image of letter	Check arm-desk position; review letter size and shape.
	Letters too narrow	Finger writing	Check positions to allow for arm movement.
		Overemphasis of straight-line stroke	Make sure straight-line stroke does not come all the way down to baseline in letters such as *l*, *b*, and *t*.
		Poor mental image of letter shape	Use transparent overlay for student's personal evaluation of shape.
			In all problems of letter shape, review letters in terms of the basic strokes.
Size	Letters too large	Exaggerated arm movement	Check arm-desk position for over-movement of forearm.
		Poor mental image of letter size	Review base and top line concepts in relation to ¼ space, ½ space, and ¾ space; use transparent overlay for student's personal evaluation of letter size.
	Letters too small or letters not uniform	Finger movement	Check arm-desk and hand-pencil positions; stress arm movement.
		Poor mental image of Letter size	Review concept of letter size (1/4 space, ½ space and ¾ space) in relation to base and top lines; use transparent overlay for student's personal evaluation of letter size.
Space	Letters in words crowded or spacing between letters uneven	Finger movement	Check arm-desk, hand-pencil positions; stress arm movement
		Poor understanding of joining strokes	Review how letters are joined; show ending stroke of one letter joined to beginning stroke of following letter; practice writing letters in groups of
	Too much space between letters and words	Exaggerated arm movement	Check arm-desk position for over-movement of forearm.
		Poor understanding of joining strokes	Review concept of spacing between words; show beginning stroke in second word starting under ending stroke of preceding word.
Alignment	Poor letter alignment along baseline	Incorrect writing position; finger movement; exaggerated arm movement	Check all writing positions; stress even, rhythmic writing movement.
		Poor understanding of baseline concept	Use repetitive exercise with emphasis on relationship of baseline to written word.

(continued)

Factor	Problem	Possible Cause	Remediation
		Incorrect use of joining strokes	Review joining strokes
Speed and ease	Writing becomes illegible under stress and speed (grades 4, 5, and 6)	Degree of handwriting skill is insufficient to met speed requirements	Improve writing positions; develop more arm movement and less finger movement.
	Writing becomes illegible when writing activity is too long	Handwriting positions have not been perfected to allow handwriting ease	Improve all writing positions, especially hand-pencil position; stress arm movement.
Slant	Back slant	Left-handedness	Correct hand-pencil and paper-desk positions.
	Vertical	Poor positioning	Correct hand-pencil and paper-desk positions.
	Too far right	Overemphasis of finger movement	Make sure student pulls slant strokes toward center of body if right handed and left elbow if left-handed.
			Use slant line instruction sheets as aid to teaching slant.
			Use transparent overlay for student's personal evaluation.
			Review all lowercase letters that derive their shape from the slant line.
			Write lowercase alphabet on chalkboard.
			Retrace all slant strokes in color chalk.

Source: Mercer, Cecil D; Mercer, Ann R., *Teaching Students with Learning Problems,* © 2005. Reprinted by permission of publisher.

Some students find it helpful to have a picture on their desk to model all of the above factors—for example, a small photo of the student sitting correctly, or with the pencil grip and with the paper on the desk in the appropriate position.

Mercer and Mercer (2005) provide activities and games for handwriting instruction and practice and the University of Maryland's Center to Accelerate Student Learning (http:// www.education.umd.edu/literacy/srsd/srsd1.htm) continue to provide excellent information regarding all aspects of written expression, including specific handwriting programs.

SPELLING

There continues to be disagreement about spelling instruction. Should students be taught directly or should they learn to spell incidentally? It is generally agreed that students with learning disabilities are not masters of incidental thought. Yet there are many who believe that this is the way they will learn how to spell. Traditionally, teaching spelling was not emphasized. Instruction in reading was paramount, as well as the belief that good spelling would follow—which never occurred. This section will discuss current thoughts on instructional practices in spelling, as well as the learning characteristics of students with spelling, disorders and ways to address these disorders.

In a third-grade classroom with students engaged in a writing assignment, when one student raised her hand and asked, "Does spelling count?" the teacher replied, "Spelling always counts!" And indeed it does. The quality of the written product is greatly reduced by poor spelling, and students with learning disabilities may be judged poorly due to their inability to spell words correctly.

Characteristics

Johnson and Myklebust (1967) used the term **revisualization** to describe the ability to write words spontaneously or from dictation. Some students with learning disabilities can read the words but cannot recall what they (or letters within the words) look like. Students who have specific disabilities in memory, discrimination, attention, or motor skills will most likely have difficulty with spelling.

It should not be surprising that students with learning disabilities have difficulty spelling. If they have a disorder in spoken language, they will likely have a disorder in reading, and if they have a reading disorder they will most likely have a written language disorder, including the ability to spell. They have mechanical difficulty, as noted by Fulk and Stormont-Spurgin (1995), which includes many spelling errors. Anyone who has observed students with learning disabilities in the classroom finds numerous spelling errors, ranging from the typical additions, substitutions, and omissions of letters to spelling that bears no relationship to the actual word.

Assessment

Most spelling assessment conducted through information spelling inventories, weekly spelling tests, and students' written products. To provide more specificity, you may want to use a more thorough diagnostic procedure. Mercer and Mercer (2001, p. 374) describe four spelling tests that can be used for this purpose:

Diagnostic Tests

Diagnostic Spelling Potential Test (Arena, 1981)
Age/Grade Level   7 Years–Adult

This test measures traditional spelling, word recognition, visual recognition, and auditory-visual recognition. The four 90-item subtests take about 25 to 40 minutes to administer. Raw scores from each subtest can be converted to standard scores, percentiles, and grade ratings.

Test of Written Spelling-4 (Larsen, Hammill, & Moats, 1999)
Age/Grade Level   1st-12th Grade

This dictated word test consists of 100 words chosen from ten basal spelling series. The test assesses the student's ability to spell words that have readily predictable spellings in sound–letter patterns as well as words whose spellings are less predictable (spelling demons). The test can be administered to individuals or small groups in about 20 minutes and yields standard scores, percentiles, spelling ages, and grade equivalents. Two equivalent forms are available.

Criterion-Referenced Tests

Brigance Diagnostic Comprehensive Inventory of Basic Skills-Revised (Brigance, 1999)
Age/Grade Level   Kindergarten-9th Grade

The test contains a section that assesses spelling skills arranged in a developmental and sequential hierarchy. Tests include spelling-dictation grade placement, initial consonants, initial clusters, suffixes, and prefixes. Also, the reference skills section contains a test on the skill of dictionary use. The instructional objectives related to each test are defined clearly. In addition to determining the student's level of achievement, the results can help the teacher develop individualized programs.

Diagnostic Spelling Test (Kottmeyer, 1970)
Age/Grade Level   2nd-6th Grade

The test measures specific phonics and structural spelling elements (e.g., doubled final consonants, nonphonetic spelling, and th spelling). The examiner says a word and a sentence using the word, and the student is required to write the word. The two 32-item tests (one for second and third grades, and one for fourth grade and above) are designed so that each item measures a particular spelling element. A grade score is computed from the total number of correct spellings. Specific information on skills not yet mastered is obtained through an analysis of the student's errors.

A spelling checklist (see Table 14-2) provided by Miller (1995), as cited in Choate (2004, p. 214), is also useful. Once you have identified specific errors or error patterns, you can develop an intervention plan.

The spelling checklist enables you to evaluate the spelling performance of your students on a

TABLE 14-2 Spelling Checklist

Student _____

Teacher _____

Skill/Error Pattern Data Source/Level/Date	Possible Problem Behaviors	Related Areas
Spelling Correctly on Tests		
__ Vowel substitutions	Performs poorly on spelling tests	Weak word
__ Recognition skills		
__ Vowel omissions	Performs inconsistently	Poor study habits
__ Consonant substitutions	Has better weekly scores than unit scores	
__ Consonant omissions	Generally does not spell	Test anxiety
	Has weak word recognition skills	Reading
Spelling Simple and Common Words		
__ Vowel substitutions	Spells poorly on tests and daily work	Weak memory skills
__ Silent letters omitted	Has serious spelling problems	
__ Sounded letters omitted	Spells word patterns	Application of spelling rules
	Reverses and transposes letters	Visual discrimination
	Exhibits weak word recognition skills	Reading
	Appears to be trying but not improving	
	Substitutes unrelated words	
Spelling Difficult Words		
__ Letter transpositions	Misspells difficult words on tests and daily work	
__ Phonetic substitution	Repeatedly misspells the same words	Generalization
	Exhibits difficulty learning homonyms	Vocabulary development
	Transposes letters	Letter–sound sequencing
	Generally is poor speller	Study habits
Spelling Correctly on Authentic Tasks		
__ Vowel substitutions	Appears to be careless speller	Motivation
__ Silent letters omitted	Frequently misspells on daily work	Generalization skills
__ Double letters omitted	Demonstrates limited proofreading skills	Dictionary skills
__ Single letter added	Scores well on tests but not on daily work	Motivation
__ Phonetic substitution	Writes illegibly	Handwriting
	Exhibits weak word recognition skills	
	Demonstrates limited vocabulary skills	

Teacher Comments

Source: From Joyce S. Choate–Editor. *Successful Inclusive Teaching: Proven Ways to Detect and Correct Special Needs,* 4/e. Published by Allyn and Bacon, Boston, MA. Copyright © 2004 by Pearson Education. Reprinted by permission of the publisher.

continuing basis. You can look for a pattern, as well as differentiate between simple and difficult words on authentic writing tasks.

Interventions

Graham (1999) discusses a number of ways in which spelling can be taught. He recommends a combination of incidental (caught) and direct instruction (taught) approaches based on his review of the literature.

Spelling words can come from a variety of sources. Students can choose words from their reading and writing. They can study frequently misspelled words, words they are most likely to use in their writing, and finally, commonly occurring spelling patterns. These overlap. Some methods for teaching spelling follow.

Test-Study Test. This is the typical form of instruction for many students. They are given a pretest, they study the words missed, and then they are tested again. If a student is a poor speller, then the pretest will merely reinforce this pattern and may not be useful.

Corrected-Test Method. Students are provided with feedback quickly, and they immediately correct their errors.

Systematic Study Strategy. Students are taught to use a specific strategy and apply it with teacher prompts.

Distributed Practice. Students study the words throughout the week rather than all at once.

Decrease the Number of Words to Be Mastered. If the number of words is decreased, some students may spell more words correctly.

Cooperative Practice. Students study the spelling words together. Some teachers use traditional cooperative learning approaches, others use a game format, and still others employ peer tutoring.

Self-Monitoring. Students record their on-task and attending behaviors and spelling productivity.

Goal Setting, Reinforcement, and Public Posting of Performance. Graham (1999) notes that this method has not been validated but is promising. In a few studies, setting a spelling goal and providing contingent reinforcement increased spelling performance.

Effective teachers use a variety of approaches to teach spelling. One ineffective approach that appears to be widely used is having students copy their misspelled words correctly three to five times. In addition to not working, this increases negative attitudes toward spelling.

A promising approach is to provide extra spelling instruction (Graham, Harris, & Fink-Chorzempa, 2003). The CASL Spelling Program teaches basic sound–letter combinations, spelling patterns involving long and short vowels, and common spelling words that fit those patterns. There are eight units (see Table 14–3) and six lessons per unit.

TABLE 14–3 Unit Spelling Patterns Taught in the CASL Spelling Program

1. Short vowel sound for /a/,/e/, and /i/ in CVC type words.
2. Short vowel sound for /o/and /u/ in CVC type words.
3. Short vowel sound for /a/ in CVC type words. Long vowel sound for /a/ in CVCe type words.
4. Short vowel sound for /o/ in DVC type words. Long vowel sound for /o/ in CVCe type words.
5. Short vowel sound for /i/ in CVC type words. Long vowel sound for /i/ in CVCe type words.
6. Short vowel sound and /ck/ at the end of monosyllabic words. Long vowel sound and /ke/ at the end of monosyllabic words.
7. Adding the suffix "ing" to monosyllabic words with a short vowel or a long vowel sound.

Graham et al. (2003) employ a five-step study strategy:

- Say the work and study the letters
- Close you eyes and say the letters
- Study the letters again
- Write the word three times without looking at it
- Check the spelling and correct any misspelling

These authors also employ games, cooperative pairs, and graphing of their results. The results have been promising, and students appeared more confident in reading and writing.

Bailet (2001, pp. 25–26) provides the following list of remedial teaching strategies for students with spelling difficulties:

1. Avoid the tendency to work quickly in order for the child to catch up. A slow, deliberate pace will result in greater long-term gains.
2. Keep activities short, approximately 5 to 10 minutes, particularly when working with new words.
3. Limit the number of words to be learned to about three to five per day, especially if these include sight words that do not fit a pattern. More words that follow a pattern (e.g., *hop, top, mop, pop*) can be practiced in one lesson.
4. Review words daily, and introduce only one or two new words each day, depending on the child's retention.
5. Aim for at least 90% accuracy in spelling words within one pattern before introducing a new pattern. This is especially important for fundamental phonics principles, including short vowels, long vowels with ending silent *e*, single consonants, consonant blends, and consonant digraphs (*sh, ch, th, wh, tch, ph*). Many examples of each pattern should be presented, including some nonsense words that fit the pattern.
6. A synthetic or alphabetic phonics approach, which requires the child to sound out each phoneme in a word and then blend them, is an essential component of most effective remedial programs for children with learning disabilities (e.g., Gillingham & Stillman's [1970] method). For some children, particularly those with a significant articulation disorder, this may be too

difficult, in which case an analytic or linguistic phonics method can be used. For these methods, the child does not sound out each phoneme, but simply says the whole word. Phonics patterns or word families still are presented systematically.

7. Use a variety of reading and spelling activities to extend practice on sight words and phonics patterns. For example, ask the child to read *-at* words (e.g., *bat, cat, fat, hat*) on cards, underlining them in sentences, spell them from dictation, spell them using letter cards, write sentences with them, and play games with them.
8. Use frequent word-sorting activities.
9. For children with strong verbal skills, have them recite specific spelling rules in conjunction with word-sorting activities.
10. Experiment with multisensory techniques. Try to incorporate visual (seeing the word), auditory (hearing the word), and tactile/kinesthetic (feeling the word through touch and muscle movement) sensation. Some children learn best by seeing, saying, and tracing each letter within a word simultaneously. Others learn better by performing these steps sequentially. The child will need to study a word in this manner many times over successive days.
11. Present a sight word on a card (e.g., *who*) and have the child read each letter, trace it, and say the whole word. Then remove that card and present a second card on which the same word has been misspelled (e.g., *woh*). Ask the child if the word is spelled correctly. Have him or her find the error and state how to correct it. If the child has difficulty, present the original card with the correct spelling of the word for comparison. Then present a third card, with the word misspelled in a different way (e.g., *how*). Go through the same procedure. Continue with several cards on the same word, including some cards on which the word has been spelled correctly.
12. After several phonics patterns and sight words have been mastered, introduce the suffixes plural *-s*, past tense *-ed,* and *-ing*. Begin with words that do not require spelling changes when the suffix is added. Extended practice will be necessary to gain complete mastery of the spelling rules associated with these suffixes.

13. For words that the child has mastered, increase reading speed to encourage automaticity by using timed drills. Do not stress response speed on words the child is still learning.
14. Provide immediate corrective feedback for any errors made during a lesson.
15. Make attractive, fun charts to show children's progress and thus provide frequent positive feedback for their efforts.

WRITTEN EXPRESSION

It should be clear by now that an integrated approach incorporating handwriting, spelling, and written expression is most effective for students with learning disabilities. Graham (1999) notes that "an overemphasis on either meaning process or form in writing instructions is not in the best interest of the child. Failure to develop competence in any of these areas is likely to hobble a child's writing process" (p. 297).

Characteristics

Not surprisingly, students with learning disabilities in handwriting and spelling will have difficulty with written expression. Johnson and Myklebust (1967) noted difficulty in formulation and syntax. Students with learning disabilities wrote less than their counterparts without disabilities, and when they did write, they had syntactic problems.

Students with learning disabilities also have difficulty coming up with ideas, planning, and revising. These students may be able to express themselves orally, but they cannot translate from oral to written language. Part of the problem may be due to a specific disability or it may be directly related to lack of instruction. It has been noted that so much time is devoted to reading that teachers never get to writing. And by the time they do, many negative attitudes and poor work habits have developed.

Figure 14-3 shows a written expression language disorder. The student is a middle school student in a cotaught inclusive classroom.

Assessment

In the past, one of the methods most frequently used to assess written language was to examine the discrepancy between oral and written language. Obviously, if students could not express their thoughts orally, they could not be expected to express them in writing. We now have more thorough, sophisticated procedures that enable teachers to identify specific problems. The following list of diagnostic and criterion-referenced tests of written expression is provided by Mercer and Mercer (2001, p. 421).

Diagnostic Tests

Oral and Written Expression (Carrow-Woolfolk, 1995)
Age/Grade Level   5–21 Years

This test measures writing skills including the use of conventions (handwriting, spelling and punctuation), the use of syntactical forms (modifiers, phrases, and sentence structures), and the ability to communicate meaningfully (relevance, cohesiveness, and organization). The examiner presents a variety of developmentally appropriate writing prompts, either verbally, with pictures, or in print, and the student writes responses in a booklet. The scale can be administered individually or in small groups in about 15 to 25 minutes and yields standard scores, grade and age equivalents, and percentiles. Computer scoring with the ASIST system provides a score profile, score narrative, suggested exercises, and a descriptive analysis.

Test of Early Written Language–2 (Hresko, Herron, & Peak, 1996)
Age/Grade Level   3–10 Years

The test includes two forms, each with a Basic Writing and a Contextual Writing subtest. The Basic Writing subtest measures a child's ability in areas such as spelling, capitalization, punctuation, sentence construction, and metacognitive knowledge. The Contextual Writing subtest measures a child's ability to construct a story when provided with a picture prompt, and the subtest focuses on areas such as story format, cohesion, thematic maturity, ideation, and story structure. Administration time is 30 to 45 minutes; the test provides standard score quotients, percentiles, and age equivalents.

You have found a secret room in your house. Describe the room and tell about your experience while you were in it.

hat was
& shiney

One sunny/cloudy day me and my mom were meving into our new house and when I was ~~putting~~ putting in the ~~living room~~ stuff I found an ancient stone ~~and~~ it said forever on it so I picked it up and put it in my poket but ~~I~~ did shew my mether or ~~father~~ farther because they would waste time and t to give it back to ye people who hend i before me. So I went ~~upstairs~~ to go in my ~~room~~ room I found a ~~closet~~ closet ~~to~~ put my ~~clothes~~ clothes in so when I ~~was~~ was loking in my closet I was amazed at hew big my room was so

FIGURE 14–3 Written Expression Language Disorder: Sample from a Middle School Student with Learning Disabilities

Test of Written Expression (McGhee, Bryant, Larsen, & Rivera, 1995)
Age/Grade Level 6–14 Years

The test includes a series of items that assess different skills associated with writing. Also, the student reads or hears a prepared story starter and uses it as a stimulus for writing an essay. The essay is scored by evaluating performance across ideation, vocabulary, grammar, capitalization, punctuation, and spelling. The test can be administered to individuals or groups and yields standard scores and percentile ranks.

Test of Written Language-3 (Hammill & Larsen, 1996) Age/Grade Level   2nd–12th grade

The test assesses cognitive, linguistic, and conventional components of written language by having the student look at pictures and write a complete story based on the pictures. Subtests with spontaneous formats (essay analysis) include contextual conventions—measures capitalization, punctuation, and spelling: contextual language—measures vocabulary, syntax, and grammar; and story construction—measures plot, character development, and general composition. Subtests with contrived formats include vocabulary—measures word usage; spelling—measures ability to form letters into words; style—measures punctuation and capitalization; logical sentences—measures ability to write conceptually sound sentences; and standards scores are provided. The test can be administered to individuals or groups in about 90 minutes, and the PRO-SCORE system allows computer scoring.

Criterion-Referenced Test

Brigance Diagnostic Comprehensive Inventory of Basic Skills–Revised (Brigance, 1999) Age/Grade Level   K–9th grade

This criterion-referenced inventory includes a grade placement test in sentence writing. The writing section also assesses the student's strengths and weaknesses in the following areas: writing cursive lowercase and uppercase letters in sequence, quality of manuscript and cursive writing, writing personal data, capitalization, punctuation, addressing envelopes, writing a personal letter, writing a letter requesting information, and writing a customer-complaint letter. A student record book tracks assessment administered, correct and incorrect responses, progress since last testing, and instruction objectives. A class record book also is available.

Graham et al., 2003, p. 596) provide a very useful checklist for assessing writing instruction in your classroom (see Table 14-4).

Interventions

Gersten and Baker (1999, p. 2) provide research-based instructional strategies for students with learning disabilities in written expression. Their meta-analysis indicates that three major components appear to be most important: *planning, writing,* and *revision.* They recommend that students be given explicit instruction on these three steps, explicit instruction on writing different types of express texts, and feedback on the quality of their work. The authors also believe that the mechanics of writing should be taught and integrated with written expression. Specifically, they recommend the following (pp. 2–3):

Planning
- Well-developed plans for writing result in better first drafts. Teachers or peers who write well can verbalize the process they go through to help students develop their own "plans of action." One type of plan of action, called a "Planning Think Sheet," uses a series of sequential, structured prompts. It specifies a topic and asks the questions, "Who (am I writing for)?," "Why am I writing?," "What do I know?," "How can I group my ideas?" and "How will I organize my ideas?" (Englert, Raphael, & Anderson, 1992). Another technique is to use semantic mapping to help students plan their writing.

Creating a First Draft
- Using a plan for action helps students create first drafts. The plan serves as a concrete map for engaging in the writing process and provides students with suggestions for what to do when they feel "stuck." The plan of action provides a permanent reminder of the content and structure of the writing task. A well-developed plan of action also gives the student and teacher a common language to use in discussing the writing. The dialogue between teacher and student represents a major advance in writing instruction over traditional methods that required students to work in relative isolation.

Revising and Editing
- Revising and editing skills are critical to the writing process. Developing methods to help students refine and edit their work has been difficult, but a few researchers have begun to develop specific strategies that appear promising. For example, Wong, Butler, Ficzere, and Kuperis (1996), in teaching

TABLE 14–4 Checklist for Classroom Writing Instruction

My Students . . .
—— Write daily and work on a wide range of writing tasks for multiple audiences, including writing at home.
—— Help each other plan, draft, revise, edit, or publish their written work.
—— Share their work with each other, receiving praise and critical feedback on their efforts.
—— Use writing as a tool to explore, organize, and express their thoughts across the curriculum.
—— Assess their progress as writers.

I Make Sure That I . . .
—— Develop a literate classroom environment where students' written work is prominently displayed and the room is packed with writing and reading material.
—— Establish a predictable writing routine where students are encouraged to think, reflect, and revise.
—— Hold individual conferences with students about their current writing efforts, helping them establish goals or criteria to guide their writing and revising efforts.
—— Make writing motivating by setting an exciting mood, creating a risk-free environment, allowing students to select their own writing topics or modify teacher assignments, developing assigned topics compatible with students' interests, reinforcing children's accomplishments, specifying the goal for each lesson, and promoting an "I can do" attitude.
—— Provide frequent opportunities for students to self-regulate their behavior during writing, including working independently, arranging their own space, and seeking help from other.
—— Conduct periodic conferences with parents, soliciting their advice and communicating the goals of the program as well as their child's progress as a writer.

To Help Students Progress as Writers I . . .
—— Model the process of writing as well as positive attitudes toward writing.
—— Provide instruction on a broad range of skills, knowledge, and strategies, including phonological awareness, handwriting and spelling, writing conventions, sentence-level skill, text structure, the functions of writing, and planning and revising.
—— Deliver follow-up instruction to ensure mastery of targeted writing, skills, knowledge and strategies.
—— Monitor students' progress as writers as well as students' strengths and needs.
—— Adjust my teaching style and learning pace as needed, conduct mini-lessons responsive to current student needs, and provide individually guided assistance with writing assignments.

Note: *Place a check next to each item that describes a feature of writing instruction in your classroom. Determine the actualization of any unchecked items that would improve the quality of writing instruction in your class.*

students to write opinion essays, used peer editing as an instructional strategy for the students. Pairs of students alternated their roles as student-writer and student-critic. The student-critic identified ambiguities in the essay and asked the writer for clarification. With help from the teacher, the students made revisions. The teacher also provided the student-writer with feedback on clarity and on the cogency of the supportive arguments. Once the clarity and cogency of the essay met the teacher's standard, the pair moved on to correct capitalization, spelling, and punctuation. Through this process, the student-writer had to explain his or her communicative intent to the peer and revise the essay to faithfully reflect it. These clarifying interactive dialogues led the student-critic and student-writer to understand each other's perspective. In this way the trainees developed a sense of audience for their writing.

Graham and Harris (1988), as cited in Mercer and Mercer (2005, pp. 393–394), recommend the following for an effective writing program:

1. Allocate time for writing instruction.
A sufficient amount of time should be allocated to writing instruction (e.g., four times per week) because students can learn and develop as writers only by writing.

2. Expose students to a broad range of writing tasks.
Students should participate in writing activities that present highly structured problem-solving situations

as well as activities that involve self-selected and expressive writing.

3. Create a social climate conducive to writing development.

The teacher needs to be encouraging in a nonthreatening environment and should try to develop a sense of community by promoting student sharing and collaboration.

4. Integrate writing with other academic subjects.

Writing should be integrated with other language arts activities to increase writing and develop skills.

5. Aid students in developing the processes central to effective writing.

The composition process can be divided into a series of discrete stages (e.g., pre-write, write, and rewrite), and students can be taught appropriate task specific and metacognitive strategies (e.g., self-instructional strategy training).

6. Automatize skills for getting language onto paper.

The teacher should provide direct instruction in mechanical skills and sentence and paragraph production, or the mechanical requirements of composing can be moved through the use of oral dictation.

7. Help students develop explicit knowledge about the characteristics of good writing.

Students should be given exposure to the characteristics of various literary compositions either through reading or teacher presentation of written or live models that incorporate a specific skill or style, or students should receive direct instruction in the structured elements representative of a particular literary style.

8. Help students develop goals for improving their written products.

Three methods for the development of more mature composing processes include conferences during which teachers act as collaborators, procedural facilitation in which external support is provided, and self-instructional strategy training.

9. Help students develop goals for improving their written products.

Goal setting and having students evaluate their own or others' written products according to specific criteria can help students accurately monitor and evaluate progress.

10. Avoid instructional practices that do not improve students' writing performances.

Skills in grammar and usage should be developed within the context of real writing tasks, and the teacher should give specific, explanatory feedback on only one or two types of frequently occurring errors at any time.

THE WRITING PROCESS

A process approach to writing has been advocated for students with written language disorders (Calkins, 1994; Graves, 1995). Mercer and Mercer (2001, p. 427) provide an overview of the stages:

- Select a topic for the written piece.
- Consider the purpose for writing (e.g., to inform, describe, entertain, or persuade).
- Identify the audience for whom the writing is intended (e.g., classmates, parents, businesspersons, or publishers).
- Choose an appropriate form for the composition based on purpose and audience (e.g., story, report, poem, script, or letter).
- Engage in rehearsal activities to gather and organize ideas for writing (e.g., drawing, talking, reading, interviewing, brainstorming ideas, and clustering main ideas and details).
- Participate in writing a collaborative or group composition with the teacher so that the teacher can model or demonstrate the writing process and clarify questions and misconceptions.

Drafting Stage

Write a rough draft, skipping every other line and allowing adequate space for revising. Emphasize content rather than mechanics, grammar, and spelling.

Revising Stage

Reread the rough draft and make changes by adding, substituting, deleting, and moving text. Share the composition in writing groups in which listeners respond with compliments as well as comments and suggestions about how to improve the composition.

Make revisions based on feedback from the writing group by crossing out, drawing arrows, and writing in the space left between the writing lines.

Editing Stage

Focus on mechanics, including capitalization, punctuation, spelling, sentence structure, word usage, and formatting considerations. Proofread the composition by reading word by word and hunting for errors (e.g., spelling, capitalization, and punctuation) rather than reading for meaning, and insert proofreading symbols to indicate needed changes. Correct as many mechanical errors as possible and, if necessary, use a dictionary or have a conference with the teacher for instruction or a mini-lesson on a needed skill.

Publishing Stage

Publish the writing in an appropriate form (e.g., make a covered booklet or contribute to a newspaper or magazine). Share the finished composition with classmates or appropriate audiences by reading it aloud in the class "author's chair" or displaying the writing on a bulletin board.

During the prewriting stage, semantic webs can be helpful. See Salend (2001, p. 360) for a sample semantic map for writing a story about a birthday party:

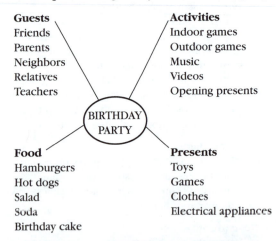

Guests
Friends
Parents
Neighbors
Relatives
Teachers

Activities
Indoor games
Outdoor games
Music
Videos
Opening presents

BIRTHDAY PARTY

Food
Hamburgers
Hot dogs
Salad
Soda
Birthday cake

Presents
Toys
Games
Clothes
Electrical appliances

LEARNING STRATEGIES

The following learning strategies are provided by Mercer and Mercer (2001, pp. 430–432):

PLEASE (Welsh, 1992)
COPS (Schumaker, Nolan, & Deshler, 1985)
TOWER

Each one will be described below.

PLEASE is a metacognitive strategy used for writing paragraphs.
P Pick a topic, an audience and the appropriate textual format.
L List information about the topic to be used in the sentence generation, ongoing evaluation and organizational planning.
E Evaluate whether the list is complete and plan how to organize the ideas that will be used to generate supporting sentences.
A Activate the paragraph with a short and simple declaration sentence.
S Supply supporting sentences based on items from the list.
E End with a concluding sentence that rephrases the topic sentence, and evaluate the written work for errors in capitalization, punctuating, spelling and appearance. (See COPS for help!)

A useful editing/proofreading strategy is **COPS.**

C Have I *capitalized* the first word and proper nouns?
O How is the *overall* appearance?
P Have I put in commas, semicolons and end *punctuation*?
S Have I *spelled* all the words correctly?

TOWER can be used for secondary level students when they have to write essays.

T Think about content
O Order topics and details
W Write the rough draft
E Look for errors
R Revise/rewrite

DIRECT INSTRUCTION IN WRITTEN LANGUAGE

Research on the effectiveness of direct instruction is well documented (Adams & Carmine, 2003). The following programs provide instruction on handwriting, spelling, and written expression (see http//:www.sra4kids.com/product_info/ direct).

Handwriting
- *Cursive Writing Program.*   for Grades 3 and 4

Spelling
- *Spelling Mastery.*   (Levels A–F Elementary). This is for Grades 1 through 6 and teaches high-utility words, sound symbolic principles, and general spelling strategies.
- *Corrective Spelling.*   This program is for Grade 4 and above and teaches 500 predictable, highly generalized rules.

Written Expression
- *Expressive Writing.*   This is for Grades 4 and above. It teaches sentence writing through sophisticated paragraph writing with copyediting.
- *Reasoning and Writing.*   This is for elementary and secondary students. It combines the teaching of language, thinking, and writing skills.

APPLICATION OF TECHNOLOGY IN WRITTEN LANGUAGE

Word processing may be the most important application of technology for students with learning disabilities (Behrmanm & Kinas Jerome, 2002). The use of grammar and spell checkers, dictionaries, and thesauruses will assist students with mechanical difficulty in writing. Also, keyboards are available in large sizes. When students are engaged in writing, they can collaborate with the teacher and fellow students, receiving instant feedback and recommendations for revision.

Students can also be provided with talking word processors that provide auditory feedback to reinforce their writing (Quenneville, 2001). A few recommended models are Intellitale II (http://www.intellitools.com), Read and Write 5.0 (http://www.

texthelp.com), and Write: Out Loud 3.0 (http://www.donjohnsston.com). Read and Write 5.0 has a word prediction feature that displays words based on frequency of use, grammatically correct usage of words, and most recently used words.

Portable note takers (see AlphaSmart 3000, Intelligent Periphernal Devices, Cupertino, CA) are efficient, allow students to focus on ideas and note taking, and require less energy when operating the device. Inspiration (http:// www.inspirations.com) provides students with graphic organizers that can assist them in the writing process. All of these devices allow for more meaningful inclusion in regular classrooms. (See DO IT—Disabilities, Opportunities, Internetworking and Technology, at http://www.mailto:doit@u.washington.edu for additional information of the application of technology to students with learning disabilities.)

For some students with learning disabilities, technological products may be useful. The Franklin Speller computer, which includes a spell checking program, provides a novel motivating experience (see the next section). It is important to recognize that these devices are not a panacea. Many students have trouble using the keyboard effectively due to attention, memory, and fine motor difficulties.

Written expression should be meaningful. Students should write daily, should see a reason for writing, and should have a variety of writing experiences. Personal journals are used in many classrooms, and many students write in them daily. Some teachers use a dialogue journal to enhance communication with their students. This method is time-consuming but extremely useful. Pen pals are another way to demonstrate to students that their writing has meaning. This can be as simple as having schools in your district establish pen pal links with schools across the country. As students receive correspondence from their pen pals, they are motivated to write back and start viewing themselves as writers.

Implications for Teachers: PowerPoint Presentations. It is not unusual to observe students in a variety of classrooms developing

PowerPoint presentations. In a high school social studies inclusive class, Mr. Zaiff and Ms. Conway divided their students into heterogeneous groups based upon their abilities. Written expression is particularly difficult for some of these students, and assigning the typical term paper would lead to failure. For this "report" on the amendments to the U.S. Constitution, students selected the amendment they wanted to present, researched it through print and Internet sources, and developed a PowerPoint program to present their findings to their classmates.

The PowerPoint presentation enabled students with learning disabilities to focus on their strengths while relying or their classmates to compensate for their weaknesses. This collaborative experience enabled the students with learning disabilities to be active participants and showcased their abilities. Due to the inclusionary practice employed by Mr. Zaiff and Ms. Conway, these students demonstrated their competence to their classmates as well as to themselves. (See http://www.actden.ww/pp. for a tutorial on PowerPoint for students who need additional help.)

SUMMARY

Written language is the highest form of expression and, for students with learning disabilities, the most difficult. Characteristics of students with handwriting, spelling, and written expression problems were presented in this chapter, as well as assessment procedures and interventions for these components of written language. Research suggests that all components are critical for success in writing, and that to focus on one over the others is a mistake. An integrated approach, as recommended by Graham and colleagues, appears to be the most logical and sensible way to address these complex problems.

SPRINGBOARDS FOR REFLECTION AND DISCUSSION

1. Observe classes in kindergarten through third grade. What kind of instruction are they receiving in handwriting, spelling, and written expression? Are the needs of the students with learning disabilities being addressed?
2. Review some commercially available handwriting and spelling programs. How could you adapt or modify them for a student with learning disabilities?
3. Review some assessment devices in the area of written language. Do they reflect current thinking on the topic? Does their use lead to recommendations that can be implemented in the classroom?
4. Interview a teacher of students with learning disabilities. How does he or she believe written language should be taught?
5. Interview a regular education teacher. How does he or she believe written language should be taught?
6. How would you develop and implement instruction in written language?
7. Observe a high school class including students with learning disabilities. Are these students competent writers? If not, how do their problems impact their learning? What recommendations can you make?
8. Speak to an adult with learning disabilities. What type and amount of instruction did he or she receive in written language? Is the situation very different in today's classrooms?

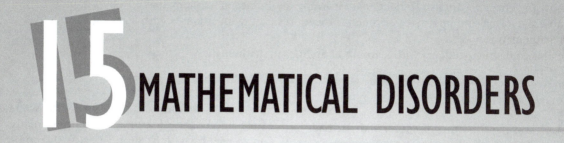

15 MATHEMATICAL DISORDERS

CHAPTER OBJECTIVES

At the end of this chapter you will:

- know the characteristics of students with learning disabilities in mathematics.
- know the formal and informal assessment procedures used with students with learning disabilities in mathematics.
- be able to instruct students with learning disabilities in mathematics.

Math was never a strong point for Matt. He had problems in all content areas, but math was particularly difficult. He focused on irrelevant details and could not remember basic facts. He is now in sixth grade and continues to struggle with math. Oddly, Matt is more concerned than his teachers or his parents. They are more worried about his reading and writing abilities; he receives extra help in school and has a private tutor. Yet, for all of Matt's struggles with math, they just dismiss it, saying, "A lot of people have difficulty in math" or "You'll use a calculator when you get older." Matt does not understand. Why are they not concerned with his inability to perform basic mathematical calculations? Why are they not worried that he never seems to understand work problems or that he doesn't "see" acute angles the way other students do? Is math less important than literacy? Will he be able to do well in life without adequate math skills?

Matt's confusion is easy to understand. When you examine the disproportionate emphasis on literacy versus mathematics, you may also wonder how important a learning disability in math is. Can you get by with it? Simply peruse the number of journals, journal articles, books, and assessment procedures devoted to each area, and the conclusion is obvious. We are far more concerned with literacy than mathematical performance. What will you as a teacher do in the classroom? Will you try to establish a balanced approach to the curriculum? Will you integrate literacy and math skills? Will you provide adequate instruction to students who are having difficulty with math? This chapter provides information on the characteristics of students with learning disabilities who have mathematical disorders, ways to assess their performance, and interventions you can use in the classroom. The emphasis will be on providing these interventions in the inclusive setting. Then, when you have students like Matt, they will realize that appropriate instruction in mathematics is as important as any other curriculum area.

Recently, increased attention has been given to students with learning disabilities in mathematics. Pedrotty-Bryant, Bryant, and Hammill (2000) note the three publications (*LD Forum, Learning Disability Quarterly,* and *Journal of Learning Disabilities*) devoted exclusively to mathematical disabilities and students with learning disabilities. In P.L. 94-142, math calculations and math reasoning are two of the seven major areas of deficiency among students with learning disabilities. IDEA 2004 continues to include these two areas. Clearly, mathematical ability is necessary for success in school and beyond. And yet, many students with learning disabilities leave high school without being competent in math (Garnett, 1998).

CHARACTERISTICS OF STUDENTS WITH MATH DISORDERS

Kroesberger and VanLuit (2003) cite difficulty with memory and inadequate use of strategies as two major characteristics of students with math disorders. Pedrotty-Bryant et al. (2000, p. 68) cite studies describing other difficulties of these students in the following areas: math fact automaticity (Garnett & Fleischner, 1983; Jordan, Levine, & Huttenlocher, 1995); use of arithmetic strategies (Geary, 1990; Goldman, Pellegrino, & Mertz, 1988); and interpretation of word problems and sentence construction (Montague & Applegate, 1993).

The number of students with math disabilities varies, but most researchers agree that approximately 6% of students have math problems (Fleischner & Manheimer, 1997). They divide this population into two groups: those with primary math disabilities (nonverbal learning disabilities) and those with math disabilities due to verbal learning disabilities or reading disorders.

Garnett (1998) cites four types of math disorders in students with learning disabilities:

- mastering basic number facts
- calculation weakness, but excellent grasp of math concepts
- learning difficulties (oral and written)
- visual-spatial aspects of mathematics

Other researchers (Bley & Thornton, 2001; Mercer & Pullen, 2005) discuss the characteristics of students with learning disabilities and how they manifest themselves in math disorders. Mercer and Pullen (2005, pp. 489–490) provide a useful chart (Table 15–1) that describes these common difficulties.

SUBTYPES OF STUDENTS WITH MATH DISORDERS

Another way to view the characteristics of students with mathematical disorders is to see if there are particular subtypes. Geary (1993) developed a taxonomy of three general subtypes of mathematical disability: procedural, semantic memory, and visuospatial. The defining characteristics (Geary, 2003, p. 205) adapted from Geary (1993, 2000) are as follows:

Procedural Subtype

Cognitive and performance features

A. Relatively frequent use of developmentally immature procedures (i.e., the use of procedures that are more commonly used by younger, academically normal children).
B. Frequent errors in the execution of procedures.
C. Poor understanding of the concepts underlying procedural use.
D. Difficulties sequencing the multiple steps in complex procedures.

Neuropsychogical features

Unclear, although some data suggests an association with left-hemispheric dysfunction and in some cases (especially for feature D above) a prefrontal dysfunction.

Genetic features

Unclear

Developmental features

Appears, in many cases, to represent a developmental delay (i.e., performance is similar to that of younger, academically normal children, and often improves across age and grade).

Relation to RD [reading disability]

Unclear

Semantic Memory Subtype

Cognitive and performance features

A. Difficulties retrieving mathematical facts, such as answers to simple arithmetic problems.
B. When facts are retrieved, there is a high error rate.
C. For arithmetic, retrieval errors are often associates of numbers in the problem (e.g., retrieving 4 to 2 + 3 = ?; 4 is the counting-string associate that follows 2, 3).
D. RTs [reaction times] for correct retrieval are unsystematic.

Neuropsychological features

A. Appears to be associated with left-hemispheric dysfunction, possibly the posterior regions for one form of retrieval deficit and the prefrontal regions for another.
B. Possible sub-cortical involvement, such as the basal ganglia.

Genetic features

Appears to be a heritable deficit.

TABLE 15–1 Learning Disabilities and Math-Related Performance

Learning Difficulty		Math-Related Performance
Visual Perception	Figure–Ground	Loses place on worksheet. Does not finish problems on a page. Has difficulty reading multi-digit numbers.
	Discrimination	Has difficulty differentiating between numbers (e.g., 6,9,; 2,5; or 17, 71), coins, the operation symbols, clock hands. Has difficulty copying shapes or problems. Has difficulty writing across paper in a straight line. Has confusion about before-after concepts (e.g., has difficulty with time or counting).
	Spatial	Has difficulty relating to directional aspects of math, which can be noted in problems with computations involving up-down (e.g., addition), left-right (regrouping), and aligning numbers. Puts decimals in the wrong place. Has difficulty spacing manipulatives into patterns or sets. Has confusion about positive and negative numbers *(directional)*.
Auditory Perception		Has difficulty doing oral drills. Has difficulty doing oral word problems. Is unable to count on from within a sequence. Has difficulty writing numbers or assignments from dictation. Has difficulty learning number patterns.
Motor		Writes numbers illegibly, slowly, and inaccurately. Has difficulty writing numbers in small spaces (i.e., writes numbers that are too large).
Memory	Short-Term	Is unable to retain math facts or new information. Forgets steps in an algorithm. Is unable to retain the meaning of symbols.
	Long-Term	Works slowly on mastering facts over time; performs poorly on review lessons or mixed probes. Forgets steps in algorithms.
	Sequential	Has difficulty telling time. Does not complete all steps in a multi-step computation problems.
Attention		Has difficulty maintaining attention to steps in algorithms or problem solving. Has difficulty sustaining attention to critical instruction (e.g., teacher modeling).
Language	Receptive	Has difficulty relating math terms to meaning (e.g., *minus, addend, dividend, regroup, multiplicand,* and *place value*). Has difficulty relating words that have multiple meaning (e.g., *carry* and *time*).
	Expressive	Does not use the vocabulary of math. Has difficulty performing oral math drills. Has difficulty verbalizing steps in solving a work problem or an algorithm.
Reading		Does not understand the vocabulary of math work problems.
Cognition and Abstract Reasoning		Has difficulty converting linguistic and numerical information into math equations and algorithms. Has difficulty in solving word problems. Is unable to make comparisons of size and quantity. Has difficulty in understanding symbols in math (e.g., $>$, $<$, $>$, x, and $=$). Has difficulty understanding the abstract level of mathematical concepts and operations.

Metacognition		Is unable to identify and select appropriate strategies for solving computation and word problems.
		Has difficulty monitoring the problem-solving process in word problems and multi-step computations.
		Is unable to generalize strategies to other situations.
Social and Emotional	Impulsive	Makes careless mistakes in computation.
		Responds incorrectly and rapidly in oral drills.
		Corrects responses frequently when asked to look at or listen to a problem again.
		Does not attend to details in solving problems.
	Short Attention/ Distractibility	Does not complete work in assigned time.
		Has difficulty doing multi-step computation.
		Starts a problem and does not finish it but goes on to next problem.
		Is off task.
	Passivity Learned Helplessness	Omits computation problems.
		Omits word problems.
		Appears disinterested.
		Lacks strategies.
	Self-esteem	Lacks confidence.
		Gives up easily.
		Becomes so tense during math test that performance is impaired.
	Anxiety	Avoids math to reduce anxiety.

Source: Mercer, Cecil D.; Pullen, Paige C., *Students with Learning Disabilities*, © 2005. Reprinted by permission of publisher.

Developmental features

Appears to represent a developmental difference (i.e., cognitive and performance features differ from that [sic] of younger, academically normal children, and do not change substantively across age or grade).

Relation to RD

Appears to occur with phonetic forms of RD.

Visuospatial Subtype

Cognitive and performance features

A. Difficulties in spatially representing numerical and other forms of mathematical information and relationships.

B. Frequent misinterpretation or misunderstanding of spatially represented information.

Neuropsychological features

Appears to be associated with right-hemispheric dysfunction, in particular, posterior regions of the right hemisphere, although the parietal cortex of the left hemisphere may be implicated as well.

Genetic features

Unclear, although the cognitive and performance features are common with certain genetic disorders (e.g., Turner's syndrome).

Developmental features

Unclear

Relation to RD

Does not appear to be related.

It is frequently noted that if a student has a reading disability, he or she will also have a mathematical disability. In the subtypes noted above, the only one that appears to be related to an RD is semantic memory. These students have difficulty retrieving basic arithmetic facts—a deficit that does not appear to improve over time.

Researchers are attempting to identify early predictors of mathematical disorders. Gersten, Jordan, and Flojo (2005) found that mathematical difficulties are not stable over time. Students who have trouble reading make slower progress in mathematics, and almost all of the students they studied had difficulty with "accurate and automatic retrieval of basic arithmetic combinations" (p. 293). The students most at risk for mathematical difficulties were those who were deficient in magnitude comparison ("which number is larger?"), counting strategies, fluent identification of number, and working memory. Gersten et al. believe that intervention should focus on the "development of fluency and proficiency with basic arithmetic combinations and the increasingly accurate and efficient use of counting strategies" (p. 302). They caution that much more research is needed (see the Special Series of the *Journal of Learning Disabilities*, 38 [4], 2005, for information on this emerging research base).

ASSESSMENT

Formal Assessment

Few standardized tests of mathematics are available for teachers. The large number of tests for reading further emphasizes the relative neglect of mathematics. This problem has received increased study, but the gap remains wide. Cohen and Spenciner (2003, p. 284) provide information on these assessment devices (see Table 15-2).

Criterion-Referenced Assessment

Teacher-made tests are material specific and relate to the curriculum but are not always possible to develop. The Brigance Diagnostic Inventories are commercially available criterion-referenced tests. Rather than comparing your students to a standardized sample, they allow you to compare their performance to a well-defined area of the curriculum. Cohen and Spenciner (2003, p. 293) list the mathematical skills assessed in the various inventories (see Table 15-3).

Error Analysis

Many teachers use error analysis to identify error patterns in order to understand the errors and remediate them. Ashlock (1998) was one of the first to describe this process. For example, in the problem below, the student subtracted the smaller number from the larger number, regardless of the position.

$$\begin{array}{r} 47 \\ -29 \\ \hline 22 \end{array}$$

Some students are confused about the sequence of the algorithm or may not know basic number facts. Cohen and Spenciner (2003, pp. 294–295) provide the following common errors that your students may display:

Addition and Subtraction
- lack of understanding of regrouping
- confusion of 1's and 10's in carrying and writing
- forgetting to carry 10's and 100's

TABLE 15–2 Standardized Tests of Mathematics

Name	Ages/Grades	Group/Individual
Diagnostic Screening Test Math(DSTM) (Gnagey, 1980)	Grades 1 through 10	Individual or group
KeyMath-R/NU (Connolly, 1998)	Grades K through 9	Individual
Slossdon-Diagnostic Math Screener (S-DMS)	Ages 6 years through	Individual or group
(Erford & Boykin, 1996)	13 years	Individual or group
Stanford Diagnostic Mathematics Test (4th ed.)	Grades 1 through 8	Individual or group
(Harcourt Brace Educational Measurement, 1995)		
Test of Early Mathematics Ability (Tema-2)	Ages 3 years through	Individual
(Ginsburg & Baroody, 1990)	8 years, 11 months	
Test of Mathematical Abilities–2 (TOMA-2)	Grades 3 through 12	Individual
(Brown, Cronin, & McEntire, 1994)		

TABLE 15–3 Brigance Inventories

Name	Ages/Grades	Mathematical Skills
BRIGANCE *Inventory of Essential Skills* (Brigance, 1981)	Grades 4 through 12	Numbers Number Facts Computation of Whole Numbers Fractions and Mixed Numbers Decimals Percents Measurement Metrics Math Vocabulary Money and Finance
BRIGANCE *Comprehensive Inventory* *of Basic Skills Revised* (Brigance, 1999)	Pre-K through 9	Numbers Number Facts Computation of Whole Numbers Fractions and Mixed Numbers Decimals Percents Measurement/Geometry Metrics Time Money
BRIGANCE *Assessment of Basics Skills,* *Spanish Edition* (Brigance, 1984)	Grades K through 6	Number Sequences Operations Measurement
BRIGANCE *Inventory of Diagnostic* *Early Development* (Brigance, 1991)	Ages birth to 7 years	Number Concepts Rote Counting Reads Numerals Numeral Comprehension Ordinal Position Numbers in Sequence Writes Following and Preceding Numerals Writes Numerals Dictated Addition Combinations Subtraction Combinations Recognition of Money Time
BRIGANCE *Diagnostic Life Skills Inventory* (Brigance, 1994)	Vocational Secondary Adult education	Money Operations Finance Money Management
BRIGANCE *Diagnostic Employability Skill Inventory* (Brigance, 1995)	Vocational Secondary Adult education Job training	Operations Fractions Measurement Geometry Math Vocabulary

- regrouping when it is not required
- incorrect operation (the student subtracts instead of adding)
- lack of knowledge of basic number facts

Multiplication and Division
- forgetting to carry in multiplication
- carrying before multiplying
- ignoring place value in division
- recording the answer from left to right
- lack of alignment of work in columns
- lack of knowledge of basic number facts

Fractions
- incorrect cancellation
- failure to reduce to lowest common denominator
- ignoring the remainder
- incorrect conversion of mixed numbers to fractions

Word Problems
- difficulty in reading
- inability to relate to context of problem
- inability to understand the language and vocabulary of the problem
- difficulty in identifying the relevant and the irrelevant information
- difficulty in identifying the number of steps required to solve the problem
- trouble in doing mathematical operations (addition, subtraction, multiplication, division)

Curriculum-Based Assessment

In order to assess what is being taught, many teachers employ curriculum-based measurement. To develop a survey test, you must carry out the five steps below (Mercer & Mercer, 2005, pp. 414–415):

1. Identify a sequence of successive skills included in the school curriculum.
2. Select a span of math skills to be assessed.
3. Construct select items for each skill within the range selected.
4. Administer and score the survey test.
5. Display the results in a box plot, interpret the results, and plan instruction.

Specific directions for administration and scoring are provided by Mercer and Mercer in Figure 15–1 (2005, p. 416).

Other Classroom-Based Assessment Procedures

Many teachers develop their own tests based upon the skills to be taught, and others find interviewing students helpful in trying to identify specific areas of concern. Fleishner and Manheimer (1997) recommend the use of clinical interviews. They suggest the following conversation for the computation problem (p. 399):

$$\begin{array}{r} 77 \\ + \quad 7 \\ \hline 174 \end{array}$$

E. I see that you said the answer to 77 plus 7 is 174. Would you tell me how you get this answer?

S. Well, I said 77 plus 7. Then I said 7 plus 7 is 14. Then I wrote down the 4. Then I said 7 plus 7 is 7. So I wrote down the 7. But I still had to carry the 1. So I put it in front of the answer.

If she offered similar explanation for her errors the teacher would be able to develop an intervention plan based upon her feedback. This can be useful for a host of other problems, including word problems. It can be time consuming and some teachers have students work in pairs to identify the problem.

Assessment is an ongoing process. In order to develop reasonable and sensible interventions, you must continually monitor students' progress.

INTERVENTIONS

Most students with math disabilities will be educated in the regular classroom, using materials and methods that are typically inappropriate for their needs. The National Council of Teachers of Mathematics (NCTM) published a list of standards to be employed with all students (Principles and Standards for School Mathematics, 2000). The emphasis was on problem solving and real-life mathematical applications (see http://www.nctm.org/standards/standards.htm).

The initial publication did not fully address the needs of students with learning disabilities, nor did

Administration Directions

The following steps are recommended for administering 2 minute timings to individuals or groups.

1. Select the appropriate measurement (i.e., survey test or specific skill probe) and pass it face down to students.
2. Give standardized directions at the beginning of the administration. Also, use specific instructions for different parts of the test.

    "The sheets I just passed out are math problems." If a single skill probe is used, tell the students the operation: "All problems are _____ (addition, subtraction, multiplication, or division)." If multiple skill probe is used, say: "There are different types of problems on the sheet. There are some addition, subtraction, and multiplication problems. Look at each problem closely before you compute."

    "When I say 'Begin,' turn the sheet over and answer the problems. Start with the first problem at the beginning of the first row. Touch the problem. Work across the sheet and then go to the beginning of the next row. If you are unable to do a problem, mark an $\times$ on it and go to the next problem. If you finish one page go to the next page. Do you have any questions?"

    "Ready, start."
3. Monitor student work to ensure that students are following the directions (i.e., working in successive rows). Watch for students who want to skip around and do the easy problems.
4. When 2 minutes have elapsed, say: "Stop. Put your pencils down."

Scoring Procedures

1. Underline each correct digit.
2. Score numerals written in reverse from ε for 3 as correct.
3. Score a correct digit in the proper place (column) as correct.
4. Award full points (number of digits used in solving a problem) when the student has a correct answer, even if the work is not shown.
5. If the student displays work and the answer is incorrect, give credit for each digit done correctly.
6. Do not count numerals written for regrouping purposes (i.e., carried numbers).
7. Do not count remainders of zero.
8. When an X or zero is placed correctly as a placeholder, count it as one digit correct.
9. Give credit for any correct digits, even if the problem has not been completed.
10. Total the number of correct digits and record it on the paper.

Sample Scoring of Student Copy

$$
\begin{array}{r} 2 \\ + 4 \\ \hline 6 \end{array}
\qquad
\begin{array}{r} 12 \\ + 26 \\ \hline 38 \end{array}
\qquad
\begin{array}{r} 38 \\ \times\ 9 \\ \hline 342 \end{array}
$$

1 digit correct   2 digits correct   3 digits correct

```
     12 R42
63 )798   (4 digits correct)        1    +    1    =
    63x   (3 digits correct with x) ─         ─
    168   (3 digits correct)        4         3
    126   (3 digits correct)        3    +    4    =        7
     42   (2 digits correct)        ──        ──          ──
                                    12        12          12

                                  (3 digits  (3 digits  (3 digits
                                  correct)   correct)   correct)
    15 digits correct             9 digits
```

FIGURE 15-1 Curriculum-Based Measurement Administration Directions and Scoring Procedures for Math

Source: Mercer, Cecil D.; Mercer, Ann R., *Teaching Students with Learning problems*, © 2005. Reprinted by permission of publisher.

the 2000 publication. Mercer and Pullen (2005, p. 483) cite the following criticisms:

1. The standards make only modest reference to students with disabilities (Giordano, 1993; Hofmeister, 1993; Hutchinson, 1993; Rivera, 1993).
2. The standards are not based on replicable, validated, instructional programs. Research-supported instructional programs for students with moderate to mild disabilities are especially lacking (Hofmeister, 1993; Hutchinson, 1993; Rivera, 1993). For example, Hutchinson states that there is "no evidence to support the claim that exposure to the proposed content and experiences will result in mathematical power for students with disabilities" (p. 20).
3. The standards promote an endogenous constructivist approach (self-discovery) for teaching math to all students. The position ignores the wealth of teaching practices generated from the process-product research (Englert, Tarrant, & Mariage, 1992) that have proven to be effective with students who have moderate-to-mild disabilities. Moreover, strict adherence to endogenous constructivism does not recognize the promising findings being generated from constructivists who promote a directed discovery (exogenous) approach or constructivists who advocate a guided discovery (dialectical) approach.

Given this disparity, it is crucial that both regular and special educators develop collaborative practices to meet the needs of students with learning disabilities who have difficulty in mathematics (see the next section for an example of how two teachers, a special educator and a regular educator, utilized station teaching in their inclusive classroom).

Best Practices: Math Stations. The class consisted of 18 heterogeneous students, 5 of whom had learning disabilities. All of them loved working at stations and participating in hands-on learning. All students had the opportunity to use manipulatives, apply mathematical reasoning, and work cooperatively with their classmates.

The students had to demonstrate an understanding of a variety of hands-on math activities that had already been taught. The teachers planned to review time, patterning, adding, and problem solving.

The students were divided into four groups and sat at group tables. The groups were labeled by shapes, and the captains had a star next to their names. The captains were chosen for different reasons—some for their learning levels and others because the teachers felt it would increase their self-esteem.

The teachers discussed each station thoroughly with the students and modeled an example from each station. They were reminded of the rules and expectations during the rotations. A bell would ring when they were asked to move.

Group	Group	Group	Group
*Matthew	*Robert	*Anthony	*Jack
Danielle	Ian	Brooke	Casey
Derick	Emily	Jessica	Jonathan
Adara	Amanda	David	Maria
Kyle		Nathaniel	

Station 1: *Independent Station*

Each student had a pattern book that he or she had to complete using unifix cubes. As the children worked through the book, the patterns increased in difficulty.

Station 2: *Jewelry Station*

Each student received a piece of string with a knot on one end. They were asked to string different colored beads to make patterns—for example, ABAB, ABBA, and ABC. The teacher associate clapped twice to alert the students to clear the string and create a new pattern.

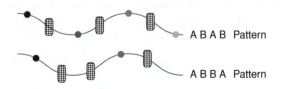

A B A B Pattern

A B B A Pattern

Station 3: *Paradise Island*

Each student had an island math mat and shells. They had to listen to a math story and place the appropriate number of shells on their island. At the end of the story, the children were asked to add their shells together to tell how many shells there were in all. Throughout this activity, the children were able to self-check with the teacher model.

Example: You are walking on the beach, and you find three shells. As you continue to walk, you find two more shells. How many shells are there altogether?

Station 4: *What Time Is It?*

Each student was handed a little clock with color-coded hands. The hour hand was red, and the minute hand was blue. They were asked to set their clocks on different hours.

Example 1: Pretend it is snack time; put your clock on 1:00. The students were able to self-check with the teacher's clock. They were asked to complete many more examples before they were handed new clocks.

Small Clocks

Next, they were given a wipe board card with a clock missing its hands. On the bottom of the card, there was room to write the time drawn on the clock. The teachers played the same game as above, except that the students had to draw and write the times.

Example 2: What time do we go to specials? 2:00. The students filled the card out, and then the captain checked each member of the group. Students could also look at the teacher's clock.

Wipe Board Card

After each group rotated around the room once, each captain gave the class his or her "captain report." Each captain reported something he or she had learned about the station and enjoyed.

GENERAL PRINCIPLES OF MATHEMATICAL INSTRUCTION

Teachers need to spend adequate time on mathematics instruction despite the dearth of research on specific instructional procedures. Lock (1996) recommends the following to enhance student performance in math:

- Increasing instructional time
- Using effective instruction
- Varying group size
- Using real-life examples
- Varying reinforcement styles

Increasing Instructional Time

Providing enough time for instruction is crucial. Too often, "math time," according to Usnick and McCoy (cited in McCoy & Prehm, 1987), includes a long stretch of independent practice in which students complete large numbers of math problems without prior feedback from the teacher. Instructional time is brief, often consisting of rapid modeling of the skill without a period of guided practice. By contrast, small–group practice in which students with math disabilities complete problems and then check within the group for the correct answer, use self-checking computer software programs, and receive intermittent teacher interaction are positive modifications for increasing the time spent on mathematics instruction. Additionally, time must be provided for students to engage in problem solving and other math "thinking" activities beyond simple computation even before students show mastery of the computational skills. Hammill and Bartel (1990) suggest slowing down the rate of instruction by using split mathematics instructional periods and reducing the number of problems required in independent practice.

Using Effective Instruction

Polloway and Patton (1996) suggest that the components of effective instruction play an important role in the success of students with disabilities in general duration mathematics instruction. One suggested schedule for the class includes a period of review of previously covered materials, teacher-directed instruction on the concept for the day, guided practice with direct teacher interaction, and independent practice with corrective feedback. During the guided and independent practice periods, teachers should ensure that students are allowed opportunities to manipulate concrete objects to promote their conceptual understanding of the mathematical process, identify the overall process involved in the lesson (i.e., have students talk about "addition is combining sets" when practicing addition problems rather than silent practice

with numerals on a worksheet), and write down numerical symbols such as addition or subtraction signs.

Teaching key math terms as a specific skill rather than as an outcome of basic math practice is essential for students with learning disabilities (Salend, 1994). The math terms might include words such as *sum, difference, quotient,* and *proper fraction,* and should be listed and displayed in the classroom to help jolt students' memories during independent assignments.

Varying Group Size

Varying the size of the group for instruction is another modification that can be used to create an effective environment for students with math disabilities. Large-group instruction, according to McCoy and Prehm (1987), is useful for brainstorming and problem-solving activities. Small-group instruction, on the other hand, is beneficial by allowing for personal attention from the teacher and collaboration with peers who are working on the same skills at comparable levels. The arrangement allows students at similar levels to be grouped and progress through skills at a comfortable rate. When using grouping as a modification, however, the teacher must provide flexibility in the groups so that students with math disabilities have the opportunity to interact and learn with all members of the class.

Using Real-Life Examples

Salend (1994) recommends that new math concepts be introduced through everyday situations rather than worksheets. With everyday situations as motivators, students are more likely to recognize the importance and relevance of a concept. Real-life demonstrations enable students to understand more readily the mathematical process being presented. Further, everyday examples involve students personally in the instruction and encourage them to learn mathematics for use in their own lives. Changing the instructional delivery system by using peer tutors, computer-based instruction, or reality-based assignments such as a "store" for practice with money recognition and making change also provides real-life math experiences (Hammill & Bartel, 1990).

Varying Reinforcement Styles

Adaptations and modifications of reinforcement styles or acknowledgment of student progress begin with teachers' awareness of different reinforcement patterns. Beyond the traditional mathematical reinforcement style, which concentrates on obtaining the right answer, students with mathematics disabilities may benefit from alternative reinforcement patterns that provide recognition for efforts to complete the steps in a problem, regardless of the outcome (McCoy & Prehm, 1987). By concentrating on the process of mathematics rather than on the product, students may begin to feel some control over the activity. In addition, teachers can isolate the sources of difficulty and provide for specific accommodations in those area. For example, if the student is able to replicate the steps in a long division problem but has difficulty remembering the correct multiplication facts, the teacher should reward the appropriate steps and provide a calculator or multiplication chart to help the student solve the problem.

Many of the instructional practices employed for students with mathematical disabilities appear to be rather simple. For example, consider some of these suggestions from Bley and Thornton (2001):

- Use visuals and manipulatives to illustrate important ideas
- Use visual cueing by boxing problems off from others
- Assign fewer problems
- Minimize or eliminate copying from the textbook or board
- Color-code
- Modify standard text
- Tactile cues
- Capitalize on patterns
- Use auditory cueing

- Provide models for students
- Carefully sequence in small steps
- Provide adequate practice and review

Although some of these practices are rather simple, others take some time. For example, reducing the number of problems per page is easy and often leads to success for your students. Eliminating copying can substantially reduce copying errors and minimize frustration for students who copy slowly and make frequent errors. Other practices, such as modifying the textbook, take more time and effort. However, over time, you will be able to select and simplify those pages, examples, and problems that are visually confusing.

In a review of the literature on validated practices in teaching math to students with learning disabilities, Miller, Butler, and Lee (1998) identified several effective interventions. Students benefited from strategy and self-regulation instruction. The use of manipulatives and drawings was effective for both computation and word problems. The authors also found that direct instruction was effective. The use of computer-assisted instruction was promising. Based on their findings, they noted that the following instructional procedures consistently employed:

- teacher demonstration
- opportunities to model
- guided practice
- independent practice
- ongoing measurement of student progress

For example, teachers were observed in an inclusive classroom while teaching long division. They demonstrated the procedure, employing mnemonics for the divide, multiply, subtract, and bring down operations ("Diane Makes Super Brownies"), and then asked for volunteers to compute similar problems. As one teacher demonstrated, the other one observed students carrying out the operation. It appeared that they were ready to work on their own. They would continue independent practice the next day, and the teacher would monitor their progress.

DIRECT INSTRUCTION IN MATHEMATICS

Direct instruction programs are highly structured, intensive, and provide explicit instruction to students. These evidence-based programs have been proven to be successful (Adams & Carmine, 2003; Fuchs & Fuchs, 2001; Marchard-Martella, Slocum, & Martella, 2004; Swanson, 1999). Direct instruction is a comprehensive program. Students are placed in specific levels based on the results of placement tests. Two mathematics programs are *Connecting Math Concepts* and *Corrective Mathematics.* In *Connecting Math Concepts,* students are taught math skills up to pre-algebra. The program can be used on both elementary and secondary levels. *Corrective Mathematics* has seven levels from remedial third grade to adulthood. Its seven self-contained programs teach addition; subtraction; multiplication; division basic fractions; fractions, decimals, percentages; and ratios and equations (for further information, go to http://www.sra4kids.com/product_info/direct).

A BALANCED APPROACH

Teachers often find themselves in a bind. On the one hand, the National Council of Teachers of Mathematics (1989, 2000) calls for instructional techniques that are constructivist; that is, each student builds his or her own knowledge base. This has also been referred to as **implicit instruction.** The teacher provides the experience, and students create their own knowledge base. On the other hand, there are researchers who support a direct instruction approach, also called **explicit direction.** As is the case in reading, teachers are being asked to consider a balanced approach. Fleishner and Manheimer (1997) advocate this approach because no one method is appropriate for all students. They propose the following principles (p. 413):

1. Follow this sequence, regardless of the age of your students or the topic you are including:

Concrete Representation: Use manipulative materials to introduce new topics and/or operations to students. Use manipulatives far beyond the grade in which they typically are no longer used, and use them for every topic or operation. Students with learning disabilities do not develop the ability to infer from abstract examples at the same rate as students who do not have learning disabilities.

Pictorial Representation: Ask students to represent their understanding of the topics and/or operations that you are teaching by pictures or other figures. Students with learning disabilities often have difficulty translating their understanding, based on concrete representation, to iconic representational forms. Link these systems of representation. Do this by having students talk about their reasoning and explain it to others, using both concrete and pictorial examples.

Symbolic: Be sure that students understand the symbols that represent operations in mathematics, and that they can use these appropriately in the examples that they are working on.

Abstract: Check to see if students can suggest other ways of solving problems or if they can state the steps in a way that allows other students to understand what they did.

2. Use cooperative learning groups in heterogeneously grouped classes whenever they are appropriate.
3. Maintain a balance between an emphasis on achieving solutions to real-life problems and mastery of skills, such as basic facts or procedural rules. Accommodate special needs by using such cueing systems as graph paper for recording responses, color coding for highlighting procedural steps, and calculators to check the accuracy of computation.
4. Realize that students whose primary learning disability is in reading often have related problems in achievement in mathematics. Students with learning disabilities and other students from populations that traditionally have been at-risk for academic achievement will be increasingly disadvantaged if we do not attend to their need to master the mathematics curriculum. As the economy of the United States changes from the manufacturing and agricultural bases of the past,

all students must have the skills that permit them to participate in the economy of the future, which will rest on technology and the skills to use it. Math is a critical factor for these students, and we must do all that we can to help them to meet current standards for math achievement.

A PLAN FOR TEACHING COMPUTATION OR PROBLEM SOLVING

Mercer and Mercer (2005, p. 431–432) recommend the following plan for teaching computation and problem solving. This plan is appropriate for elementary, middle, and high school students with learning disabilities.

1. Assess the student's skills and develop objectives.
2. Establish goals with the students.
3. Use effective teaching steps.

These authors provide an excellent sample lesson for teaching diverse learners, which works well in an inclusive setting. The steps are as follows (p. 159):

Step 1: *Introduce the lesson*
Use a focusing activity to gain student attention. Connect the lesson to previous learning or lesson. Identify the target skill, strategy, or content. Provide a rationale for learning the skill, strategy, or content. Discuss the relevancy of the skill, strategy, or content until an authentic context is realized. Authenticity may be achieved within the context of school activities, community events, or future demands.

Step 2: *Describe and model the skill or strategy*
The teacher requests the students to attend while the teacher demonstrates the skill or strategy. To help the students understand the demonstration, the following two procedures are used:

Procedure 1: The teacher asks a question and then answers the question. The students hear and observe the teacher think aloud while modeling metacognitive strategies.

Procedure 2: The teacher asks a question and the students help provide the answer. The students participate by answering the question and solving the problem. The teacher and the students perform the strategy together, and the teacher continues to provide modeling.

Step 3: *Use scaffolding to guide practice and interactive discourse*
Procedure 1: The teacher guides students through problem solving strategies without demonstration unless it is required. Guidance is provided as needed and the following supportive techniques are used:

- The teacher asks specific leading questions and models if necessary (e.g., "What is the first step in solving a problem?").
- The teacher provides prompts regarding declarative knowledge (e.g., "Use a variable [letter] to represent the unknown in the work problem").
- The teacher provides cues regarding procedural knowledge (e.g., "Remember to isolate the variable in solving the equation").

Procedure 2: The teacher instructs students to do the task and reflect on the process and product. The teacher provides support on an as-needed basis and uses fewer prompts and cues. The students are encouraged to become more independent.

Step 4: *Conduct independent practice to mastery*
Students are encouraged to reflect (i.e., estimate, predict, check, and create) and work without teacher assistance. Activities include group projects to explore multiple ways to solve problems (e.g., using objects, pictures, drawings, and algorithms) or the creation of authentic contexts for solving problems (e.g., conducting a survey and using math to present and describe the results). A variety of practice arrangements are used, including cooperative learning, peer tutoring, instructional games, self-correcting materials, and computer-assisted instruction.

Step 5: *Provide feedback*
Procedure 1: Focus on successes. Discuss student performance or product in terms of a predetermined learning goal. Tie student efforts and thinking processes to success.

Procedure 2: Focus on error correction. View errors as opportunities for the teacher to teach and for the students to learn. Ask students to note errors and correct. If needed, guide their correction through questions, metaphors, and modeling. Also, have students work together to correct errors.

Step 6: *Teach generalization and transfer*
Reflect on applications of new knowledge across settings and situations.

Encourage students to create meaningful math word problems related to new knowledge. Have students work on more difficult problems. For example, if they have learned multiplication facts 0 to 81, have them attempt problems such as 12 × 6 using the strategies they have learned. With word problems, challenge students to solve those involving more than one operation. Have students collaborate to solve the challenging problems.

TEACHING BASIC MATH FACTS

The majority of instructional time in mathematics for students with learning disabilities is spent on basic facts and operations (Scruggs & Mastropieri, 1998). Mercer and Mercer (2005) recommendations for teaching basic math facts.

TEACHING COMPUTATION SKILLS

The components for teaching computation are as follows (Mercer & Mercer, 2005, p. 439):

1. Provide concrete experiences to promote understanding.
   Example:

   $$4 \quad + \quad 3 \quad = \frac{3}{M}$$

2. Provides semi-concrete experiences to promote understanding.
   Example:

   $$\begin{array}{ccc} //// & + & /// \\ 4 & & 3 \end{array} = \frac{3}{M}$$

3. Provide abstract activities and practice to promote mastery.
   Example:

   $$4 \quad + \quad 3 \quad = \frac{3}{M}$$

4. Teach rules that show patterns and relationships. Example: *Zero rule:* Any number plus zero equals the number.

   $$4 \quad + \quad 0 \quad =$$

   Order rule: Addends yield the same sum regardless of their order.

   $$4 + 3 = 7 \qquad 3 + 4 = 7$$

5. Teach algorithms for solving problems.
   Example:
   Fact: $7 + 2 = \frac{2}{M}$ *Algorithm:* Start BIG and count on.

6. Use mnemonics to help students remember algorithms or problem-solving procedures.
   Example: DRAW

   D—*Discover* the sign $(+, -, \times)$.
   R-*Read* the problem ("four plus three equals blank").
   A-*Answer*, or "Draw" a conceptual representation of the problem, using lines

   $$1111 \quad 111$$

   and tallies, and check $\left(4 + 3 = \frac{2}{M}\right)$.
   W-*Write* the answer ($4 + 3 = \underline{7}$).

7. Provide a variety of practice activities to promote mastery and generalization.
   Example: Provide vertical and horizontal problems.
   Use self-correcting materials, instructional games, peer tutoring, and computer-assisted instruction for seatwork.
   Provide activities to improve the rate of responses (e.g., 1-minute probes).

8. Teach problem solving.
   Example: Have students solve a variety of word problems.
   Have students create their own word problems.
   Provide students with strategies for solving problems.

TEACHING PROBLEM SOLVING

There is now increased emphasis on problem solving (NCTM, 2000). For example, New York State proficiency examinations in mathematics place considerable emphasis on story problems. This presents major problems for students with learning disabilities, given their reading and attention difficulties. Teachers must make word problems meaningful, present them orally, use concrete examples, simply the problems, and have the students explain them in their own words. Teachers should provide additional practice, use strategies (see the discussion of mnemonics later in this chapter), and give students ample time to process the information.

Students with learning disabilities need explicit strategies for solving math and word problems. Four basic categories of addition/subtraction word problems are provided by Mercer and Pullen (2005, p. 455):

Join (elements are added to a given set)
- Jan had 7 cookies. Kevin gave her 4 more. How many does Jan have altogether? (result unknown)
- Jan has 7 cookies. How many more cookies does she need to have 11 cookies altogether? (change unknown)
- Jan had some cookies. Kevin gave her 4 more cookies. Now she has 11 cookies. How many cookies did Jan have to start with? (start unknown)

Separate (elements are removed from a given set)
- Jan had 11 cookies. She gave 7 cookies to Kevin. How many cookies does she have left? (result unknown)
- Jan had 11 cookies. She gave some to Kevin. Now she has 7 cookies. How many did Jan give to Kevin? (change unknown)
- Jan had some cookies. She gave 7 to Kevin. Now she has 4 cookies left. How many cookies did Jan have to start with? (start unknown)

Part-Part-Whole (comparisons between two disjoint sets)
- Jan has 7 oatmeal cookies and 4 chocolate cookies. How many cookies does she have?
- Jan has 11 cookies. Seven are oatmeal and the rest are chocolate. How many chocolate cookies does Jan have?

Compare
- Jan has 11 cookies. Kevin has 7 cookies. How many more cookies does Jan have than Kevin?
- Kevin has 7 cookies. Jan has 4 more than Kevin. How many cookies does Jan have?
- Jan has 11 cookies. She has 7 more cookies than Kevin. How many cookies does Kevin have?

Two mnemonic devices that are helpful in solving word problems are RIDE and SIGNS:

R *Read* the problem correctly.
I *Identify* the relevant information.
D *Determine* the operations and unit for expressing the answer.
E *Enter* the correct numbers, and calculate and check the answer.
S *Survey* the question.
I *Identify* key words and labels.
G *Graphically* draw the problem.
N *Note* the operation(s) needed.
S *Solve* and check.

Montague (1997, p. 171) suggests a metacognitive strategy for mathematical problem solving. The teacher models the strategy for the student and provides guided and independent practice.

Read (for understanding)
Say: Read the problem. If I don't understand, read it again.
Ask: Have I read and understood the problem?
Check: For understanding as I solve the problem.

Paraphrase (your own words)
Say: Underline the important information. Put the problem in my own words.
Ask: Have I underlined the important information?
What is the question?
What am I looking for?
Check: The information goes with the question.

Visualize (a picture of a diagram)
Say: Make a drawing or a diagram.
Ask: Does the picture fit the problem?
Check: The picture against the problem information.

Hypothesize (plan to solve the problem)

Say: Decide how many steps and operations are needed. Write the operation Symbols (+ − × ÷).

Ask: If I do $\dfrac{3}{M}$, what will I get? If I do $\dfrac{3}{M}$, then what do I need to do next?
How many steps are needed?

Check: That the plan makes sense.

Estimate (predict the answer)

Say: Round the numbers, do the problem in my head, and write the estimate.

Ask: Did I round up and down? Did I write the estimate?

Check: That I used the important information.

Compute (do the arithmetic)

Say: Do the operations in the right order.

Ask: How does my answer compare with my estimate?
Does my answer make sense? Are the decimals or money signs in the right places?

Check: That all the operations were done in the right order.

Check (make sure everything is right)

Say: Check the computation.

Ask: Have I checked every step? Have I checked the computation?
Is my answer right?

Check: That everything is right. If not, go back. Then ask for help if I need it.

Due to the hierarchical nature of math and the rapid pace of instruction, grade level accommodations are difficult to implement. As a teachers of students with learning disabilities in an inclusive setting, you will be collaborating with teachers who are competent in the area of mathematics. Together you should consider the prerequisite skills necessary for a particular lesson. How will you teach those skills? Are they truly "prerequisite" skills? Are there accommodations that can be made? There may be times when you will need to provide additional support. Will you provide remediation at the level of student performance or accommodation at the grade level? Through collaboration with your math counterpart, you will have to decide which approach is more appropriate at the time. This may well be an ongoing discussion.

CALCULATORS

Many teachers and parents think that the solution is a calculator. However, its use is not easy for some students to master. The following guidelines provided by Mercer and Mercer (2005, p. 461) should be followed when using calculators:

- Encourage the student to press the *Clear* key twice prior to beginning each problem on the calculator.
- Point out the sequential number configuration on the calculator and the location of the initial function keys the student will use.
- Encourage the student to watch the display panel after each entry and check the results for reasonableness (Heddens & Speer, 1997).
- Stress that weak batteries or broken calculators can produce incorrect answers (Heddens & Speer, 1997).
- Encourage the student to operate the calculator with the hand not used for writing. This facilitates the ability to record the results with one hand and operate the calculator with the other hand (Heddens & Speer, 1997).

COMPUTER-AIDED INSTRUCTION

Computer-aided instruction has been demonstrated to be effective for math instruction for students with learning disabilities; however, you may be overwhelmed by the number of choices. Babbitt (1999) provides 10 tips for software selection (also see http://www.ldonline) for a review of math software).

Tip 1—The less clutter on the screen, the better.
Most students with LD are distracted by too much stimuli coming at them at the same time. Moreover, cluttered screens often distract from the math concept

or procedure being studied. Choose programs that use simple screen displays.

Tip 2—*Procedures should match those being taught in school.*

Many LD students get confused if the same task is presented in different ways, particularly in the early stages of learning. Some computation procedures used in software differ from standard classroom presentations. Weigh the other advantages of the software before introducing this conflict into math instruction. If you decide to use software with differing procedures, take the time to carefully point out the differences and be ready to assist if confusion arises.

Tip 3—*Choose Modifiable Software.*

Software in which speed, number of problems, and instructional level can be modified will serve the needs of a wide range of students in a single classroom or an individual student over a long period of time. Some students are motivated by the necessity of a speedy response while others become frustrated by the time pressure. While some students enjoy the ever-increasing speed of Math Munchers Delux (MECC), others are very relieved to play this math matching game with the speed element turned off. Having the ability to modify the response speed is very important to effective math instruction. In addition, students vary greatly in their ability to complete a number of problems before they need feedback and a break. Individuals vary in persistence, depending on the time of day and the difficulty of the problems. This variation can best be responded to by being able to adjust the number of problems in any problem set and the starting level for each student.

Tip 4—*Choose software with small increments between levels.*

Most math software designed for all students makes rather large jumps in difficulty from one level to the next. This is particularly true of retail math software that purports to cover the entire K-8 math curriculum. Students with LD will often test out of Level 1 but then fail miserably on Level 2 because the problems have gotten too difficult too fast. Special education publishers such as Edmark (http://www.edmark.com) are more aware of this difficulty and incorporate smaller difficulty increments between levels. The other solution is to choose software that allows problem selection or construction to design an intermediate level that fits a particular student.

Tip 5—*Choose software with helpful feedback.*

Math software should provide clues to the correct answer when a student makes an error. Software might indicate the range within which the answer should lie or show a diagram to indicate the underlying concept that could help the students solve the problem on their own. Software that simply indicates [that] a student is wrong is less helpful. Fraction Fireworks (Edmark) incorporates an interesting and useful feedback technique. The fireworks celebration after a correct answer illustrates the fraction chosen.

Tip 6—*Choose software that limits the number of wrong answers for a single problem.*

A sure formula for creating student frustration is to require students to repeatedly guess on a problem they don't know. It's also a sure formula for encouraging random guessing and other non-thinking behavior. The best software will limit the number of attempts, give clues as to the correct answer, provide the correct answer, and then reintroduce that same item at a later time. Test this feature on a software program by making deliberate errors.

Tip 7—*Choose software with good record keeping capabilities.*

We know that informative performance feedback can help students understand their errors and help them set realistic but challenging goals. Software should keep records for each student. Young children might be told how many items out of the total number were correct. Older students can be given percentages correct. Information should be made available on the types of problems or the exact problems that caused difficulties. Most software will include record keeping capabilities, but preview software to be sure.

Tip 8—*Choose software with built-in instructional aids.*

The ability to accurately represent word problems can increase problem solving performance. Software that incorporates built-in instructional aids such as counters, number lines, base-ten blocks, hundreds charts, or fraction trips can give the student tools to represent a given problem and then go on to solve it. These virtual manipulatives are incorporated in such programs as Equivalent Fractions by *Sunburst* (http://www.sunburst.com). A colleague and I have done some preliminary work with students using concrete manipulatives with software when built-in instructional aids were not available. Students found the aids very helpful as they solved fraction comparison problems.

Tip 9—Select software that simulates real-life solutions.

In real life there is usually more than one way to solve a problem. Money, time, and problem-solving software is more effective if it allows multiple roads to problem solution. Making Change by *Attainment Company, Inc.* (http://www.attainment-inc.com), for example, is a very helpful program because it combines decisions (where can I buy this item on my shopping list?) with multiple solution routes (students can select any combination of bills and coins to pay for items as long as they give the clerk enough money).

Tip 10—Remember, software is a learning tool— not the total solution!

Instructional software is a tool in effective math instruction and learning. With color, graphics, animation, sound and interactivity, it can capture and hold the attention of students so that they persist in mathematics tasks. Software can use these same features to present mathematics in imaginative and dynamic ways. When modifiable, it can support learning at the child's pace and on the child's level. It is important, however, to combine direct teacher instruction with technology-assisted instruction. In most instances, concept development with concrete materials and clear procedural instruction should precede software use. Pencil and paper tasks still have a role to play in student learning. Problem solving should occur with and without technology use. While well-designed math software can support student learning in a positive manner, software can rarely stand on its own. Instruction must precede software use and then extend beyond the software to apply the math concepts, procedures, and problem solving in many new settings.

MIDDLE AND HIGH SCHOOL STUDENTS

In a review of the literature on mathematics instruction for middle and high school students with learning disabilities, Maccini and Hughes (1997) found that most studies focused on lower-level math skills. To examine the problem solving of middle and high school students, Cass, Cates, and Smith (2003) utilized a multiple baseline design. Students were trained to use manipulatives to solve area and perimeter problems. Concrete manipulatives, as well as modeling, guided practice, and independent practice, were effective in teaching students problem-solving skills. This is one of the few studies that addresses geometry concepts.

Middle school students with learning disabilities were taught algebra using an explicit instruction model (Witzel, Mercer, & Miller, 2003). The model utilized a concrete-to-representational-to abstract approach. The results indicated that teachers of middle and high school students with learning disabilities must actively involve students. Presenting algebraic concepts solely on an abstract level may not be effective. When students were asked how teachers could help them with algebra, they cited additional support, caring teachers who could reduce the complexity of the task, relevant activities and materials, and the ability to work in groups (Kortering, deBettencourt, & Braziel, 2005).

If you are teaching mathematics to secondary school students with learning disabilities, it is imperative that you collaborate, since curriculum demands for high-stakes assessments are greater than in the elementary years. The mathematics teacher's lack of knowledge regarding learning disabilities and your limited knowledge of secondary mathematics necessitate consultation and collaboration (Magiera, Smith, Zigmond, & Gerbauer, 2005). Unfortunately, Magiera et al. observed only limited collaboration in their study. (See Chapter 7 for additional information on collaboration).

MATH ANXIETY

Mercer and Pullen (2005) note that "many students with learning disabilities have a history of math failure" (p. 521). This can lead to negative attitudes and anxiety about mathematics. Teachers must promote a positive attitude. Mercer and Pullen (2005, p. 521) provide the following guidelines:

1. Involve students in setting challenging but attainable instruction goals. Goal setting has a powerful influence on student involvement and effort (Locke & Latham, 1990).
2. Provide students with success by building on prior skills and using task analysis to simplify the instructional sequence of a math skill or concept. Use charts to give students feedback on how well they are doing.
3. Discuss the relevance of a math skill to real-life problems. Use word problems that are part of a student's daily life.
4. Communicate positive expectancies of students' abilities to learn. Students need to sense that the teacher believes they will achieve in math.
5. Help students understand the premise that their own effort affects outcomes regarding achievement. Constantly point out that what they do influences both success and failure. The premise helps students realize that their behavior directly influences what happens to them. In turn, they realize that they are in control of their own learning.
6. Model an enthusiastic and positive attitude toward math and maintain a lively pace during math instruction.
7. Reinforce students for effort on math work and stress that errors are learning opportunities.

SUMMARY

Mathematics is an area of relative neglect in the field of learning disabilities. Although many students experience difficulty in math, there is much less emphasis on math instruction than on literacy. Geary (2003, p. 210) states:

In comparison to simple arithmetic, relatively little research has been conducted on the ability of children with MD [mathematics disabilities] to solve more complex arithmetic problems (but see Russell

& Ginsburg, 1984), and even less has been conducted in other mathematical domains. Even in the area of simple arithmetic, the cognitive and neural mechanisms that contribute to the problem-solving characteristics of children with MD are not fully understood and are thus in need of further study. Other areas that are in need of attention include the development of diagnostic instruments for MD; cognitive and behavioral genetic research on the comorbidity of MD and other forms of MD and ADHD; and, of course, the development of remedial techniques. If progress over the last 10 years is any indication, we should see significant advances in many of these areas over the next 10 years.

This chapter has provided information on the characteristics of students with learning disabilities in mathematics. Formal and informal assessment procedures were discussed, and interventions for students with several math disorders were provided. The chapter concluded with sections on math anxiety and the selection of computer software.

SPRINGBOARDS FOR REFLECTION AND DISCUSSION

1. Why do you think there is so much emphasis on literacy and so little emphasis on mathematics for students with learning disabilities?
2. Observe elementary and secondary level resource rooms. How much instruction time is allocated to mathematics? How much to reading?
3. Interview teachers of students with learning disabilities. How important do they think it is to teach math to these students?
4. Interview the director of assessment in a local school district. What mathematical assessment tools does he or she employ?
5. Observe a high school math class that utilizes co-teaching. How do the teachers divide the responsibility? How do they plan? How

comfortable does the special educator feel in the area of mathematics?

6. Review a popular math series used in a local public school. How well does it meet the needs of students with learning disabilities in mathematics?

7. What are some ways that calculators can be used by students with learning disabilities in mathematics?

8. How can computer software be employed with students with learning disabilities in mathematics?

CHAPTER 16

SOCIAL-EMOTIONAL AND BEHAVIORAL ASPECTS OF LEARNING DISABILITIES

CHAPTER OBJECTIVES

At the end of this chapter you will:

- understand the importance of the social side of learning disabilities.
- be able to assess social aspects of learning disabilities.
- be able to work collaboratively with mental health professionals.
- be able to collaborate on the development and implementation of a functional behavioral assessment and a behavior intervention plan.
- be able to implement a variety of interventions to address the social aspects of learning disabilities in your classroom.

Josh had a lot going for him. He was a physically attractive high school student and a good athlete, had a supportive family, and lived in an excellent school district. The only thing he was missing was a social life. Josh was diagnosed with a learning disability in second grade in the early 1970s. With a lot of hard work, extra help, tutoring, and other aids, he was performing well in school. He attended the resource room, went for extra help before school, and was able to maintain a B average. His parents were very satisfied with his school performance. What puzzled them was his lack of friends, his loneliness, never being asked to play at someone's house when he was younger, and, as an adolescent, being excluded from after-school and weekend activities that engaged other teenagers. When they shared their concern with the resource room teacher, they were disappointed with his response. Essentially, he told them that his major concern was academics, not social issues, and that Josh was one of his best students. He admitted knowing very little about these problems and did not know what

to do about them. He recommended that they try to find a therapist who could help Josh.

Much has changed since the 1970s about the way we view the social side of learning disabilities. A seminal article by Bryan (1974) called attention to the fact that there is more to learning disabilities than academic performance. If Josh's parents expressed those same concerns today, they would find a completely different response. The literature on the social and emotional aspects of learning disabilities has greatly increased. And while there is a debate regarding causality and interventions, it is clearly not an area of neglect.

What would you do if you had a student similar to Josh? How would you respond to his parents? How will you address the social and emotional needs of your students with learning disabilities? This chapter provides answers to these questions by discussing the social and behavioral characteristics of students with learning disabilities, ways to assess social and emotional behaviors, and interventions to ensure that all the needs of your students will be met.

CHARACTERISTICS OF SOCIAL-EMOTIONAL AND BEHAVIORAL COMPONENTS OF LEARNING DISORDERS

The current federal government definition of learning disabilities (see Chapter 2) does not mention

their social-emotional or behavioral components. However, there are two other definitions that address this concern. The Learning Disabilities Association of America (LDA), previously known as the Association for Children with Learning Disabilities (ACLD), defines learning disabilities as

a chronic condition of presumed neurological origin, which selectively interferes with development, integration, and/or demonstration of verbal and/or nonverbal activities. Specific learning disabilities exist as ... distinct handicapping condition[s] and [vary] in [their] manifestations and in degree of severity. Throughout life, the condition can affect self-esteem education, vocational, *socialization* [emphasis added], and/or daily living activities. (ACLD, 1985, p.1)

The Interagency Committee on Learning Disabilities (ICLD) proposed the following definition to Congress (1987, p. 222):

Learning disabilities is a generic term that refers to a heterogeneous group of disorders manifested by significant difficulties in the acquisition and use of listening, speaking, reading, writing, reasoning, or mathematical ability, or of social skills. These disorders are intrinsic to the individual and presumed to be due to central nervous system dysfunction. Even though a learning disability may occur concomitantly with other handicapping conditions (e.g., sensory impairment, mental retardation, social and emotional disturbance), the socio-environmental influences (e.g., cultural differences, insufficient or inappropriate instruction, psychogenic factors), and especially attention deficit disorders, all of which may cause learning problems, a learning disability is not the direct result of those condition or influences.

Elksnin and Elksnin (2004) note that the National Joint Committee on Learning Disabilities (NJCLD, 2001) acknowledges social-emotional deficits but does not believe they constitute a learning disability on their own. The NJCLD's definition of learning disabilities (2001, p. 31) is as follows:

Learning disabilities is a general term that refers to a heterogeneous group of disorders that is manifested by significant difficulties in the acquisition and use of listening, speaking, reading, writing, reasoning, or mathematical abilities. These disorders are intrinsic to the individual, presumed to be due to central nervous system dysfunction, and may occur across the life span. Problems in self-regulatory behaviors, social perception, and social interaction may exist with learning disabilities but do not by themselves constitute a learning disability. Although learning disabilities may occur concomitantly with other handicapping conditions (for example, sensory impairment, mental retardation, serious emotional disturbance), or with extrinsic

influences (such as cultural differences, insufficient or inappropriate instruction), they are not the result of those conditions or influences.

The lack of recognition of social-emotional factors in the federal government's definition of learning disabilities is in stark contrast to the perceptions of parents and school personnel regarding the characteristics of students with learning disabilities. It is also out of sync with the large body of research over the last 30 years that has documented the social-emotional and, to a lesser degree, behavioral components of learning disabilities. Bryan, Burstein, and Ergul (2004) note that the social problems of students with learning disabilities have been well documented. They exist across age, race, and ethnicity, settings, roles, methods, measures, and countries. These authors divide the social-emotional components of a learning disability into six categories:

1. Self-concept
2. Affect (emotions)
3. Social information processing
4. Social cognition
5. Communication competence and social behavior

Each will be discussed below.

Self-Concept

Intuitively, you may assume that all students with learning disabilities have poor self-concepts as a side effect of poor school performance. According to Bryan et al. (2004), this is the most widely researched topic in the field of learning disabilities. These students do rate themselves lower on academic achievement (what some refer to as - **academic self-concept**) but they are inconsistent when it comes to their social status. Some of your students may not be able to assess their social status accurately for many reasons.

Affect (Emotions)

There is very little in the professional literature on the impact of affect (emotions) on social relations and learning in persons with learning disabilities. Mercer and Pullen (2005) discuss concerns related to isolation, depression, loneliness, and suicide, but at present very little data are available (see the following section). Clearly, teachers of students with learning disabilities need to be alert for signs that a child is lonely, depressed, or suicidal; the most effective way to approach this issue is in a collaborative manner. They should speak with mental health professionals in their school (psychologists, social workers, school counselors), become competent in identifying students who have difficulty, and know when to refer them to an appropriate professional. Collaboration is critical because these problems are beyond the training of most classroom teachers, and they must know when to get help.

Best Practices: Collaborating on Social-Emotional Concerns. In the area of social-emotional issues related to learning disabilities, collaboration is critical. There is a danger that the teacher will try to solve the problem alone, not knowing when to involve the school psychologist, counselor, and/or social worker. Particularly in suicidal ideation and depression, it is critical to alert trained professionals. Conversely, the classroom teacher may not think that social-emotional issues are his concern. He may believe that his job is to focus on academic intervention and leave the social-emotional issues to the school's mental health professionals. The instructional support team (IST) described in Chapter 5 is a good mechanism for considering how these issues will be handled. They can be addressed at the first meeting, allowing professionals working together to make sound decisions. The IST will also be able to decide if the situation warrants immediate attention, as in depression or suicidal ideation, and get help fast. Collaboration is also necessary to implement and develop the Functional Behavioral Assessment (FBA) and the Behavior Intervention Plan (BIP). This involves not only the expertise of a variety of school personnel, but also input from the student's family.

Social Information Processing

Bryan et al. (2004) discuss two types of normal information processing:

1. Social perception
2. Nonverbal perception

The former is the ability to understand expressions, physical space, and language. Students with learning disabilities often misinterpret social cues.

Nonverbal Perception. Nonverbal perception is typically measured by labeling photographs, student films, and everyday emotions (happy, sad, angry, etc.). Kavale and Forness (1996) and Swanson and Malone (1992) report that students with learning disabilities consistently perform worse then their counterparts without disabilities. These students are aware of their problems in this area. The term **nonverbal learning disabilities** has also been used to describe some of these students (Rourke, 1989, 1995). In addition to a host of difficulties (graphomotor, reading, comprehension, mathematical reasoning, and certain tasks in science), these students have severe social/behavioral problems (Torgesen, 2002).

Social Cognition

Typically, students with learning disabilities perform worse than their peers without disabilities in generating solutions to social problems. Weiner (2004) notes that they have difficulty interpreting nonverbal information, such as facial expressions, body language, and physical proximity.

Communicative Competence

Bryan et al. (2004) cite a study by Lapadat (1991) that examined practical skills. The findings indicated that students with learning disabilities have consistent difficulty. Citing the research of Donahue and Bryan (1984), Henry and Reed (1995), and Nippold (1993), they note that students with learning disabilities display problems in "topic selection," initiation, and maintenance, conversational turn taking, requesting and producing clarification, narrative production, presenting logical opinions and different points of view, gaze and eye contact, being tactful when formulating and delivering messages, and comprehension of humor and slang (p. 47).

Social Behavior

A number of studies reported by Bryan et al. (2004, pp. 47–48) cite negative or inappropriate behaviors of students with learning disabilities. These include:

- Lack of skills in initiating and sustaining positive social relationships (Gresham, 1997; Heiman & Margalit, 1998).
- Acting more aggressively and exhibiting more negative verbal and nonverbal behaviors (McConaughy, Mattison, & Peterson, 1994; Sigafoos, 1995).
- Some are shy and withdrawn, while others are disruptive (Clare & Leach, 1991; McIntosh, Vaughn, & Zaragoza, 1991).
- More disruptive, less cooperative, insensitive and less tactful (Pearl, Donahue, & Bryan, 1985).
- Attention–seeking behavior (Perlmuter, 1983).

Weiner (2004) examined peer relations among students with learning disabilities and supported the conclusion of Bryan and her colleagues. Students with learning disabilities were less likely to be socially accepted. Although they had the same number of friends as their peers, their friends tended to be younger and they were more likely to be lonely (although there is little evidence on loneliness). Another area addressed by Weiner was bullying. Students with learning disabilities and those with ADHD are more likely to be victimized (McNamara & McNamara, 2000; Mishna, 2003; Olweus, 2003). While there is little research on the relationship between bullying and learning disabilities, the limited number of studies suggests that these students are likely victims (Mishna, 2003).

Bullies want to dominate and control others. They attempt to do this in a number of ways. They may use aggressive behaviors ranging from verbal taunts, name calling, and spreading vicious rumors among their classmates to threatening other children and sometimes carrying out their threats. Bullies often engage in physical aggression, and may steal money and other valuables from their victims. Bullying is characterized by the persistence of these pernicious attacks; they are frequent and ongoing (McNamara & McNamara, 2000).

There are two types of victims: passive and provocative. The passive victim is physically weak and does not fight back. The provocative victim is more restless and irritable, frequently teasing and picking on others. Many students with learning disabilities and/or ADHD fall into the latter category. This type of victim appears to have poor impulse control; he or she acts out and then becomes a victim.

Victims tend to be physically weaker than bullies. They are also anxious and insecure children who usually have poor social skills, which sets them apart from other youngsters in their class, play group, or camp. Most victims have a difficult time making friends and sustaining friendships.

School personnel need to be aware of the following signs of victimization in schools (McNamara & McNamara, 1997, pp. 18–19):

- Being (repeatedly) teased, called names, taunted, belittled, ridiculed, intimidated, degraded, threatened, given orders, dominated, subdued.
- Being made fun of and laughed at in a derisive and unfriendly way.
- Getting picked on, pushed around, shoved, punched, hit, kicked (and not being able to defend themselves adequately).
- Becoming involved in "quarrels" or "fights" in which they are fairly defenseless and from which they try to withdraw (maybe crying).
- Having their books, money, or other belongings taken, damaged, or thrown around.
- Having bruises, injuries, cuts, scratches, or torn clothing that can't be explained.
- Often being alone and excluded from the peer group during breaks and lunchtime, not seeming to have a single good friend in the class.
- Being among the last chosen in the team games.

- Trying to stay close to the teacher or other adults during breaks.
- Having difficulty speaking up in class.
- Appearing distressed, unhappy, depressed, and tearful.
- Showing sudden or gradual deterioration of schoolwork.

The increase in school violence and the heightened awareness of bullying in our schools have led many schools to adopt antibullying programs. These range from isolated, one-time assembly-type events to more thorough schoolwide programs (see the next section). According to Mishna (2003, p. 344), "it is necessary to evaluate current antibullying interventions to determine their effectiveness for students with learning disabilities."

Best Practices: Developing and Implementing Schoolwide Programs to Combat Bullying. The most effective antibullying program is a schoolwide program developed through collaboration of the school and the community (McNamara & McNamara, 1997). The goals of such a program are two:

1. To reduce, if not eliminate, the bully/victim problem in and out of school
2. To prevent future bullying

Victims need to feel safe in school, and bullies need to learn how to assert themselves in more socially acceptable ways.

All school personnel and community members need to become aware of the serious nature of bullying. One way to do this is to give students a questionnaire. Once schools have developed an awareness of the problem, they can then address it. Without such awareness, they will resort to ineffective, outdated interventions that have little, if any, chance of success.

Most schoolwide programs have three major components:

1. Clear-cut rules
2. Reinforcement for students who obey the rules
3. Consequences for not following the rules

These components must be supported by the entire school, as well as by community members.

The first step in implementing an antibullying program is to provide training for the school staff. As previously noted, many parents and teachers do not recognize the severity of the problem. Children who are bullied frequently report that they cannot depend on adults in authority positions to do anything about the problem. Therefore, the first step is to create awareness. Typically, bullying is much more pervasive than most teachers think. Once they recognize the nature of the problem, they are ready to learn how to deal with it.

Training should provide appropriate role models, intervention strategies, and support for victims. Additionally, staff members can use literature or videos as supplements. Many books provide excellent examples of dealing with bullies, empathizing with victims, and instituting preventive strategies; there are videos that do the same.

What can teachers do to reduce bullying in their classrooms? Although a schoolwide approach is necessary to change the school environment, the individual teacher is critical for the success of any program. Just as parents model appropriate behavior at home, teachers do so in class. Classrooms where teachers provide a warm, supportive environment and clear, consistent rules regarding bullying send a strong message to their students. Teachers must be aware of the characteristics of bullies and their victims, and know when and where to get help at school and in the community.

If a child is a loner, which many victims are, a classroom teacher can find something the child does well and have him or her work with other, less competent students. This child could be placed with some cooperative, empathetic students who will work together and include him or her in the group. Groups can receive reinforcement for cooperative behaviors and point out how well the victim performed. The teacher can try to make the child attractive to be with either by demonstrating his or her competence or by reinforcement of the child's group. Over time, there is a higher probability that these students will involve the child in their group.

Victims of bullying are not good athletes, so they are usually the last ones selected by teams. There is absolutely no reason why this should happen in a school. In this controlled environment, teachers should not allow students to select their partners, groups, or teams because, invariably, children who are passive victims will not be selected. Some children are never selected as laboratory partners, and when the teacher chooses a partner, the partner moans in disgust. Random selection of partners or placing a victim with a popular child can eliminate this humiliating experience. Finally clear, consistent consequences for the negative behaviors of other students must be provided.

There are children who eat lunch every day alone and then go to the playground for recess by themselves. Teachers can provide some supervision in the lunchroom, assign seats, and/or reinforce children who eat together in a cooperative manner. They can also find caring youngsters who will include the isolated child in their group. Attention must be paid to those situations that allow the inappropriate isolation of victimized students.

Whether the social-emotional and behavioral aspects of a learning disability are due solely to the disability itself or result from the disability is not clear (Weiner, 2004). What is clear is that teachers need to address these concerns in the classroom.

The social problems of students with learning disabilities exist in all settings (Bryan et al., 2004). Therefore, whether working in a self-contained classroom, a resource room, or an inclusive classroom, the teacher must be aware of the issues and characteristics discussed above. The following section addresses the assessment of social-emotional and behavioral aspects of learning disabilities.

ASSESSMENT

Mercer and Pullen (2005) note that "several instruments and procedures are required to assess social and emotional behavior. Helpful information may be obtained from teachers, parents, students and peers, as well as records of social development and educational history" (p. 555). To do this, classroom teachers need to work collaboratively with school psychologists, social workers, school counselors, and mental health professionals in the community, using both formal and informal measures.

FORMAL ASSESSMENT

Table 16-1 deals with standardized measures to assess the social-emotional and behavioral concerns of students with learning disabilities (Cohen & Spenciner, 2003, pp. 421–424). Typically, the school psychologist or social worker will provide information on completing these instruments (e.g., Conner's Rating Scales). Other instruments, such as the Child Behavior Checklists, may be administered by a school psychologist with input from the teachers.

INFORMAL ASSESSMENT

A number of informal measures, such as self-report instruments and sociometric techniques, have been suggested by Mercer and Pullen (2005) as part of the assessment process. McNamara (1998) suggests direct measurement of student behavior.

A behavioral approach demands precision from identification of the behavior to evaluation of the effectiveness of the intervention plan. Therefore, the teacher must define exactly what behaviors are to be increased or decreased—for example, to increase in-seat behavior, to decrease the number of times Joseph talks out, to increase the raising of hands to ask a question, or to decrease the number of times John hits Louis. All of these behaviors can be observed and measured: we can count the frequency or duration of each. Most, if not all, classroom behaviors can be stated in observable and measurable terms.

TABLE 16-1 Assessment of Social-Emotional and Behavioral Problems

Assessment Concern	Name of Instrument	Grade or Age Range	Technical Characteristics	Comments
Attention Hyperactivity Social Skills Behavior	ADD-H: Comprehensive Teacher's Rating Scale (ACTeRS), Second Edition (Ullmann, Sleator, & Sprague, 1991)	K–8	Internal consistency adequate; test-retest reliability ranges from .78–.82	Scores are converted to percentiles and can be plotted on a summary profile sheet.
Hyperactivity Impulsivity	Attention-Deficit/Hyperactivity Disorder Test (Gilliam, 1995)	3 yrs–23 yrs	High internal consistency and test-retest reliability; evidence of content, construct, and criterion-related validity; concurrent validity established with the Conners' Rating Scales and ADD-H Comprehensive Teacher's Rating Scale	Based on the diagnostic criteria of DSM-IV. Can be completed by teachers and parents.
Withdrawn, anxious and Depressed Somatic Complaints Delinquent Behavior Aggressive Behavior Social Problems Attention and Hyperactivity	Child Behavior Checklists (CBCL/1 1½–5 (Achenbach & Resorla, 2000); (CBCL/6–18) Achenbach, 2001); (YABCL/18-30) (Achenbach, 1977) and Caregiver-Teacher Report Form for Ages 1½–5 (Achenbach, 2000); Teacher Report Form for Ages 6–18 (Achenbach 2001b)	1 yr 6 months through 30 yrs	Interrater, test-retest, and internal consistency are adequate. Construct validity and criterion-related validity are adequate	Use direct observation
Attention Hyperactivity	Conner's Rating Scales-Revised (Conners, 1997)	3 yrs to 17 yrs (Parent) and Grades 4–12 (Teacher)	Internal and test-retest reliability adequate; construct validity adequate; continued research on predictive validity needed	Conner's Rating Scales-Revised included parent, teacher, and adolescent self-report and ADHD/DSM-IV Scales
Problem Behavior Social Skills	Social Skills Rating System (Gresham & Elliott, 1990)	Pre-K through 12th grade	Good technical characteristics	Separate questionnaires for preschool, elementary, and secondary level students. Separate forms designed for teachers and parents; self-report form for students

Following is a list of typical problem student behaviors. Column A presents the problems in behavioral terms, and Column B defines the target behaviors.

Column A	Column B
Student never pays attention	Increase the percentage of time the student spends on task (eye contact with the teacher, looking at textbook, writing when appropriate)
Student is very hostile	Deceases the number of times the student hits another student
Student has no friends in class	Increase the number of positive comments made to the student by fellow classmates; increase time spent with other students
Student has a poor self-concept	Increase the number of positive self-statements; decrease negative comments regarding work or self.
Student is always interrupting	Increase the number of times the student waits his or her turn to speak
Student wanders around the room	Increase in-seat behavior
Student is never on time	Increase on-time behavior during a specific period
Student does not respect others' property	Decrease the number of times the student defaces another student's work
Student appears to have a great deal on his or her mind	Decrease off-task behavior (looking out the window, lack of eye contact, not following directions)
Student is very aggressive	Decrease the number of times the student pushes another student

As this list shows, refinement of the description of behavior allows teachers to focus on a specific behavior, communicate more effectively with colleagues, administrators, and parents, and begin to collect data on the frequency and duration of students' behaviors. Accurate recording keeping is vital for a behavioral approach to classroom management. Often teachers believe that the paperwork associated with this approach is overwhelming. They should seek help from the school psychologist or IST for help in implementing these procedures.

Many recording methods are available to teachers, but these three appear to be most applicable:

1. Event recording
2. Duration recording
3. Time sample recording

Event Recording

Event recording involves collecting data on raw frequencies of behavior. It is used for discrete events that typically last for less than 2 minutes, Such as the number of times a child is out of his or her seat, comes late to class, talks out, or hits classmates.

The teacher must be able to collect the data in a manner that does not interfere with his or her ability to move about the room and teach. The author has found a wrist golf counter the best device for this purpose. It allows the teacher to move, and is readily available and inconspicuous. Other ways in which events can be recorded are by marking a piece of adhesive tape adhered to the wrist, moving small objects (paper, tokens, toothpicks, etc.) from one pocket to another, or using a small tally sheet or index card. Usually a 30-minute observation period is adequate. Below is a record of the number of times a student called out during instruction time.

Date	Time	Number of Events
5/20	9:30–10:00	20
5/29	10:00–10:30	15
6/2	11:30–1:20	18

Duration Recording

When behaviors occur for a long period of time, duration recording is the most appropriate procedure. Certain behaviors, such as temper tantrums, leaving the classroom, talking, and time off the task, may not occur frequently but may occur for a relatively long period of time. When a behavior occurs for more than 2 or 3 minutes, collecting data on the time elapsed may be a more meaningful recording procedure. Below is a record of the amount of time a student was off the task during reading instruction.

Date	Time	Total Duration
11/1	9:00–9:05	15 min
	9:30–9:40	
11/5	9:00–9:10	25 min
	9:20–9:30	
	9:35–9:40	
11/15	9:10–9:12	12 min
	9:17–9:22	
	9:30–9:35	

Although a stopwatch is the most accurate way to collect these data, the minute hand on a wall clock or wristwatch can be used as long as the recorder keeps accurate records of the time elapsed.

Time Sample Recording

The observation period is divided into equal intervals. If a student emits the target behavior at the end of the interval, it is recorded as a plus; if not, it is recorded as a minus. In Figure 16–1, a 30-minute period is divided into ten 3-minute intervals in order to record the percentage of time a student is in his seat. Using a stopwatch, wall clock, or wristwatch, the teacher observes the student during each 3-minute segment. At the 6-minute interval, the student was out of his seat; therefore, a minus was recorded. This process continues until the 30-minute segment ends. The percentage of time the student spent in the seat is obtained by dividing the number of intervals into the number of intervals of in-seat behavior and converting this figure to a percentage. In this case, the student was in his seat 50% of the time.

Although a 30-minute interval is used most often, longer observation intervals may be necessary for specific behaviors.

Charting Baseline Data

All behavioral data can be displayed in a similar fashion on a graph. The ordinate (vertical axis) is labeled with a scale representing the behaviors emitted in terms of frequency or percentage, and the abscissa (horizontal axis) is labeled with the time dimensions, such as minutes, days, or observations (Alberto & Troutman, 1995). Collect and display data in such a way that you will be able to evaluate the effectiveness of the intervention plan. Typically, baseline data are collected for at least 1 week; then an intervention plan is implemented. A more detailed explanation of each of these stages follows.

Educational decisions should be based on factual information, not intuition or feelings. The first step in this process is to establish the **baseline,** which can be defined as the operant level of behavior—that is, the level of behavior prior to intervention. Therefore, during the first 5 days of data collection, the student must be unaware of the procedure so that an accurate reading can be obtained. Typically, the baseline will last for 5 days, but you must examine the data prior to moving on to the next stage. In baseline A (see Figure 16–2), a desirable behavior such as remaining in the seat is increasing; therefore, you can simply continue recording baseline data. In baseline B, an undesirable behavior, such as yelling out, is decreasing by itself; therefore, you should not implement an intervention but instead continue to observe the behavior and record baseline data. A stable baseline is illustrated in baseline C. It is going up and down but within reasonable parameters; therefore, it is appropriate to intervene.

Functional Behavioral Assessment (FBA)

FBA is "a collection of methods of gathering information and antecedents, behaviors and consequences in order to determine the reason (function) of behavior" (Gresham, Watson, & Skinner, 2001,

+	–	+	–	+	–	+	–	+	–
3	6	0	12	15	18	21	24	27	30

FIGURE 16–1   In-Seat Behavior (30-minute intervals)

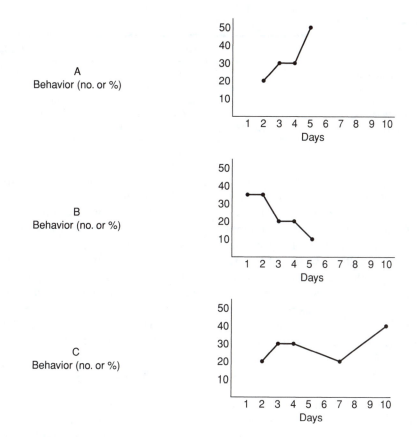

A
Behavior (no. or %)

B
Behavior (no. or %)

C
Behavior (no. or %)

FIGURE 16–2   Three Types of Baselines

p. 158). Many teachers and administrators think of FBAs as suited only for students with behavior disorders or emotional disturbances, yet the IDEA 1997 amendments state that students should be given behavioral support if their behavior impacts on their learning or that of their classmates. This must be included on their IEP. It is also provided in IDEA 2004. The FBA is a reasonable way to address these concerns. Whether it should or must be used is open to legal interpretation, but, schools are wise to conduct an FBA in these cases. A student with a disability who is suspended for more than 10 days must have an FBA and a Behavior Intervention Plan (BIP). The BIP will be discussed later in this chapter. (Teachers may think that a student with a learning disability will not display significant behavioral problems, but

for a number of reasons this is not the case; see the next section.)

An FBA requires the following:

- Identifying target behavior(s)
- Collecting data
- Identifying events that happened before and after the behaviors(s) (see Table 16-2)
- Formulating a hypothesis about the function(s) of the behavior(s)

Implications for Teachers: Learning Disability or Emotional Disturbance (Behavior Disorder).   Many teachers of students with learning disabilities assume that if the primary concern is behavioral, then the classification should be

TABLE 16–2 ABC Chart

	A (Antecedent)	B (Behavior)	C (Consequence)
1.	Reading instruction	Calls out	Verbal reprimand
2.	Written assignment	Does not complete task	Staying during recess
3.	During instruction	Inattentive	Verbal reprimand
4.	Math instruction	Bothering classmates	Move seat
5.	Traveling from classroom to resource room	Late to resource room	Give warning

emotional disturbance or behavior disorder. They may anticipate a social-emotional-behavioral overlay due to the presence of a learning disability but not significant behavioral problems. These assumptions and expectations may lead to a lack of appropriate behavioral intervention and/or transfer of this responsibility to the psychologist, counselor, or social worker. All teachers of students with learning disabilities should be well versed in classroom and behavior management principles and techniques because there is a high probability that they will encounter behavior problems.

Why aren't these students classified as having an emotional disturbance or behavior disorder? One reason may be the disproportionately large number of students classified as having learning disabilities. Clearly, a number of these students are being referred for behavioral reasons but are being classified as having learning disabilities. Parents may be reluctant to accept the classification of emotional disturbance (behavior disorder), and the learning disability classification is more palatable. Alternatively, the school district may not have done an adequate job of documenting the behavior problem. Whatever the reason, the teacher should not be surprised if behavioral issues overshadow academic ones. This may be especially true as the student progresses through school with limited academic success.

Developing a Behavior Intervention Plan (BIP)

Much of the information concerning direct measurement of student behavior is applicable to the FBA. Shippen, Simpson, and Crites (2003, pp.

43-44) provide a useful guide to its development (see Figure 16-3).

Once the data are collected and analyzed, a hypothesis is developed to attempt to explain the functions of the behavior(s). Is the student avoiding tasks because he or she cannot perform them adequately? Is the student calling out to get the teacher's attention? Once the function is determined, the BIP can be developed.

It is virtually impossible to do this alone; it must be a collaborative effort. Scott, Liaupsin, Nelson, and Jolivette (2003, p. 17) provide guidelines for team-based FBA tasks (see Table 16-3).

An important component of the FBA is **manifest determination:** is the behavior related to (or caused by) the disability? In the case of students with learning disabilities and ADHD, is the inability to control impulses that leads to inappropriate behavior due to the disability? Is the student able to control the behavior and follow school rules? This has been a topic of concern in the popular press, and teachers frequently comment that students get away with too much by blaming it on their disability. This was a contentious issue in the 1977 and 2004 reauthorizations of IDEA

Manifest determination continues to be part of IDEA 2004, with additional provisions related to suspension and educational services. If there are unique circumstances, a change in placement may be considered on a case-by-case basis if the student violates the school's conduct code. IDEA 2004 shifts the burden of proof from the school to the parents.

Student who are removed from the current placement must receive educational services that enable them to continue to participate in the

Student Name: _____ School: _____ Meeting Date: _____

Submitting Teacher _____ Beginning Date: _____ Review/End Date: _____

Functional Behavioral Assessment Worksheet
(Sequence Analysis)

Antecedent	Behavior Concern	Consequence

Committee Determined Target Behaviors

1. _____
   _____

2. _____
   _____

3. _____
   _____

The following persons attended and participated in the FBA meeting:

Name:	Position	Date
_____	Parent	____
_____	LCA Representative	____
_____	Special Education Teacher	____
_____	Student	____
_____	General Education Teacher	____
_____	_____	____

Method for Reporting Progress to Parent: Frequency for Reporting Progress to Parent:

☐ progress report
☐ parent conference   _____
☐ other   _____

II. Functional Behavioral Assessment   _____

Target Behavior 1. _____

Baseline Assessment Method: *Baseline Frequency of Target Behavior:*

Parent interview   _____
Teacher interview   _____
Checklists   _____
Systematic observation   _____
Frequency counts of target behaviors   _____
Sequence analysis (required)   _____
Norm-referenced assessments   _____

(*continued*)

FIGURE 16–3   Functional Behavioral Assessment Guide

Target Behavior II. _____

Baseline Assessment Method: *Baseline Frequency of Target Behavior:*
   Parent interview   _____
   Teacher interview   _____
   Checklists   _____
   Systematic observation   _____
   Frequency counts of target behaviors   _____
   Sequence analysis (required)   _____
   Norm-referenced assessments   _____

Target Behavior III. _____

Baseline Assessment Method: *Baseline Frequency of Target Behavior:*
   Parent interview   _____
   Teacher interview   _____
   Checklists   _____
   Systematic observation   _____
   Frequency counts of target behaviors   _____
   Sequence analysis (required)   _____
   Norm-referenced assessments   _____

Purpose of Target Behavior 1:

1. To obtain something?   yes   no   what? _____
2. To escape/avoid something? yes   no   what? _____
3. Other factors?   yes   no   what? _____
Hypothesis: _____
Replacement Behavioral Goal: _____
Necessary Skills?   yes   no, needs additional instruction in _____

Purpose of Target Behavior II:

1. To obtain something?   yes   no   what? _____
2. To escape/avoid something? yes   no   what? _____
3. Other factors?   yes   no   what? _____
Hypothesis: _____
Replacement Behavioral Goal: _____
Necessary Skills?   yes   no, needs additional instruction in _____

Purpose of Target Behavior III:

1. To obtain something?   yes   no   what? _____
2. To escape/avoid something? yes   no   what? _____
3. Other factors?   yes   no   what? _____
Hypothesis: _____
Replacement Behavioral Goal: _____
Necessary Skills?   yes   no, needs additional instruction in _____

FIGURE 16–3 (*continued*)

Source: From "A Practical Guide to FBA" by M. E., Shippen, R. G. Simpson, and S. A. Crites. Teaching Exceptional Children, 35, 2003, 36–44. Copyright © 2003. Published by The Council for Exceptional Children. Reprinted with permission of the publisher.

TABLE 16–3 Guidelines for Team-Based Functional Behavior Assessment

Tasks	Considerations
Develop a Team	• Represent persons who have interactions with student • Invite parents • Involve student as appropriate • At least one person on team is familiar with FBA
Define Problem Behavior	• All team members collaborate to define the problem • Create observable and measurable definition • Define the conditions under with behavior occurs
Share Data and Observations	• Summarize existing date (referrals, reports, etc.) • Team members discuss their interactions with student • Discuss appropriate and inappropriate behaviors
Analyze Patterns	• Consider how the environment predicts behavior • Identify predictable antecedents and consequences • Analyze both appropriate and inappropriate behavior
Hypothesize Function	• Create a testable statement of behavior's function • Define when the behavior is likely to occur • Define how consequences maintain the behavior

Source: From "Ensuring Student Success Through Team-Based FBA" by J. M. Scott, C. J. Liaupin, C. M. Nelson, and K. Jolinette. *Teaching Exceptional Children,* 35, 2003, 16–21. Copyright © 2003. Published by The Council for Exceptional Children. Reprinted with permission of the publisher.

general education curriculum and progress toward meeting their IEP goals. They must also receive an FBA and a BIP that address their behavioral problems.

INTERVENTIONS

Behavior Intervention Plan

Once the teacher has assessed the functions of the behavior(s), a BIP must be developed, including specific measurable goals. Salend (2001, p. 236) poses the following questions that can guide the teacher in developing a BIP:

1. What antecedents and consequences can I change to increase/decrease the behavior?
2. What strategies, curricular adaptation, and physical design modification can I use to increase/decrease the behavior?
3. Which of these changes are most likely to be effective, acceptable, easy to use, culturally sensitive, least intrusive and beneficial to others and the learning environment?

The BIP, like the FBA, must be developed in a collaborative manner. Scott et al. (2003, p. 19) provide tasks and considerations for the team (see Table 16-4).

Social Skills Training

In the past, social skill training appeared to be the most widely used intervention for the social-emotional and behavior problems of students with learning disabilities p. 41. Kavale and Forness's (1995) meta-analysis of its efficacy was not encouraging. The "training did not appear to influence significantly the social functioning of students with Specific Learning Disabilities" p. 41. They suggest that we view social skills training as experimental. Weiner (2004) cites Weiner and Sunohara's (1998) study, which recommends methods parents can use to improve the student's social relationships, such as making the home an inviting place for friends and encouraging nonacademic activities.

Bryan et al. (2004) note that individualized interventions geared to the needs of the student

TABLE 16–4 Developing the Behavior Assessment Plan: Tasks and Considerations

Tasks	Considerations
Identify a replacement behavior	• Determine an appropriate behavior as replacement • Be sure that the replacement can access same function • Choose skills to maximize immediate success
Design instruction	• Determine whether student has replacement skills • Select teaching examples and sequences • Design instruction to teach how, when, when, where and why
Arrange the environment to facilitate success	• Consider potential failures and prevent • Develop prompts, cues, and routines for success • Arrange the environment to set student up for success
Plan for reinforcement	• Determine the natural reinforcer for behavior • Make natural reinforcer immediately available
Plan for negative consequences	• Ensure that negative consequences do not provide desired function • Use the smallest consequences necessary to get desired effect • Fade to natural consequences
Define criteria for success and monitor	• Define measurable criteria for desired performance • Measure behavior over time • Compare performance to criteria and evaluate intervention success

Source: From "Ensuring Student Success Through Team-Based FBA" by J. M. Scott, C. J. Liaupin, C. M. Nelson, and K. Jolinette. Teaching Exceptional Children, 35, 2003, 16–21. Copyright © 2003. Published by The Council for Exceptional Children. Reprinted with permission of the publisher.

(rather than classroom-based interventions) are more likely to be effective. Cartledge and Milburn (1995) prepared a five-step model that can be used for individualize social skill training:

- *Providing Instructions.* Students with learning disabilities require direct instruction for those skills that capable learners appear to learn incidentally. You must provide explicit instructions about the skills to be taught. The teacher must provide the students with sufficient information to enable them to understand what is expected of them. Often students act in an inappropriate fashion because it was assumed that they knew how to behave. This approach makes no such assumption; it provides the student with the instruction necessary to comprehend what the expected behavior is prior to engaging in a violation of a social skill.
- *Exposure to a Model.* Instructions alone will be insufficient to bring about an increase in social skill. Students must have an opportunity to observe individuals who model the appropriate behavior. This can be done in a number of ways— through the use of role playing, pictorial representations, films, slides, books, and the like.

Ample exposure to appropriate models will enable students to see how the social skills can be manifested in a wide variety of settings and under different conditions.

- *Rehearsals.* Students should be encouraged to think about the setting in which the social skill is to be demonstrated and to practice the skill. Some students find the use of visual imagery very helpful. They try to imagine the situation in the classroom and "see" themselves carrying out the appropriate social skill successfully. Role playing is also helpful when rehearsing a social skill. Students can try the social skill as other students play the role of the teacher and other students.
- *Performance Feedback.* During the rehearsal of social skills the teacher must evaluate the student's performance. Although these activities are enjoyable in and of themselves, the goal is to increase the students' ability to increase their social skills. Therefore, feedback must be given to enable them to redefine their understanding of the procedure. The feedback should be immediate and overwhelmingly positive.... Students should be provided with frequent positive

feedback regarding their performance. At times, neutral comments may need to be made about a specific skill, but all efforts must be made to ensure that students do not receive punitive rewards regarding their ability to rehearse the social skill.

- *Practice.* When the social skill has been demonstrated in the special education setting, the student is ready to generalize the skill. It is obvious that this is the goal of social skill training: it is not sufficient to display these behaviors in isolation. Ample opportunity must be given for practicing the skill, and reinforcement must be given contingent upon performing the skill in training.

Social skills do not develop in isolation. The cultural patterns of the students' community have an impact on the skills they use in the classroom. To clarify cultural distinctions, Cartledge, Lee, & Feng (1995) provide information on the four largest minority groups in the United States. Given the disproportionately large number of culturally and linguistically diverse students classified as having learning disabilities, it is imperative that teachers learn this information.

APPLIED BEHAVIOR ANALYSIS

Classroom teachers need to apply sound behavioral principles in their classrooms. Over four decades of research support the use of these principles and techniques in a wide variety of classroom settings specifically related to students with learning disabilities (McNamara, 1998). Reinforcement, punishment, token economies, and contracting will be discussed below.

Teacher approval, perhaps the most easily accessible reinforcement technique, should be used in special and regular classrooms to increase appropriate student behavior. Reinforcing appropriate behavior and (to a great extent) ignoring inappropriate behavior should be management tools used by all teachers. Other reinforcers that can be employed in the mainstream class are free

time, privileges, star stickers, notes, positive notes to parents, and the like.

Reinforcement

Anything that increases a behavior is a reinforcer (McNamara & McNamara, 1995). The contingent use of reinforcement—that is, applying reinforcement after an appropriate behavior—increases a wide variety of behaviors used by children and adolescents in school. There is also consistent evidence that teacher attention (proximity, verbal and nonverbal approval) may act as an effective reinforcement for preschool and school-age children.

Punishment

A punishment is anything that decreases the strength of a behavior. It is imperative that teachers be aware of its negative effects because students tend to associate the punisher with the punishment. This will clearly interfere with the establishment of good rapport between teacher and student. Also to be considered is the effect of modeling this behavior for students who view the teacher as a standard for appropriate behavior. In most cases, behaviors can be changed through the systematic use of reinforcement techniques. However, there may be times when a negative consequence is necessary to change a behavior.

Token Economies

Token economies have been employed in various environments, including the classroom. Briefly, this system involves having students earn tokens (or points, stars, checks, etc.) when they use desired behaviors. At a later time, usually the end of the week, the student can exchange the tokens for prizes—edibles, toys, classroom privileges, or virtually anything that can serve as a reinforcer. Tokens are not a cureall, nor are they ends in themselves. Teachers must also realize that the record keeping involved in using tokens is extensive and may not represent a cost-effective use of time.

Student's Name					

HOMEWORK

Subject	Mon	Tues	Wed	Thurs	Fri
Reading					
Math					
Spelling Hand writing					

I will complete _____ homework assignments.

My reward will be _____

Teacher _____ Date _____

(signature)

Student _____ Date _____

(signature)

FIGURE 16–4   Sample Homework Contract

CONTRACTING

If students are to succeed, there must be improved communication between regular and special educators regarding the students' homework contracts to reinforce appropriate behavior and improve academic and social behaviors. Contracts can be used for special subjects, academic subjects, homework assignments, or other similar educational areas that need specific attention. An example of a homework contract is presented in Figure 16–4. The teacher and the student jointly decide on the number of assignments that must be completed and the reward that will be given.

Conflict Resolution

Johnson and Johnson (1995) developed the *Teaching Students to Be Peacemakers Program* to teach students how to resolve conflicts. It has six steps:

1. *Create a cooperative context.*   Considerable evidence and practical experience demonstrate that when individual are in competition, they will strive for a "win" in conflicts and not try to solve the problem. A problem-solving approach requires the disputants to recognize their long-term interdependence and the need to maintain effective working relationships with each other—conditions that exist only in a cooperative context.

2. *Teach students to recognize when a conflict is and is not occurring.*   Many students see conflicts as always involving anger, hostility, and violence. They do not recognize conflicts as such when they lead to laughter, insight, learning, and problem solving.

3. *Teach students a concrete and specific procedure for negotiating agreements.*   Everyone involved can thus achieve their goals while maintaining or even improving the quality of their relationship. Telling students to "be nice," or "talk it out," or "solve your problem" is not enough.

4. *Teach students to use a concrete and specific mediation procedure.*   Give them enough practice in using this procedure to develop some expertise. If students are to mediate their schoolmates' conflicts, they must know how to do so. This initial training in the nature of conflict and how to negotiate and mediiate usually consists of approximately thirty half-hour lessons.

5. *Implement the peer mediation program.*   Working in pairs at first, the mediator's role is rotated so [that] each student is a mediator.

6. *Continue the training in negotiating and mediation procedures weekly throughout first through twelfth grades to refine and upgrade students' skills.* To become competent in resolving conflicts takes years an years. Any thought that a few hours of training is enough to ensure constructive conflict management is terribly misguided.

The research on the effectiveness of the program has been very positive. Johnson and Johnson (1995) believe that conflicts can be constructive and valuable. To summarize:

- Conflicts can increase achievement and long-term retention of academic material.
- Conflicts are the key to using higher-level cognitive and moral reasoning and healthy cognitive, social, and psychological development.
- Conflicts focus attention on problems that have to be solved and energize us to solve them.
- Conflicts clarify who you are, what your values are, what you care about and are committed to, and how you may need to change.

Academic Interventions

Providing appropriate instruction is critical in addressing the social side of learning disabilities. Effective proven interventions, faithfully carried out, will increase the probability of academic success. Elbaum and Vaughn (2003) examined self-concept intervention for students with learning disabilities. They found that students who perceive themselves to be low in academic skills, but are average or above-average in all other areas of self-concept, probably need academic intervention more than counseling. The authors suggest that on the elementary level academic intervention may be effective, while on the secondary level course work may be necessary. Consider a high school student who has struggled throughout her school career. It seems reasonable that this student may need counseling beyond academic intervention, since the emotional overlay of the learning disability may become overwhelming (see the next section).

Implications for Teachers: Counseling or Academic Intervention? The school psychologist was very upset by Mark's drawing of a boat that was sinking. As it was descending, awaiting, it was a huge shark, much larger than normal, with its wide-open mouth exposing a row of sharp teeth. If the boat continued to sink, it would fall directly into the shark's mouth. The psychologist interpreted the drawing as a signal that Mark felt overwhelmed and feared dying. He wanted Mark to receive counseling as soon as possible and notified Marks's parents of his concern. The classroom teacher was less alarmed. She thought Mark's attitude was fairly realistic. Mark was experiencing great academic difficulty in her third-grade classroom. When she reviewed his school records, she learned that school had always been a problem for him. He was always well behaved, but no matter how hard he tried, he could not read. She felt that Mark's drawing represented the way he viewed himself in school—as continuing to sink and never able to keep afloat. While the psychologist wanted counseling, the teacher wanted extra help for reading instruction.

What do you think? Do you believe that students with learning disabilities develop emotional and behavioral problems as a result of their poor academic performance? Or do you think that these problems are part of the neurological makeup of students with learning disabilities? Does Mark have a poor self-concept because he can't read? If so, then the intervention should be reading instruction. However, if you believe the reason is that students with learning disabilities have poor self- concepts, then your intervention will be different. You need to decide.

TEACHING SOCIAL-EMOTIONAL BEHAVIORS THROUGH THE CURRICULUM

Given the current research suggesting the limitations of group-based commercial social skills traing (SST) programs, it may be worthwhile to try teaching positive social-emotional behaviors in your classroom. One concern of teachers is the lack of time to provide social-emotional and behavioral intervention, particularly in the modern era of high-stakes testing and emphasis on academic subjects. Infusing SST through literacy instruction appears to be an effective and efficient method.

Three ways in which teachers can do this are through bibliotherapy, folk literature, and experiential learning activities and games (Forgan & Gonzalez-DeHass, 2004). Bibliotherapy involves using books to help people solve problems. The teacher can identify a particular social-emotional or behavioral issue to address and select books portraying that concern. Bibliotherapy can also be employed for problem solving (see Anderson, 2000; Forgan, 2003). Cartledge and Kleefeld (1994) used folk literature to teach social skills, and Forgan (2002) and de la Cruz, Cage, and Lian (2000) employed games to teach appropriate social skills. Forgan and Gonzalez-DeHass (2004, p. 26) provide the following literature synopsis on the infusion of social skills training into the academic curriculum:

- One approach for overcoming the dilemma of either teaching academics or social skills is to infuse social skills instruction into the academic curriculum (Sugai & Lewis, 1996) and literacy instruction in particular (Anderson, 2000; Bauer & Balius, 1995; Cartledge & Kiarie, 2001; Forness & Kavale, 1996; Gresham et al., 2001).
- By infusing social skills training into the academic curriculum, students receive vastly more time devoted to social skills training than when these programs are offered as an isolated area of instruction that traditionally amounts to a total of 30 hours or less (Forness & Kavale, 1996; Gresham et al., 2001).
- Training that is divorced from meaningful settings may result in a lack of transfer of social skills. Literature activities offer an ideal opportunity to teach skills through a medium that can be perceived as meaningful to students' lives (Korinek & Popp, 1997).
- Literacy affords students the natural tendency to read a book in search of answers, and teachers

can use children's literature books to help students learn to solve problems and enhance self-concept. Bibliotherapy allows students to see that they are not the only ones to encounter such problems and learn that there is more than one solution to a problem. It helps them discuss the problem or freely create a constructive course of action to solve it (Alex, 1993).

- *Working Together: Building Children's Social Skill Through the Literature* allows students the opportunity to relate *with a folk literature* character so that skills are presented in a natural context of literacy rather than as a separate entity; this program has been successfully used to increase the social skills of middle-school adolescents with behavior disorders (Blake, Wang, Cartledge, & Gardner, 2000).

Forgan and Gonzalez-DeHass (2004, pp. 26, 28, 29) also provide tables of useful print and Internet resources (see Tables 16–5 and 16–6).

MODELING AND REINFORCING A KIND, CARING CLASSROOM ENVIRONMENT

As noted earlier in the chapter, students with learning disabilities are at risk for victimization. Creating a classroom environment that reinforces empathy, kindness, caring, and inclusive friendships is important. Using an applied behavioral approach, you can identify specific kind and caring behaviors and display them in your classroom. Some teachers keep flip chart lists of all the kind and caring behaviors that students use. Anyone in the classroom can add to the list. For example, one student observes another fellow student assisting someone with a written assignment; the student can then go to the flip chart and write, "Louise helped Alan with an essay." Weekly, the teacher and the class review the list and comment on the behavior. Some teachers provide reinforcement contingent on a specific number of acts of kindness and caring; others provide spontaneous and sporadic reinforcements.

TABLE 16–5 Print Resources for Infusing Social Skills

Title	Author	ISBN #	Publisher	Web Site
Children's Literature: An Issues Approach (3rd ed)	Marsha Kabakow Rudman	0-8013-1469-0	Addison-Wesley	www.aw.com
Adventures in Peacemaking: A Conflict Resolution Activity Guide for School-Age Prog.	William J Kreidler And Lisa Furlong	0-93438-711-7	Project Adventure, Inc.	www.pa.org
Teaching Conflict Resolution Through Children's Literature	William J. Kreidler	0-590-49747-2	Scholastic	www. scholastic.com
Teacher Problem Solving Through Children's Literature	James Forgan	1-56308-981-5	Teacher Ideas Press	www.teachrid-eas press.com
Silver Bullets: A Guide to Initiative Problems, Adventure Games, and Trust Activities	Karl Rhonke	0-8403-5682-X	Kendall/Hunt Publishing	www.kendall-hunt. com
Quicksilver	Karl Rhonke and Steve Butler	0-7872-0032-8	Kendall/Hunt Publishing	http://www.kendall-hunt. com
Problem Solver	Patti Waldo	0-930599-05-5	Thinking Publications	www.thinking-publications.com
Communicate	Patty Mayo and Patti Waldo	0-930599-04-7	Thinking Publications	www.thinking-publications.com
Communicate, Jr.	Patty Mayo and Nancy Gajewski	0-939599-68-3	Thinking Publications	www.thinking-publications.com

Source: From "How to Infuse Social Skills Training into Literacy Instruction" by J.W. Forgan and A. Gonzalez-DeHass. Teaching Exceptional Children, 36, 2004, 24–30. Copyright © 2004. Published by The Council for Exceptional Children. Reprinted with permission of the publisher.

It is important to comment on these good deeds and reinforce the kind way students talk to each other, treat each other, and care for each other. The process begins with teachers modeling the behavior and can make the classroom a welcoming environment for all students, especially those for whom it is not always friendly.

Providing Positive Behavioral Support (PBS)

IDEA 2004 requires schools to provide "positive behavioral supports" to ensure that every student receives a free, appropriate public education. Schoolwide positive behavioral supports "define, teach and support appropriate behaviors in a way that establishes a culture of competence within schools" (OSEP Technical Assistance Center, 2003, p. 1). PBS has been employed with preschoolers (Stormont, Lewis, & Beckner, 2005), in primary grades (Stormont, Espinosa, Knipping, & McCathren,

2003), on the playground (Lewis, Powers, Kelk, & Newcomer, 2002), and schoolwide (Flannery, Sugai, & Eber, 2002; Lewis & Sugai, 1999; Lewis, Sugai, & Colvin, 1998).

The major components of PBS are as follows (OSEP Technical Assistance Center, 2003, p. 2):

1. *Behavioral Expectations Are Defined.* A small number of clearly defined behavioral expectations are defined in positive, simple rules. Examples are:
   - Be Respectful, Be Responsible, Be Safe; or
   - Respect Yourself, Respect Others, and Respect Property.
2. *Behavioral Expectations Are Taught.* The behavioral expectations are taught to all students in the building, and are taught in real contexts. The goals of the teaching are to take broad expectations (like Be Respectful) and provide specific behavioral examples. (In class: being respectful means raising your hand when you want to speak or get help. During lunch or in the hall:

TABLE 16–6 Internet Resources on Social Skills

Title	Social Skills Genre	Web Site
Carnegie Library of Pittsburgh	Bibliotherapy	www.clpgh.org/kids/booknook/bibliotheraphy
ERIC Digest on Bibliotherapy	Bibliotherapy	eric.indiana.edu/ieo/digest/d177.html
International Reading Assoc. Bibliotherapy		
Special Interest Group	Bibliotherapy	www.reading.org/dir/sig/sigbibli.html
Project Adventure Inc.	Experiential Social Skills	www.pa.org
National Association of School		
Psychologists: Infusing Social Skills	Social Skills in Academics	www.naspcenter.org/factsheets/ social skills_fs.html
Infusing Social Skills	Social Skills in Academics	www.nrel.org/sdrs/areas/issues/ envrnmt/drugfree/sa300.htm
Learning Disabilities On-Line	Social Skills in Academics	www.ldonline.com
American Guidance	Social Skills Curricula	www.agsnet.com

Source: *From "How to Infuse Social Skills Training into Literacy Instruction" by J. W. Forgan and A. Gonzalez-DeHass. Teaching Exceptional Children, 36, 2004, 24–30. Copyright © 2004. Published by The Council for Exceptional Children. Reprinted with permission of the publisher.*

being respectful means using a person's name when you talk to him or her.) Teaching appropriate behavior involves much more than simply telling students what behaviors they should avoid. Behavioral expectations are taught using the same teaching norms applied to other curricula. The general rule is presented, the rationale for the rule is discussed, positive examples ("right way") are described and rehearsed, and negative examples ("wrong way") are described and modeled. Students are given an opportunity to practice the "right way" until they demonstrate fluent performance.

3. *Appropriate Behaviors Are Acknowledged.* Once appropriate behaviors have been defined and taught, they need to be acknowledged on a regular basis. Some schools do this through formal systems (tickets, rewards); others do it through social events. Schools that are successful in creating a competent culture typically establish a pattern in which adult interactions with students are "positive" four times as often as they are "negative." To achieve this standard, some strategy is needed to build and maintain positive adult initiations to students (both in class and outside of class).

4. *Behavioral Errors Are Corrected Proactively.* When students violate behavioral expectations, clear procedures are needed for providing information to them that their behavior was unacceptable and preventing that unacceptable

behavior from resulting in inadvertent rewards. Students, teachers, and administrators all should be able to predict what will occur when behavioral errors are identified.

Typically, the development and implementation of schoolwide PBS utilizes a team approach similar to that of the IST (see Chapter 5). This inclusive, positive collaborative model can be helpful in addressing the behavioral needs of your students (see Lewis & Sugai, 1999, and Scott, 2003, for specific information on developing and implementing PBS).

Self-Regulation

Students with learning disabilities need to develop methods for assessing and evaluating their own social-emotional behavior. This self-regulation process takes four common forms (Reid, Trout, & Schwartz, 2005): self-monitoring, self-monitoring plus reinforcement, self-reinforcement and self-management.

Self-Monitoring. Students are taught to observe and record their own behavior. They also learn to become more aware of their performance, whether behavioral (such as calling out) or academic (such as a writing task). You can provide verbal or pictorial cues for your students. Some teachers take a

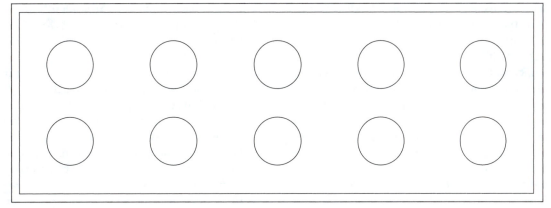

FIGURE 16–5 "Did I Raise My Hand?"

picture (using a digital camera) of the student displaying the desirable behavior and point to it. Others place a simple chart on the student's desk to enable the student to observe and record the behavior. For example, one teacher made a simple chart labeled "Did I raise my hand?" with 10 circles below it. The student was required to identify "hand raising" and place a line through a circle each time he raised his hand (see Figure 16–5).

Self-Monitoring Plus Reinforcement. External reinforcement increases the probability that the student will develop self-monitoring skills. Clearly, not all students will need this step. However, in the initial stages of a self-regulation program, it may be necessary.

Self-Reinforcement. Students self-monitor a particular behavioral (or academic) goal and identify the reinforcer. Once they reach the goal, they receive the reinforcement. For example, your student may decide that when she raises her hand 10 times in a row, she will receive a coupon that can be redeemed later for a reward. She may also decide that she can report to her parents the accomplishment of the goal. This student is identifying the goal, the reinforcement, and when to receive it. She is becoming actively involved in regulating her behavior.

Self-Management. Mace, Belfioe, and Hutchinson (2001) describe this form of self-regulation. Students must monitor, rate, and compare their behavior to their goal (or a initially agreed-upon goal). They must also compare their self-evaluations to the teacher's rating of their behavior. Typically, they receive reinforcement contingent on the degree of congruency between the teacher's evaluation and their own.

There is a body of evidence to support the use of self-regulation techniques. Two meta-analyses were performed. Graham and Harris (2003) reviewed studies of students with learning disabilities and found that self-regulation techniques were effective in improving their written language skills. Reid et al. (2005) found that self-regulatory techniques "can produce meaningful improvement in students' on-task behavior, academic productivity and accuracy, and reduction of inappropriate or disruptive behaviors of students with ADHD" (p. 374). For students with learning disabilities or ADHD, these appear to be powerful tools.

SUMMARY

The social side of learning disabilities cannot be ignored. Leaders in the field fear that the emphasis on high-stakes testing and academics will leave teachers little time to address this critical area. Add to this the absence of social skills in the federal government's definition of learning disabilities, and many are concerned. These problems have been well documented. Researchers, teachers, and parents have noted the social-emotional and behavioral difficulties of students with learning disabilities. And while some interventions lack support (e.g., social skills training), these concerns must be addressed. This chapter has discussed the social-emotional and behavioral problems of students with learning disabilities, ways to assess these problems, and interventions currently employed. Professionals in this field must continue to conduct research and implement research-based interventions, ever aware that public policy impacts on our practice.

SPRINGBOARDS FOR REFLECTION AND DISCUSSION

1. Interview a parent of a student with a learning disability. How has the social aspect of the disability impacted the student's life? How has it impacted the family? Does the parent think it is adequately addressed in the school?

2. Interview a teacher of students with learning disabilities. How much of the teacher's day is devoted to social-emotional and behavioral issues? How does the teacher prioritize academic and behavioral instruction?

3. Observe a student with learning disabilities in the classroom. How do the student's social-emotional behaviors affect him or her? How do they affect the student's classmates? How are these social-emotional behaviors addressed?

4. Speak to mental health professionals (psychologists, school counselors, social workers). How do they deal with the social issues of students with learning disabilities? How do they work with classroom teachers?

5. Examine the literature on bullying and design an antibullying program that can be carried out in your school.

6. What are some ways in which you can infuse SST into the curriculum?

REFERENCES

Abel, E. L. (1995). An update on incidence of FAS: FAS is not an equal opportunity birth defect. *Neurotoxicology and Teratology, 17*(4), 437–443.

Abramowitz, A. J., O'Leary, S. G., & Rosen, L. A. (1987). Reducing off-task behavior in the classroom: A comparison of encouragement and reprimands. *Journal of Abnormal Psychology, 15,* 153–163.

Achenbach, T. M. (2000). *Caregiver-teacher report form for ages 1¹/₂-5 (C-TRF/1¹/₂-5).* Burlington, VT: ASEBA.

Achenbach, T. M. (2001a). *Child behavior checklist for ages 6–18 (CBC/6–18).* Burlington, VT: ASEBA.

Achenbach, T. M. (2001b). *Teacher report form for ages 6–18 (TRF/6–18).* Burlington, VT: ASEBA.

Achenbach, T. M., & Rescorla, L. A. (2000). *Child behavior checklist for ages 1¹/₂-5 (CBC/1¹/₂-5).* Burlington, VT: ASEBA.

Adam, M. J. (1990). *Beginning to read: Thinking and learning about print.* Cambridge, MA: MIT Press.

Adams, G., & Carmine, G. (2003). Direct instruction. In H. L. Swanson, K. R. Harris, & S. Graham (Eds.), *Handbook of learning disabilities* (pp. 403–416). New York: Guilford Press.

Adams, G. L., & Englemann, S. (1996). *Research as direct instruction: 25 years beyond DISTAR.* Portland, OR: Educational Achievement Systems.

Adelman, P. B., & Vogel, S. A. (1993). Issues in the employment of adults with LD. *Journal of Learning Disabilities,* 16, 219–232.

Advocates for Children. (1992). *Segregated and second rate: Special education in New York.* New York: Author.

Agran, M., King-Sears, M. E., Wehmeyer, M. L., & Copeland, S. R. (2003). *Student directed learning.* Baltimore: Paul H. Brookes.

Alberto, P. A., & Troutman, A. C. (1995). *Applied behavior analysis for teachers* (4th ed.). Upper Saddle River, NJ: Merrill/Prentice Hall.

Alberto, P. A., & Troutman, A. C. (2003). *Applied behavior analysis for teachers* (6th ed.). Upper Saddle River, NJ: Merrill/Prentice Hall.

Alex, N. K. (1993). *Bibliotherapy* (Report NO.EDO-CS-93-05). Bloomington: Indiana University, Office of Educational Research and Improvement, (ERIC).

Algozzine, B., Christenson, S., & Ysseldyke, J. (1982). Probabilities associated with the referral to placement process. *Teacher Education and Special Education, 5,* 19–23.

Allen, R. V., & Allen, C. (1982). *Language experience activities* (2nd ed.). Boston: Houghton Mifflin.

Allington, R. L. (1984). So what is the problem? Whose problem is it? *Topics in Learning Disabilities, 3*(4), 91–99.

Alternative Testing. (2002). National Council for Learning Disabilities. Retrieved October 12, 2003, from http://www.ldonline.org.

American Academy for Pediatrics. (1998). Learning disabilities, dyslexia, and vision. *Pediatrics, 102*(5), 1217–1219.

American Academy for Pediatrics. (2001). Clinical practice guide: Treatment of the school age child with attention deficit hypertension disorder. *Pediatrics, 108*(4), 1033–1044.

American Psychiatric Association. (1994). *Diagnostic and statistical manual of mental disorders* (DSM-IV; 4th ed.). Washington, DC: Author.

American Speech-Language-Hearing Association. (1999). *Guidelines for the roles and responsibilities of the school-based speech-language pathologists.* Rockville, MD: Author.

Anderson, P. L. (2000). Using literature to teach social skills to adolescents with LD. *Intervention in School and Clinic, 35,* 271–279.

Anderson, P. L., Cronin, M. E., & Miller, J. H. (1986). Referral reasons for learning disabled students. *Psychology in the Schools, 23,* 388–395.

Anderson, P. L., Kazmierski, S., & Cronin, M. E. (1995). Learning disabilities, employment discrimination, and the ADA. *Journal of Learning Disabilities, 28,* 196–204.

Anthony, R. J., Johnson, T. D., Mickelson, N. I., & Preece, A. (1991). *Evaluating literacy: A perspective for change.* Portsmouth, NH: Heinemann.

Apling, R. N., & Jones, N. L. (2005). *IDEA 04: Analysis of changes made by P. L. 108-446.* Washington, DC: Congressional Research Service, Library of Congress.

Arena, J. (1981). *Diagnostic spelling test.* Novato, CA: Academic Therapy Publications.

Artiles, A., & Ortiz, A. (Eds.). (2002). *English language learners with special education needs: Identification, assessment and instruction.* McHenry, IL: Delta Systems.

Artiles, A., & Trent, S. (1997a). Forging a research program on multicultural preservice teacher education in special education: A proposed analytic scheme. In J. Lloyd, E. Kame'enui, & D. Chard (Eds.), *Issues in educating students with disabilities* (pp. 275–304). Mahwah, NJ: Erlbaum.

Artiles, A. J., & Trent, S. C. (1997a). Overrepresentation of minority students in special education: A continuing debate. *Journal of Special Education, 27*(4), 410–437.

Ashlock, R. B. (1998). *Error patterns in computation* (7th ed.) Upper Saddle River, NJ: Merrill/Prentice Hall.

Association for Children with Learning Disabilities. (1985). Definition of the condition of specific learning disabilities. *ACLD Newsbriefs, 158,* 1-3.

Association for Children with Learning Disabilities. (1986). ACLD definition: Specific learning disabilities. *ACLD Newsbriefs,* 15-16.

Ausubel, D. P. (1960). The use of advance organizers in the learning and retention of meaningful verbal material. *Journal of Educational Psychology, 51,* 267-272.

Babbit, B. C. (1999). 10 tips for software rel for math instruction. Retrieved February 11, 2005, from http://www.ldonline.org/ld—indepth/technology/Babbitt_math_tips.html.

Baddeley, A. D. (1986). *Working memory.* London: Oxford University Press.

Bagnato, S. J., & Neisworth, J. T. (1990). *System to plan early childhood services (SPECS).* Circle Pines, MN: American Guidance Service.

Bailet, L. L. (2001). Development and disorders of spelling in the beginning school year. In A. M. Bain, L. L. Bailet, & L. C. Moats (Eds.), *Written language disorders: Theory into practice* (2nd ed., pp. 1-42). Austin, TX: PRO-ED.

Bain, A. M. (1995). *Handwriting survey.* Unpublished manuscript.

Bain, A. M., Bailet, L. L., & Moats, L. C. (2001). *Written language disorders: Theory into practice.* Austin, TX: PRO-ED.

Barkley, R. A. (1997). *ADHD and the nature of self-control.* New York: Guilford Press.

Barkley, R. A. (1998). *Attention deficit hyperactivity disorder: A handbook for diagnosis and treatment* (2nd ed.). New York: Guilford Press.

Barkley, R. A. (2003). Forward. In G. J. Du Paul & G. Stover, *ADHD in the Schools* (pp. ix-xi). New York: Guilford Press.

Bateman, B. (1965). An education view of a diagnostic approach to learning disorders. In J. Hellmuth (Ed.), *Learning disorders* (Vol. 1, pp. 219-239). Seattle, WA: Special Child Publications.

Batshaw, M. G. (2002). *Children with disabilities* (5th ed.). Baltimore: Paul H. Brookes.

Bauer, A. M., & Shea, T. M. (2003). *Parents and schools: Creating a successful partnership for students with special needs.* Upper Saddle River, NJ: Merrill/Prentice Hall.

Bauer, M. S., & Balius, F. A. (1995). Storytelling: Integrating therapy and curriculum for students with serious emotional disturbances. *Teaching Exceptional Children, 27*(2), 24-28.

Bayley, N. (1993). *Bayley scales of infant development* (2nd ed.). San Antonio, TX: Psychological Corporation.

Behrmann, M., & Kinas Jerome, M. (2002). *Assistive technology for students with mild disabilities.* Update (2002). ERIC Digest (E623).

Belson, L. (2003). *Technology for exceptional learner.* Boston: Houghton Mifflin.

Bender, W. N. (2004). *Learning disabilities: Characteristics, identification, and teaching strategies* (5th ed.). Boston: Allyn & Bacon.

Benz, M. R., Lindstrom, L., & Yovanoff, P. (2000). Improving graduation and employment outcomes with students with disabilities: Predictive factors and students' perspective. *Exceptional Children, 66,* 509-529.

Bernstein, D. K. (2002). The nature of language and its disorders. In D. K. Bernstein & E. Tiegerman-Farber (Eds.), *Language and communication disorders in children* (5th ed., pp. 2-26). Boston: Allyn & Bacon.

Bernstein, D. K., & Tiegerman-Farber, E. (2002). *Language and communication disorders in children.* (5th ed.). Boston: Allyn & Bacon.

Biklin, D., & Zollers, N. (1986). The focus on advocacy in the LD field. *Journal of Learning Disabilities, 19,* 579-586.

Blake, C., Wang, W., Cartledge, G., & Gardner, R. (2000). Middle school students with serious emotional disturbances serve as social skills trainers and reinforcers for peers with SED. *Behavioral Disorders, 25,* 280-298.

Bley, N. S., & Thornton, C. A. (2001). *Teaching mathematics to students with learning disabilities* (4th ed.). Austin, TX: PRO-ED.

Bligh, T. (1996). Choosing and using picture books for mini-lessons with middle school students. *Reading and Writing Quarterly: Overcoming Learning Difficulties, 12*(4), 333-349.

Block, A. K. (2000). *Special education law and delingual children: An overview.* Charlotte, VA: Institute of Law, Psychiatry and Public Policy.

Bloom, L. (1970). *Language development: Forum and function of emerging grammars.* Cambridge, MA: MIT Press.

Bloom, L. (1988). What is language? In L. Bloom & M. Lahey, *Language development and language disorders* (pp. 1-19). Needham, MA: Macmillan.

Bloom, L., & Lahey, M. (1978). *Language development and language disorders.* New York: Wiley.

Boehm, A. (2000). *Boehm test of basic concepts (Boehm—3)* (3rd ed.). San Antonio, TX: Psychological Corporation.

Boehm, A. (2001). *Boehm test of basic concepts—preschool* (3rd ed.). San Antonio, TX: Psychological Corporation.

Bos, C. S., & Vaughan, S. (1994). *Strategies for teaching students with learning and behavior problems* (3rd ed.). Boston: Allyn & Bacon.

Bos, C. S., & Vaughan, S. (1998). *Strategies for teaching students with learning and behavior problems* (4th ed.). Boston: Allyn & Bacon.

Bowman, B. T., Donovan, M. S., & Burns, M. S. (Eds.). (2001). *Eager to learn: Educating our preschoolers.* Washington, DC: National Academy Press.

Bracken, B. A. (1998). *Bracken basic concept scale* (rev.). San Antonio, TX: Psychological Corporation.

Bradley, R., Danielson, L., & Hallahan, D. P. (Eds.). (2002). *Identification of learning disabilities: Research to Practice.* Mahwah, NJ: Erlbaum.

Bricker, D. (Ed.). (1993). *Assessment, evaluation, and programming system (AEPS) for infants and children: Vol. 1*

AEPS measurement for birth to three years. Baltimore: Paul H. Brookes.

Bricker, D., & Pretti-Frontczak, K. (Eds.). (1996). *Assessment, evaluation, and programming system (AEPS) for infants and children: Vol. 3 AEPS measurement for three to six years.* Baltimore: Paul H. Brookes.

Bricker, D., & Squires, J. (1999). *Ages and stages questionnaire (AQS).* Baltimore: Paul H. Brookes.

Brier, N. (1989). The relationship between learning disability and delinquency: A review and reappraisal. *Journal of Learning Disabilities, 22*(9), 546-553.

Brier, N. (1994). Targeted treatment for adjudicated youth with learning disabilities: Effects on recidivism. *Journal of Learning Disabilities, 27,* 215-222.

Brigance, A. H. (1981). BRIGANCE® *inventory of essential skills.* No. Billerica, MA: Curriculum Associates.

Brigance, A. H. (1984). BRIGANCE® *assessment of basic skills—Spanish edition.* No. Billerica, MA: Curriculum Associates.

Brigance, A. H. (1991). BRIGANCE® *inventory of early development* (rev.). No. Billerica, MA: Curriculum Associates.

Brigance, A. H. (1994). BRIGANCE® *Life skills inventory.* No. Billerica, MA: Curriculum Associates.

Brigance, A. H. (1995). BRIGANCE® *employability skills inventory.* No. Billerica, MA: Curriculum Associates.

Brigance, A. H. (1998). BRIGANCE® *Preschool screen for three- and four-year-old children.* No. Billerica, MA: Curriculum Associates.

Brigance, A. H. (1999). BRIGANCE® *comprehensive inventory of basic skills—revised.* No. Billerica, MA: Curriculum Associates.

Brigham, F. J., Gustashaw, W. E., III, & St. Peter Brighan, M. (2004). Scientific practice and the tradition of advocacy in special education. *Journal of Learning Disabilities, 37,* 200-206.

Broadbent, W. H. (1872). On the cerebral mechanism of speech and thought. *Proceedings of the Royal Medical and Chirurgical Society of London* (pp. 25-29). London: Anonymous.

Broca, P. (1879). Anatomie Comparée des circonvolutions cérbrales. *Revue Anthropologique, 1,* 387-498.

Brooks-Gunn, J., & Duncan, G. J. (1997, Summer–Fall). The effects of poverty on children. *The Future of Children, 7*(2), 55-71.

Brophy, J., and Good, T. (1974). *Teacher–student relationships: Causes and consequences.* New York: Holt, Rinehart, and Winston.

Brown, A. L. (1978). Knowing when, where, and how to remember: A problem of metacognition. In R. Glaser (Ed.), *Advances in instructional psychology.* (Vol. 1, pp. 77-165). Hillsdale, NJ: Erlbaum.

Brown, A. L., Day, J. D., & Jones, R. S. (1983). The development of plans for summarizing texts. *Child Development, 54,* 968-979.

Brown, J. I., Fisco, V. V., & Hanna, G. S. (2000). *Nelson-Denny reading test.* Itasca, IL: Riverside.

Brown, V. L., Cronin, M. E., & McEntire, E. (1994). *Test of mathematical ability* (2nd ed.). Austin, TX: PRO-ED.

Brown, V. L., Hammill, D. D., & Wiederholt, J. L. (1995). *Test of reading comprehension—3.* Austin, TX: PRO-ED.

Brownell, K. D., Colletti, G., Ersner-Hershfield, R., Hershfiled, S. M., & Wilson, G. T. (1977). Self-control in school children: Stringency and leniency in self-determined and externally imposed performance standards. *Behavior Therapy, 8,* 442-455.

Brownell, R. (Ed.). (2000). *Expressive one-word picture vocabulary text.* Novato, CA: Academic Therapy.

Bryan, T. (1974) Peer popularity of learning disabled children. *Journal of Learning Disabilities, 7,* 621-625.

Bryan, T., Burstein, K., & Ergul, C. (2004). The social-emotional side of learning disabilities: A science-based presentation of the state of the art. *Learning Disability Quarterly, 27,* 45-52.

Buck, G. H., Polloway, E. A., Smith-Thomas, A., & Cook, K. W. (2003). Prereferral intervention processes: A survey of state practices. *Exceptional Children, 69,* 349-360.

Bulgren, J., & Lenz, K. (1996). Strategic instruction in the content areas. In D. D. Deshsler, E. S. Ellis, & B. K. Lenz (Eds.), *Teaching adolescents with learning disabilities* (2nd ed., pp. 409-473). Denver, CO: Love.

Bulgren, J. A., Schumaker, J. B., & Deshler, D. D. (1988). Effectiveness of a concept teaching routine in enhancing the performance of LD students in secondary-level mainstream classes. *Learning Disability Quarterly, 11,* 3-17.

Burnette, J. (2000). Assessment of culturally and linguistically diverse students for special education eligibility (604). Retrieved October 20, 2005, from http://www.Ericec.org/digests/e604.html.

Butler, A. (n.d.). *The elements of a whole language program.* Crystal Lake, IL: Rigby.

Calkins, L. M. (1994). *The art of teaching writing.* Portsmouth, NH: Heinemann.

Camp. R. (1992). Assessment in the context of schools and school change. In H. H. Marshall (Ed.), *Redefining student learning: Roots of educational change,* (pp. 241-263). Norwood, NJ: Ablex.

Cannon, L. (1997). Preface. *Learning Disabilities: A Multidisciplinary Journal, 8*(1), iii-iv.

Carnine, D. (1997). Instructional design in mathematics for students with learning disabilities. *Journal of Learning Disabilities, 30*(2), 134-141.

Carnine, D., Silbert, J., & Kame'enui, E. J. (1990). *Direct instruction reading.* Upper Saddle River, NJ: Merrill/ Prentice Hall.

Carnine, D., Silbert, J., & Kame'enui, E. J. (1997). *Direct instruction reading* (3rd ed.). Upper Saddle River, NJ: Merrill/Prentice Hall.

Carrow-Woolfolk, E. (1996). *Oral and written language scales.* Minneapolis: American Guidance Service.

Carter, J., & Sugai, G. (1988). Teaching social skills. *Teaching Exceptional Children, 20*(3), 68-71.

Carter, J., & Sugai, G. (1989). Survey on prereferral practices: Responses from state departments of education. *Exceptional Children, 55,* 298-302.

Cartledge, G., & Kiarie, M. W. (2001). Learning social skills through literature for children and adolescents. *Teaching Exceptional Children, 34*(2), 40-47.

Cartledge, G., & Kleefield, J. (1994). *Working together: Building children's social skills through folk literature.* Circle Pines, MN: American Guidance Service.

Cartledge, G., Lee, J. W., and Feng, H. (1995). Cultural diversity: Multicultural factors in teaching social skills. In C. Cartledge & J. F. Milburn (Eds.), *Teaching social skills to children and youth* (pp. 328-355). Boston: Allyn & Bacon.

Cartledge, G., & Milburn, J. F. (Eds.). (1980). *Teaching social skills to children.* New York: Pergamon.

Case, R., Kurland, M., & Goldberg, J. (1982). Operational efficiency and the growth of short-term memory span. *Journal of Experimental Child Psychology, 33,* 386-404.

Cass, M., Cates, D., Smith, M., & Jackson, C. (2003). Effects of manipulative instruction: Solving area and operative problems by students with learning disabilities. *Learning Disabilities Research and Practice, 18,* 112-120.

Catts, H. W., & Kamki, A. G. (Eds.) (1999). *Language and reading disabilities.* Boston: Allyn & Bacon.

Cavuto, G. (2003). *Naturalistic, classroom-based reading assessment: A problem solving, approach.* Dubuque, IA: Kendall/Hunt.

Cawley, J. F., & Foley, T. E. (2002). Connecting math and science for all students. *Teaching Exceptional Children, 34,* 14-19.

Cawley, J. F., & Reines, R. (1996). Mathematics as communication. *Teaching Exceptional Children, 28*(2), 29-34.

CEC Today. (April–May 1999). *Primer on IDEA'97.* Reston, VA: Council for Exceptional Children.

Chalfant, J. C., and Pysh, M. V. (1989). Teacher assistance teams: Five descriptive studies on 96 teams. *Remedial and Special Education, 10*(6), 49-58.

Chalfant, J. C., Pysh, M. V., & Moultrie, R. (1997). Teacher assistance teams: A model for within building problem solving. *Learning Disability Quarterly, 2,* 85-96.

Chard, D. J. (2004). Maintaining the relationship between science and special education. *Journal of Learning Disabilities, 37,* 213-217.

Chittenden, T. (1991). Authentic assessment, evaluation, and documentation of student performance. In V. Perrone (Ed.), *Expanding student assessment* (pp. 23-31). Alexandria, VA: Association for Supervision and Curriculum Development.

Choate, J. S. (Ed.). (2004). *Successful inclusion teaching: Proven ways to detect and correct special needs* (4th ed.). New York: Pearson Education.

Choate, J. S., Bennett, T. Z., Enright, B. E., Miller, L. J., Poteet, J. A., and Rakes, T. A. (1987). *Assessing and programming basic curriculum skills.* Boston: Allyn & Bacon.

Choate, J. S., Enright, J. S., Enright, B. E., Miller, L. J., Poteet, J. A., & Rakes, T. A. (1995). *Curriculum-based assessment and programming.* Boston: Allyn & Bacon.

Choate, J. S., & Evans, S. S. (1992). Authentic assessment of special learners: Problem or promise. *Parenting School Failure, 27,* 1, 6-9.

Choate, J. S., & Rakes, T. A. (2004). Reading to construct meaning to comprehend. In J. S. Choate (Ed.), *Successful inclusive teacher* (4th ed., pp. 86-129). Boston: Pearson Allyn & Bacon.

Chomsky, N. A. (1957). *Syntactic structures.* The Hague: Mouton.

Chomsky, N. A. (1965). *Aspects of the theory of syntax.* Cambridge, MA: MIT Press.

Cienion, M. (1968). Some aspects of a learning-resource room. In J. I. Arena (Ed.), *Successful programming: Many points of view.* Pittsburgh: Association for Children with Learning Disabilities.

Clare, P., & Leach, D. (1991). Classroom and playground instruction of students with and without disabilities. *Exceptional Children, 57,* 212-224.

Clay, M. (1985). *The early detection of reading difficulties* (3rd ed.). Portsmouth, NH: Heinemann.

Clements, S. D. (1966). Minimal brain dysfunction in children: Terminology and identification: Phase one of a three-phase project. *NINDS Monographs, 9,* Public Health Service Bulletin No. 1415. Washington, DC: U.S. Department of Health, Education, and Welfare.

Cohen, L. G., & Speciner, L. J. (2003). *Assessment of children and youth with special needs.* Boston: Allyn & Bacon.

Cohn, P. (1998). Why does my stomach hurt? How individuals with learning disabilities can use cognitive strategies to reduce anxiety and stress at the college level. *Journal of Learning Disabilities, 31*(5), 514-516.

Congressional Digest. (2005). *Special education reform.* Bethesda, MD: Congressional Digest Corporation.

Connell, P. J. (1986). Teaching subjecthood to language-disordered children. *Journal of Speech and Hearing Research, 39,* 518-526.

Conners, C. K. (1997). *Conners' Rating Scales* (rev.). North Tonawanda, NY: Multi-Health Systems.

Connolly, A. J. (1998). *KeyMath—revised/normative update: A diagnostic inventory of essential mathematics.* Circle Pines, MN: American Guidance Service.

Conte, R. (1998). Attention disorders. In B. Y. L. Wong (Ed.), *Learning about learning disabilities* (2nd ed., pp. 67-105). San Diego, CA: Academic Press.

Cooney, J. B., & Swanson, H. L. (1987). Memory and learning disabilities: An overview. In H. L. Swanson (Ed.), *Advances in learning and behavioral disabilities: Memory and learning disabilities* (Suppl. 2, pp. 1-40). Greenwich, CT: JAI Press.

Cortiella, C. (2005). IDEA 04: Improving transition planning and results. National Center for Learning Disabilities. Retrieved June 22, 2005, from http://www.ld.org/newsletter/0205 newsler/0205feature2.cfm.

Cortiella, C., & Horowitz, S. (2004). *The No Child Left Behind Act: Implication for students with learning disabilities.* Presented at the Learning Disability Association International Conference, Atlanta, March 17-20.

Council for Exceptional Children, Division for Children with Learning Disabilities. (1967). *Working definition of learning disabilities.* Unpublished manuscript.

Court, C., & Givon, S. (2003). Group intervention: Improving social skills of adolescents with learning disabilities. *Teaching Exceptional Children, 35,* 49-55.

Craig, S., Hull, K., Haggart, A. G., & Perez-Selles, M. (2000). Promoting cultural competence through teacher assistance teams. *Teaching Exceptional Children, 32,* 14-23.

Crockett, J. B. (2004). Taking stock of science in the schoolhouse: Four ideas to foster effective instruction. *Journal of Learning Disabilities, 37,* 189-199.

Cruickshank, W. M., Bentzen, F.A.,Ratzeburg, F. H., & Tannhauser, M. T. (1961). *A teaching method of brain-injured and hyperactive children.* Syracuse, NY: Syracuse University Press.

Cutting, L. E., & Denckla, M. B. (2004). Genetic disorders and learning disabilities: Closing remarks and future research questions. *Learning Disability Research and Practice, 19,* 174-176.

Davies, D. (1991). Schools reaching out: Family, school, and community partnerships for student success. *Phi Delta Kappan, 72*(5), 376-380, 382.

Davis, D.T., Kroth, R., James, A., & Van Curen, S. (1991). *Family involvement guides* (2nd ed.). Plantation, FL: South Atlantic Regional Resource Center.

Delacato, C. H. (1959). *The treatment and prevention of reading problems: The neurological approach.* Springfiled, IL: Charles C. Thomas.

Delacato, C. H. (1963). *The diagnosis and treatment of speech and reading problems.* Springfiled, IL: Charles C. Thomas.

Delacato, C. H. (1966). *Neurological organization and reading.* Springfiled, IL: Charles C.Thomas.

De la Cruz, R. E., Cage, C. E., & Lian, M. G. J. (2000). Let's play Mancala and Sungka! Learning math and social skills through ancient multicultural games. *Teaching Exceptional Children, 32*(3), 38-42.

Deno, E. (1970). Special education as educational capital. *Exceptional Children, 37,* 229-237.

Deno, S. L. (1985). Curriculum-based measurement: The emerging alternative. *Exceptional Children, 52,* 219-232.

Dent, H. (1994). Testing African American children: The struggle continues. *Psych Discourse, 25,* 5-9.

Denton, C., & Mathes, P. (2002, Summer). Reading Recovery. *Practice Alerts, 7.* Washington, DC: Council for Exceptional Children.

Deshler, D. D., Alley, G. R., Warner, M. M., & Schumaker, J. B. (1981). Instructional practices for promoting skill acquisition and generalization in severely learning disabled adolescents. *Learning Disability Quarterly, 4*(4), 415-421.

Deshler, D. D., Ellis, E. S., & Lenz, B. K. (1996). *Teaching adolescents with learning disabilities: Strategies and methods* (2nd ed.). Denver, CO: Love.

Deshler, D. D., & Lenz, B. K. (1989). The strategies instructional approach. *Internatinoal Journal of Learning Disabilities, Development and Education, 36,* 203-224.

Deshler, D. D., & Putnam, M. L. (1996). Learning disabilities in adolescents: A perspective. In D. D. Deshsler, E. S. Ellis, & B. K. Lenz (Eds.), *Teaching adolescents with learning disabilities* (2nd ed., pp. 1-8). Denver, CO: Love.

Deshler, D. D., & Schumaker, J. B. (1988). An instructional model for teaching students how to learn. In J. L. Graden, J. E. Zins, & M. J. Curtis (Eds.), *Alternative educational delivery systems:Enhancing instructional options for all students* (pp. 391-411). Washington, DC: National Association of School Psychologists.

Deshler, D. D., and Schumacher, J. B. (1989). Learning strategies: An instructional alternative for low achieving adolescents. *Exceptional Children, 52,* 583-589.

Deshler, D., Schumaker, J., Lenz, B., Bulgren, J., Hock, M., Knight, J., & Ehren, B. (2001). Ensuring content-area learning by secondary students with learning disabilities. *Learning Disabilities Research & Practice, 16*(2), 96-108.

Dickinson, D. L., & Verbeek, R. L. (2002). Wage differentials between college graduates with and without learning disabilities. *Journal of Learning Disabilities, 35*(2), 175-184.

Dimino, J., Taylor, R., & Gersten, R. (1995). Synthesis of the research on story/grammar as a means to increase comprehension. *Reading and Writing Quarterly, 11,* 53-72.

DLD (Division for Learning Disabilities) and DR (Division for Research) of the Council for Exceptional Children. (2001, Spring). *Current Practice Alerts: High-Stakes Assessment, Alert 4,* 1-4.

Donahue, M., & Bryan, T. (1984). Communicative skills and peer relations of learning disabled adolescents. *Topics in Language Disorders, 4,* 10-21.

Donovan, M. S., & Cross, C.T. (2002). *Minority students in special and gifted education.* Washington, DC: National Academy Press.

Douglas, V. A. (1984).The psychological processes implicated in ADD. In L. M. Bloomingdale (Ed.), *Attention deficit disorder: Diagnostic, cognitive and therapeutic understanding* (pp. 147-162). New York: Spectrum.

Dowling, W. D. (1991). Learning disabilities among incarcerated youth. *Journal of Continuing Education, 42,* 180-185.

Duane, D. D. (1989). Comment on dyslexia and neurodevelopmental pathology. *Journal of Learning Disabilities, 22,* 219-220.

Dunn, L. M. (1968). Special education for the mildly retarded: Is much of it justifiable? *Exceptional Children, 35,* 5-22.

Dunn, L.M., & Dunn, L.M. (1997). *Peabody picture vocabulary test* (3rd ed.). Circle Pines, MN: American Guidance Service.

Du Paul, G. J., & Stover, G. (2003). *ADHD In the Schools* (2nd ed.). New York: Guilford Press.

Edge, D., & Franken, M. (1996). *Building parent and community involvement in education: Importance of research in parent involvement* (part one of three series). [video]. Louisville: Kentucky Education Television and University of Louisville.

Ehri, L., Nunes S., Willows, D., Schuster, B., Yaghoub-Zadeh, Z., & Shanahan, T. (2001). Phonemic awareness instruction helps children learn to read: Evidence from the National Reading Panel's meta-analysis. *Reading Research Quarterly, 36*, 250-287.

Elbaum, B., & Vaughn, S. (2003a). For which students with learning disabilities are self-concept interventions effective? *Journal of Learning Disabilities, 36*(2), 101-108.

Elbaum, B., & Vaughn, S. (2003b). Self-concept and students with learning disabilities. In H. L. Swanson, K. R. Harris, & S. Graham (Eds.), *Handbook of learning disabilities* (pp. 229-241). New York: Guilford Press.

Elksnin, L. K., & Elksnin, N. (1989). *Facilitating successful vocational/special education programs for mildly handicapped adolescents through collaborative consultation with parents.* Paper presented at the Fifth Annual Conference on Career Development, Atlanta (ERIC Document Reproduction Service No. ED 320-360).

Elksnin, L. K., & Elksnin, N. (2004). The social-emotional side of learning disabilities. *Learning Disabilities Quarterly, 27*, 3-8.

Ellis, E. S. (1989). A model for assessing cognitive reading strategies. *Academic Therapy, 24*(4), 407-424.

Ellis, E. S. (1994). An instructional model for integrating content-area instruction with cognitive strategy instruction. *Reading and Writing Quarterly: Overcoming Learning Difficulties, 1*, 63-90.

Ellis, E. S., & Colvert, G. (1996). Writing strategy instruction. In D. D. Deshler, E. E. Ellis, & B. K. Lenz (Eds.), *Teaching adolescents with learning disabilities: Strategies and methods* (2nd ed., pp. 127-209). Denver: Love.

Ellis, E. S., & Friend, P. (1991). The adolescent with learning disabilities. In B.Y. K. Wong (Ed.), *Learning about learning disabilities* (pp. 506-561). Orlando, FL: Academic Press.

Ellis, E. S., & Lenz, B. K. (1987). A component analysis of effective learning strategies for LD students. *Learning Disabilities Focus, 2*(2), 94-107.

Ellis, E. S., & Lenz, B. K. (1996). Perspective on instruction in learning strategies. In D. D. Deshler, E. E. Ellis, & B. K. Lenz (Eds.), *Teaching adolescents with learning disabilities: Strategies and methods* (2nd ed., pp. 9-60). Denver: Love.

Engelman, S., Becker, W. C., Hanner, S., & Johnson, G. (1978). *Corrective reading program: Series guide.* Chicago: Science Research Associates.

Engelman, S., Becker, W. C., Hanner, S., & Johnson, G. (1988). *Corrective reading program: Series guide* (rev. ed.). Chicago: Science Research Associates.

Englert, C. S., Mariage, T. V., Garmon, M. A., & Tarrant, K. L. 1998). Accelerating reading progress in early literacy project classrooms: Three exploratory studies. *Remedial and Special Education, 19*, 142-159.

Englert, C. S., Raphael, T. E., & Anderson, L. M. (1992). Socially-mediated instruction: Students' knowledge and talk about writing. *Elementary School Journal, 92*, 411-449.

Englert, C. S., Tarrant, K. L., & Mariage, T.V. (1992). Defining and redefining instructional practice in special education: Perspectives on good teaching. *Teacher Education and Special Education, 15*, 62-86.

Erford, B. T., & Boykin, R. R. (1996). *Slosson-diagnostic math screener.* East Aurora, NY: Educational Publications.

Eysenck, H. J., & Schoenthaler, S. J. (1997). Raising IQ level by vitamin and mineral supplementation. In R. J. Sternberg and E. Grigorenko (Eds.), *Intelligence, Heredity, and Environment* (pp. 363-392). Cambridge: Cambridge University Press.

Famularo, J. (2005). Preschool special education program. Bellmore, NY: Bellmore Union Free School District.

Farr, R., & Tone, B. (1994). *Portfolio and performance assessment: Helping students evaluate their progress as readers and writers.* Fort Worth, TX: Harcourt Brace.

Feingold, B. (1975). *Why your child is hyperactive.* New York: Random House.

Fernald, G. M. (1943). *Remedial techniques in basic school subjects.* New York: McGraw-Hill.

Fernald, G. M., & Keller, H. (1921). The effect of kinesthetic factors in the development of word recognition in the case of non-readers. *Journal of Educational Research, 4*, 355-357.

Ferri, B. A., Connor, D. J., Solis, S., Valle, J., & Volpitta, J. (2005). Teachers with LD: Ongoing negotiations with discourses of disability. *Journal of Learning Disabilities, 38*, 62-78.

Field, S., Martin, J., Miller, R., Ward, M., & Wehmeyer, M. (1990). *A practical guide to teaching self-determination.* Reston, VA: Council for Exceptional Children.

Field, S., Price, L., & Patton, J. R. (2003). Epilogue. *Remedial and Special Education, 24*, 380-383.

Field, S., Sarver, M., & Shaw, S. (2003). Self-determination: A key to postsecondary education for students with learning disabilities. *Remedial and Special Education, 24*(6), 339-349.

Flagler, S. (1996). *Infant-preschool play assessment scale.* Lewisville, NC: Kaplan.

Fleischner, J. E., & Manheimer, M. A. (1997). Math interventions for students with learning disabilities: Myths and reality. *School Psychology Review, 26*, 397-413.

Fletcher, J. M., Lyon, G. R., Baumes, M., Stueberg, K. K., Cranus, D. J., Olson, R. K., Shaywitz, S. E., & Shaywitz, B. A. (2002). Classification of learning disabilities: An evidence-based evaluation. In R. Bradley, L. Danielson & D. P. Hallahan (Eds.), *Identification of learning disabilities: Research to practice* (pp. 185-250). Mahwah, NJ: Erlbaum.

Fletcher, J. M., & Martinez, G. (1994). An eye-movement analysis of the effects of notopic sensitivity connection on passing and comprehension. *Journal of Learning Disabilities, 27*, 67-70.

Forgan, J. W. (2002). Using bibliotherapy to teach problem-solving. *Intervention in School and Clinic, 38*(2), 75-82.

Forgan, J. W. (2003). *Teaching problem-solving through children's literature.* Englewood, Co: Libraries Unlimited.

Forgan, J. W., & Gonzalas-De Hass, A. (2004). How to infuse social skills training into literacy instruction. *Teaching Exceptional Children, 36*, 24-30.

Forness, S. R., & Kavale, K. A. (1996). Treating social skill deficits in children with learning disabilities: A meta-analysis of the research. *Learning Disability Quarterly, 19*, 2-13.

Foster, G. G., Ysseldyke, J. E., Casey, A., & Thurlow, M. L. (1974). The congruence between reason for referral and placement outcome. *Journal of Psychoeducational Assessment, 2*, 209-217.

Fradd, S. H., & Cook, L. (2002). *Collaboration skills for school professionals* (4th ed.). Boston: Allyn & Bacon.

Fradd, S. H., & Hallman, C. L. (1983). Implications of psychological and educational research for assessment and instruction of culturally and linguistically different students. *Learning Disability Quarterly, 6*, 468-478.

Fradd, S. H., & Weismantel, M. J. (1989). Developing and evaluating goals. In S. H. Fradd & M. J. Weismantel (Eds.), *Meeting the needs of culturally and linguistically different students: A handout for educators* (pp. 34-64). Boston: College Hill.

Frankenburg, W. K., Dodds, J., Archer, P., Bresnick, B., Maschka, P., Edelman, N., & Shapiro, M. (1990). *Denver—II.* Denver, CO: Denver Developmental Materials.

Friend, M., & Cook, L. (2003). *Interaction: Collaboration skills for school professionals* (4th ed.). New York: Longman.

Frostig, M. (1973). Learning problems in the classroom. *Prevention and remediation.* New York: Grune and Stratton.

Fuchs, D., & Fuchs, L. S. (1989). Mainstream assistance team to accommodate difficult to teach students. In G. Stoner, M. R. Shinn, & H. M. Walker (Eds.), *Interventions for achievement behavior problems* (pp. 241-267). Washington, DC: National Association of School Psychologists.

Fuchs, D., & Fuchs, L. S. (1994). *Reintegration of students with learning disabilities into the mainstream: A two-year study.* Paper presented at the annual convention of the Council for Exceptional Children, Denver, CO, April 6-10.

Fuchs, L. S., & Fuchs, D. (2001). Principles for the prevention and intervention of mathematical difficulties. *Disabilities Research and Practice, 6*, 85-95.

Fuchs, L. S., Fuchs, D., & Speece, D. L. (2002). Treatment validity as a unifying construct for identifying learning disabilities. *Learning Disabilities Quarterly, 25*, 33-45.

Fulk, B. M., & Stormont-Spurgin, M. (1995). Spelling interventions for students with learning disabilities. *Journal of Special Education, 28*, 488-513.

Galaburda, A. M. (1988). The pathogenesis of childhood dyslexia. In F. Plum (Ed.), *Language, communication and the brain* (pp. 127-138). New York: Raven Press.

Galaburda, A. M. (1990). The testosterone hypothesis: Assessment since Geschwind and Behan, 1982. *Annals of Dyslexia, 40*, 18-38.

Galaburda, A. M. (2005). Neurology of learning disabilities: What will the future bring? The answer comes from the successes of the recent past. *Learning Disability Quarterly, 28*(2), 107-109.

Galda, L., Cullinan, B. E., & Strickland, D. S. (1997). *Language literacy and the child* (2nd ed.). New York: Harcourt Brace.

Gallagher, J. J. (2000). The beginnings of federal help for young children with disabilities. *Topics in Early Childhood Special Education, 20*(1), 3-6.

Garner, A., & Lipsky, D. K. (1987). Beyond special education: Toward a quality system for all students. *Harvard Educational Review, 37*, 307-395.

Garnett, K. (1998). Math learning disabilities: Discussion for *Learning Disabilities,* Journal of the Council of Exceptional Children. Retrieved April 14, 2003, from http://www.ldonline.org/ld_indepth/math_skills/garnet.html.

Garnett, K., & Fleischner, J. E. (1983). Automation and basic fact performance of normal and learning disabled children. *Learning Disability Quarterly, 6*, 223-230.

Geary, D. C. (1993). Mathematical disabilities: Cognitive, neuropsychological, and genetic components. *Psychological Bulletin, 114*, 345-362.

Geary, D. C. (2000). Mathematic disorders: An overview for educators. *Perspective, 26*, 6-9.

Geary, D. C. (2003). Learning disabilities in arithmetic: Problem-solving differences and cognitive defects. In H. L. Swanson, K. R. Harris, & S. Graham (Eds.), *Handbook of learning disabilities* (pp. 199-212). New York: Guilford Press.

Gelzheiser, L. M. (1987). Reducing the number of students identified as learning disabled: A question of practice, philosophy or policy? *Exceptional Children, 54*, 145-150.

Gerber, P. J. (1992). At first glance: Employment for people with learning disabilities at the beginning of the Americans-with-Disabilities-Act era. *Learning Disability Quarterly, 15*(4), 330-332.

Gerber, P. J. (2003). Adults with learning disabilities redux. *Remedial and Special Education, 24*, 324-327.

Gersten, R., & Baker, S. (1999). *Reading comprehension instruction for students with learning disabilities: A research synthesis.* Washington, DC: Keys to Successful Learning Summit.

Gersten, R., & Baker, S. (2001). Teaching expressive writing to students with learning disabilities: A meta-analysis. *The Elementary School Journal, 101*, 251-272.

Gersten, R., Jordan, N. C., & Flojo, J. R. (2005). Early identification and interaction for students with mathematical difficulties. *Journal of Learning Disabilities, 38*, 393-304.

Gersten, R., Schiller, E. P., & Vaughn, S. (Eds.). (2000). *Contemporary special education research: Synthesis of the knowledge base on critical instructional issues.* Mahwah, NJ: Erlbaum.

Gilliam, J. E. (1995a). *Attention-deficit/hyperactivity disorder test.* Austin, TX: PRO-ED.

Gilliam, J. E. (1995b). *Gilliam autism rating scale.* Austin, TX: PRO-ED.

Gillingham, A., & Stillman, B. (1960). *Remedial training for children with specific disability in reading, spelling, and penmanship* (7th ed.). Cambridge, MA: Educators Publishing Service.

Ginsburg, H. P., & Baroody, A. J. (1990). *Test of early mathematic ability* (2nd ed.). Austin, TX: PRO-ED.

Giordano, G. (1993). Fourth invited response: The NCTM standards: A consideration of the benefits. *Remedial and Special Education, 14*(6), 28-32.

Glatthorn, A. A. (1990). Cooperative professional development: A tested approach, not a panacea. *Remedial and Special Education, 11*(4), 62.

Gnagey, T. D. (1980). *Diagnostiic screening tests math.* East Aurora, NY: Slosson Education Publication.

Goforth, F. S. (1998). *Literature and the learner.* Belmont, CA: Wadsworth.

Goldman, S. R., Pellegrino, J. W., & Mertz, D. L. (1988). Extended practice of basic addition facts: Strategy changes in learning disabled students. *Cognition and Instruction, 5,* 223-265.

Gottlieb, J., Alter, M., Gottlieb, B. W., & Wishner, J. (1994). Special education in urban America: It's not justifiable for many. *Journal of Special Education, 27,* 453-465.

Gottlieb, J., Gottlieb, B. W., & Trogone, S. (1991). Parent and teacher referrals for psychoeducational evaluation. *Journal of Special Education, 25,* 155-167.

Graden, J. L., Casey, A., & Christenson, S. L. (1985). Implementing a prereferral intervention system: Part I. The model. *Exceptional Children, 51*(5), 377-383.

Graham, S. (1999). Handwriting and spelling instruction for students with learning disabilities: A review. *Learning Disability Quarterly, 22,* 78-98.

Graham, S., Berninger, V., Weintraub, N., & Schafer, W. (1998). The development of handwriting fluency and legibility in grades 1 through 9. *Journal of Educational Research, 92,* 42-52.

Graham, S., & Harris, K. R. (1988). Instructional recommendations for teaching writing to exceptional students. *Exceptional Children, 54,* 506-512.

Graham, S., & Harris, K. R. (2000). The role of self-regulation and transcription skills in writing and writing development. *Educational Psychologist, 35,* 3-12.

Graham, S., & Harris, K. R. (2002). Prevention and intervention for struggling writers. In M. Shinn, G. Stoner, & H. Walker (Eds.), *Interventions for academic and behavior problem II: Prevention and remedial approaches* (pp. 589-610). Bethesda, MD: National Association of School Psychologists.

Graham, S., & Harris, K. R. (2003). Students with learning dis abilities and the process of counting: A meta-analysis of SRSD studies. In H. L. Swanson, K. R. Harris, & S. Graham (Eds.), *Handbook of learning disabilities* (pp. 323-344). New York: Guilford Press.

Graham, S., Harris, K. R., & Fink-Chorzempa, B. (2003). Extra spelling instruction: Improving spelling, writing and reading right from the start. *Teaching Exceptional Children, 35,* 66-68.

Graham, S., Harris, K., & Larsen, L. (2001). Prevention and intervention of writing disabilities. *Learning Disabilities Research & Practice, 16*(2), 62-73.

Graham, S., & Miller, L. (1979). Spelling research and practice: A unified approach. *Focus on Exceptional Children,*

Graham, S., & Weintraub, N. (1996). A review of handwriting research: Progress and prospects from 1980 to 1994. *Educational Psychology Review, 8*(1), 7-87.

Graham, S., Weintraub, N., & Berninger, V. (1980). Handwriting remediation and principles: A unified approach. *Focus on Exceptional Children, 12,* 2.

Graham, S., & Weintraub, N. (1996). A review of handwriting research: Progress and prospects from 1980 to 1993. *Educational Psychology Review, 8,* 7-87.

Graham, S., Weintraub, N., & Berninger, V. (1998). The relationship between handwriting style and speed and legibility. *Journal of Educational Research, 91*(5), 390-296.

Graham, S., Weintraub, N., & Berninger, V. (2001). Which manuscript do primary grade children write legibly? *Journal of Educational Psychology, 93,* 488-497.

Grant, R. (1973). Strategic training for using text headings to improve students' processing of content. *Journal of Reading, 36*(6), 482-488.

Graves, D. H. (1994). *A fresh look at writing.* Portsmouth, NH: Heinemann.

Gregg, N. & Scott, S. (2000). Definition and documentation: Theory measurement and the courts. *Journal of Learning Disabilities, 31*(1). 5-13.

Gresham, F. M. (1989). Assessment of treatment integrity in school consultation and pre-referral intervention. *School Psychology Review, 18,* 37-50.

Gresham, F. M. (1997). Social competency and students with behavioral disorders: Where we've been, where we are, and where we should go. *Education and Treatment of Children, 20,* 233-249.

Gresham, F. M., & Elliot, S. N. (1990). *Social skills rating system.* Circle Pines, MN: American Guidance Service.

Gresham, F. M., Watson, T. S., & Skinner, C. H. (2001). FBA: Principles, procedures, and future directions. *School Psychology Review, 30,* 156-172.

Grossman H. (1996). *Special education in a diverse society.* Boston: Allyn & Bacon.

Guralnick, M. J. (Ed.). (1997). *The effectiveness of early intervention.* Baltimore: Paul H. Brookes.

Hagen, J. W. (1967). The effect of distraction on selective attention. *Child Development, 38,* 385-694.

Hallahan, D. P., Gajar, A. H., Cohen, S. G., & Tarver, S. G. (1978). Selective attention and focus of control in learning disabled and normal children. *Journal of Learning Disabilities, 11,* 231-236.

Hallahan, D. P., Lloyd, J. W., Kauffman, J. M., Weiss, M., & Martinez, E. A. (2005). *Learning disabilities: Foundation, characteristics and effective teaching.* Boston: Pearson/ Allyn & Bacon.

Hallahan, D. P., & Mercer, C. D. (2002). Learning disabilities: Historical perspectives. In R. Bradley, L. Danielson, & D. P. Hallahan (Eds.), *Identification of learning disabilities: Research to practice* (pp. 1–67). Mahwah, NJ: Erlbaum.

Hallerick, R. L. (1969). The creative learning center. *Elementary School Journal, 69,* 259–264.

Hambleton, R. K., & Murphy, E. (1992). A psychometric perspective on authentic measurement. *Applied Measurement in Education, 5*(1), 1–16.

Hammill, D. D. (1990). On defining learning disabilities: An emerging consensus. *Journal of Learning Disabilities, 23,* 74–84.

Hammill, D. D., & Bartel, N. R. (Eds.). (1971). *Educational perspective in learning disability.* New York: Wiley.

Hammill, D. D., & Bartel, N. R. (Eds.). (1990). *Teaching students with learning and behavior problems* (5th ed.). Boston: Allyn & Bacon.

Hammill, D. D., Brown, V. L., Larsen, S. C., & Wiederholt, J. L. (1994). *Test of adolescent and adult language* (3rd ed.). Austin, TX: PRO-ED.

Hammill, D. D., & Larsen, S. C. (1974). The effectiveness of psycholinguistic training. *Exceptional Children, 41,* 514.

Hammill, D. D., & Larsen, S. C. (1996). *Test of written language* (3rd ed.). Austin, TX: PRO-ED.

Hammill, D. D., & Newcomer, P. L. (1997). *Test of language development—intermediate* (3rd ed.). Austin, TX: PRO-ED.

Hanson, F. A. (1993). Testing testing: *Social consequences of the examined life.* Berkeley: University of California Press.

Harcourt Brace Educational Measurement (1995). *Stanford diagnostic reading text 4* (4th ed.). San Antonio, TX: Harcourt Brace Educational Assessment.

Harris, K. R., & Graham, S. (1997). *Making the writing process work: Strategies for composition and self-regulation.* Cambridge, MA: Brookline Books.

Harris, K. R., & Graham, S. (1999). Programming intervention research: Illustrations from the evolution of self-regulated strategy development. *Learning Disabilities Quarterly, 22,* 251–262.

Harris, K. R., Graham, S., & Mason, L. (2003). Self-regulated strategy development in the classroom: Part of a balanced approach to writing instruction for students with disabilities. *Focus on Exceptional Children, 35*(7), 1–16.

Harrison, P. L., Kaufman, A. S., Kaufman, N. L., Bruininks, R. H., Rynders, J., Ilmer, S., Sparrow, S. S., & Cicchetti, D. V. (1990). *AGS early screening profiles.* Circle Pines, MN: American Guidance Service.

Harry, B. (2002). Response to learning disabilities: Historical perspective. In R. Bradley, L. Danielson, & D. P. Hallahan (Eds.), *Identification of learning disabilities: Research to practice* (pp. 75–79). Mahwah, NJ: Erlbaum.

Harry, B., Allen, N., & McLaughlin, M. (1995). Communication versus compliance: African-American parents' involvement in special education. *Exceptional Children, 61,* 364–77.

Hazel, J. S., & Schumaker, J. B. (1988). Social skills and learning disabilities: Current issues and recommendations for future research. In J. F. Kavangh & T. J. Truss (Eds.), *Learning disabilities: Proceedings of the national conference* (pp. 293–344). Parkton, MD: York Press.

Hearne, D., & Stone, S. (1995). Multiple intelligences and underachievement: Lessons for individuals with learning disabilities. *Journal of Learning Disabilities, 28*(7), 439, 448.

Heddens, J. W., & Speer, W. R. (1987). *Today Part II: Activities and instructional ideas* (9th ed.). Upper Saddle River, NJ: Merrill/Prentice-Hall.

Heddens, J. W., & Speer, W. R. (1997). *Today's mathematics: Part I concepts and classroom methods* (10th ed.). New York: Wiley.

Heiman, T., & Margalit, M. (1998). Loneliness, depression, and social skills among students with mild mental retardation in different educational settings. *Journal of Special Education, 32,* 154–163.

Henry, F. M., & Reed, V. A. (1995). Adolescents' perceptions of the relative importance of communication skills. *Language, Speech, & Hearing Services in Schools, 26,* 263–273.

Henry, N. A., & Flynn, E. S. (1990). Rethinking special education referral: A procedural manual. *Intervention in School and Clinic, 26,* 22–24.

Herr, C. M., & Bateman, B. D. (2003). Learning disabilities and the law. In H. L. Swanson, K. R. Harris, & S. Graham (Eds.), *Handbook of learning disabilities* (pp. 256–272). New York: Guilford Press.

Heubert, J. P., & Hauser, R. M. (1999). *High stakes: Testing for tracking, promotion and graduation.* Washington, DC: National Academy Press.

Hinshelwood, J. (1917). *Congenital word-blindness.* London: H. K. Lewis.

Hobbs, N. (1978). Classification options: A conversation with Nicholas Hobbs on exceptional children. *Exceptional Children, 44,* 494–497.

Hocutt, A. M. (1996). Effectiveness of special education: Is placement the critical factor? *The Future of Children, 6*(1), 77–102.

Hoffman, A. J. (2000). Meeting the challenges of learning in adulthood. Baltimore, MD: Paul H. Brookes.

Hoffman, A. (2003). Teaching decision making to students with learning disabilities by promoting self-determination. ERIC Digest (ED 470036).

Hoffman, J. V., Roser, N. L., & Battle, J. (1993). Reading aloud in classrooms: From the modal toward the "model." *The Reading Teacher, 46*(6), 496–503.

Hofmeister, A. M. (1993). Elitism and reform in school mathematics. *Remedial and Special Education, 14*(6), 8–13.

Holloway, J. (2001, March). Inclusion and students with learning disabilities. *Educational Leadership,* 86–88.

Horowitz, S. H. (2005). Adolescents and young adults with LD: Transition and now. National Center for Learning Disabilities. Retrieved March 17, 2006, from http://www.ld.org/newsltr/0205newsltr/0205research.cfm.

House, J. E., Zimmer, J. W., & McInerney, W. F. (1991, Winter). Empowering teachers through the intervention team assistance team. *CASE in Point*, 5-8.

Hresko, W. P., Herron, S. R., & Peak, P. K. (1996). *Test of early written language* (2nd ed.). Austin, TX: PRO-ED.

Hresko, W. P., Reid, D. K., & Hammill, D. D. (1982). *Prueba del desarrollo inicial del lenguaje*. Austin, TX: PRO-ED.

Hresko, W. P., Reid, D. K., & Hammill, D. D. (1999). *Test of early language development*. (3rd ed.). Austin, TX: PRO-ED.

Hughes, C. A., Schumaker, J. B., Deshler, D. D., & Mercer, C. D. (1993). *Learning strategies curriculum: The test-taking strategy* (rev. ed.). Lawrence, KS: Edge Enterprises.

Hutchinson, N. L. (1993). Second invited response: Students with disabilities and mathematics education reform—Let the dialogue begin. *Remedial and Special Education, 14*(6), 20-23.

Hynd, G. W., Marshall, R., & Gonzalez, J. (1991). Learning disabilities and presumed central nervous system dysfunction. *Learning Disability Quarterly, 14*, 283-296.

Individuals with Disabilities Education Improvement Act (IDEA). (1997). P.L. 105-17. 105th Cong., 1st Sess.

Individuals with Disabilities Education Act of 2004. P.L. 108-446. 108th Cong., 2nd Sess.

Interagency Committee on Learning Disabilities. (1987). *Learning Disabilities: A report to the U.S. Congress*. Bethesda, MD: National Institute of Health.

Interagency Committee on Learning Disabilities (Ed.). (1988). *Learning disabilities: A report to the U.S. Congress*. Washington, DC: U.S. Government Printing Office.

Irlen, H. (1991). *Reading by the colors: Overcoming dyslexia and other disabilities through the Irlen method*. Garden City Park, NY: Avery.

Janiga, S. J., & Costenbader, V. (2002). The transition from high school to postsecondary education for students with learning disabilities: A survey of college service coordinators. *Journal of Learning Disabilities, 35*, 462-469.

Jenkins, J. R., & Mayhall, W. F. (1976). Development and evaluation of a resource teacher program. *Exceptional Children, 43*, 21-30.

Jimenez, J. E., del Rosario Ortiz, M., Rodrigo, M., Hernandez-Valle, I., Ramirez, G., Esteves, A., O'Shanahan, I., & Tralave, M. (2003). Do the effects of computer-assisted practice differ for children with reading disabilities with and without IQ-achievement discrepancies? *Journal of Learning Disabilities, 36*, 34-47.

Jimenez, J. E., Siegel, L. S., & Rodrigo Lopez, M. (2003). The relationship between IQ and reading disabilities in English-speaking Canadian and Spanish children. *Journal of Learning Disabilities, 36*, 19-33.

Johnson, D. J., & Myklebust, H. R. (1967). *Learning disabilities: Educational principles and practices*. New York: Grune & Stratton.

Johnson, D. W., & Johnson, R. T. (1995). Peacemakers: Teaching students to resolve their own and schoolmates' conflicts. In E. L. Myen, G. A. Vergason, & R. J. Whelan (Eds.), *Strategies for teaching exceptional children in inclusive settings* (pp. 311-329). Denver, CO: Love.

Johnson, E. R., Stodden, R. A., Emanuel, E. J., Luecking, R., & Mack, M. (2002). Current challenges facing secondary education and transition services. What research tells us. *Exceptional Children, 68*, 519-531.

Johnson, G. O. (1962). Special education for the mentally handicapped. *Exceptional Children, 29*, 62-69.

Johnson, L. J., Pugach, M. C., & Hammittee, D. (1988). Barriers to effective special education consultation. *Remedial and Special Education, 9*, 41-47.

Johnson, L. J., Zorn, D., Kai Yung Tam, B., Lamontagne, M., & Johnson, S. A. (2003). Stakeholders' views of factors that impact successful interagency collaboration. *Exceptional Children, 69*, 195-209.

Johnson-Martin, M. N., Attermeier, S. M., & Hacker, B. J. (1990). *The Carolina curriculum for preschoolers with special needs*. Baltimore: Paul H. Brookes.

Jordon, N. C., Levine, S. C., & Huttenlocher, J. (1995). Calculation abilities of young children with different patterns of cognitive functioning. *Journal of Learning Disabilities, 28*, 53-67.

Kalyanpur, M., & Harry, B. (1999). *Culture in special education: Building reciprocal family-professional relationships*. Baltimore: Paul H. Brookes.

Kalyanpur, M., & Rao, S. (1991). Empowering low-income black families of handicapped children. *American Journal of Orthopsychiatry, 61*(4), 523-532.

Kame'enui, E. J., Carnine, D. W., Dixon, R. C., Simmons, D. G., & Coyne, M. D. (2000). *Effective teaching strategies that accommodate diverse learners*. Upper Saddle River, NJ: Merrill/Prentice Hall.

Kandt, R. S. (1984). Neurological examination of children with learning disorders. *Pediatric Clinics of North America, 31*, 297-315.

Kass, C., & Myklebust, H. (1969). Learning Disability: An educational definition. *Journal of Learning Disabilities, 2*, 377-379.

Kaufman, A. S., & Kaufman, N. L. (1993). *Kaufman survey of early academic and language skills*. Circle Pines, MN: American Guidance Service.

Kaufman, J. M. (1993). How we might achieve radical reform of special education. *Exceptional Children, 60*, 6-16.

Kavale, K. A., & Forness, S. R. (1995). Social skill deficits and training: A meta-analysis of research in learning disabilities. *Advances in Learning and Behavioral Disabilities, 9*, 119-160.

Kavale, K. A., & Forness, S. R. (1996). Social skill deficits and LD: A meta-analysis. *Journal of Learning Disabilities, 29*, 226-237.

Kavale, K. A., & Mostert, M. P. (2004). Social skills interventions for individuals with learning disabilities. *Learning Disabilities Quarterly, 27*, 31-44.

Kephart, N. (1971). *The slow learner in the classroom*. Upper Saddle River, NJ: Merrill/Prentice Hall.

King-Sears, M. E. (2001). Three steps for gaining access to the general education curriculum for learners with disabilities. *Interactions in School and Clinic, 37,* 67-76.

King-Sears, M. E., & Mooney, J. E. (2004). Teaching content in an academically diverse class. In B. Lenz, D. D., Deshler, & B. R. Kissan (Eds.), *Teaching content to all: Evidence-based inclusive practices in middle and secondary school* (pp. 221-257.) Boston: Pearson Allyn & Bacon.

Kirk, S. A. (1962). *Educating exceptional children.* Boston: Houghton Mifflin.

Kirk, S. A. (1963). Behavioral diagnosis and remediation of learning disabilities. In *Proceedings of the conference on the exploration into problems of the perceptually handicapped child.* Evanston, IL: Fund for the Perceptually Handicapped Child.

Kirk, S. A. (1976). Samuel A. Kirk. In J. M. Kauffman & D. P. Hallahan (Eds.), *Teaching children with learning disabilities: Personal perspectives* (pp. 239-269). Columbus, OH: Merrill.

Kirk, S. A., & Chalfant, J. (1984). *Academic and developmental learning disabilities.* Denver, CO: Love.

Kirst, M. (1991). Improving children's services. *Phi Delta Kappan, 72,* 615-618.

Kline, F. M., Schumaker, J. B., & Deshler, D. D. (1991). Development and validation of feedback routines for instructing students with learning disabilities. *Learning Disabilities Quarterly, 14,* 191-207.

Kling, B. (2000). Assert yourself: Helping students of all ages develop self-advocacy skills. *Teaching Exceptional Children, 32*(3), 66-70.

Klinger, J. K., & Vaughn, S. (1999). Students' perceptions of instruction in inclusive classrooms: Implication for students with learning disabilities. *Exceptional Children, 66,* 23-27.

Klinger, J. K., & Vaughn, S. (2002). The changing roles and responsibilities of an LD specialist. *Learning Disabilities Quarterly, 25,* 19-32.

Knotek, S. (2003). Bias in problem solving and the social press of students' study teams: A qualitative investigation. *Journal of Special Education, 37,* 2-14.

Koegal, R. L., & Covert, A. (1972). The relationship of self-stimulation to learning in autistic children. *Journal of Applied Behavior Analysis, 5,* 381-387.

Kohler, P. D., & Field, S. (2003). Transition-focused education: Foundation for the future. *Journal of Special Education, 37,* 174-183.

Korinek, L., & Popp, P. A. (1997). Collaborative mainstream integration of social skills with academic instruction. *Preventing School Failure, 41,* 148-152.

Kortering, L. J., de Bettencourt, L. U., & Braziel, P. M. (2005). Improving performance in high school algebra: What students with LD are saying. *Learning Disabilities Quarterly, 28,* 191-203.

Kottmeyer, W. (1970). *Teacher's guide to remedial spelling.* New York: McGraw-Hill.

Krackendoffel, E. A., Robinson, S. M., Deshler, D. D., & Schumaker, J. B. (1992). *Collaborative problem solving.* Lawrence, KS: Edge Enterprises.

Kroesberger, E. H. & VanLuit, J. E. H. (2003). Mathematics intervention for children with special education needs: A meta-analysis. *Remedial and Special Education, 24*(2), 97-114.

Kronick, D. (1973). *Social development of learning disabled persons.* San Francisco: Jossey-Bass.

Kroth, R. L., & Edge, D. (1997). *Strategies for communicating with parents and families of exceptional children* (3rd ed.) Denver, CO: Love.

Kroth, R. L., & Otteni, H. (1985). Parent education programs that work: A model. *Focus on Exceptional Children, 15*(8), 1-16.

Kruger, L. J., Struzziero, J., Watts, R., and Vocca, D. (1995). The relationship between organizational support and satisfaction with teacher assistance teams. *Remedial and Special Education, 16,*(4), 203-211.

Kussmaul, A. (1877). Word deafness and word blindness. In H. von Ziemssen & J. A. T. McCreery (Eds.), *Cyclopedia of the practice of medicine* (pp. 770-778). New York: William Wood.

Lahey, M. (1988). *Language disorders and language development.* Needham, MA: Macmillan.

Lapadat, J. C. (1991). Pragmatic language skills of students with language and/or LD: A quantitative synthesis. *Journal of LD, 24,* 147-158.

Larsen, S. C., Hammill, D. D., & Moats, J. C. (1999). *Test of written spelling* (4th ed.). Austin, TX: PRO-ED.

Learning Disability Roundtable. (2002). *Finding common ground.* Washington, DC: National Joint Committee on Learning Disabilities.

Lehmann, J. P., Davies, T. G., & Laurin, K. M. (2000). Listening to student voices about postsecondary education. *Teaching Exceptional Children, 32*(5), 60-65.

Lenz, B. K., Alley, G. R., & Schumaker, J. B. (1987). Activating the inactive learner: Advance organizers in the secondary content classroom. *Learning Disability Quarterly, 10*(1), 53-67.

Lenz, B. K., Bulgren, J., & Hudson, P. (1990). Content enhancement: A model for promoting the acquisition of content by individuals with learning disabilities. In T. E. Scruggs & B. Y. L. Wong (Eds.), *Intervention research in learning disabilities* (pp. 122-165). New York: Springer-Verlag.

Lenz, B. K., & Hughes, C. A. (1990). A word identification strategy for adolescents with learning disabilities. *Journal of Learning Disabilities, 23,* 149-158, 163.

Lenz, B. K., Schumaker, J. B., Deshler, D. D., & Beals, V. L. (1984). *The learning strategies curriculum: The word identification strategy.* Lawrence: University of Kansas Center for Research on Learning.

Leong, C. K. (1999). What can we learn from language in China? In I. Lundberg, T. T. Tonnessen, & I. Austard (Eds.), *Dylexia: Advances in theory and practice* (pp. 117-139). Dordrecht: Kluwer Academic.

Lerner, J. (2006). *Learning disabilities and related disorders: Characteristics and teaching strategies.* Boston: Houghton Mifflin.

Lerner, J., Lowenthal, B., & Egan, R. (2003). *Preschool children with special needs: Children at-risk and children with disabilities.* Needham Heights, MA: Allyn & Bacon.

Leung, B. (1996). Quality assessment priorities in a diverse society. *Teaching Exceptional Children, 28*(3), 42–45.

Lewis, R. B. (1998). Assistive technology and learning disabilities: Today's realities and tomorrow's promises. *Journal of Learning Disabilities, 31*, 16–26.

Lewis, R. B., & Doorlag, D. H. (2006). *Teaching special students in general education classroom* (7th ed.). Upper Saddle River, NJ: Merrill/Prentice Hall.

Lewis, T. J., Powers, L. J., Kelk, M. J., & Newcomer, L. (2002). Reducing problem behavior on the playground: An investigation of the application of school-wide positive behavior supports. *Psychology in the School, 39*, 181–190.

Lewis, T. J., & Sugai, G. (1999). Effective behavior support: A systems approach to proactive schoolwide management. *Focus on Exceptional Children, 31*(6), 1–24.

Lewis, T. J., Sugai, G., & Colvin, G. (1998). Reducing problem behavior through a school-wide system of effective behavior supports: Investigation of a school-wide social skills training program and contextual interventions. *School Psychology Review, 27*, 446–459.

Lewis-Palmer, T., Flannery, K. B., Sugai, G., & Eber, L. (2002). *Applying a system approach to school-wide discipline in secondary school: What we are learning and need to know.* Arlington, VA: Council for Children with Behavioral Disorders.

Lindsley, O. R. (1991). From technical jargon to plain English for application. *Journal of Applied Behavior Analysis, 24*, 449–458.

Lloyd, J. W., & Hallahan, P. P. (2005). Going forward: How the field of learning disabilities has and will continue to contribute to education. *Learning Disabilities Quarterly, 28*, 133–136.

Lochner, P. A. (2000). *Instructional support teams.* Seaford, NY: Executive Educational Solutions.

Lochner, P. A., & McNamara, B. E. (1989, April). *Meeting the needs of the atypical learner.* Paper presented at the annual convention of the Council for Exceptional Children, Toronto.

Lock, R. H. (1996, Winter). Adapting mathematics instructions in the general education classroom for students with mathematical disabilities. L. D. Forum: Council for Learning Disabilities, Winter. Retrieved June 15, 2004 from http:// www.ldonline.org/ld_indepth/math-skills/adopt_ld.html.

Lock, R. H., & Layton, C. A. (2001). Succeeding in secondary education through self-advocacy. *Teaching Exceptional Children, 34*(2), 66–71.

Locke, E. A., & Latham, G. P. (1990). A theory of goal setting and task performance: 1969–1980. *Psychological Bulletin, 90*, 125–152.

Losen, D., & Orfield, G. (Eds.). (2002). *Racial inequality in special education.* Cambridge, MA: Harvard University Press.

Lynch, E. W., & Hanson, M. J. (Eds.). (1998). *Developing cross-cultured competence: A guide for working with young children and their families* (2nd ed.). Baltimore: Paul H. Brookes.

Lyon, G. R. (1995a). Research initiatives in learning disabilities: Contributions from scientists supported by the National Institute of Child Health and Human Development. *Journal of Child Neurology, 10*(Suppl. 1), 120–126.

Lyon, G. R. (1995b). Toward a definition of dyslexia. *Annals of Dyslexia, 45*, 3–27.

Lyon, G. R. (1999). The NICHD research program in reading development, reading disorders, and reading instruction. Retrieved January 21, 2004, from http://www.ncld.org/research/keys99_nichd.cfm.

Lyon, G. R. (2001). Rethinking learning disabilities. In *rethinking special education for a new century.* Retrieved November 10, 2003, from: www.ppionline.org.

Lyon, G. R. (2002). *The current status and impact of U.S. reading research.* Keynote address at the meeting of the National Association of University Centers for Excellence in Developmental Disabilities, Bethesda, MD.

Lyon, G. R. (2005). Why scientific research must guide educational policy and instructional practices in learning disabilities. *Learning Disabilities Quarterly, 28*, 140–143.

Lyon, G. R., Fletcher, J. M., Shaywitz, S. E., Shaywitz, B. A., Torgessen, J. K., Woods, E. B., Schulte, A., & Olson, R. (2001). Rethinking learning disabilities. In C. E. Finn, Jr., A. J. Rotherham, & C. R. Hokanson, Jr. (Eds.), in *Rethinking special education for a new century* (pp. 259–288). Washington, D C: Thomas B. Fordham Foundation.

Maccini, P., & Hughes, C. A. (1997). Mathematics intervention for adolescents with learning disabilities. *Learning Disabilities Research and Practice, 12*(3), 168–176.

Mace, F. C., Belfiore, P. J., & Hutchinson, J. M. (2001). Operant theory and research in self-regulation. In B. Zimmerman & D. Schunk (Eds.), *Learning and academic achievement: Theoretical perspectives* (pp. 39–65). Mahwah, NJ: Erlbaum.

MacMillan, D. L. (1971). Special education for the mildly retarded: Servant or savant. *Focus on Exceptional Children, 29*, 1–11.

MacMillan, D. L., Gresham, F. M., & Bocian, K. M. (1998a). Discrepancy between definitions of learning disabilities and school practices: An empirical investigation. *Journal of Learning Disabilities, 31*, 314–326.

MacMillan, D. L., Greshman, F. M., & Bocian, K. M. (1998b). Curing mental retardation and causing learning disabilities: Consequence of using various WISC-III IQs to estimate aptitude of Hispanic students. *Journal of Psychoeducational Assessment, 16*, 36–54.

MacMillan, D. L., & Saperstein, G. N. (2002). Learning disabilities as operationally defined by schools. In R. Bradley, L. Danielson, & D. P. Hallahan (Eds.), *Identification of learning disabilities: Research to Practice* (pp. 287-333). Mahwah, NJ: Erlbaum.

Madaus, J. W. (2005). Navigating the college transition maze: A guide for students with learning disabilities. *Teaching Exceptional Children, 37,* 32-37.

Madaus, J. W., Folley, T. E., McGuire, J. M., & Ruban, L. M. (2002). Employment self-disclosure of postsecondary graduates with learning disabilities: Rates and rationales. *Journal of Learning Disabilities, 35*(4), 364-369.

Madaus, J. W., & Shaw, S. F. (2004). Section 504: The differences in the regulations regarding secondary and postsecondary education. *Intervention in School and Clinic, 40,* 81-87.

Magiera, K., Smith, C., Zigmond, N., & Gerbauer, K. (2005). Benefits of co-teaching in secondary mathematics classes. *Teaching Exceptional Children, 37*(3), 20-24.

Maheady, L. Towne, R., Algozzine, B., Mercer, J., & Ysseldyke, J. (1983). Minority overrepresentation: A case for alternative practices prior to referral. *Learning Disabilities Quarterly, 64,* 448-456.

Maher, C.A., & Bennett, R. E. (1984). *Planning and evaluating special education services.* Upper Saddle River, NJ: Merrill/Prentice Hall.

Maher, C.A., & Illback, R. J. (1985). Implementing school psychological programs: Description and application of the DURABLE approach. *Journal of School Psychology, 23*(1), 81-89.

Maldonado-Colon, E. (1991). Development of second language learners' linguistic and cognitive abilities. *The Journal of Educational Issues of Language Minority Students, 9,* 37-48.

Malian, I. M., & Nevin, A. (2002). A review of self-determination literature: Implications for practitioners. *Remedial and Special Education, 23,* 68-74.

Malmgren, K., Abbot, R. H., & Hawkins, J. D. (1999). Learning disabilities and juvenile delinquency: Rethinking the link. *Journal of Learning Disabilities, 32,* 194-200.

Mann, L. (1979). *On the trail of process.* New York: Grune & Stratton.

Mann, L., & Phillips, W. A. (1967). Fractional practices in special education: A critique. *Exceptional Children, 33,* 311-317.

Manset, G., & Semmel, M. J. (1997). Are inclusive programs for students with disabilities effective? A comparative review of a model program. *Journal of Special Education, 31,* 155-180.

Marchand-Martella, N. E., Slocum, T. A., & Martella, R. C. (Eds.). (2004). *Introduction to direct instruction.* Boston: Pearson.

Mardell-Czudnowski, C., & Goldenberg, D. S. (1998). *Developmental indicators for the assessment of learning—3 (DIAL—3)* (3rd ed.). Circle Pines, MN: American Guidance Service.

Martin, E.W. (2002). Response to learning disabilities: Historical perspective. In R. Bradley, L. Danielson & D. P. Hallahan (Eds.), *Identification of learning disabilities: Research to practice* (pp. 82-87). Mahwah, NJ: Erlbaum.

Mastropieri, M.A., & Scruggs, T. E. (1998). Constructing more meaningful relationships in the classroom: Mnemonic research into practice. *Learning Disabilities Research and Practice, 13*(3), 138-145.

Mastropieri, M. A., & Scruggs, T. E. (2005). Feasibility and consequences of response to intervention: Examination of the issues of scientific evidence as a model for the identification of individuals with learning disabilities. *Journal of Learning Disability, 38,* 525-531.

Mastropieri, M. A., Scruggs, T. E., & Fulk, B. J. M. (1990). Teaching abstract vocabulary with the keyword method: Effects on recall and comprehension. *Journal of Learning Disabilities, 23,* 92-96.

Mastropieri, M. A., Scruggs, T. E., Graetz, J., Norlad, J., Garchizi, W., & McDuffie, K. (2005). Case studies in co-teaching in the content areas: Successes, failures, and challenges. *Intervention in School and Clinic, 40,* 260-270.

Mayan, I., & Nevin, A. (2005). A review of self-determination literature: A guide for practitioners. *Remedial and Special Education, 23,* 68-75.

Mayer, R. E. (1987). *Educational psychology: A cognitive approach.* Boston: Little, Brown.

McConaughy, S., Mattison, R. E., & Peterson, R. L. (1994). Behavioral/emotional problems of children with serious emotional disturbances and L.D. *School Psychology Review, 23,* 8-15.

McCoy, E. M., & Prehm, H. J. (1987). *Teaching mainstreamed students. Methods and techniques.* Denver, CO: Love.

McGhee, R., Bryant, B. R., Larsen, S. C., & Rivera, D. M. (1995). *Test of written expression.* Austin, TX: PRO-ED.

McGrady, H. J. (2002). A commentary on empirical and theoretical support for direct diagnosis of learning disabilities by assessment of intrinsic processing weaknesses. In R. Bradley, L. Danielson, & D. P. Hallahan (Eds.), *Identification of learning disabilities: Research to practice* (pp. 623-633). Mahwah, NJ: Erlbaum.

McIntosh, R., Vaughn, S., & Zaragoza, N. (1991). A review of social interventions for students with LD. *Journal of Learning Disabilities, 24,* 451-458.

McLesky, J., & Waldron, N. L. (2002). Inclusion and school change: Teachers' perceptions regarding curricular and instructional strategies. *Teacher Educational Special Education, 25,* 41-54.

McNamara, B. E. (1989). *The resource room: A guide for special educators.* Albany: State University of New York Press.

McNamara, B. E. (1999). *Learning disabilities: Appropriate practices for a diverse population.* Albany: State University of New York Press.

McNamara, B. E., & McNamara, F. J. (1993). *Keys to parenting a child with A.D.D.* Hauppauge, NY: Barron Educational.

McNamara, B. E., & McNamara, F. J. (1995). *Keys to parenting a child with a learning disability.* Hauppauge, NY: Barron Educational.

McNamara, B. E., & McNamara, F. J. (1997). *Keys to dealing with bullies.* Hauppauge, NY: Barron Educational.

McNamara, B. E., & McNamara, F. J. (2000). *Keys to parenting a child with A.D.D.* (2nd ed.). Hauppauge, NY: Barron Educational.

Meisels, S. J., Marsden, D. B., Wiske, M. S., & Henderson, L. W. (1997). *Early screening and inventory (ESI—R)* (rev.). Ann Arbor, MI: Rebus.

Mellard, D. F. (1998). Screening for learning disability in adult literacy programs. In B. Lenz, N.A. Sturomski, & M.A. Corley (Eds.), *Serving adults with learning disabilities: Implications for effective practice* (pp. 13–28). Washington, DC: National Adult Literacy and Learning Disability Center, Academy for Educational Development.

Mellard, D. F., & Lancaster, P. E. (2003). Incorporating adult community resource in students' transition planning. *Remedial and Special Education, 24,* 359–369.

Menchetti, B. M., & Garcia, L. A. (2003). Personal and employment outcomes of person-centered career planning. *Educational and Training in Developmental Abilities, 38,* 145–156.

Mercer, C. D. (1997). *Learning disabilities.* Columbus, OH: Merrill.

Mercer, C. D., Jordan, L., Allsopp, D., & Mercer, A. (1996). Learning disabilities definitions and criteria used by the state education departments. *Learning Disability Quarterly, 19*(2), 217–232.

Mercer, C. D., & Mercer, A. R. (2001). *Teaching students with learning problems* (6th ed.). Upper Saddle River, NJ: Merrill/Prentice Hall.

Mercer, C. D., & Mercer, A. R. (2005). *Teaching students with learning problems* (7th ed.). Upper Saddle River, NJ: Merrill/Prentice Hall.

Mercer, C. D., & Pullen, P. C. (2005). *Students with learning disabilities* (6th ed.). Upper Saddle River, NJ: Merrill/Prentice Hall.

Messick, S. (1987). *Assessment in the schools: Purposes and consequences.* (Research Report RR-87-51). Princeton, NJ: Educational Testing Service.

Miller, L. J. (1992). *First STEPS: Screening test for evaluating preschoolers.* San Antonio, TX: Psychological Corporation.

Miller, L. J. (1995). Spelling and handwriting. In J. S. Choate, B. E. Enright, L. J. Miller, J. A. Poteet, & T. A. Rakes (Eds.), *Curriculum-based assessment and programming* (3rd ed., pp. 241–285). Boston: Allyn & Bacon.

Miller, L. J., Sanchez, J., & Hynd, G. W. (2003). Neurological correlates of reading disorders. In H. L. Swanson, K. R. Harris, & S. Graham (Eds.), *Handbook of learning disabilities* (pp. 242–255). New York: Guilford Press.

Miller, S., Butler, F., & Lee, K. (1998). Validated practices for teaching mathematics to students with learning disabilities:

A review of the literature. *Focus on Exceptional Children, 31*(1), 1–24.

Miller, S., & Mercer, C. (1997). Education aspects of mathematics disabilities. *Journal of Learning Disabilities, 30*(1), 47–56.

Minskoff, E. H., & DeMoss, S. (1993). Facilitating successful transition: Using the TRAC model to access develop academic skills needed for vocational competence. *Learning Disability Quarterly, 16,* 161–170.

Mishna, F. (2003). Learning disabilities and bullying: Double jeopardy. *Journal of Learning Disabilities, 36,* 336–347.

Monroe, M. (1928). Methods for diagnosis and treatment of cases of reading disability. *Genetic Psychology Monographs, 4,* 341–456.

Monroe, M. (1932). *Children who cannot read.* Chicago: University of Chicago Press.

Montague, M. (1997). Cognitive strategy instruction in mathematics for students with learning disabilities. *Journal of Learning Disabilities, 30,* 164–177.

Montague, M., Applegate, B., & Marquard, K. (1993). Cognitive strategy instruction and mathematical problem-solving performance of students with learning disabilities. *Learning Disabilities Research & Practice, 8,* 223–232.

Morgan, W. P. (1896). A case of congenital word blindness. *British Medical Journal, 2,* 1378.

Moses, N., Klein, H. B., & Altman, E. (1990). An approach to assessing and facilitating causal language in adults with learning disabilities based on Piagetian theory. *Journal of Learning Disabilities, 23,* 220–228.

Moses, S. (1990). School psychologists raise sights. *APA Monitor, 21*(11), 36.

Mull, C., Sitlington, P. L., & Alper, S. (2001). Postsecondary education for students with learning disabilities: A synthesis of the literature. *Exceptional Children, 68*(1), 97–118.

Mullen, E. M. (1995). *Mullen scales of early learning.* Circle Pines, MN: American Guidance Service.

Murawski, W. W., & Swanson, H. L. (2002). A meta-analyses of co-teaching research: Where are the data? *Research and Special Education, 22,* 258–267.

Murray, C. (1976). *The link between learning disabilities and juvenile delinquency: Current theory and knowledge* (Grant No. 76JN-99-0009). Washington DC: Juvenile Justice and Delinquency Prevention Operative Task Group, Law Enforcement Administration, U.S., Department of Justice.

Myers, P., & Hammill, D. D. (1990). *Learning disabilities: Basic concepts, assessment practices, and instructional strategies.* Austin, TX: PRO-ED.

National Advisory Committee on Handicapped Children. (1968). *Special education for handicapped children* (First Annual Report). Washington, DC: Department of Health, Education, and Welfare.

National Center for Learning Disabilities. (2002). No child left behind and students with learning disabilities: Ensuring full participation and equal accountability: Retrieved May 1, 2004, from http://www.ld.org/advocacy/nclb_policy.cfm

National Center for Learning Disabilities. (2004). IDEA 2004: Changes to the identification and eligibility procedures for specific learning disabilities. Frequently asked questions. Retrieved March 19, 2005, from http://www.ld.org/advocacy/IDEA04FedReg.CFM.

National Center for Learning Disabilities. (2005a). Changes to the identification and eligibility procedures for specific learning disabilities: Frequently asked questions. Retrieved March 19, 2005, from http://www.ld.org/advocacy/IDEA04FedReg.cfm.

National Center for Learning Disabilities. (2005b). *Guide to frequently asked questions: Individuals with Disabilities Education Improvement Act.* Washington, DC: Author.

National Council of Supervisors of Mathematics. (1988). *Twelve components of essential mathematics.* Minneapolis, MN: Author.

National Council of Teachers of Mathematics. (2000). *Principles and standards for school mathematics.* Reston, VA: Author.

National Information Center for Children and Youth with Disabilities (NICHCY). (1997). Module 8: Least restrictive environment background text. Retrieved April 12, 2004, from http://www.nickey.org/Trainpkg/traintext/8txt.htm.

National Joint Committee on Learning Disabilities. (1981). *Learning disabilities: Issues and definition.* Unpublished manuscript. (Available from The Orton Dyslexia Society, 724 York Road, Baltimore, MD 21204. Reprinted in *Journal of Learning Disabilities, 20,* 107-108.

National Joint Committee on Learning Disabilities. (1988). Letter to NJCLD member organizations.

National Joint Committee on Learning Disabilities. (2001). *Collective perspectives on issues affecting learning disabilities: Position papers, statements, and reports.* Austin, TX: PRO-ED.

National Joint Committee on Learning Disabilities. (2002). *Finding common ground.* Washington, DC: The 2002 Learning Disabilities Roundtable.

National longitudinal transition study-2 (NLTS2). (2005). Menlo Park, CA: SRI International.

National Reading Panel. (2000). Teaching children to read: An evidence-based assessment of the scientific research literature on reading and implications for reading instruction. Washington, DC: National Institute of Child Health and Human Development. Retrieved April 12, 2004 from: www.nichd.nih.gov/publications/nrp/smallbook.htm.

Neil, M., & Medina, N. (1989). Standardized testing: Harmful to educational health. *Phi Delta Kappan, 70,* 689-697.

National Research Council. (2000). *Neurons to neighborhoods.* Committee on Integrating the Sciences of Early Childhood Development, Board on Children, Youth and Families, J. P. Shonkoff and D. A. Phillips (eds.). Washington, DC: National Academy Press.

Neubert, D. A., & Moon, M. S. (2000). How a transition profile helps students prepare for life in the community. *Teaching Exceptional Children, 33*(2), 20-25.

Neufeld, P. (2006). Comprehensive instruction in content area classes. *The Reading Teacher, 59,* 302-311.

Newcomer, P. L. (1999). *Standardized reading inventory—2.* Austin, TX: PRO-ED.

Newcomer, P. L., & Hammill, D. D. (1997). *Test of language development primary* (3rd ed.). Austin, TX: PRO-ED.

New York State United Teachers. (2000, December), *Consultant teacher services.* (Information Bulletin 990038.) Albany, NY: Author.

Nippold, M. (1993). Developmental markers in adolescent language: Syntax, semantics, and pragmatics. *Language Speech and Hearing Services in Schools, 24,* 21-28.

Office for Civil Rights (1989). *The civil rights of students with hidden disabilities under Section 504 of the Rehabilitation Acts of 1973.* Washington, DC: Author.

Office for Civil Rights (1998). *1997 Elementary and secondary schools civil rights compliance report: National state projections.* Washington, DC: Author.

Olweus, D. (2003). A profile of bullying at school. *Educational Leadership, 60*(6), 12-17.

Orton, S. (1937). *Reading, writing, and speech problems in children.* New York: W. W. Norton.

OSEP Technical Assistance Center on Positive Behavioral Interventions & Supports. (2003). *Schoolwide PBS.* Retrieved January 21, 2005, from http://www.pbis.org/english/Schoolwide_ PBS.htm.

Overton, S. (2005). *Collaborating with families.* Upper Saddle River, NJ: Merrill/Prentice Hall.

Palincsar, A. S., & Brown, A. L. (1984). Reciprocal teaching of comprehension fostering and comprehension monitoring activities. *Cognition and Instruction, 1*(2), 117-175.

Parent Center, Albuquerque Public School. (1995).

Park, J., Turnbull, A. P., & Turnbull, H. R. (2002). Impacts of poverty on the quality of life in the future of children with disabilities. *Exceptional Children, 68*(2), 151-170.

Pastor, P. N., & Reuben, C. A. (2002). Attention deficit disorder and learning disability: United States, 1997-98. In *National Center for Health Statistics: Vital Health Statistics* (DHHS Publication No. PHS 2002-15 34). Hyattsville, MD: Department of Health and Human Services.

Patton, J. R., & Polloway, E. A. (1992). Learning disabilities: The challenge of adulthood. *Journal of Learning Disabilities, 25,* 410-416.

Pearl, R., Donahue, M., & Bryan, T. (1985). The development of tact: Children's strategies for delivering bad news. *Journal of Applied Developmental Psychology, 6,* 141-149.

Pedrotty Bryant, D., Bryant, B. R., & Hammill, D. D. (2000). Characteristic behaviors of students with LD who have teacher-identified math weakness. *Journal of Learning Disabilities, 33,* 168-178.

Peenan, J. (1995, September). Danger signs of overrepresentation of minorities in special education. *C.E.C. Today,* p. 7.

Pemberton, J. B. (2003). Communicating academic progress as an integral part of assessment. *Teaching Exceptional Children, 35,* 16-29.

Pennington, B. F., & Gilger, J. W. (1996). How is dyslexia transmitted? In C. H. Chase, G. D. Rosen, & G. F. Sherman (Eds.), *Developmental dyslexia: Neural, cognitive, and genetic mechanisms* (pp. 41-61). Baltimore: York Press.

Perlmutter, B. F. (1983). Sociometric status and related personality characteristics of mainstreamed learning disabled adolescents. *Learning Disabilities Quarterly, 6,* 20-30.

Pertsh, C. F. (1936). *A comparative study of the progress of subnormal pupils in the grades and in special classes.* Unpublished doctoral dissertation, Teachers College, Columbia University.

Pffifner, L. J., & O'Leary, S. G. (1993). School-based psychological treatments. In J. L. Matson (Ed.), *Handbook of hyperactivity in children* (pp. 234-255). Boston: Allyn & Bacon.

Phelps-Terasaki, D., & Phelps-Gunn, T. (1992). *Test of pragmatic language.* Austin, TX: PRO-ED.

Pike, K., Compain, R., & Mumper, J. (1994). *New connections: An integrated approach to literacy.* New York: HarperCollins.

Pike, K., Compain, R., & Mumper, J. (1997). *New connections: An integrated approach to literacy* (2nd ed.). New York: Longman.

Pike, K., & Salend, S. J. (1995). Authentic assessment strategies. Alternative to norm-referenced testing. *Teaching Exceptional Children, 28* (1), 15-21.

Pollitt, E. H., Ma, H., & Harahap, H. (1994). Stunting and delayed motor development in rural West Java. *American Journal of Human Biology, 6*(5), 627-635.

Polloway, E. H., & Patton, J. R. (1996). *Strategies for teaching learners with special needs* (6th ed.). Columbus, OH: Merrill.

Ponte, C. R., Zins, J. E., & Graden, J. L. (1988). Implementing a consolidation-based service delivery system to decrease referrals for special education. A case study of organizational considerations. *School Psychology Review, 17,* 89-100.

Poteet, J. A., Choate, J. S., & Stewart, S. C. (1993, October). Performance assessment and special education: Practices and prospects. *Focus on Exceptional Children,* 1-13.

Poteet, J. A., Choote, J. S., & Stewart, S. C. (1996). Performance assessment and special education: Practices and prospects. In E. L. Meyer, G. A. Vergasor, & R. J. Whelan (Eds.), *Strategies for teaching exceptional children in inclusive settings* (pp. 209-242). Denver, CO: Love.

Pressley, M. (1986). The relevance of the good strategy user model to the teaching of mathematics. *Educational Psychologist, 21,* 139-161.

Pressley, M. (1994). Embracing the complexity of individual differences in cognition: Studying good information processing and how it might develop. *Learning and Individual Differences, 6,* 259-284.

Pressley, M., Cariglia-Bull, S. D., & Schneider, W. (1987). Short-term memory, verbal competence, and age as predictors of an imaginary structural effectiveness. *Journal of Experimental Child Psychology, 43,* 194-211.

Price, L. A., & Gerber, P. J. (2001). At second glance: Employers and employees with learning disabilities in the Americans with Disability Act era. *Journal of Learning Disabilities, 34*(3), 202, 211.

Pugach, M. C., & Johnson, L. J. (1989). Preferred interventions: Progress, problems, and challenges. *Exceptional Children, 56,* 217-226.

Quality Education for Minorities. (1990). *Education that works: An action plan for the education of minorities.* Cambridge, MA: Quality Education for Minorities Project.

Quenneville, J. (2001). Tech tools for students with LD: Infusion into inclusive classrooms. *Preventing School Failure, 45,* 167-170.

Ramp, A. (1999). How to tell parents their child has a disability. *CEC Today, 5*(8), 6.

Rapport, M. D. (1987). *The attention training system: User's manual.* DeWitt, NY: Gordon System.

Rapport, M. D., Stover, G., Du Paul, G. J., Birmingham, B. K., & Tucker, S. (1985). Methylphenidate in hyperactive children: Differential effects of dose on academic, learning, and social behavior. *Journal of Abnormal Child Psychology, 13,* 227-244.

Raskind, W. H. (2001). Current understanding of the genetic basis of reading and spelling disability. *Learning Disability Quarterly, 24,* 141-158.

Raskind, W. H., Goldberg, R. J., Higgins, E. L., & Herman, K. L. (2006). Predictors of success in individuals with learning disabilities: Results from a twenty-year longitudinal study. Retrieved January 7, 2006, from http://www.ldonline.org/ld_indepth/general_info/predictor_of_success.html.

Rea, P. J., McLaughlin, V. L., & Walther-Thomas, C. (2002). Outcomes for students with learning disabilities in inclusive and pull-out programs. *Exceptional Children, 68,* 203-222.

Reger, R. (1969). *Resource room program: Outline and concept.* Erie County, NY: BOCES 1.

Reger, R. (1972). Resource rooms: Change agents or guardians of the status quo? *The Journal of Special Education, 6,* 355-359.

Reger, R. (1973). What is a resource room program? *Journal of Learning Disabilities, 6,* 607-614.

Reid, R., Trout, A. L., & Schwartz, M. (2005). Self-regulation intervention for children with ADHD. *Exceptional Children, 71,* 361-378.

Reiff, H. (2004). Reframing the learning disability experience redux. *Learning Disabilities Research and Practice, 19,* 185-198.

Reiter, D. (1986). *The role of the resource room teacher.* Master's thesis, Hofstra University.

Reith, H., & Polsgrove, L. (1994). Curriculum and instructional issues in teaching secondary students with learning disabilities. *Learning Disabilities Research and Practice, 9,* 118-126.

Reschly, D. J. (2005). Learning disabilities identification. Primary intervention, secondary intervention, and then what? *Journal of Learning Disabilities, 38,* 510-515.

Rhodes, L. K., & Shanklin, N. L. (1993). *Windows into literacy: Assessing learners k-8.* Postmouth, NH: Heinemann.

Rice, D., & Zigmond, N. (2000). Co-teaching in secondary schools. *Learning Disabilities Research and Practice, 15,* 190-197.

Rivera, M. D. (1993). Third invited response: Examining mathematics reform and the implications for students with mathematics disabilities. *Remedial and Special Education, 14*(6), 24-27.

Robbins, M., & Glass, G. V. (1969). The Doman-Delacato rationale: A critical analysis. In J. Hellmuth (Ed.), *Educational therapy: Vol II* (pp. 321-377). Seattle, WA: Special Child Publications.

Rodis, P., Garrod, A., & Boscardin, M. L. (2001). *Learning disability and life stories.* Needham Heights, MA: Allyn & Bacon.

Roffman, A. J. (2000). *Meeting the challenges of learning disabilities in adulthood.* Baltimore: Paul H. Brookes.

Rosen, L. A., O'Leary, S., Joyce, S. A., Conway, G., & Pfiffner, L. (1984). The importance of prudent negative consequences for maintaining the appropriate behavior of hyperactive students. *Journal of Abnormal Child Psychology, 12,* 581-604.

Ross, A. O. (1976). *Psychological aspects of learning disabilities and reading disorders.* New York: McGraw-Hill.

Rourke, B. P. (1989). *Nonverbal learning disabilities: The syndrome and the model.* New York: Guilford Press.

Rourke, B. P. (1995). *Syndrome of nonverbal learning disabilities: Neurodevelopmental manifestations.* New York: Guilford Press.

Russell, R. L., & Ginsberg, H. D. (1984). Cognitive analysis of children's mathematical difficulties. *Cognition and Instruction, 1,* 217-244.

Sabatino, D. A. (1972). Resource rooms: The renaissance in special education. *The Journal of Special Education, 6,* 335-347.

Salend, S. J. (1983). Self-assessment: A model for involving students in the formation of their IEPs. *Journal of School Psychology, 21,* 65-70.

Salend, S. J. (1994). *Effective mainstreaming: Creating inclusive classrooms* (2nd ed.). Upper Saddle River, NJ: Merrill/Prentice Hall.

Salend, S. J. (2001). *Creating inclusive classrooms: Effective and reflective practices for all students* (4th ed.). Upper Saddle River, NJ: Pearson Education.

Salend, S. J. (2005). *Creating inclusive classrooms: Effective and reflective practices for all students* (5th ed.). Upper Saddle River, NJ: Pearson Education.

Salend, S. J., & Salinas, A. (2003). Language differences or learning difficulties. *Teaching Exceptional Children, 35,* 36-43.

Salvia, J., & Ysseldyke, J. E. (1995). *Assessment in special and remedial education* (5th ed.). Boston: Houghton Mifflin.

Salvia, J., & Ysseldyke, J. E. (2001). *Assessment* (7th ed.). Boston: Houghton Mifflin.

Sax, C. L., & Thoma, C. A. (2002). *Transition assessment: Wise practices for quality lives.* Baltimore: Paul H. Brookes.

Scarborough, H. S. (1990). Very early language deficits in dyslexic children. *Child Development, 61,* 1728-1743.

Scarborough, H. S. (1998). Predicting the future achievement of second grades with reading disabilities: Contribution of phonemic awareness, verbal memory, rapid memory, and I.Q. *Annals of Dyslexia, 48,* 115-136.

Schensul, J. J. (1995). *Comments on ethnicity, culture and cultural competence.* Hartford, CT: Institute for Community Research.

Schneider, W. (1993). Acquiring expertise: Determinants of exceptional performance. In K. A. Heller, F. J. Monks, & A. H. Passow (Eds.), *International handbook of research and development of giftedness and talent* (pp. 311-324). New York: Pergamon.

Schor, D. P. (1983). The neurological examination. In J. A. Blackman (Ed.), *Medical aspects of developmental disabilities in children birth to three: A resource for special-service providers in the educational setting* (pp. 173-177). Iowa City: University of Iowa Press.

Schrag, J. A. (2000, October) *Discrepancy approaches for identifying learning disabilities.* Alexandria, VA: National Association of State Directors of Special Education, Project Forum, Quick Turn Around.

Schumaker, J. B., Nolan, S. M., & Deshler, D. D. (1985). *Learning strategies curriculum: The error monitoring strategy.* Lawrence: University of Kansas Center for Research on Learning.

Schwartz, A. A., Jacobson, J. W., & Holburn, S. C. (2002). Defining person centeredness: Results of two consensus methods. *Education and Training in Mental Retardation and Developmental Disabilities, 35,* 235-249.

Scott, J. M., Liaupin, C. J., Nelson, C. M., & Jolinette, K. (2003). Assuring student success through team-based FBA. *Teaching Exceptional Children, 35,* 16-21.

Scott, S. S., McGuire, J. M., & Shaw, S. F. (2003). Universal design for instruction: A new paradigm for adult instruction in postsecondary education. *Remedial and Special Education, 24,* 369-379.

Scott, T. (2003). Making behavior intervention planning decisions in a schoolwide system of positive behavior support. *Focus on Exceptional Children.* Retrieved August 18, 2005, from http://www.findarticles.com/p/articles/mi_qu3813/is_200309/ain9280001.

Scruggs, T. E., & Mastropieri, M. A. (1989). Mnemonic instruction of LD students: A field-based evaluation. *Learning Disability Quarterly, 12,* 119-125.

Scruggs, T., & Mastropieri, M. A. (2000). On babies and bathwater: Addressing the problems of identification of learning disabilities. *Learning Disability Quarterly, 25,* 155-168.

Scruggs, T., & Mastropieri, M. A. (2004). Science and schooling for students with LD: A discussion of the symposium. *Journal of Learning Disabilities, 37,* 270-278.

Semel, E., Wiig, E. H., & Secord, W. (1996). *Clinical evaluation of language fundamentals* (3rd ed.). San Antonio, TX: Psychological Corporation.

Shankweiler, D., Liberman, I. Y., Mark, S. L., Fowler, L. A., & Fischer, F. W. (1979). The speech code and learning to read. *Journal of Experimental Psychology: Human, Learning & Memory, 5,* 531-545.

Shapiro, B., Church, R. P., & Lewis, M. E. B. (2002). Specific learning disabilities. In M. L. Batshaw (Ed.), *Children with disabilities* (5th ed., pp. 417-422). Baltimore: Paul H. Brookes.

Share, D. L., & Silva, P. A. (2003). Gender bias in IQ-discrepancy and post-discrepancies definitions of reading disabilities. *Journal of Learning Disabilities, 36,* 4-14.

Shattuck, M. (1946). Segregation versus non-segregation of exceptional children. *Journal of Exceptional Children, 12,* 235-240.

Shaw, S.F., Cullen, J. P., McGuire, J. M., & Brinckerhoff, C. C. (1995). Operation analyzing a definition of learning disabilities. *Journal of Learning Disabilities, 28*(9), 586-597.

Shaywitz, S. E. (2003). *Overcoming dyslexia.* New York: Alfred A. Knoff.

Shaywitz, S. E., Fletcher, J. M., Holahan, J. M., Shneider, A. E., Marchione, K. F., Stuebing, K. K., Francis, D. J., Pugh, K. R., & Shaywitz, B. A. (1999). Persistence of dyslexia: The Connecticut longitudinal study at adolescence. *Pediatrics, 104*(6), 1351-1359.

Shaywitz, S. E., & Shaywitz, B. A. (1988). Hyperactivity attention deficits. In J. K. Kavanagh & T. J. Truss (Eds.), *Learning disabilities: Proceedings of the national conference* (pp. 369-523). Parkton, MD: York Press.

Shaywitz, S. E., & Shaywitz, B.A. (2003). Neurobiological indices of dyslexia. In H. L. Swanson, K. R. Harris, & S. Graham (Eds.). *Handbook of learning disabilities* (pp. 514-531). New York: Guilford Press.

Shippen, M. E., Simpson, R. G., & Crites, S. A. (2003). A practical guide to FBA. *Teaching Exceptional Children, 35,* 36-44.

Siegel, L. (1989). IQ is irrelevant to the definition of learning disabilities. *Journal of Learning Disabilities, 22,* 469-479.

Siegel, L. S. (2003a). Basic cognitive processes in reading disabilities. In H. L. Swanson, K. R. Harris, & S. Graham (Eds.), *Handbook of learning disabilities,* (pp. 158-181). New York: Guilford Press.

Siegel, L. S. (2003b). I.Q. discrepancies and the diagnosis of L. D. Instruction to the special issue. *Journal of Learning Disabilities, 36,* 2-3.

Sigafoos, J. (1995). Factors associated with aggression vs. aggression and self-injury among persons with intellectual disabilities. *Developmental Disabilities Bulletin, 23,* 30-39.

Sigman, M., & Whaley, S. E. (1998). The role of nutrition in the development of intelligence. In U. Neisser (Ed.), *The rising curve* (pp. 155-182). Washington, DC: American Psychological Association.

Silver, L. B. (1987). The "magic cure": A review of the current controversial approaches to treatment of learning disabilities. *Journal of Learning Disabilities, 20,* 498-504.

Silver, L. B. (1995). Controversal therapies. *Journal of Child Neurology, 10*(Suppl 1), 96-100.

Simmons, D. C., Gunn, B., Smith, S. B., & Kame'enui, E. J. (1994). Phonological awareness: Applications of instructional design. *LD Forum, 19*(4), 9-13.

Sitlington, P. L. (1996). Transition to learning: The neglected component of transition programming for individual with learning disabilities. *Journal of Learning Disabilities, 29,* 31-39.

Skinner, B. F. (1957). *Verbal behavior.* New York: Appleton-Century-Crofts.

Smith, B. J., Strain, P. S., Snyder, P., Sandall, S. R., McLean, M. E., Broudy-Ramsey, A., & Sumi, W. C. (2002). DEC recommended practices: A review of 9 years of E1/ECSE research literature. *Journal of Early Intervention, 25,* 108-119.

Smith, C. R. (2004). *Learning disabilities: The interaction of students and their environment* (5th ed.) Boston: Pearson Education.

Smith, T. E. C. (2002). Section 504: What teachers need to know. *Intervention in School and Clinic, 37,* 259-266.

Smith, T. E. C., Dowdy, C. A., Polloway, E. A., & Blalock, G. E. (1997). *Children and adults with learning disabilities.* Boston: Allyn & Bacon.

Sousa, D. A. (2001). *How the special needs brain learns.* Thousand Oaks, CA: Corwin Press.

Sparks, R. L., & Javorsky, J. (1999). The Boston University lawsuit: Introduction to the special issues. *Journal of Learning Disabilities, 32,* 284-285.

Sparks, R. L., Philips, L. G., & Jarvorsky, J. (2002). Students classified as LD who received course substitutions for the college foreign language requirement: A replication study. *Journal of Learning Disabilities, 35*(6), 482-499.

Sparrow, S. S., Balla, D. A., & Cicchetti, D. V. (1998). *Vineland social-emotional early childhood scales (SEEC).* Circle Pines, MN: American Guidance Service.

Spekman, N. J., Goldenberg, R. J., & Herman, K. L. (1993). An exploration of risk and resilience in the lives of individuals with learning disabilities. *Learning Disabilities Research and Practice, 8,* 11-18.

Spekman, N. J., Herman, K. L., & Vogel, S. A. (1993). Risk and resilience in individuals with learning disabilities: A challenge to the field. *Learning Disabilities Research and Practice, 8,* 11-18.

Stage, S. A., Abbot, R. D., Jenkins, J. R., & Berninger, V. W. (2003). Predicting response to early reading intervention from verbal IQ, reading-related language disabilities, attention ratings and verbal IQ–reading discrepancies: Failure to validate discrepancy model. *Journal of Learning Disabilities, 36,* 24-33.

Stanton-Chapman, T. L., Chapman, D. A., & Scott, K. G. (2001). Prediction of learning disabilities from information available on birth records. *Journal of Early Intervention, 24,* 193-206.

Steere, D. E., & Cavaiuolo, D. (2002). Connecting outcomes, goals, and objectives in transition planning. *Teaching Exceptional Children, 34*(6), 54–59.

Steinberg, J. (1997, June). Special education practices in New York faulted by U.S. *New York Times,* pp. 1, 22.

Stern, D. (2002, Spring). Building the bridge between community college and work for students with learning disability. *Perspective,* 17–20.

Steward, S. R., & Cegelka, P. T. (1995). Teaching reading and spelling. In P. T. Cegelka & W. H. Berdine (Eds.), *Effective instruction for students with learning difficulties* (pp. 265–301). Boston: Allyn & Bacon.

Stormont, M., Espinosa, L., Knipping, N., & McCathren, R. (2003, Fall). Supporting vulnerable learners in the primary grades: Strategies to prevent early school failure. *Early Childhood Research & Practice, 5*(2). Retrieved January 21, 2005, from http://ecrp.uiuc.edu/v5n2/stormont.html.

Stormont, M., Lewis, T. J., & Beckner, R. (2005). Positive behavior support systems: Applying key features in preschool settings. *Teaching Exceptional Children, 37,* 6, 42–49.

Strauss, A. A., & Kephart, N. C. (1955). *Psychopathology and education of the brain-injured child, Vol. II: Progress in therapy and clinic.* New York: Grune & Stratton.

Strauss, A. A., & Letinen, L. E. (1947). *Psychopathology and education of the brain-injured child.* New York: Grune & Stratton.

Sugai, G., & Lewis, T. J. (1996). Preferred and promising practices for social skills instruction. *Focus on Exceptional Children, 29,* 1–16.

Swanson, H. L. (1983). Relations among metamemory, rehearsal activity and word recall in learning disabled and nondisabled readers. *British Journal of Educational Psychology, 53,* 186–194.

Swanson, H. L. (1986). Do semantic memory deficiencies underlie disabled readers' encoding processes? *Journal of Experimental Child Psychology, 41,* 461–488.

Swanson, H. L. (1987). Verbal coding deficits in the recall of pictorial information by learning disabled readers: The influence of a lexical system. *American Educational Research Journal, 24,* 143–170.

Swanson, H. L. (1988). Learning disabled children's problem solving: Identifying mental processes underlying intelligent performance. *Intelligence, 12,* 261–278.

Swanson, H L. (1999). Reading comprehension and working memory in skilled readers: Is the phonological loop more important than the executive system? *Journal of Experimental Child Psychology, 72,* 1–31.

Swanson, H. L., Ashbaker, M., & Lee, C. (1996). Working memory in learning disabled readers as a function of processing demands. *Journal of Child Experimental Psychology, 61*(3), 242–275.

Swanson, H. L., Cochran, K., & Ewers, C. (1989). Working memory and reading disabilities. *Journal of Abnormal Child Psychology, 17,* 745–756.

Swanson, H. L., & Cooney, J. (1985). Strategy transformations in learning disabled children. *Journal of Learning Disabilities, 8,* 221–231.

Swanson, H. L., Cooney, J. D., & O'Shaughnessy, T. E. (1998). Memory and learning disabilities. In B. Y. Wong (Ed.), *Learning about learning disabilities* (2nd ed., pp. 107–162.) San Diego, CA: Academic Press.

Swanson, H. L., Cooney, J. D., & O'Shaughnessy, T. E. (2004). In B.Y.L. Wong (Ed.), *Memory and learning disabilities,* (3rd ed., pp. 41–92). Amsterdam: Elsevier/Academic Press.

Swanson, H. L., Cooney, J. D., & Overholser, J. D. (1988). The effects of self-generated visual mnemonics on adult learning disabled readers' word recall. *Learning Disabilities Research, 4,* 26–35.

Swanson, H. L., Hoskyn, M., & Lee, C. (1999). *Intervention for students with learning disabilities: A meta-analysis of treatment outcomes.* New York: Guilford Press.

Swanson, H. L., & Malone, S. (1992). Social skills and learning disabilities: A meta-analysis of the literature. *School of Psychology Review, 21,* 427–443.

Swanson, H. L., & Rathgeber, A. J. (1986). The effect of organizational dimension on memory for words in learning-disabled and nondisabled readers. *Journal of Educational Research, 79,* 155–162.

Swanson, H. L., & Rhine, B. (1985). Strategy transformations in learning disabled children's math performance: Clues to the development of expertise. *Journal of Learning Disabilities, 18,* 596–603.

Swanson, H. L., & Saez, L. (2003). Memory difficulties in children and adults with learning disabilities. In H. L. Swanson, K. R. Harris, & S. Graham (Eds.), *Handbook of learning disabilities* (pp. 182–198). New York: Guilford Press.

The Center for Universal Design. (1997). *Environments and products for all people.* Raleigh: North Carolina State University Press.

Thomas, C., Correa, V. I., & Morsink, C. V. (1995). *Interactive teaming: Consultation and collaboration in special programs.* Upper Saddle River, NJ: Merrill/Prentice Hall.

Thomas, S. B., & Rapport, M. J. K. (1998). The least restrictive environment: Understanding the direction of the courts. *The Journal of Special Education, 32*(2), 66–78.

Thomas, C., Rogan, P., & Baker, S. R. (2001). Student involvement in transition planning: Unheard voices. *Educational and Training in Mental Retardation and Developmental Disabilities, 36,* 42–54.

Thomas, P. J. (2004). Language: The foundation of learning. In J. S. Choate (Ed.), *Successful inclusive teaching* (pp. 152–177). Boston: Pearson Allyn & Bacon.

Thompson, J. B., & Raskind, W. H. (2003). Genetic influences on reading and writing disabilities. In H. L. Swanson, K. R. Harris, & S. Graham (Eds.), *Handbook of learning disabilities* (pp. 256–272). New York: Guilford Press.

Tiegerman-Farber, E. (2002). Interactive teaching: The changing role of the speech-language pathologist. In D. K. Bernstein & E. Tiegerman-Faber (Eds.), *Language and communication disorder* (pp. 354–386). Boston: Allyn & Bacon.

Tierney, R. J., Carter, M. A., & Desai, L. E. (1991). *Portfolio assessment in the reading-writing classroom.* Norwood, MA: Christopher-Gordon.

Tomlinson, C. A. (2002). Invitation to learn. *Educational leadership, 60*(1), 6–10.

Tomlinson, C. A. (2003). Deciding to teach them all. *Educational Leadership, 61,* 6–11.

Tomilson, C. A., & Doubet, K. (2005). Reach them to teach them. *Educational Leadership, 62,* 8–15.

Tomlinson, C. A., & Eidson, C. C. (2003). *Differentiate in practice: A resource guide for differentiating curriculum.* Alexandria, VA: Association for Supervision and Curriculum Development.

Torgesen, J. K. (1979). What shall we do with psychological processes? *Journal of Learning Disabilities, 12,* 514–521.

Torgesen, J. (1998). Catch them before they fall. *American Educator, 22*(1&2), 32–39.

Torgesen, J. K. (2002). Empirical and theoretical support for direct diagnosis of learning disabilities by assessment of intense processing weaknesses. In R. Bradley, L. Danielson, & D. P. Hallahan (Eds.), *Identification of learning disabilities* (pp. 565–613). Mahwah, NJ: Erlbaum.

Torgesen, J. K. (2004a). Learning disabilities: An historical and conceptual overview. In B. Y. L. Wong (Ed.), *Learning about learning disabilities* (3rd ed., pp. 3–40). Amsterdam: Elsevier/Academic.

Torgesen, J. K. (2004b, Fall). Preventing early reading failure—and its devastating downward spiral: The evidence for early intervention. *American Educator,* 6–9.

Torgeson, J. K., & Bryant, B. R. (1994). *Test of phonological awareness.* Austin, TX: PRO-ED.

Tucker, D. L., & Bakken, J. P. (2000). How do your kids do at reading? And how do you assess them? *Teaching Exceptional Children, 32*(6), 14, 19.

Turnbull, R. H., & Turnbull, A. (2001). *Exceptional lives: Special education in today's schools* (3rd ed.). Upper Saddle River, NJ: Merrill/Prentice Hall.

Turnbull, A., & Turnbull, R. H. (2005). *Families, professionals, and exceptionality: Collaborating for empowerment* (5th ed.). Upper Saddle River, NJ: Merrill/Prentice-Hall.

Ullmann, R. K., Sleator, E. K., & Sprague, R. L. (1991). *ADD-H: Comprehensive teacher's ratings scale (ACTeRS)* (2nd ed.). Champaign, IL: Metritech.

U.S. Department of Education. (2000). *To assure the free appropriate public education of all children with disabilities* (Twenty-Second Annual Report to Congress on the implementation of the Individual with Disabilities Education Act). Washington, DC: U.S. Government Printing Office.

U.S. Department of Education. (2002). *To assure the free, appropriate public education of all children with disabilities* (Twenty-Fourth Annual Report to Congress on the implementation of the Individual with Disabilities Education Act). Washington, DC: U.S. Government Printing Office.

U.S. Department of Education, Office of Civil Rights. (1999). *1988 elementary and secondary school civil rights compliance report projected values for the nation.* Washington, DC: Author.

U.S. Department of Education, Office of Special Education and Rehabilitation Services, Office of Special Education Program. (2003). Identifying and treating attention deficit hyperactivity disorder: A resource for school and home. Washington, DC: Author.

U.S. Office of Education. (1976). Education of handicapped children. 41 Federal Register, *41*(230), 52404–52407.

U.S. Office of Education. (1977). Definition and criteria for defining students as learning disabled. Federal Register, *42*(250), 65082–65085.

Usnick, V. E. (1992). Multidigit addition: A study of an alternative sequence. *Focus on Problems in Mathematics, 14,* 53–62.

Van Etten, C., & Adamson, G. (1973). The fail-save program: A special education continuum. In *Instructional Alternatives for Exceptional Children* (pp. 156–165). Reston, VA: Council for Exceptional Children.

Van Reusen, A. K., Bos, C. S., Schumaker, J. B., & Deshler, D. D. (1987). *The learning strategies curriculum: The educational planning strategy.* Lawrence, KS: Edge Enterprises.

Vaughn. S., & Elbaum, B. (1999). The self-concept and friendships of students with learning disabilities: A developmental perspective. In R. Galliune (Ed.), *Developmental perspectives on children with high incidence disabilities* (pp. 81–107). Mahwah, NJ: Erlbaum.

Vaughn, S., & Fuchs, L. S. (2003). Redefining learning disabilities as inadequate response to instruction: The promise and potential problems. *Learning Disabilities Research and Practice, 18,* 137–146.

Vaughn, S., Gersten, R., & Chard, D. J. (2000). The underlying message in LD intervention research: Findings from research syntheses. *Exceptional Children, 9,* 47–66.

Vaughn, S., & Klinger, J. K. (1998). Students' perceptions of inclusion and resource room settings. *The Journal of Special Education, 32,* 79–88.

Vaughn, S., & Linan-Thompson, S. (2003). What is so special about special education for students with learning disabilities? *The Journal of Special Education, 37,* 140–147.

VORT Corporation. (1995). *Hawaii Early Learning Profile (HELP) for preschoolers.* Palo Alto, CA: VORT Corporation.

Voress, J. K., & Maddox, T. (1998). *Developmental assessment of young children.* Austin, TX: PRO-ED.

Vygotsky, L. S. (1978). *Mind in society: The development of higher psychological processes.* Cambridge, MA: Harvard University Press.

Wagenberg, R. (2003). *Classroom modifications.* Dix Hills, NY: Half Hollow Hills Central School District.

Wagner, M., Newman, L., Camero, R., Garza, N., & Levine, P. (2005). *After high school: A first look at the postschool experience of youth with disabilities*. A report from the National Longitudinal Transition Study-2 (NLTS2). Menlo Park, CA: SRI International.

Waldron, N. L., & McLeskey, J. (1998). The effects of an inclusive school program on students with mild and severe learning disabilities. *Exceptional Children, 65*, 395-405.

Wallace, G., & Hammill, D. D. (2002). *Comprehensive receptive and expressive vocabulary test* (2nd ed.). Austin, TX: PRO-ED.

Weiner, J. (2004). Do peer relationships foster behavioral adjustment in learning disabilities? *Learning Disabilities Quarterly, 27*, 21-30.

Weiner, J., & Sunohara, G. (1998). Parents' perceptions of the quality of friendships of their children with learning disabilities. *Learning Disabilities Research and Practice, 13*(4), 242, 257.

Weintraub, N., & Graham, S. (1998). Writing legibly and quickly: A study of children's ability to adjust their handwriting to meet common classroom demands. *Learning Disabilities Research and Practice, 11*, 295-305.

Weiss, A. L. (2002). Planning language intervention for young children. In D. K. Bernstein & E. Tigerman-Farber (Eds.), *Language of communication disorders* (pp. 256-314). Boston: Allyn & Bacon.

Weiss, M. P., & Lloyd, J. W. (2002). Congruence between roles and actions of secondary special educators in co-taught and special education settings. *The Journal of Special Education, 36*(2), 58-68.

Weiss, M. P., & Lloyd, J. W. (2003). Conditions for co-teaching: Lessons from a case study. *Teacher Education and Special Education, 26*, 27-41.

Welsh, M. (1992, Spring). The PLEASE strategy: A metacognitive learning strategy for improving the paragraph writing of students with mild learning disabilities. *Learning Disabilities Quarterly, 12*(2), 119-128.

Wesson, C. L., & King, R. P (1996). Portfolio assessment and special education students. *Teaching Exceptional Children, 28* (2), 44-49.

Wiederholt, J. L. (1974). Historical perspectives on the education of the learning disabled. In L. Mann & D. Sabatino (Eds.), *The second review of special education* (pp. 103-152). Philadelphia: JSE Press.

Wiederholt, J. L., & Bryant, B. (2001). *Gray oral reading test-4.* Austin, TX: PRO-ED.

Wiederholt, J. L., Hammill, D. D., & Brown, V. (1983). *The resource room teacher* (2nd ed.). Boston: Allyn & Bacon.

Wiig, E. H., & Semel, E. M. (1980). *Language assessment and intervention for the learning disabled* (2nd ed.) Boston: Allyn & Bacon.

Wiig, E. H., & Semel, E. M. (1984). *Language assessment and intervention for the learning disabled* (2nd ed.) Boston: Allyn & Bacon.

Will, M. C. (1986). Educating children with learning problems: A shared responsibility. *Exceptional Children, 52*, 411-415.

Williams, K. T. (1997). *Expressive vocabulary test.* Circle Pines, MN: American Guidance Service.

Wisconsin Education Association Council. (1996). Special education inclusion (updated 2001). Retrieved May 2, 2005, from http://www.weac.org./resource.

Witte, R. H., Philips, L., & Kakela, M. (1998). Job satisfaction of college graduates with learning disabilities. *Journal of Learning Disabilities, 31*(3), 259-265.

Witzel, B., Mercer, C., & Miller, M. (2003). Teaching algebra to students with learning difficulties: An investigation of an excellent instructional model. *Learning Disabilities Research and Practice, 18*, 121-131.

Wolf Nelson, N. (2002). Language intervention in school settings. In D. K. Bernstein & E. Tigerman-Faber (Eds.), *Language and communication disorders in children* (pp. 315-353). Boston: Allyn & Bacon.

Wolf Nelson, N. (2005). The context of discourse difficulty in classroom and clinic: An update. *Topics in Language Disorders, 25*, 322-331.

Wong, B. Y. L. (Ed.). (2004). *Learning about learning disabilities* (3rd ed.). Amsterdam: Elsevier/Academic Press.

Wong, B. Y. L., Butler, D. L., Ficzere, S. A., & Kuperis, S. (1997). Teaching adolescents with learning disabilities and low achievers to plan, write, and revise compare-contrast essay. *Learning Disabilities Research and Practice, 9*, 78-90.

Wong, B. Y. L., & Donahue, M. (Eds.).(2002). *The social dimensions of learning disabilities.* Mahwah, NJ: Erlbaum.

Wong, B. Y. L., & Jones, W. (1982). Increasing metacomprehension of learning disabled and normal achieving students through self-questioning training. *Learning Disability Quarterly, 5*, 228-240.

Wood, F. B., & Grigorenko, E. L. (2001). Emerging issues in the genetics of dyslexia: A methodological review. *Journal of Learning Disabilities, 34*, 503-511.

Woodcock, R. W. (1991). *Woodcock language proficiency battery—revised English form.* Itasca, IL: Riverside.

Woodcock, R.W., McGrew, K. S., & Mather, N. (1998). *Woodcock-Johnson psychoeducational battery—III.* Itasca, IL: Riverside.

Woodcock, R. W., & Munoz-Sandoval, A. F. (1995). *Woodcock language proficiency battery—Spanish form.* Itasca, IL: Riverside.

Woodcock, R. W., & Munoz-Sandoval, A. F. (2001). *Woodcock/Munoz language survey, normative update.* Itasca, IL: Riverside.

Worrall, R. S. (1990). Detecting health fraud in the field of learning disabilities. *Journal of Learning Disabilities, 23*, 207-212.

Ysseldyke, J. E. (1983). Current practices in making psychoeducational decisions about learning disabled students. *Journal of Learning Disabilities, 16*, 209-219.

Ysseldyke, J. E. (2002). Response to learning disabilities: Historical perspectives. In R. Bradley, L. Danielson, & D. P. Hallahan (Eds.), *Identification of learning disabilities: Research to practice* (pp. 185–250). Mahwah, NJ: Erlbaum.

Ysseldyke, J. E. (2005). Assessment and decision making for students with learning disabilities: What if this is as good as it gets? *Learning Disabilities Quarterly, 28,* 125–128.

Ysseldyke, J. E., & Algozzine, B. (1995). *Special education: A practical approach for teachers* (3rd ed.). Boston: Houghton Mifflin.

Zigmond, N. (1995). Models for delivery of special education services to students with learning disabilities in public schools. *Journal of Child Neurology, 10*(Suppl 1), S86–S91.

Zigmond, N., & Magiera, K. (2001, Autumn). *Co-teaching. Practice Alerts, 6.* Washington, DC: Council for Exceptional Children.

Zimmerman, B. (2000). Attaining self-regulation: A social cognitive perspective. In M. Boekaerts, P. Pintrilk, & M. Zeidner (Eds.), *Handbook of self regulation* (pp. 13–29). San Diego, CA: Academic Press.

Zimmerman, I. L., Steiner, V. G., & Pond, R. E. (1992). *Preschool language scale-3.* San Antonio, TX: Psychological Corporation.

NAME INDEX

Getman, G., 22
Gilger, J. W., 43
Gilliam, J. E., 276
Gillingham, A., 20, 223, 238
Ginsburg, H. D., 267
Ginsburg, H. P., 252
Glass, G. Y., 22
Glatthorn, A. A., 81
Gnagey, T. D., 252
Goforth, F. S., 219
Goldberg, J., 64
Goldberg, R. J., 186
Goldenberg, D. S., 147
Goldman, S. R., 249
Goldstein, K., 20
Goldstein, M., 62
Goldstein, S., 62
Gonzalez, J., 39
Gonzalez-DeHass, A., 288, 289, 290
Gottlieb, B. W., 8, 87, 199
Gottlieb, J., 8, 10, 87, 199
Graden, J. L., 70, 71, 81
Graetz, J., 109
Graham, S., 229, 234, 237, 238, 239, 241, 242, 292
Graves, D. H., 243
Gregg, N., 180
Gresham, F. M., 273, 276, 278, 288
Grigorenko, E. L., 43
Grossman, H., 101
Gunn, B., 217
Guralnick, M. J., 144
Gustashaw, W. E. III, 35

Hacker, B. J., 152
Hagen, J. W., 50
Haggart, A. G., 112
Hallahan, D. P., 3, 4, 5, 18, 19, 20, 21, 22, 23, 25, 35, 50, 51, 134
Hallahan, P. P., 14
Hallerick, R. L., 133
Hambleton, R. K., 101
Hammill, D. D., 3, 4–5, 13, 18, 22, 48, 133, 134, 196, 197, 235, 241, 248, 258, 259
Hanner, S., 23
Hanson, F. A., 101
Hanson, M. J., 119
Harris, K. R., 229, 237, 242, 292

Harrison, P. L., 147
Harry, B., 10, 119
Hauser, R. M., 162
Hawkins, J. D., 161
Hazel, J. S., 160
Heddens, J. W., 264
Heiman, T., 273
Henderson, L. W., 148
Henry, F. M., 272
Herman, K. L., 180, 186
Herr, C. M., 34, 35
Herron, S. R., 239
Heubert, J. P., 162
Higgins, E. L., 186
Hinshelwood, J., 19
Hocutt, A. M., 130
Hoffman, A. J., 175
Hoffman, J. V., 219
Holburn, S. C., 178
Holloway, J., 130
Horowitz, S., 33, 176, 177, 186
Hoskyn, M., 216
House, J. E., 87
Hresko, W. P., 197, 239
Hudson, P., 65
Hughes, C. A., 65, 266
Hull, K., 112
Hutchinson, J. M., 291
Huttenlocher, J., 249
Hynd, G. W., 39, 43

Illback, R. J., 71
Ingersoll, B., 62
Irlen, H., 44

Jacobson, J. W., 178
James, A., 118
Janiga, S. J., 179, 181
Javorsky, J., 181, 182
Jenkins, J. R., 90, 133
Jimenez, J. E., 90
Johnson, D., 22, 145
Johnson, D. J., 134, 145, 193, 202, 209, 229, 235, 239
Johnson, D. W., 286, 287
Johnson, E. R., 178
Johnson, G., 23
Johnson, G. O., 133
Johnson, L. J., 70, 178

Johnson, R. T., 286, 287
Johnson, S. A., 178
Johnson, T. D., 97
Johnson-Martin, M. N., 152
Jolinette, K., 283, 284
Jones, N. L., 29, 30
Jones, R. S., 65
Jones, W., 63
Jordan, N. C., 249, 251
Jordan, L., 7
Joyce, S. A., 59

Kai Yung Tam, B., 178
Kakela, M., 185
Kalyanpur, M., 119
Kame'enui, E. J., 164, 165, 216, 217
Kamki, A. G., 194
Kandt, R. S., 42
Kass, C., 4, 6
Kaufman, A. S., 153
Kauffman, J. M., 51, 134
Kavale, K. A., 23, 272, 284, 288
Kazmierski, S., 180
Kelk, M. J., 290
Keller, H., 20
Kephart, N., 20, 21, 22, 145
Kiarie, M. W., 288
Kinas Jerome, M., 245
King, R. P., 98, 99
King-Sears, M. E., 163, 167, 184
Kirk, S., 3, 4, 6, 20, 21, 22
Kirst, M., 101
Kleefeld, J., 288
Klein, H. B., 202
Kline, F. M., 65
Kling, B., 182
Klinger, J. K., 108, 137
Knipping, N., 290
Knotek, S., 70
Kohler, P. D., 177
Korinek, L., 288
Kortering, L. J., 266
Kottmeyer, W., 235
Krackendoffel, E. A., 87
Kreidler, W. J., 289
Kroesberger, E. H., 248
Kroth, R. L., 118
Kuperis, S., 241

SUBJECT INDEX

Impulsivity, 51
Inclusion
  adolescents and, 163
  language disorders (oral)
    and, 204–205
  principles of, 129, 130–132
Indirect services, 136
Individualized Education Program
    (IEP), 26, 28–29, 30
  conference, 121–122
  example of, 113–114
  teams, 111–112
Individualized Transition
    Educational Plan (ITEP),
    177–178
Individuals
  needs and inclusion, 130–131
  use of term, 27
Individuals with Disabilities
    Education Improvement
    Act (IDEA)
  case law, 34–35
  legislative history of, 29
  1990 passing of, 27
  1997 version, 27–29
  summary of, 31–32
  transition requirements, 178
  2004 reauthorization of, 2, 29
*Infant-Preschool Play Assessment
    Scale,* 152
Informal Reading Inventory (IR),
    213, 214, 215
Information processing, 58
  instructional strategies, 65–66
Inspiration, 223
Inspiration, 223, 245
Institute of Medicine (IM), 39
Instructional strategies
  for ADHD, 60–61
  for adolescents, 165–167
  for information processing,
    65–66
  for memory, 62–65
  prereferral, 72
  resource room teachers
    and, 134
Instructional support team (IST),
    71, 87, 272
  referral form, 72, 76–77

Intellectual functioning
  discrepancy, achievement-,
    7–8, 30
  problems with, 89–91
Intellitale II, 245
Interagency Committee on
    Learning Disabilities (ICLD),
    6–7, 27, 271
International Dyslexia Association
    (IDA), 5, 19, 125, 224
International Reading Association
    (IRA), 5
Internet, use of the, 122–123, 125
Irlen Institute for Perceptual and
    Learning Disabilities, 44
Iron deficiency, 40

Journal of Learning Disabilities,
    35–36, 90, 91, 248
Juvenile delinquency, link between
    learning disabilities and,
    160–161

*Kaufman Survey of Early
    Academic and Language
    Skills (K-SEALS),* 153
KeyMath, 252
Kidspiration, 223
*Kurzweil Educational
    Systems,* 223

Language
  analysis of written, 170
  components of, 191–192
  defined, 191
  development of normal, 191
  development theories, 192–193
  form, 191
  sample, 195
Language disorders, oral, 12
  assessment of, 194–198
  behavior associated with, 194, 195
  characteristics of, 193–194
  comprehension
    problems, 201–202
  computer programs, 204
  culturally and linguistically
    diverse students and, 199–201
  examples of, 190

  inclusion, 204–205
  intervention plans, 201–204
  language production
    problems, 202
  in preschoolers, 146
  sentence formation, 202, 204
  word finding, 202, 204
  word meaning, 203–204
Language disorders, written
  direct instruction, 244–245
  handwriting, 228–234
  learning strategies, 244
  spelling, 234–239
  technology, use of, 245–246
  writing process, 243–244
  written expression, 239–243
Language experience
    approach, 218
Laterality, 19–20, 41–42
Laws
  federal government, 24–35
  governing adults, 180
  governing preschoolers, 143
Lawsuits, 34–35
LD Forum, 248
Lead poisoning, 40
League of School Reaching
    Out, 118
Leadership Training Institution
    (LTI), 25
Learning disabilities
  achievement-intellectual
    functioning discrepancy, 7–8
  ADHD and, 55
  central nervous system
    dysfunction, 8
  characteristics of, 3, 11–13
  defined, 2–7, 270–261
  defined by schools, 8–9
  gender differences, 9–10
  identification of, 13
  introduction of term, 20, 21
  minority status, 10–11, 13–14
Learning disabilities, causes of
  genetic, 43–44
  medical, 41–43
  perinatal factors, 40
  postnatal factors, 40–41
  prenatal factors, 39–40